Chaucer and
the Italian Trecento

I wil myselven al hyt drynke...

... with David,

Piero

Nardo di Cione (died 1366), detail showing Dante, and perhaps Boccaccio and Petrarch, centre to left, in the group of the blessed. From the Last Judgement fresco in the Cappella Strozzi, Santa Maria Novella, Florence.

Chaucer and the Italian Trecento

EDITED BY
PIERO BOITANI

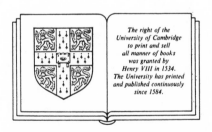

The right of the
University of Cambridge
to print and sell
all manner of books
was granted by
Henry VIII in 1534.
The University has printed
and published continuously
since 1584.

Cambridge University Press

CAMBRIDGE

LONDON   NEW YORK   NEW ROCHELLE

MELBOURNE   SYDNEY

Published by the Press Syndicate of the University of Cambridge
The Pitt Building, Trumpington Street, Cambridge CB2 1RP
32 East 57th Street, New York, NY 10022, USA
10 Stamford Road, Oakleigh, Melbourne 3166, Australia

First published 1983
Reprinted 1984
First paperback edition 1985

Printed in Great Britain at the
University Press, Cambridge

Library of Congress catalogue card number: 82–17772

British Library cataloguing in publication data

Chaucer and the Italian Trecento.
1. Chaucer, Geoffrey – Criticism and
interpretation
I. Boitani, Piero
820'.1   PR1924
ISBN 0 521 23998 2   hard covers
ISBN 0 521 31350 3   paperback

To the memory of Jack Bennett

Contents

Contributors

JOHN LARNER is *Professor of Medieval History, University of Glasgow.*

JANET COLEMAN is *Lecturer in Political Thought, University of Exeter.*

WENDY CHILDS is *Lecturer in History, University of Leeds.*

†J. A. W. BENNETT was *Professor of Medieval and Renaissance Literature, University of Cambridge (1963–78).*

PIERO BOITANI is *Professor of English, University of Rome.*

DAVID WALLACE is *Fellow of St Edmund's House, Cambridge.*

BARRY WINDEATT is *Fellow of Emmanuel College, Cambridge.*

ROBIN KIRKPATRICK is *Lecturer in Italian, University of Cambridge.*

NICHOLAS HAVELY is *Lecturer in English and Related Literature, University of York.*

PETER GODMAN is *Fellow of Pembroke College, Oxford.*

ENRICO GIACCHERINI is *Lecturer in English, University of Pisa.*

Preface

In a very particular way, this book is the child of J. A. W. Bennett, who had felt the need of it for many years. We wish he could have seen it in print and the least we can do is to dedicate it to his memory.

I think I am interpreting the feelings of all contributors in thanking Patrick Boyde, Derek Brewer, Helen Cooper, Peter Dronke, Jill Mann, Nicholas Mann, Derek Pearsall, Eric Stanley and J. B. Trapp for the assistance they have given us at the various stages of work on our essays. Finally, I wish to thank the President and Fellows of the Accademia Nazionale dei Lincei for granting us permission to reprint J. A. W. Bennett's essay.

PIERO BOITANI

Rome, March 1982

Note on the Texts

Chaucer's works are quoted from F. N. Robinson's edition of *The Works of Geoffrey Chaucer*, 2nd edn. (London, 1957). Different readings of single words or punctuation have at times been chosen by contributors. The text of Dante's *Divina Commedia* is that edited by G. Petrocchi (Milan, 1966–7). Other works by Dante are quoted from *Le Opere di Dante*, Testo Critico della Società Dantesca Italiana (Florence, 1921). We have used the Mondadori edition of *Tutte le Opere di Giovanni Boccaccio*, general editor V. Branca (Milan 1967–) whenever possible. Other editions of works by Boccaccio and the editions of Petrarch and all other authors are quoted in the notes. References to the classics, unless otherwise specified, are to the Loeb edition.

Note on the Illustrations

The illustrations that have been chosen for this book are particularly relevant to our subject. Those on the jacket reproduce two pieces of sculpture. One is a detail from the tomb of Giovanni da Legnano by Pier Paolo delle Masegne (1386?), now in the Museo Civico, Bologna. It shows clerks listening to a lecture presumably being given by Giovanni himself. Giovanni is the 'Lynyan' mentioned by Chaucer's Oxford Clerk in one breath with Petrarch. He 'enlumyned al Ytaille' 'of philosophie, / Or lawe, or oother art particuler' (Prologue to the *Clerk's Tale*, 31–5). The second piece of sculpture is the equestrian statue of Bernabò Visconti, from his tomb (1370) by Bonino da Campione, in the Castello Sforzesco, Milan. It is emblematic of the celebration of secular rulers in fourteenth-century Italy. Medieval knight and Roman emperor merge into one image. Chaucer, who went to Milan to negotiate with Bernabò in 1378, celebrated him as 'god of delit, and scourge of Lumbardye' in the *Monk's Tale* (2399–406).

The frontispiece shows Dante, and perhaps Boccaccio and Petrarch, in the group of the blessed, from the Last Judgement fresco in the Cappella Strozzi, Santa Maria Novella, Florence. In his *Commentarii*, Ghiberti attributes this fresco to Nardo di Cione alone, who died in 1366. In the *Lives*, Vasari maintains that it is the work of Nardo's younger brother, Andrea di Cione, called 'Orcagna', in collaboration with his brother 'Bernardo' or 'Leonardo'. Nothing is known of Orcagna after 1368. In any case the fresco would have been painted before Chaucer's visit to Florence in 1372–3, and he might have seen it. Here (from centre to left) Dante and two characters who have been traditionally identified as Boccaccio and Petrarch, are celebrated together – a sign of the fact that they might have already been associated as the greatest 'Florentine' men of letters by the 1360s, when Boccaccio and Petrarch were still alive. (*Reproduced by permission of Alinari.*)

PIERO BOITANI

Introduction

I like to think of the Italian Trecento as beginning on Good Friday, 1300, when Dante entered the dark wood and started his journey through Hell, Purgatory and Paradise, and ending with the competition for the Florence Baptistery doors in 1400, in which Ghiberti gained the victory over Brunelleschi. There is exactly that much continuity and change in the century as between those two events. But of course these are just two images I am very fond of – reality was much more varied and complex than this, and one could easily choose different emblematic events, for instance the proclamation of the Jubilee by Boniface VIII on 22 February 1300 (and the fresco by Giotto that celebrates it in St John Lateran) and the death of St Catherine of Siena on 29 April 1380 in Rome, after the 'Babylonian Captivity' in Avignon, the return of the papacy to Rome and the beginning of the Great Schism. Or again, perhaps the Trecento begins with the writing down – in French – of the Venetian Marco Polo's *Il Milione* in a Genoese jail between 1298 and 1299, and the disappearance of the Genoese Vivaldi brothers in the Atlantic in 1291, in the course of an expedition 'per mare Oceanum . . . ad partes Indiae' – two 'tydynges' that might have interested Chaucer the traveller on his visit to Genoa. The century might be thought to end with Manuel Chrysoloras' first lectures on Greek at Florence in 1397. The Trecento is the first 'golden' century in Italian culture after Augustus, Trajan and Constantine, and a century in which the Middle Ages, classical antiquity and the roots of modern European culture meet. It was indeed fortunate that Chaucer visited Italy and read Italian literature in the second half of this century.

After the books devoted in the past to *Chaucer and the French Tradition* by Charles Muscatine and to *Chaucer and the English Tradition* by Ian Robinson, the need for some kind of comprehensive work on Chaucer and the Italian tradition was undoubtedly felt. We have tried to put some new questions or to ask ourselves some old questions in a new way. The essays in this volume are meant to be source-studies inasmuch as a source-study implies a source, an author who transforms it, and a final product. In our case the sources are several: Italy and Italian culture in the Trecento, England and English culture in the fourteenth century – the contexts, that is, of Chaucer's activity as a poet – and the Italian texts that we know Chaucer used.

It is impossible to judge the extent of Chaucer's indebtedness to Italian literature without first assessing what Chaucer *could* have found in Italy, what his image of that country could have been like, and what contemporary English culture stimulated him to look for there. The first two essays in this volume are therefore devoted to Italy and England, the political, economic, social, cultural and artistic developments that the former underwent in the Trecento, and the shape English culture was taking in the fourteenth century. There are divergences, incomprehensions (Petrarch and his circle referred to the English as 'barbari Britanni'), but also common roots and similarities. Janet Coleman questions old assumptions in this respect and points to Avignon as the great crucible of European culture during the 'Babylonian Captivity' of the papacy there; and John Larner shows how Italian culture itself changed between the time of Dante and that of Petrarch and Salutati.

Thus, the first two essays in this collection aim at sketching in the background, at comparative cultural history. The third article brings fourteenth-century Italy and England together. Here, Wendy Childs examines the relationships between the two countries as established by friars, prelates, university clerks, shipmen, pilgrims and merchants – the very protagonists of the *Canterbury Tales*. The Wife of Bath had been to Rome, and the Clerk – so he says – to Padua. Chaucer himself had of course travelled to Italy at least twice (1372–3 and 1378). But perhaps, being a wine-merchant's son, young Geoffrey had early heard of the 'vernage of Venyce' that the alliterative *Morte Arthure* mentions. Later in life, as high officer in the King's Customs, he certainly knew that 'ducat in Venyse' – 'of which', he says in the *House of Fame*, 'to lite al in my pouche is'. He must have handled quite a few florins – those coins the very name of which bore witness to their Florentine connections. As J. A. W. Bennett points out in his essay, the painter of Diana's temple in the *Knight's Tale* 'with many a floryn [he] the hewes boghte' – as Giotto and Simone Martini and the Lorenzetti brothers must also have done. It is in the real world of 'rekenynges' that Chaucer first met Italy and Italians.

Yet accounts and books, 'labour', business and literature were never totally separate for him. And the world of Italian literature in the Trecento was an exciting one. The three greatest Italian writers of all time were trecento authors. Dante, who had dared to write a work to which both earth and Heaven had set hand, had died only fifty years before. Petrarch, who was crowned 'lauriat poete' in Rome, died not long after one of Chaucer's visits, in 1374. And Boccaccio, who started lecturing on Dante in Florence shortly after Chaucer's visit, died only in 1375. He was a devotee of Dante and a dear friend of Petrarch's.

Whether or not Chaucer was himself aware of the overwhelming shadow that this most famous triad of poets seems to have cast on the whole Trecento, it was both inevitable and lucky that he should know first and probably exclusively the works of Dante, Boccaccio and Petrarch. Italian culture was of course, as both John Larner and David Wallace show, more varied and decentralized than the predominantly Florentine image of the triad would suggest. Naples, Venice, Padua, Bologna and Lombardy were important centres. Yet Dante, Boccaccio and Petrarch must have appeared as a striking *avant-garde* to the Chaucer who came to them from an essentially Anglo-French culture. The Italian poets were steeped in tradition – a background that was Chaucer's own – and yet built on it a new world. The classics, medieval Latin culture, and courtly and French literary forms were absorbed and re-cast to produce something unknown in European literature before. With Boccaccio, the romance moved in all possible directions, including the epic. Dream-poetry became 'triumphal' vision in the hands of both Boccaccio and Petrarch. Mythography was organized into a coherent encyclopedia by critical principles, biography came into vogue again as a literary and historical genre. Above all, the status of the modern poet and of poetry in general was tenaciously defended and exalted. Dante presented himself as both a prophet and Virgil's ideal successor, Petrarch was crowned on the Capitol, Boccaccio talked of poetry as theology. Moreover, Dante's poem was being commented on as if it were a classic, Peter Lombard or the Bible itself. Finally, the worlds of literature and history were inextricably fused in the *Commedia* as well as – albeit in a different manner – in the *De Casibus Virorum Illustrium*. The essays in this volume take due account of this and thus form a coherent whole. A general, introductory article such as John Larner's discusses Ugolino and Bernabò Visconti as historical figures, and later contributors take them up in the context of literature.

The second part of this volume is devoted to Chaucer's relationship with the great writers of the Trecento – the subject of an essay written fifty years ago by Mario Praz, whose pioneering influence, we hope, is still felt here. J. A. W. Bennett looks at the way in which Chaucer's mind worked with Dante's and Boccaccio's poems, going from and through one to the other, transforming their images, imbibing their sense of the importance of the classics and of poetry. His article, the opening pages of which take up topics touched on in the first three chapters of this volume, establishes the main lines of inquiry that are followed in the subsequent essays. What was Chaucer's image of Dante, how did he approach him, how deeply was he influenced by him, what, in short, did Dante mean to Chaucer is a question that dominates not only my own essay on the subject, but also, for instance, Robin Kirkpatrick's on the *Decameron* and the *Canterbury Tales*. This is a piece of work that is certainly not source-study, but comparative literature. In the same vein, Nicholas Havely explores the relevance of the friar-figures in Boccaccio and Chaucer. We have tried, in other words, to ask ourselves not only how a work of literature influences another, but also how their relation to each other influences *our* view, our perception of the literature of the fourteenth century.

The puzzling, elusive and somewhat mysterious relationship of Chaucer to the trecento writers offers a unique opportunity for this kind of analysis. Here was the greatest poet of fourteenth-century England meeting the greatest poets of Italy – a phenomenon that is rare in literary history yet not uncommon in Anglo-Italian relations. How did his reading of Dante, Boccaccio and Petrarch affect his own work? The parallels and differences between Boccaccio's exploration of themes, forms, structures and styles – both in his vernacular and his Latin works – and Chaucer's continuous experiments with narrative, are the subject of six essays in this collection. David Wallace lays the ground with a thorough examination of all Boccaccio's early works and focuses particularly on the *Amorosa Visione*. Barry Windeatt takes up the *Filostrato* and asks not 'what Chaucer really did with it' but what the *Troilus* would be without it. I read the *Teseida* as a model of narrative, style and iconography with which Chaucer wrestles throughout his career. Robin Kirkpatrick examines the way in which Dante's *Commedia* influences the themes and the forms of Petrarch's *Canzoniere*, Boccaccio's *Decameron* and Chaucer's *Canterbury Tales*. The story of Griselda, which fascinates all three writers, is but a particular case of that more general topic. Peter Godman sets the *De Casibus*, *De Mulieribus* and *Genealogie* in their cultural context and examines their relevance for Chaucer, in particular for the *Legend of Good Women* and the *Monk's Tale*.

These, then, are some of the questions we ask and try to answer. We have deliberately avoided facing other problems, though they lurked in the background and made our research more exciting.

Where did Chaucer find Petrarch's sonnet, 'S'Amor non è'; why does he seem to attribute to Petrarch works written by Boccaccio; why does he never mention Boccaccio by name; and who is 'Lollius' – these are, at present, insoluble problems, and furthermore they do not fit in with the kind of approach to the history of culture and literature we adopted at the beginning of our enterprise.

We have also avoided another problem that might well have fitted in with our research – the presence of a sonnet by Petrarch in the *Troilus*. E. H. Wilkins and in particular Patricia Thomson have studied this in articles to which we felt we could add nothing substantial. Furthermore, this is an isolated problem, which does not recur in Chaucer's works. Interesting and fascinating as a singular accident in the history of literature, it could be seen as a simple case of missed opportunity for Chaucer as well as for fourteenth-century English literature. As literary form, the Petrarchan sonnet does not seem to have any effect on Chaucer, and the *Canzoniere* as a whole – which alone could have given him a full idea of the beauty of Petrarch's lyric as well as fascinated him with its themes of love, death and poetry – seems to have been unknown to him. The 'lauriat poete' Chaucer knew was the Latin translator of the Griselda and perhaps the author of at least one of the *Trionfi*, the 'Triumphus Fame'. But Chaucer would have found what might have interested him in that poem – the celebration of poets – in Boccaccio's *Amorosa Visione* or in Dante's Limbo (and indeed in the whole *Divine Comedy*).

We have, then, by no means exhausted all the questions about Chaucer's relationship to the Italian Trecento that could be asked. To use two lines of Dante that Chaucer had certainly read,

> Forse di retro a noi con miglior voci
> Si pregherà perché Cirra risponda.

We hope that our volume will stimulate further research in the subject, and the purpose of Enrico Giaccherini's Bibliography here is precisely that of providing future students with all the tools necessary to start anew.

Of the contributors to this book, three are historians or historians of culture, and the others students of literature, either English or Italian, who have done and are doing work on the Trecento and on fourteenth-century English literature. Two are Italian, one American, six British and two New Zealanders by birth. We feel that in a collective volume of comparative literature these are not insignificant facts.

JOHN LARNER

Chaucer's Italy

I

If, before first setting out for Italy, Chaucer had opened Bartholomew
the Englishman's *De proprietatibus rerum* (a standard encyclopedia
of the age, soon to be rendered into English by Trevisa, already, some
eighty years before, translated into the speech of Mantua) he would
have found there a description of the peninsula based upon information from Isidore and Pliny together with a laconic but clear-cut
summary of its more recent reputation:

Amonge alle þe weste cuntreys and londes of Europa, Italy bereþ þe prys
þerynne ben noble ilondes and solempne hauens of þe see, and provynces
ful of alle rycchesses, and citees most ful of people and with most stronge
walles and dyches and with oþer array of werre, with plente of golde and
of sulder.[1]

It was a bland formulation, one that would have given little help for
the tasks ahead. The reality he was to meet was very much more
complex. Here was a land deeply divided, politically, economically,
socially, and one about which any generalization at all might seem
precarious.

Political divisions loomed large. It is true that, as compared with the
second half of the thirteenth century, the general virulence of faction-
struggles within the individual city-states had diminished. Their naked
ferocity, symbolized by the murder of Ugolino della Gherardesca and
of his kinsmen at Pisa in 1288[2] – that incident which was so to move
Dante and, through him, Chaucer – was giving way to often no less
bloody but more narrowly limited conflict within signorial families.
At the same time, however, external conflicts had grown and differences in the character of the towns had intensified. Anyone who
travelled in the peninsula was called upon at each stage of the journey,
to make sharp revision of attitudes and expectations. Each of the cities
that Chaucer visited, for example, was subject to different experiences
of government and society. Genoa, whose ships traded over an area
bounded by the North Sea, the Atlantic coast of Africa and the

Crimea, and whose commercial power had drawn it into a secular rivalry with Venice, was the ruler of a maritime economic empire. Yet her commune was dominated by an oligarchy torn by complex rivalries. These divisions, which had recently brought the city for a brief period in subjection to the Visconti (1353–6), now spawned a series of dictators (ruling with the title of 'Doge'), whose periodic rise and fall was conditioned by the balance of power among the *alberghi* or kin-groupings of its nobility. Within a generation its inherent instability was to lead to a long-term loss of independence. Florence, by contrast, had an economy that was founded on banking and the production of luxury textiles for the export market. It was ruled by a noble–merchant oligarchy that, though menaced by internal division and by proletarian discontent – whose dual development was to lead to the rising of the *Ciompi*, those at the bottom of society, in 1378 – displayed a more vigorous capacity for survival. The city, with its subject territories, remained as one of the major powers in the complex political chessboard of the peninsula, and its upper classes were shortly to develop their fascinating, however misleading, ideology of their devotion to 'Italian liberty'.

Very different was the *signoria* (or rule by one single person or family) of the Visconti, who had firmly established themselves as Lords of Milan by the 1320s and who had thenceforth extended their rule throughout much of Lombardy and Piedmont. Their autocratic government brought peace between hitherto rival communes and ensured a strong measure of harmony within the oligarchies of the cities over which they ruled. Their marriage-alliances of the 1360s into the royal houses of France and England had been a recognition of the family's status as a European power. Yet, even when the hostile propaganda of their enemies has been discounted, their rule was accompanied by all that violence and aggression characteristic of absolute régimes. From 1355 the family was headed by Galeazzo II and his brother, Bernabò. On Galeazzo's death in August 1378 Bernabò was to assume control. Chaucer's 'God of delyt and scourge of Lumbardie', brutal, coarse-humoured, boastful of his cruelties, Bernabò was for the next seven years the strongest political force in northern Italy. In 1385, however, Galeazzo's son, Giangaleazzo, wearying of the contempt and subordination to which his uncle exposed him, executed against him that bold and treacherous *coup d'état* which (immediately before the tragedy of 'erl Hugelyn') the Monk was to recall in the *Canterbury Tales*.[3]

Beyond these societies lay others which Chaucer was not to know personally but which were often influential in the cultural formation of the age: in the north very many communes and *signorie*, each tenaciously seeking to preserve its own sovereignty; in the south the kingdoms of Naples and of Sicily. Naples in particular, though now in the seventies distracted by the difficulties facing Queen Giovanna I, still possessed something of that rich amalgam of influences that, as David Wallace shows in a later chapter,[4] had, in the days of King Robert I (1309–43), formed the mind of the young Boccaccio. There was a sense in which the peregrinations of men like Dante and Petrarch and Boccaccio had produced from the diversity of Italy something like an 'Italian' culture. Yet the political contrasts remained. These were matched – it was something that would have struck a poet with particular force – by strong linguistic divisions. The Genoese, Florentines, and Milanesi whom Chaucer was to meet spoke not so much different dialects (for that would be to presuppose that there existed at the time some generally accepted standards of Italian speech) as different languages, languages that could be seen by Italians of the Middle Ages as being as remote from each other as from non-Italian speech. So in his chronicle Salimbene de Adam, by origin from Parma, remarks of a friend, Fra Bernabò of Reggio (d. 1285), that he was an accomplished linguist who spoke French, Tuscan, and Lombard fluently.[5] Did 'Italy' then in fact exist? From compatriots with experience of the peninsula, men of action like Edward Despencer or John Hawkwood, Chaucer would no doubt have learnt that it was a word without meaning. From English students at Italian universities he might have received a more nuanced judgement. There were writers who spoke of Italy (Petrarch's 'most holy land, dear to God . . . fair mother, glory of the world'), who wrote of themselves – however much it remained a literary idea – as Italians. There were some writers in Tuscan speech who seemed to have created – certainly in verse, less surely in prose – a common literary language. But outside Tuscany it was a written rather than a spoken tongue, something to be not absorbed but learnt – as one of the greatest Italian authors of the nineteenth century was to write of it in his own day – 'quasi come una lingua morta' ('almost like a dead language').[6]

Of this multilingual Italy, Bartholomew, in his encyclopedia, had stressed one particular characteristic. It was predictable that an Englishman whose country had been open since the twelfth century to the operations of north-Italian merchants and financiers, should have emphasized: 'solempne hauens of þe see, and provynces ful of alle rycchesses', 'plente of golde and of sulder', and it was these things perhaps that persuaded him that 'Italy bereþ þe prys'. Yet here again diversity predominated. Bartholomew's formula disguised the reality

of a land that was often very poor (often much poorer than its
northern neighbours) and of an economy that was, in all but a few
sectors, underdeveloped. Some Italians, of course, enjoyed great wealth.
The expansion of commerce from the eleventh century had made
certain ports masters of an *entrepôt* trade in the goods of the Eastern
world. Some financial companies had developed banking facilities in
over a hundred towns throughout Europe and had made the gold florin
of Florence and the gold ducat of Venice the principal units of international currency. In its turn this commerce, essentially concerned
with luxuries and the money market, had given the leading merchants
in its principal centres – Venice, Genoa, Florence, Pisa and Siena – an
ultimate control of political life within their communities.

This control, however, had not altered the basic social fabric of the
communes.[7] The 'commercial revolution' had brought with it no
'emergence of a dominant bourgeoisie' nor any general *embourgeoise-
ment* of society. For here – it was one of the greatest contrasts between
northern Italy and the rest of Europe – there was no necessary and
inevitable antithesis between 'merchant' (in so far as the word was
used of those participating in long-distance trade and international
finance) and 'noble'. In Italy, where city and countryside were much
more intimately linked than in the northern world and where the
contrast, 'merchant of the town, noble of the countryside', did not exist
the great mercantile families were either noble in origin or had become
or were becoming nobles and the principal aim of those with wealth
but no lineage was to assimilate in all ways to the life-styles and values
of the nobility. In the thirteenth century, it is true, most north-Italian
towns had witnessed the *popolo* movement, an attack from below upon
noble privileges and an attempt to widen the political base of the noble
oligarchies. A distinguished sociological historian has, indeed, recently
sought to show that developments in art and literature of the time
were intimately connected with this phenomenon. ('The art of Giotto
and his followers would have been impossible without the psychological stamp of the *popolo*.'[8]) Yet the reality is that, once its leaders
had been incorporated within the ruling class, the *popolo* everywhere
declined and that, even in the centres of great commerce, it was the
nobility who remained as rulers. By their very participation in trade,
of course, they differed from the nobility of the northern world, and
yet at the same time they were very different from any English
merchant. Those Genoese with whom Chaucer is found in contact –
the *cavaliere* Jacopo Provano and his son. Saladino; 'the king's merchant', Giovanni de' Mari (whose ancestor had been an admiral of the
Emperor Frederick II); Antonio d'Oria (whose forebears had fought by

the side of Richard Coeur-de-Lion at the siege of Acre) – saw themselves, and were seen by contemporaries, in a much more exalted light,
and enjoyed very much greater social esteem, as well as political power,
than the aldermen of Edward III's London.

In Florence, again, as a characteristic oligarch – one whom Chaucer
might well have met – one could take the lawyer, Lapo da Castiglionchio, a humanist, a friend of Petrarch and Boccaccio, a powerful
politician, whose brother Francesco died in England in the service of
the Alberti banking-house. Castiglionchio's *Ragionamento*, a discourse
on the character of nobility, dwells lovingly on his eminence of blood
and the *vita cortese* of his ancestors, asserts that his kindred took part
only in 'noble' long-distance trade 'and in no vile occupation', and
offers a striking reminiscence of how, at university, he had put down
a fellow-student who had come of villein stock. It is not easy to
describe a man like this as a 'bourgeois'. Yet for his contemporaries
outside the large commercial towns and in the *signorie* the claims of
blood counted still higher and here power rested unequivocally with
landowners.

II

These were the men who gave patronage in *trecento* Italy. It is true
that in this period there can be discerned the growth of an ethos that
might be described as 'bourgeois', a subculture distinguished by such
things as the use of account-books in double entry, unremitting
exchange of commercial letters, the keeping of *ricordi* or diaries,
treatises of secular morality offering prudent counsels of thrift and
self-interest, the sort of culture in which the self-made merchant of
Prato, Francesco Datini, lived.[9] Yet most of the 'high culture' of the
fourteenth century was kindled by older, more conservative ideals.
In some ways one of the strongest secular messages that Dante
communicates in the *Commedia* is the yearning to create a world in
which nobles pursued chivalric virtue, the world of:

> le donne e' cavalieri, li affanni e li agi
> che ne 'nvogliava amore e cortesia

> (The ladies and the knights, the trials and the feasts
> Which bound our hearts in love and *courtoisie*)

– that world which Guido del Duca recalls in Romagna (*Purg.*, XIV,
109–11) and Marco Lombardo in northern Italy (*Purg.*, XVI, 115–26).
If again, 'the human comedy' of the *Decameron* be 'a mercantile
epic' – a judgement based, presumably, on some of its subject matter

or on (difficult) assumptions about the 'mercantile rationality' that might be supposed to inform it rather than on its style or prejudices – it is very far from being a 'bourgeois epic'. Its full title – *Il libro chiamato Decameron cognominato Prencipe Galeotto*, with its invocation of Prince Galehaut, 'li sires des Lontaines Illes', model of *courtoisie* – reminds us how far it is a work rooted in chivalric and courtly traditions.

In one sense, that is, this culture had something very much in common with that of northern Europe. It principally differed from that of the North in that it was developed upon the basis of educational systems[10] that were largely dominated by laymen and, however traditional in form, primarily shaped to meet the interests of laymen rather than clerics. Again, in response to the needs of commerce and (perhaps more to be stressed) as an effect of the emergence in the thirteenth century of a large number of highly bureaucratized governments whose bureaucracies were manned at all levels by laymen rather than clerics, education was more widely available in northern Italy than in the non-Italian world. By the end of the thirteenth century lay schools had become common; in the fourteenth, governments came more and more frequently – particularly in the smaller city-states where private enterprise was likely to be insufficient to meet demand – to establish their own grammar schools. In the greater centres – as the figures, however exaggerated, offered by Giovanni Villani for Florence in 1338 imply[11] – literacy was widely diffused and there were many schools.

If primary and secondary education provided a base, the universities too, no doubt, had some influence on literary culture. Their development was uneven. Some ten new *studia* were founded in Italy in the Trecento, yet apart from Perugia and Pavia they enjoyed at the time little success. Of older foundations Bologna and Padua still succeeded in attracting students from outside the peninsula, though others, such as Naples, languished in the second half of the century. Normally there were two basic faculties: law (civil and canon), and medicine (to which the arts faculty was subjoined), medical studies including philosophy, natural philosophy and astrology. In arts, one reads very occasionally of lectures given on the Latin poets but teaching was mainly confined to grammar-school-type courses in Latin grammar, rhetoric and logic as a preparation for higher studies in law or medicine. Though admiration for Roman law may have produced an admiration for the Roman world and played some part in the growth of humanism, university studies were largely conceived of as satisfying vocational ends and it would be rash to overstress their influence outside these areas. Dante, whose learning persuaded the following generation that he had been to a university, is unlikely ever to have gone; Petrarch and Boccaccio could both, perhaps, be described as 'drop-outs'.

Almost all teaching in the universities was in the hands of laymen and – it is something again that emphasizes the 'secularity' of Italy in comparison with the northern world – theology was hardly ever taught in them. Yet, of course, religion still played a decisive role in society and was still a most prominent shaping factor in trecento culture. Here Chaucer, faithful son of the *ecclesia anglicana*, could find that same blending of a 'catholic' faith, linked with local elements, known to him in his homeland. Here – though expressed with more particular virulence, since it incorporated the national consciousness of intellectuals – was the same general contempt for the Roman *curia*, exiled to an alien Avignon in the 'Babylonian Captivity' (1309–77), and then later the same weary despair at the outbreak of the Great Schism (1378). Here, in the attacks launched by Dante and Marsiglio of Padua against all forms of temporal jurisdiction claimed by the Church, were the same sentiments that were to lead John of Gaunt to offer patronage to Wyclif at the beginning of his public career. Here was the same mass of parochial clergy of very limited professional competence whose defects were balanced by the vigorous influence of the mendicant orders in popular religious life.[12]

Yet despite their evident vigour, the orders of friars had not escaped the harsh, almost instinctive anticlericalism general among many articulate elements in society. Such sentiments did not however imply any repudiation of orthodoxy; rather the reverse. In Italy, after the thirteenth century, very little heresy flourished, merely a thin trickle found among the *Fraticelli*, those 'Spiritual Franciscans' who taught the doctrine of the absolute poverty of Christ and who waited for the imminent appearance of 'the last Emperor' and 'the Angelic Pope'. Against dissent stood the ecclesiastical inquisitors, whose activity, however resented, was probably of less importance in preserving orthodoxy than that of secular governments. Assisted by the strongly local character of a religious life in which each bishop formed his own diocesan calendar, the commune, which was often coterminous with the diocese, increasingly came to provide for its citizens a form of, as it were, civic religion in which religious feeling and local patriotism blended in harmony, in which the captured battle-wagons of its enemies were placed inside the cathedral, and saints whose feast-days fell on days of military victories were raised to a new prominence within the local pantheon. If Westminster Abbey and Saint Denis glorified the northern monarchies, the cathedrals of Santa Reparata in Florence and of Santa Maria in Siena exalted the communes.

Those communes, whether oligarchies or *signorie*, were caught in a system of rivalries and alliances, which generated almost constant war. Bartholomew's 'most stronge walles and dyches and with oþer array of werre' were indeed a major feature of the Italy that Chaucer visited. Throughout the second half of the fourteenth century war came in some ways to assume a still darker character in that the mercenary companies that constituted the main armies of the Italian powers were composed of and commanded by non-Italians, men like Werner Urslingen, 'Enemy of God, Pity, and Mercy', Albrecht Sterz, and that 'cher et foial Johan Haukwode' with whom in 1378 Chaucer was ordered to negotiate. Yet this very conflict between rival powers, certainly the continual competition for status between them, can in some way explain the particular richness of high culture within the peninsula in this century. For with it went a search for the exaltation of the fame of their cities, which led to the channelling of large sums into the patronage of the arts. Nor was this something directed simply at outsiders; their unity and strength menaced always by internal faction, governments sought through architecture, sculpture and painting to stimulate cohesion and loyalty to commune or *signoria*.

It was largely as a result of such calculation that the century following 1250 had seen the building of the great *duomi* of Siena, Florence, Orvieto and Arezzo; in the 1380s the beginning of the new cathedral at Milan showed that the instinct still lived. In these projects it was lay governments that built, adorned and maintained the buildings; clerics were sometimes explicitly, always implicitly, excluded from any of the decisions to be made. 'Civic religion' played a part too in the making of the very numerous other local churches that were erected at the time. When in 1293 the Dominican Fra Remigio Girolami argued that the new church of Santa Maria Novella in Florence should 'exceed all other churches not for our honour but for the honour of the Florentine people' he was touching a chord likely to provoke the warmest response. Hand in hand with these developments went the construction of government buildings – *palazzi comunali*, *loggie*, and signorial castles and palaces – and the first attempts at town-planning 'for the greater beauty of the city'. With architecture came patronage of the other arts, of that sculpture and painting which was seen primarily in this age as an adornment of building and which was very often designed specifically to spell out the messages of the various civic religions. It was an environment where there was a large, guaranteed, state-aided market for the visual arts and where large numbers of painters and sculptors were employed.

Whether these arts evoked any powerful response in Chaucer, whether his silence before the heritage and current production of Italian artists[13] indicates indifference, incomprehension, or simple deference to conventions of what was communicable in literature, it is not easy to say. There were literary precedents for descriptions of symbolic temples and statuary, but writers were still taking only their first tentative steps towards speaking of what they felt before a real building or painting. Chaucer, too, though he might admire the strength of a castle or feel reverence before a painting of a Madonna, would not, like the tourist of today, look in Italy for 'Art', since that was something which had not yet been invented. For him, as for almost all his contemporaries, building, painting and sculpture would be considered as artefacts with primarily functional purposes (interior decoration, glorification of government, excitement of religious feeling), brought into being by an *artista* (whose contemporary meaning was 'artisan') in the same spirit that any other artisan work was produced. It was still only in limited circles, and still only occasionally, that a few great individuals – Giotto, Simone Martini – were hailed as intellectual creators whose work rose above the other 'mechanical arts' and could be considered as adding to the glory of their cities.

Visually, the visitor from the north would be struck first by the landscape (which, at that time, was in some areas, just beginning to take on something of the character it has today) and the character of light – things that within the peninsula (it is a commonplace, but one worth stressing, to emphasize its geographical and climatic disunity) change very sharply from region to region – and then by the architecture of the cities. This too varied greatly, yet overall he would sense the way in which the thrust to the sky of the northern Gothic churches had ended. Here was a world where the traditions of the basilica – however much since the thirteenth century overlaid by Gothic innovators – still ruled. At Florence, in those buildings begun back in the 1290s – the cathedral (still in the 1370s unfinished), Santa Maria Novella and Santa Croce – Gothic structural engineering had been compromised to native traditions, to those of the Romanesque San Miniato and of the Baptistry (which, Chaucer would be told – it was a legend but universally believed – had once been a temple to that 'myghty Mars the rede' who had been – men said, still was – the city's tutelary deity). Under a Tuscan sun windows became much smaller. With a still-enduring classical search for harmony came shorter columns and lower roofs, and so no need for flying buttresses.

Here the emphasis lay on horizontal rather than vertical lines. Even in Lombardy, so much closer to the Gothic world, the new cathedral of Milan to be begun in 1386 – which its builders may themselves have believed to have been modelled on French or Burgundian patterns – still today, under its eighteenth- and nineteenth-century accretions, reveals itself as a traditional low-set Lombard church. Verticality in the Italian cities was to be found more in secular building: in the ascending mass of the Palazzo Vecchio and in the hundreds of fortress towers from which the nobles fought out their conflicts.

Those churches and palaces were decorated with paintings and sculptures. Outside the both more and less than wholly aesthetic expectations that a man of the time would bring to them, Chaucer's awareness of these things would be different from that of most educated people today. The modern tourist walks, with his guide-book, through galleries in which have been placed works which have been divorced from the context for which they were designed and which are generally arranged according to the teachings of art-history, chronologically and under 'schools'. Before long he forms sequences and relationships in his mind. He learns how the *maniera greca* of the thirteenth century, which had sought to produce majestic cult-images, without setting, depth, or sense of spatial relationships, had given way to the manner of Giotto (d. 1337), to a new art seeking volumetric presentation, psychological realism, individualization of character and, hence, drama. He becomes aware of how at the various regional centres Giottesque influence was accepted or adapted; how, for example, at Florence it led to an emphasis upon space and volume; how in Siena – as exemplified in Simone Martini (d. 1344), and (though in a more robust and realistic vein) in Ambrogio Lorenzetti (d. c. 1347) – to a more linear, lyric, illustrative style. He learns that at this time in Tuscany there emerged the first beginnings of portraiture and landscape naturalism and, looking forward, he sees towards the end of the century the coming of the 'International' or 'International Gothic' style. At the same time he is conscious of how in each region local styles persist. He discovers, for example, that, in the 1370s, painters in Lombardy and the Veneto like Altichiero, Avanzo and Giusto de' Menabuoi, were working in traditions of Giottesque realism, that at the same time Venetian artists were continuing to pursue modified Byzantine traditions, and the Bolognesi, again, perfecting another blend of realism and graphic refinement.

So too in sculpture, which our tourist comes to see as interacting with the developments in painting. Tracing classical sources in the work of Nicola Pisano (d. c. 1284) and the influence of French Gothic in Giovanni Pisano (d. after 1314) and Arnolfo di Cambio (d. *c.* 1302), he learns to think of these men as the originators of modern sculptural traditions. From them he plots the diffusion of the new styles through the Pisan Giovanni di Balduccio to Milan, through Andrea Pisano at Florence, through the Siennese Tino di Camaino and Lorenzo Maitani to Naples and Orvieto respectively; and so on. His aesthetic experience, that is to say, is organized historically and he can attempt to deal with the mass of different sensation to which he is exposed by categorizing it. This would not have been possible for Chaucer, who lived in an age when art was very little written about and there were no guide-books that discussed works of art in an aesthetic spirit. What he perhaps saw in, for instance, Florence – a hieratic Byzantine Madonna painted by Margaritone d'Arezzo (d. 1293), together with other pervasive survivals of the *maniera greca*; a Giotto crucifixion; the domestication to homely images of the Christ-story in such followers of Giotto as Bernardo Daddi and Taddeo Gaddi; Andrea Pisano's reliefs in the Campanile or his bronze doors in the Baptistry – would all have been timelessly undifferentiated in his mind as 'what is in Florence'. Although it is not at all improbable that he might be moved very deeply by this or that work, one wonders how far the very profusion of the arts would permit a man on his king's business to penetrate very deeply into understanding them as a whole.

There was, after all, so much to be seen. From the thirteenth century churches were filled with panels and the fruits of the new fresco technique, while the walls of nobles' houses too, and the residences of governments, were covered with paintings. Walking through some-where like Azzone Visconti's palace in Milan; pausing to look at its game preserves, fishpools and enclosures for rare animals and birds, with their lions, bears and ostriches; passing through the cloistered courtyard whose fountain, surmounted by an angel with the banner of the Visconti, had a basin in which were sculpted the navies of the Romans and Carthaginians; perhaps praying afterwards in its private chapel, San Gottardo, with its frescoes of the life of the Madonna, its gold, silver and ivory decorations; admiring its campanile ('quod videre', says the chronicler, 'est quaedam magna delectatio'); hearing its clock striking, it seems probable that only a generalized sense of richness and magnificence would remain.[14] If, in the great hall, he saw Giotto's representation of *Vanagloria and Nine Worthies* (among whom was Azzone himself), was he excited or bewildered by them? He may already have been familiar with something of the Giottesque manner. From what is known of the work of the King's Master of the Painters, Hugh of St Albans, at Westminster, pronounced 'Italian'

influence has been deduced (and, indeed, on his death in 1368, Hugh
had left to his wife 'a panel of six pieces of Lombardy which cost me
£20').[15] Yet this is not to say that Chaucer would necessarily like what
he saw. Petrarch himself, writing as late as 1370, had underlined its,
for contemporaries, still *avant-garde* and élitist flavour, in referring to
'the work of the distinguished painter, Giotto ... whose beauty
amazes the masters of the art, although the ignorant cannot understand it'.[16] If anything stood out it would be perhaps the equestrian
statue of 'grete Barnabo Viscounte', 'quae est mirabilis et pulchra',
executed by Bonino da Campione, 'sculpted in marble, armed as if
setting out for war, brandishing his baton of command'; which
Bernabò had placed in his own lifetime over the high altar of San
Giovanni in Conca.[17]

Whatever his reaction to its art, that Chaucer should show a direct
interest in the vernacular literature of Italy is something that, with
benefit of hindsight, may seem much more inevitable.[18] Yet the
element of inevitability could be overstressed. In the first place there
was the problem of obtaining Italian texts. Commercial *scriptoria* do
not seem to have yet produced many works – outside basic university
texts, account-books, and note-books – that had not been specifically
commissioned from them. Libraries of the monasteries and Orders of
friars rarely possessed any vernacular manuscripts. Works in French
and, to a lesser extent, Italian, could, it was true, be found in signorial
libraries. The inventory of the largest of these collections, that of the
Visconti library at Pavia in 1426 – by which date the collection had
grown considerably from what it had been in the 1370s – details 988
books, of which 90 were in French and 52 in Italian, and Chaucer in
his stay of perhaps a month and a half in Lombardy might have been
allowed to consult them. But for any prolonged study, it seems
probable, he would have been dependent on the invitation of private
acquaintances who would be willing to lend him for copying works
from their own collections. Yet this was an age when few even wealthy
men possessed any specifically literary works at all. If Boccaccio owned
a considerable library it was because he had transcribed it himself;
if Petrarch possessed some 200 books it was because he could afford to
employ some 5 or 6 copyists.[19]

Then, again, in his work for the Crown, Chaucer had no need to
learn any Italian language. Italian merchants and nobles used French
as a *lingua franca*; Italian officials, it goes without saying, knew Latin.
Any version of Italian he acquired must have been obtained orally, for
no Italian grammars or dictionaries existed. To have done this would
not have been difficult for someone with a good ear, yet for any

Englishman casually coming into contact with the Italian world, and preoccupied with matters of government, there existed literatures in languages that were much more immediately accessible. There were, for instance, the Latin books of the friars: works like St Bonaventura's *Life of St Francis*, Giovanni da San Gimignano's *Meditations on the Life of Christ*, the *Legenda* or lives of the saints by Jacopo da Voragine, and Jacopo da Cessole's sermonizing tract, the *Book of Chess* (these last two of extraordinary popularity throughout the whole of Europe in the later Middle Ages, eventually to be translated and published by Caxton). In less conservative vein there were works like the *Commentary on Valerius Maximus* by the Augustinian Dionigi da Borgo San Sepolcro and for that matter all the Latin prose and verse of Dionigi's friend, Francesco Petrarca. Or again in the romance tongues there existed a treasury of narrative verse that was immediately open to the northern visitor, one popular among all classes and diffused everywhere in northern and central Italy. Italians were still composing epics (would continue to do so in the early fifteenth century) in Franco-Italian, a hybrid language in which the *langue d'oeil* overwhelmingly predominated, but to which certain Italian elements were added. The themes of these works were drawn from the *matière de France*, from stories of Charlemagne and the Paladins; their spirit, however, was now generally adapted to the ethos of the courtly–epic genre and 'the most beautiful stories of Arthur'. They were sung by the *cantastorie*, the singers of tales in the market-place, and at the same time they found a prominent place (written on parchment, often illuminated with miniatures) among the *codices* of signorial libraries.

There was, that is to say, enough literature in Italy to have kept Chaucer entertained and stimulated without his ever having learnt any Italian. That he should have felt the need to have begun to elicit the sense of Tuscan, the language of a region in which, as it seems, he did not stay for any length of time, was not, that is to say, in any way casual but rather the fruit of a very powerful intellectual and literary curiosity. Without depreciating the many authors and different styles to be found in Tuscan literature of the Trecento – from that of the friars, to the *cantari*, to the work of the *poeti giocosi*, to the *novelle* – at the focus of that curiosity there no doubt lay, above all else, the authority and reputation of Dante and the place that in the fifty years after his death Dante had achieved as supreme defender of the claims of vernacular literature.

III

Vernacular literature in that age needed defenders. Latin, language of international exchange, of learning, of the great pagans and early Fathers, a language that bestowed immediate power, seemed, long before the full flood of classical revival, to be inevitably superior to any vulgar tongue. (It was indeed to be believed for a long time yet that in the Roman world men had used their local Italian in their everyday concerns but had reserved Latin for their more serious purposes.) Accordingly writers in the vernacular enjoyed small official esteem and governments offered them little patronage. The communal oligarchies ignored them. In the signorial courts they might eke out a meagre existence as *uomini del corte* – as it were, high-class minstrels – a life of 'the salt taste of another's bread' and 'the hard path which leads up and down another's stairs'. For all his skill in Latin, it was the life of Dante, preoccupied with his *volgare* poem, in exile: 'a ship without sail or helm, driven to diverse ports and estuaries and shores, blown by the dry wind of wretched poverty'. Petrarch, by contrast, enjoyed from his late thirties very considerable prosperity. The papacy endowed him with benefices; the Courts showered him with gifts. Yet in all this, it was the Latinist, not the poet of the *Canzoniere*, who was being rewarded. It was a Latin 'rethorike sweete' and a Latin 'poetrie' that had won him the laurel crown, and when at the marriage-feast of Prince Lionel of England and Valentina Visconti in 1368 he had been invited to sit at the top table it was because his hosts had hoped from him a commemoration not in Italian but in the language of the immortal past. So too Boccaccio was able to secure patronage as an author only when he had emerged as a humanist.

Against this consensus one man had asserted the dignity of common speech. He had moreover, it should be added, demonstrated the dignity of an Italian rather than any non-Italian common speech. Despite the achievements of the Sicilian school and the early *dolce stilnovisti*, writers in Italian in the second half of the thirteenth century had not been able to escape the suggestion that their works, already of minor importance in that they were written in the vernacular, stood still further condemned in that they were written in an inferior vernacular. Several of the most remarkable Italian poets of the thirteenth century, men like the Mantuan Sordello, the Bolognese Rambertino Buvalelli, the Genoese Lanfranco Cigala, had chosen to write in Provençal rather than in their own languages. Other writers in verse, we have already seen, had believed – and continued to believe throughout the fourteenth century – that they could best engage an Italian audience by writing in a predominantly French Franco-Italian. Several prose authors, too, had written in a pure *langue d'oeil* and justified their choice, as Dante's master, Brunetto Latini, had done (and his words were to be echoed by others), on the grounds that: 'this speech is the most delightful and most common to all people'.[20] It had been Dante, who in opposition to such attitudes, in opposition to 'those wicked men of Italy who praise the common speech of other nations and despise their own' (*Convivio*, I, XI), had vindicated the cause of a native tongue. In part this was through his defence of the vernacular in the *Convivio*; in part through his attempt (abandoned by the time he had begun the *Commedia*) to discover, in the *De Vulgari Eloquentia*, the elements of a common Italian literary language to be created from all the regional languages of Italy. Yet his supreme validation of an Italian *volgare* lay, of course, not in theory but in practice, in the writing of the *Commedia* in Florentine speech.

In fact the manuscript traditions of both the *Convivio* and the *De Vulgari Eloquentia* suggest that neither work was well known in the fourteenth century (though where known they were, no doubt, influential). The *Vita Nuova*, copied by Boccaccio and echoed in his and Petrarch's works, was, again on the manuscript evidence, not widely diffused. The shorter poems were dispersed in numerous collections, frequently joined to the works of other authors who had vaingloriously attached Dante's name to their own productions. Of still more restricted fame in this period were the Latin *Epistolae*, and then the *Monarchia*, which, burnt by the ecclesiastical authorities in 1329, lived a clandestine (often anonymous and untitled) life throughout the Middle Ages, its continued survival often menaced by indignant readers. (In the upper margin of the Znojmo manuscript appear the words: 'This book appears to me schismatic, compiled at the request of the late Lewis of Bavaria. I commit to your judgement whether it should be passed to the inquisitor of heretics or simply completely destroyed.') In the manuscript culture of the Trecento, that is to say, 'the complete works of Dante' (or 'of Boccaccio' or 'of Petrarch') were not available. That in these circumstances Chaucer should have been introduced to at least Book IV of the *Convivio* is rather remarkable. Not at all surprising, however, is his access to the *Commedia* (of which over 100 manuscripts survive from the fourteenth century) for it was inevitably this work to which most Italians would have drawn the attention of a foreign poet. In popular circles, among the *illiterati*, those with no or limited facility in Latin, it had achieved instant success, not simply in Tuscany, but in all the provinces of Italy. That success was matched among those of academic temperament; by

1380 there existed some ten commentaries upon all or part of the work, which, line by line, explained the difficulties and elaborated upon the felicities it presented. For Chaucer, the poem's frequent allusions to obscure figures and incidents from the political life of Dante's own day (so obscure that the trecento commentators are often at a loss to explain them), and, perhaps still more for one raised in very different political traditions, its imperial ideology, may have presented difficulties. On the other hand with the classical and Biblical allusions, the discussions of philosophy, natural science and theology – all those things that perplex the modern reader – he may be presumed to have been at home. Above all there was, too, the directness of the poetry.

Yet once again the inevitability of Chaucer's approach to Dante must be called in question. For within his lifetime certain Italians of the day, leaders in thought and literature, would, moved by other preoccupations and enthusiasms, have treated inquiries about the Dante who had died some fifty years before with a certain weariness, would, amidst the general laudations, have themselves offered only faint-hearted praise.

IV

Since Dante's death in 1321 much had changed in Italy. Its economy had contracted and famine struck now more frequently. (If Chaucer's first visit to Italy had come a year later, in 1374–5, he would have arrived to view those harrowing scenes which accompanied a general *carestia*.) Again, for the first time since the eighth century, bubonic plague had struck at and become rooted in the peninsula. From the initial and most violent attack in 1347–8 to the end of the 1370s it is likely that its population was reduced by between a third and a half.

For the effects that the coming of plague may be supposed to have had upon the 'collective Italian consciousness' – and upon, more specifically, the sensibilities of Boccaccio, Petrarch and Tuscan painters of the second half of the century – large claims have been made.[21] 'The year 1348 has left us alone and forlorn, for it has taken from us what the wealth of the Caspian or of India cannot replace. These losses are irreparable.' So Petrarch in the first letter of the *Familiares*. Yet how far men who lived through the Black Death moved to more melancholy, sober, conservative and pessimistic world views, how far, if indeed they did so, their change of heart is to be explained by circumstances (such as advancing age) quite remote from the plague, is not at all clear. Nor is it easy to think of any means by which arguments for the intellectual and spiritual consequences of the pandemic might be either validated or rejected.

The Black Death quite apart, there were good reasons enough for Dante's work to have been seen by men of the 1370s as very much the product of a previous generation and as representing interests in some ways remote from their own day. Dante had grown up in a Florence to which knowledge of scholasticism, of Aristotle, of St Thomas, had come rather late, and he had embraced all these, one might almost say, with the enthusiasm of a latecomer seeking to catch up. Yet by his death, Thomism was in retreat before new systems of thought that in the course of the fourteenth century were to gain much greater prominence. The teaching of Duns Scotus (d. 1308) denied that the world-order had been created through participation in the divine mind but asserted that it had arisen purely through the inscrutable command of the divine will. Much more radically, William of Ockham (d. 1347) developed an epistemology that placed the Godhead beyond all scutiny of the human intellect. Italian theologians began to draw sharp boundaries between faith and reason and to launch attacks upon the use of Aristotle in the search for knowledge of the divine. At the level of polemic, at least, all speculative reasoning in natural theology came increasingly to be condemned as 'Averroism'.

At the same time Augustinian thought revived to challenge the supreme scholastic confidence in the capacity of man to attain justification through a combination of grace and works. At Paris Gregory of Rimini (d. 1358), at Oxford Thomas Bradwardine (d. 1349), argued from God's 'absolute power' against 'the proud self-conceit' of those who (like Dante, Par., v, 19–22; Monarchia, I, xii, 6) had so emphatically asserted that 'lo maggior don' granted to man was 'della volontà la libertate'. Discussions of these complex issues filled the schools and filtered down to the audience of the Nun's Priest's Tale (4424–43). Ultimately perhaps all these debates on 'necessitee condicioneel' and

> 'Wheither that Goddes worthy forwiting
> Streyneth me nedely to doon a thing'

provoked in the lay mind, whether in England, whether in Italy, the conviction that the whole of that sacred science in which theologus Dantes had studied so passionately was something best left to the professionals. None the less, if the rediscovery of Augustinian theology had limited consequences, Augustine spirituality – if it be not too arbitrary to distinguish between them – enjoyed a new popularity. Characteristic of the new age was the Milleloquiam Veritatis Augustini of Bartolomeo da Urbino (d. 1350), a carefully indexed anthology of the saint's writings published together with commendatory verses by Petrarch. It was, one might almost say, inevitable that in the new age the work that, at the top of Mount Ventoux, Petrarch should pull from his pocket should prove to be Augustine's *Confessions*.[22]

Though in the *Commedia* Augustine had appeared in the celestial rose and the decretalists had been reproved for failure to study his writings, it is obvious that Dante sets far greater store by many other Christian sages. Faced with the saint's condemnation of the Roman Empire – to isolate just one issue – the poet's reserves were inevitable. Here again a wide divide opened up between his thought and the coming age. If for Dante the death of Henry VII had not at all signified the end of precious imperial hopes – so that, as is now known, the *Monarchia* that gave them their fullest expression was to be the last work he wrote – men of the next generation (indeed most men of his own generation) were more likely to write and think, like Marsiglio of Padua in his *Defensor Pacis* (best dated to shortly after 1326; translated into Tuscan in 1363), in terms of their own commune rather than of any universal power. If like Petrarch they dreamt dreams of an Italy freed from 'the pilgrim swords of barbarian fury', they entrusted their hopes to men like Cola di Rienzo rather than to foreigners from across the Alps. For all effective purposes, the Empire, a major constituent of Dante's vision of the world, had ceased to exist.

But still more than all these questions of political and philosophic viewpoint – which, of course, were not absolutely fixed between generation and generation (even Boccaccio is found transcribing St Thomas' commentary on Aristotle's *Ethics*; and the Dominicans continued to champion the saint of their Order) – the question of language itself still lay between past and present. The very greatness of Dante imposed its own barrier here. However useful it might be for a foreigner to introduce into his work Dantesque phrases, ideas and themes, for an Italian their unsolicited arrival in his mind and on his page could often have the effect – as the poetry of Boccaccio reveals – of a jarring reiteration in an inappropriate context of the all-too-familiar. Petrarch declared himself aware of the danger, sought to sidestep it by refusing to own any manuscript of Dante's work, and perhaps through that distancing was able to transmute his influence more harmoniously. Yet, this aside, what still remained at issue was the whole vexed question of the potentialities of the *volgare*, whether it could indeed be considered as the best medium for the writing of great literature. Dante's own classical knowledge, his immense dependence upon Virgil, his insistent demand for the instantaneous recognition of a very wide range of classical allusion, might all suggest, whatever the greatness of his poetry, the priority and primacy of the classical world and so too of its language.

Such reflections gained powerful reinforcement from the development of humanist studies in Dante's own lifetime. From the 1290s, small groups of friends in towns all over Italy – in Padua, Verona, Vicenza, Venice, Milan, Bologna, Florence and Naples – are found coming together informally to study the classical texts and attempting to reproduce something of the spirit of the classics in their own writings. The movement gained impetus from the transfer of the papacy to Avignon. Italians following the papal *curia* to the north or 'provided' to French benefices came then for the first time into contact with the libraries of northern and central France, which were much richer in classical texts than any in Italy. It was so that Petrarch, in the household of Cardinal Giovanni Colonna, came to discover Cicero's *Pro Archia* at Liège, and that Landolfo Colonna, as Canon of Chartres, came across and passed on to Petrarch Books XXVI–XL of Livy. The residence of the papacy at Avignon, again, by the very affront it offered to the national consciousness of intellectuals, stimulated study of that distant world in which Italy had been supreme. As a result, to some of Petrarch's contemporaries, to men seeking authentic knowledge of the classical world, attempting to plumb the secrets of a true Roman style, overmuch concern with the *volgare*, fruit of an age and culture that it was difficult not to think of as inferior, might very well suggest a certain misdirection of mind. If the verse correspondence of Dante and Giovanni del Virgilio be authentic, such a reaction was certainly being expressed towards the end of Dante's life. Why, asked Giovanni, are you writing your great work in Italian? Why throw pearls prodigally before swine; why clothe the Castalian sisters in unworthy dress?

In the next generation these were questions that were to echo insistently in the mind of Francesco Petrarca (1304–74), the most influential literary figure in Italy in the age of Chaucer, and one too whose mind and art reveal the divisions that had opened between past and present in the course of his life. Brought up as a boy in alien Avignon, dislike of the present in which he lived had been one element in that kindling of his passion for the *notitia vetustatis*, for knowledge of the Roman past. From this had sprung his textual criticism, his laudatory histories of the classical world ('For what else is history, all of it, but praise of Rome?'), and the Latin verse of the *Bucolicum Carmen* and the epic *Africa*. In these labours, which were destined to shape decisively the course of European intellectual life, his vision of the great past was always subordinate, however, to a profound adherence to the central beliefs of Christianity. Hence much of his energies too were devoted to works, very congenial to his nature, of a moralizing cast. Born of an unphilosophic and unsystematic intellect, their content fluctuated with the mood of the author. If the *De vita solitaria* praises monastic withdrawal from the world, the *De remediis utriusque fortunae*, despite occasional efforts to syncretize pagan stoicism and Christian hope, appears to have a primarily rhetorical character (no doubt the explanation of its success) and to lack any overarching theme. The central ambiguity of Petrarch's view of life appears most clearly in the *Secretum*, made public only after his death. This, a dialogue or examination of conscience between 'Franciscus' and 'Augustinus', sets the soul of the author in disturbed confrontation with a pure Christianity that is contemptuous of pagan *virtus* and secular dreams of glory. There is a profound contrast here with the moral system of Dante. For Petrarch, 'doubting everything with the sole exception of what I hold it sacrilege to doubt', has – in this most characteristic of his age – no vision of the world in which all is doctrinally united, can only grasp from moment to moment at the appearance of truth.

The same message appears in the collections of his Latin correspondence, the *Familiares* and *Seniles*. Ostensibly modelled on the letters of Cicero *Ad Atticum*, which he had found in the Chapter Library of Verona, they display a strong moralizing strain, to which are added popularization of the humanist programme and attacks upon those advocating rival intellectual interests, upon students of medicine and law and upon the followers ('disciples of that rabid dog, Averroes') of Aristotelian philosophic and scientific interests. They reveal a constant self-absorption in small things as in great, and it is this appeal to the self outside social institutions that, as in the moral philosophy, appears as the ultimate value asserted:

Finding in the whole world no place of quiet and solace, return to your own room and to yourself; keep vigil with yourself; speak with yourself; hold silence with yourself; stand still with yourself...Make for yourself at the centre of your soul a place where you may hide, where you may rejoice, where you may rest undisturbed, where Christ may dwell with you (*Familiares*, XV, 7).

All through his life, side by side with these interests, Petrarch devoted himself to that cultivation of Tuscan verse which was to make him a leading influence in the European lyric tradition. Of the widest appeal in his own age was the *Triomphi*, an allegorical vision of a not unconventional cast, begun when he was aged about fifty. Of much greater originality was the *Canzoniere*, his collection of *Fragmenta*, of *rime sparse*, brought together for the first time in 1342, and subsequently reordered, added to, and, no less than eight times, revised. Here individual poems of love (together with some verses of political interest) are gathered into a loose unity to tell the story of the poet's meeting with Laura, his love for her, her death and his emotions in the years after her death. Within the courtly and *stilnovisti* traditions yet moving to less learned and doctrinal conceptions of love than those found within them, Petrarch here again places his own self, his own changing moods of hope and fear, grief and joy, at the centre of his verse. At the end the reader remains above all with the vision of the pensive and solitary poet considering ('though speech be vain') the sadness of 'his' Italy, remembering (though mortal pleasure is 'a brief dream') the beauty of his lady, and finding meaning only within his own soul.

It cannot be thought that Petrarch, who devoted himself so frequently to the revision of the *Canzoniere*, considered at any profound level that his *volgare* writings were indeed, as he spoke of them, 'my trifles in the *volgare*' (a phrase that itself echoes Horace's ironic self-depreciation). Yet, amidst all his surrenders to mood, a certain intellectual conviction forced him to think of them as inferior to compositions in Latin. Was it possible, after all, that anything could compare with the language of Rome? As a result he was little disposed to regard with an oversympathetic eye the work of others who ventured into common speech. Hence the praise with pursed lips that – in that year in which Chaucer was in Florence – he bestows on the *Decameron* ('published, I take it, during your early years ... If I told you that I had read it, I should deceive you. It is a very big book, written in prose, one for the multitude' (*Seniles*, XVII, 13)). Hence too the terms in which, some fourteen years before, he had written to Boccaccio repudiating the suggestion that he might envy Dante:

... a certain poet, our fellow-townsman, popular indeed in his style, undoubtedly noble in matter ... Those who wish me ill say that I hate and despise him, seeking by this means to draw on me the hatred of the crowd with whom he is most popular ... to him without hesitation I grant the palm of eloquence in the *volgare*. Is it very likely that I should envy one who dedicated his whole life to those things which I pursued only as the flower and first fruits of my early life? What for him was not the only but certainly the principal craft, was for me a game, a solace, and a mental exercise ... you tell me he could have, if he wished, turned to the other [Latin] style: I fully agree ... yet to what he turned is evident ... Why should one who doesn't even envy Virgil, envy anyone, unless by chance I should envy the applause and harsh murmurings in his favour of fullers, innkeepers, and wool-workers, whose praise, which I am happy to lack, shames who receives it?[23]

The tone of this letter, its very diversions from the truth, reflect the inner disturbance of a great Italian poet who is here repudiating one aspect of his own greatness. To see in its words simply the *invidia* that their author was specifically disclaiming is to ignore the intellectual force of the arguments against the *volgare* in his own generation. We, after all, know, as the fourteenth century did not, the subsequent history of neo-Latin and of Italian and other vernacular literatures. We do not need to ask, not simply whether this or that great work, but whether great literatures, great traditions, could exist outside Latin speech. The power of Petrarch's thought here is curiously well illustrated in the defence of Dante by its principal opponent, Petrarch's friend, Giovanni Boccaccio (1313–75). For what is so striking in Boccaccio's defence of Dante are the elements of misrepresentation within it.

Significant here, for instance, is Boccaccio's composition of the 'Ilaro' letter, found in the author's own hand in codex XXIX, 8 (the *Zibaldone boccacesco*) of the Medici–Laurenziana library.[24] The monk Ilaro is represented here as describing his meeting with Dante. He tells of how the poet had explained to him that he had begun to write the *Commedia* in Latin (he offers us the first three lines of this version) but, how on realizing that the liberal arts were in decline, had decided to turn instead to Italian. The purpose of this – how shall one describe it? – *novella* is clearly to show that Dante not alone could have produced, but actually wanted to produce, a work comparable to the *Africa*, that he could be considered as a man of the highest culture in the terms of Petrarch's own generation. This claim is a major theme too in Boccaccio's *Trattatello in Laude di Dante*. This, the first extended biography of the medieval world that did not treat of a saint or political figure, presents, not without the assistance of a certain strong creative fantasy (with, for example, supernatural intervention to ensure posthumous discovery of the author's lost cantos, etc.), the picture of a man 'given to our age by the special grace of God' in order that 'dead poetry' might be reborn. It seeks to show that despite Dante's marriage and political commitments (i.e. his adherence to the *vita activa*, now unfashionable in intellectual circles) he was a man acceptable to the new age in that his learning embraced all that knowledge of and skill in Latin required by the humanists.

It might even be, as has recently been argued (though the contention seems to be rejected by most scholars), that in his eagerness to show his hero as a creative writer in Latin verse Boccaccio himself wrote the

Ecloghe that pass under the names of Dante and Giovanni del Virgilio.[25] However that may be, Boccaccio's lifelong struggle to persuade the intellectuals of his own generation that they need fear no shame in sharing the enthusiasms of the *vulgus* ended in triumph. Symbol of his success was his appointment as public *lector* on the *Commedia* at Florence in 1373. An Italian poet had now been raised to the status of a classic, had been granted public recognition by the élite of the commune, could stand thenceforth, alongside 'Virgile, Ovyde, Omer, Lucan, and Stace' (*Troilus and Criseyde*, v, 1792).

V

Of Boccaccio as an author in the *volgare* and of his influence on Chaucer subsequent essays will speak in detail. From the 1350s the influence of Petrarch also drew him to Latin essays in rhetorical moralism (the *De Casibus Virorum Illustrium* and the *De Claris Mulieribus*), and to an intensification of that interest in the classical world he had always shown. From that interest came the *De Montibus* (a dictionary of classical geography) and the *Genealogie Deorum Gentilium* (a study of classical mythology), works that are distinguished more by compilatory diligence and scholarship than creativity. In all this, Boccaccio's humility before the world of the past served as an essential complement to Petrarch's attempts to revive antiquity. In particular his efforts to secure Leontius Pilatus as teacher and translator of Greek in Florence laid the foundations for the flowering of Attic scholarship in the city from the 1390s.

At the same time, of course, Boccaccio was directing the flow of Italian high culture in directions remote from Chaucer's experience. It was perhaps fortunate that the English poet came to Italy when and where he did. If he had joined Prince Lionel in 1368 he might have encountered Petrarch at Milan and have been treated to a discourse on the vanity of vernacular literature. As it is he came to Florence in 1373 at a time when the layman Dante was about to be canonized as a classic. Some twenty years later, again, he would have encountered a world where the triumphs of Tuscan literature seemed to be part not of a living but of a past age. Sacchetti's lines on the death of Boccaccio:

> or è mancata ogni poesia
> e vote sono le case di Parnaso[26]

had a prophetic character: henceforth poetry was lacking and the houses of Parnassus were empty. Henceforth, without necessarily repudiating the claims of the *volgare* (whose true worth was still, however, a subject of debate), the patrician world was turning to 'civic humanism' and the Greek offered by Chrysoloras.

It was turning, that is, to studies that, through their very closeness to the preoccupations of city-state society, were to prove for a long time difficult to transplant in English soil. Those few who sought to do so in the fifteenth century – men like Humphrey of Gloucester, William Grey, John Tiptoft, Robert Flemynge – remained largely isolated and uninfluential.[27] Caxton's choice of titles for print notoriously ignores Italian high culture. What that choice did include, however, was, of course, that one English author who, gifted with a more striking perception and, also, coming to Italy in a particularly auspicious decade, had been able to wrest something of its poetry for himself and his fellow-countrymen.

Notes

1 *On the properties of things: Trevisa's translation of Bartholomaeus Anglicus' De proprietatibus rerum; a critical text*, ed. M. C. Seymour, vol. II (Oxford, 1975), pp. 773–4 (Lib. XV, cap. lxxix). For the Italian translation: V. Cian, 'Vivaldo Belcalzer e l'enciclopedismo italiano delle origini', *Giornale storico della letteratura italiana*, suppl. 5 (Turin, 1902).

2 The killing of Ugolino, Count of Donoratico, by Archbishop Ruggieri degli Ubaldini and his party was not chronicled by contemporaries with any precision. Yet it is clear that Dante's representation of it changes, at least in some ways, the historical circumstances, either in response to his poetic imagination or because the story had been distorted by popular rumour in the intervening twenty-five years. Three of Ugolino's relatives who were murdered with him were in fact grown men, the other, it seems likely, about fifteen years old. See S. S. Bernardi, 'Ugolino' in *Enciclopedia dantesca*, ed. U. Bosco, vol. V (Rome, 1976), pp. 795–7, and R. Piattoli, 'Ubaldini, Ruggieri', *ibid.* pp. 772–4.

3 On the political life of these governments in the period see V. Vitale, *Breviario della storia di Genova*, vol. I (Genoa, 1955); *Storia di Milano* of the Fondazione Treccani degli Alfieri, vol. V (Milan, 1955) (and a good brief account in English in D. M. Bueno de Mesquita, *Giangaleazzo Visconti* (Cambridge, 1941), chapters 1–3); G. A. Brucker, *Florentine Politics and Society 1343–1378* (Princeton, 1962).

4 See pp. 145–7 below.

5 Salimbene de Adam, *Cronica*, ed. G. Scalia (Bari, 1966), p. 864.

6 On this subject, see B. Migliorini, *Storia della lingua italiana*, 3rd edn. (Florence, 1961), chapters 4–6 (abridged English trans., London, 1966), and C. Dionisotti, *Geografia e storia della letteratura italiana* (Turin, 1967), pp. 75–102.

7 On Italian society in this period, see P. Jones, 'Economia e società nell' Italia medievale: il mito della borghesia' in his *Economia e società nell' Italia medievale* (Turin, 1980); L. Martines, *Power and Imagination: City-states in Renaissance Italy* (Harmondsworth, 1980); J. Larner, *Italy in the age of Dante and Petrarch* (London, 1980).

8 Martines, *Power and Imagination*, p. 74.

9 A. Sapori, 'La cultura del mercante medievale italiano' in his *Studi di storia economica (Secoli xiii–xiv–xv)*, 3rd edn., vol. I (Florence, 1955), pp. 59–93; I. Origo, *The Merchant of Prato*, rev. edn. (Harmondsworth, 1963); F. Melis, *Aspetti della vita economica medievale*, vol. I (Florence, 1962).

10 There is no modern general treatment of education in Italy in this period, though G. Manacorda, *Storia della scuola in Italia* (Milan–Palermo–Naples, 1913), vol. I, pt 2, and H. Rashdall, *The Universities of Europe in the Middle Ages*, new edn. of F. M. Powicke and A. B. Emden (Oxford, 1936), are still very valuable. In addition to those bibliographical indications in J. Larner, *Culture and Society in Italy, 1290–1420* (London, 1971), pp. 373–4, see J. K. Hyde, 'Commune, University and Society in Early Medieval Bologna' in *Universities in Politics*, ed. J. W. Baldwin and R. W. Goldthwaite (Baltimore, 1972); and N. G. Siraisi, *Arts and Sciences at Padua: The 'Studium' of Padua before 1350* (Toronto, 1973).

11 Villani (*Cronica*, ed. G. Dragomanni (Florence, 1845), vol. III, p. 324 (Lib. XI, cap. xciv)) asserts that in that year 8000–10,000 children of the city were being taught to read, that 1000–2000 were at business schools, and 550–600 at grammar schools. On this claim, see Larner, *Culture and Society*, p. 189. The study of literacy in Italy (as elsewhere) will, no doubt, be stimulated by the establishment of the *Seminario permanente* on *Alfabetismo e cultura scritta* held by the Istituto di Storia medievale e moderna della Facoltà di Lettere e Filosofia of the University of Perugia. The *Notizie* of this unit, edited by A. B. Langeli and A. Petrucci, have appeared from time to time since March 1980.

12 See G. Miccoli, 'La storia religiosa' in the Einaudi *Storia d' Italia*, vol. II, 1 (Turin, 1974).

13 Among a vast literature, valuable introductory studies on the fine arts are: G. Weise, *L'Italia e il mondo gotico* (rev. Italian trans. of the German original of 1939, Florence, 1956); P. Murray, *The Architecture of the Italian Renaissance*, 2nd edn. (London, 1969), chapter 1; J. White, *Art and Architecture in Italy 1250–1400* (Harmondsworth, 1966); A. Smart, *The Dawn of Italian Painting 1250–1400* (London, 1978).

14 Azzone's residence, built in 1336, was inherited by Galeazzo II, who, according to Pietro Azario (*Liber gestorum in Lombardia*, ed. F. Cognasso, R[erum] I[talicarum] S[criptores], XVI, 4, p. 152), destroyed all of it, apart from San Gottardo, in the course of building a new palace. Others think its core survived until the rebuilding of the cathedral. For its description, see Galvano della Fiamma, *Opusculum de rebus gestis ab Azone, Luchino et Johanne Vicecomitibus*, ed. C. Castiglione, R.I.S., XII, 4, pp. 16–17.

15 See E. W. Tristram, *English Wall Painting of the Fourteenth Century* (London, 1955), pp. 46, 58; J. H. Harvey, 'Some London Painters of the 14th and 15th centuries', *Burlington Magazine*, LXXXIX (1937), 303.

16 T. E. Mommsen, *Petrarch's Testament* (Ithaca, 1957), pp. 79–80.

17 Azario, *Liber gestorum in Lombardia*, pp. 133–4. It was a work that impressed other chroniclers. See *Annales Mediolanensis*, ed. Muratori, R.I.S., XVI, col. 800; and (following the *Annales*) Giovanni de' Mussi, *Chronicon Placentinum*, ed. Muratori, R.I.S., XVI, cols. 544–5. Today in the Castello Sforzesco, Milan, it is illustrated in J. Pope-Hennessy, *Italian Gothic Sculpture*, 2nd edn. (London, 1972), no. 62 and fig. 52. See the dust-jacket of the present volume.

18 Most useful introductory studies: vol. III, 'Il Trecento', of the *Storia della Letteratura Italiana*, ed. E. Cecchi and N. Sapegno (Milan, 1965); J. H. Whitfield, *A Short History of Italian Literature* (Harmondsworth, 1960), chapters 1–4; *Petrarca*, ed. R. Amaturo, 2nd edn. (Bari, 1974); V. Branca, *Boccaccio medievale*, 2nd edn. (Florence, 1975) and *Giovanni Boccaccio: Profilo biografico* (Florence, 1977).

19 There is no general study of Italian libraries and book production in the century, but see Larner, *Culture and Society*, pp. 178–88, and bibliographies there, pp. 372–3. R. A. Pratt's 'Chaucer and the Visconti Libraries' (*E.L.H.*, VI (1939), 191–9) could not, of course, take into consideration the scholarship of E. Pellegrin, *La Bibliothèque des Visconti et des Sforza* (Paris, 1955).

20 See Brunetto Latini, *Li livres dou Tresor*, ed. F. J. Carmody (Berkeley, 1948),

p. 18: 'por cou que la parleure est plus delitable et plus commune a toutes langages'; Martin da Canal, *Les Estoires de Venise*, ed. A Limentani (Florence, 1972), p. 2: 'porce que lengue franceise cort parmi le monde et est la plus delitable a lire et a oir que nulle autre'.

21 R. N. Watkins, 'Petrarch and the Black Death: From fear to monuments', *Studies in the Renaissance*, XIX (1912), 196–223. Millard Meiss' sketch (in his *Painting in Florence and Siena after the Black Death* (Princeton, 1951), chapter 7) of Boccaccio's spiritual development from the mid-century is weakened by the discovery that Boccaccio was actually recopying the *Decameron* round about 1370. On plague and culture, Larner, *Culture and Society*, pp. 122–49. To this should be added H. van Os, 'The Black Death and Sienese painting', *Art History*, IV (1981), 237–49; and the articles by C. K. Fengler; N. R. Fabbri and N. Rutenberg; and M. Plant in the section 'Painting and Sculpture after the Black Death' in *The Art Bulletin*, LXIII (1981), 374–425.

22 See U. Mariani, *Il Petrarca e gli Agostiniani*, 2nd edn. (Rome, 1959); H. A. Oberman, 'Fourteenth-century religious thought, a premature profile', *Speculum*, III (1978), 80–93. For hostile comments by Italian Augustinian friars of the Trecento upon Aristotelianism and upon the use of philosophy by theologians (comments known to and influential upon the Augustinian Luther) see A. Zumkeller, 'Die Augustiner-theologen Simon Fidati von Cascia und Hugolin von Orvieto und Martin Luthers Kritik an Aristoteles', *Archiv für Reformationsgeschichte*, LIV (1963), 15–37; H. A. Oberman, 'Headwaters of the Reformation', in *Luther and the Dawn of the Modern Era*, ed. H. A. Oberman (Leiden, 1974), pp. 70–3. For Thomist survival, however, P. O. Kristeller, *Le Thomisme et la pensée italienne de la Renaissance* (Montreal–Paris, 1967).

23 *Familiares*, XXI, 15. For the most recent discussion of this letter see G. Paparelli, 'Due modi opposti di leggere Dante: Petrarca e Boccaccio' in *Giovanni Boccaccio Editore e Interprete di Dante*, ed. Società Dantesca Italiana (Florence, 1979), pp. 73–90.

24 P. Rajna, 'Testo della lettera di Frate Ilario e osservazioni sul suo valore storico' in *Dante e la Lunigiana* (Milan, 1909), pp. 234–85. For discussion see, above all, G. Billanovich, 'La leggenda dantesca del Boccaccio: Dalla lettera di Ilaro al Trattatello in laude di Dante' in his *Prime ricerche dantesche* (Rome, 1947), pp. 35–53, 78–83.

25 On this issue, G. Rossi, 'Dossier di un' attribuzione, Dieci anni dopo', *Paragone*, CCVI (1968), 61–125; and, in rebuttal, E. Cecchini, 'Giovanni del Virgilio, Dante, Boccaccio. Appunti su un' attribuzione controversa', *Italia medioevale e umanistica*, XIV (1971), 25–56; G. Padoan, *Il pio Enea, l'empio Ulisse. Tradizione classica e intendimento medievale in Dante* (Ravenna, 1977), pp. 223–51.

26 F. Sacchetti, *Il libro delle Rime*, ed. A. Chiari (Bari, 1936), p. 194.

27 See D. Hay, 'England and the Humanities in the Fifteenth Century' in *Itinerarium Italicum: The Profile of the Italian Renaissance in the Mirror of its European Transformation* (Dedicated to P. O. Kristeller), ed. H. A. Oberman and T. A. Brady (Leiden, 1975), pp. 305–67. For important new contributions on fourteenth-century Italian literature in its context – Court, city, schools, Universities, religious orders – see the essays by A. Roncaglia, F. Gaeta, J. Le Goff, R. Antonelli, C. Bologna, V. De Caprio and G. Ricuperati in vol. I ('Il letterato e le istituzioni') of the Einaudi *Letteratura Italiana*, gen. ed. A. Asor Rosa (Turin, 1982).

JANET COLEMAN

English Culture in the Fourteenth Century

In the early fourteenth century and much more so by the end of the century, there were few English men and women of high or low degree who had little contact with a town and its market. And because of the economic and judicial ramifications that related most fourteenth-century English towns to a city and thence to the nation, most men and women were brought within the ambit of written law. Most men and women knew people who could read to some degree even when they could not do so themselves. Consequently, there were few who escaped being at least on the margins of a functional literacy.[1]

Furthermore, although England in the fourteenth century may have been a network of differing local customs, local dialects, local traditions and select ways of recalling that tradition, especially in times of crisis against outside enemies, there was constituted a unified nation, if we may judge from the host of documents that speak of things English whilst devoted to the particularities of some aspect of government administration, to specific legal wrangles and to literary entertainment. Men from whatever city, county or region defined themselves as Englishmen most vehemently in the first instance, by distinguishing themselves from the French, against whom they fought in an episodic war that endured for over one hundred years.[2] Cities and towns were, indeed, self-governing units, many by the end of the thirteenth century having their own charters of liberties, their own courts of justice and their own officials and mayors, elected from amongst the influential burgesses in the name of the rest.[3] But such local self-government, even when it became oligarchic tyranny of the rich merchants over rival craft guilds and over the less rich or over the ordinary, poor, labouring citizenry, was never seen to be divorced from central royal government and its centralized justice. If the king were weak, even dominated by his courtiers or paramours, even if he were killed – an event repeated twice in the century: Edward II and Richard II – there appears to have been little concern that England would disintegrate without its nominal head and become a congeries of self-governing cities with incompatible local traditions. This is quite distinct from contemporary Italy. Why was this the case?

Now it is true that England was not, like Italy, invaded by foreigners, although the French harried the coasts during periods of the Hundred Years War; it is also true that she 'created' a national unity by enlisting men of whatever social degree to fight for the king against the 'unjust' French across the sea, and this enabled men of low degree to return home rich with booty or from the ransom of captives and move up the social scale. Here indeed was the policy of 'imperial expansion' and something of a citizen militia that every republican political theorist from Cicero to Machiavelli would advocate as a means of uniting a nation at home and creating wealth from plunder. But at the same time there was little ostensible national pride in a common vernacular language (although Edward III had roused passions by insisting that the French wanted to invade England and destroy the English language)[4] and there simply was no written literary *tradition* in English to speak of.[5] A common history of the nation, when written at all, was composed half from myth, half from a common European stock of Latin and French writings cobbled together, most often by monks who, in having chosen the monastic vocation, indicated their own class allegiance: they, like many of their secular ecclesiastical and noble counterparts with connections with the royal Court, had more affinities with an international chivalric and aristocratic code maintained by a relatively small portion of the European population, whose manners were more like one another's than like those of the men and women they ruled.[6] What, then, can be pointed to as a substantial English experience, in which people could somehow participate, if it was not a distinct literary tradition? I think we must look to the English Parliament, which was seen by the articulate 'middle class' and gentry to be an objective instrument of participatory unity, a means of self-government on a national scale, where rules were thought to be self-imposed, particularly in terms of financial grants to subsidize royal policy. Parliament was a national court and a national legislature and, perhaps most important for the unsubtle mind, it was a place where money was granted to the king not merely by men who came there as 'petitioners' but by men who were at the same time representatives of local interests. Theirs became a power to 'answer' as well as petition, that is, to give their own opinions in the sphere of taxation, as well as to make requests of royal justice.[7] By the end of the fourteenth century, English life, especially at Court and in the urban centres of international trade and finance like London, was dominated by money and a bourgeoisie. That portion of the 'Commons' whose voice was heard with increasing frequency were the rulers of the nation, for it was they who made the money and could lend it to the Crown.

We should point not only to Parliament but more particularly to the House of Commons, which, developing in political importance during the fourteenth century, participated in drawing up authoritative decisions to bind all the king's subjects legally. By the reigns of Edward III and Richard II, the Commons were sharing functions with the Lords as their equals in authority; in practice, they were *more* than equal to the authority of the Lords because, in the sphere of taxation,[8] the Commons spoke for the men with the money and the international credit – the gentry and burgesses (in urban politics they were 'the common council') – and they called the tune of patronage and of policy at home and abroad. Not only would members of Parliament see that justice was done by the king's ministers, but they petitioned for annual parliaments because they saw it as *their* task to ensure the practice of – technically, 'the dispensing of' – a uniform royal justice. The generality of Englishmen were specially interested in that aspect of 'the business of Parliament' referred to as 'the dispensing of justice'. Parliament was seen to be, and in fact was, by the third quarter of the century, not only *the* high court, judicially above other courts in the land, but also 'an omnicompetent organ of government at the summit of lay affairs in England'.[9] And it was seen as such, so far as we can tell, even by those who would never have direct personal access to its functions.

A 'commune petition' of 1352: ROLLS OF PARLIAMENT II, 237 (8), (9):

And now...the said Lord William [de Shareshull, C.J.K.B.] told the Commons that if they had any petitions concerning grievances done to common people, or to help improve the Law, they should put them forward to parliament. And it was also told to the Prelates and Lords that each should attend to the trying of the petitions of individual persons in the places appointed for them. And then, following long discussion and deliberation by the Commons with the 'Communalte', and when the advice of some of the magnates had been conveyed to them both regarding an aid to be assigned to our Lord the King to withstand the malice of his adversary [of France] and with respect to the making of petitions touching the common people of the land, the said Commons came before our Lord the King and all the magnates in parliament and showed how the common people of the land were much impoverished as well by the deadly plague which lately occurred there...as by other harsh taxes, tallages and many other adversities that had befallen them. But notwithstanding these mischiefs, and having regard to necessary measures of defence appropriate

to the deliverance of the realm of England from the great malice of its
enemies, they presented to our Lord the King in full parliament a roll
containing the aid which they had ordained and, being of one accord, had
unanimously granted to our Lord the King in his great necessity, and also
the petitions touching the 'commune' of the land, in respect of which they
asked our Lord the King for a good and prompt response.[10]

I think we can say that whoever is meant when reference is made to
'the Commons' consulting 'the "Communalte"' that is, whatever
group is directly represented in Parliament by a 'commune petition' as
set out above, it includes, in fact is dominated by, that portion of the
population that is well within the margins of functional literacy,
because some form of literacy had become a survival skill. That portion
of the population with an active stake in the financial balance of the
nation, who were trained in the lay professions or in commerce and
who participated in some major public aspect of urban life in addition
to earning a wage through a craft or skill – Chaucer's little group of
guildsmen: the Weaver, the Tapestry-Weaver, Carpenter, Dyer and
Haberdasher who 'wel semed ech of hem a fair burgeys / To sitten in
a yeldehalle on a deys ... for to ben an alderman' (General Prologue,
369–72) – comprised the spokesmen for the interests of the Commons.[11]
Such men and their women, whose skills included literacy, even of a
sophisticated kind and in several languages – Anglo-Norman, Latin
and English – were entertained and instructed, edified and amused by
the literature of Geoffrey Chaucer, John Gower, William Langland and
lesser literary lights, during the last twenty-odd years of the century.
But why, if parliamentary rolls and Court documents were recorded
primarily in Anglo-Norman and Latin, did Chaucer, Langland, and
even Gower, write in English? And if the royal Court read Anglo-
Norman romances with ease and collected Latin texts in their libraries,
why compose in English at all? Where did their readership and
audience obtain its literacy in any of these languages in the first
instance? Furthermore, how did such multi-linguistic skills contribute
to a conception of a unified nation that, at least in political terms,
showed England to have some of the desired characteristics that a
Petrarch or a Cola di Rienzo would wish for in a united Italy?

Most men and women spoke some regional variant of Middle English
and would have been familiar with ancient stories and local customs as
rehearsed by older members of a community whose memories were
exercised concerning 'how it had always been done in the past'.
They would use the memory tricks of a culture dependent on an oral
verse tradition that passed on the valued characteristics of heroes and

heroines by means of the rhymed or alliterative collocation, the formulaic memory tag. Most men would also have some contact with traditions written on the page or at least they would know of laws that were not only held fast by the memory. If there was a formal social role as yet for the minstrel who would tell and retell the romances, the saint's life, the local tale during a winter night's entertainment, repeating what an audience already knew and wished to hear again, there is also evidence that his role was changing, certainly by mid-century. He was being replaced by the professional poet, who composed in order to be read as well as heard. The minstrel came to depend less on what he freely composed from traditional formulae than on stories written by others and committed to memory – the minstrel was a 'mere' rehearser of other men's creations if we accept the testimony of the author of *Wynnere and Wastoure*.[12] To paint an even wider canvas, we can say that by the second half of the century the earlier clerical and anonymous nature of written literature had changed, in part because patterns of literary patronage were changing, and authorial responsibility became a feature of later fourteenth-century composition. If you wanted to be a professional entertainer, to tell a story and be a poet in the last quarter of the century, the methods available, as Chaucer describes them, were either to memorize every word of someone else's story (using the original author's language, even if your own diction were plainer), or to find new words and make up a tale, fantasize, or even lie, and then one word or another would do. If engaged in the latter exercise, then Chaucer advises you to use language that is 'ful brode', plain, like Christ's in holy writ. You will get your message across all the better without high rhetoric. But was there a high rhetorical style that could be used, in Latin or in English, by the end of the century?

> For this ye knowen al so wel as I,
> Whoso shal telle a tale after a man,
> He moot reherce as ny as evere he kan
> Everich a word, if it be in his charge,
> Al speke he never so rudeliche and large,
> Or ellis he moot telle his tale untrewe,
> Or feyne thyng, or fynde wordes newe.
> He may nat spare, althogh he were his brother;
> He moot as wel seye o word as another.
> Crist spak hymself ful brode in hooly writ,
> And wel ye woot no vileynye is it.
> Eek Plato seith, whoso that kan hym rede,
> The wordes moote be cosyn to the dede.
>   (General Prologue, 730–42)

When English came to be used as a literary language, in a remarkably short space of time – it took a century if not less to produce
Chaucer – it emerged first as a language that borrowed many of the
organizational techniques that were more common to French and Latin
texts that served it as models. One major way in which English became
the status language at the end of the fourteenth century was by means
of developing itself as a medium of translation from other languages
that already possessed extensive literary traditions. Without an
exalted, written, literary tradition of its own other than the 'plain
and vigorous style' of some realistic complaint poetry, the English
language often took on literary associations from other languages.
Chaucer's English, and in particular, how he tells us his stories, owes,
it seems, far more to French, Latin and Italian literature than it does
to whatever we can surmise about native oral traditions. His poetic
apprenticeship seems to have been spent in *translatio* – literally, translating or paraphrasing, glossing, explaining or commenting on a
classical Latin tradition (Ovid, Boethius), on Boccaccio and Dante, and
on the *Roman de la Rose* and its sequels. Indeed, this could be taken
epistemologically to be the way one develops the very rudiments of
literacy and learns to compose grammatically in general: in fourteenth-
century England one copied formulae (see the school-books like *Cato*,
containing excerpts from the Latin classics like Seneca, Virgil and
Ovid, and the books of model letters known as formularies) and if one
wished to write in English, one transferred the formula to English,
finding words to suit in the new language the structure and content of
the old, the Latin or Anglo-Norman model. We can return to this later
in order to help to explain Chaucer's (and Gower's) dependence on
relatively few but seminal texts of the later Latin/Roman period, and
his early dependence on Dante and Boccaccio. My reason for raising
the issue of *translatio* at this point is that English society was coming
to be increasingly open to lay (as opposed to exclusively ecclesiastical)
governance, and if one wanted employment other than working the
land, one needed somehow to learn the written skills of recording and
copying documents in Latin and Anglo-Norman. These languages had
venerable written traditions in the spheres of legal theory and theology.
On the practical side they provided formulae for land conveyancing,
legal practice, religious instruction and after-hours entertainment.
A manorial court would require men, at first ecclesiastics and then
gradually laymen, with skills to record, according to traditional
formulae, the legal relations and financial dealings and accounts that
were increasingly needed by landowners if they were to defend their
possessions before the king's law, particularly against those without

land but with money ready to purchase. It was becoming more difficult to enforce traditions in the realm of property and rights merely by appealing to those traditions 'held from time out of mind'. Where were your documents, your proofs? *Quaestio quid juris?* ('What law applies?').

The language of legal cases for the thirteenth and earlier fourteenth centuries tells us very little other than the formulaic expression of men's relations with one another. And as Milsom has argued, such formulae disguise the real changes in a society like England's.[13] England was changing from a society where feudal and mutual relationships obtained regarding duties and mutualities of dignity concerning degree (thirteenth century) to a society where relations were increasingly reified, individualized and were discussed in terms of private property *rights* of singular persons. Feudal duties came to be commuted to some one-sided financial equivalent by the end of the thirteenth century. The written formula that records what went on in a court does not, except by accident and where a scribe is inexperienced, tell us of this gradual change in relations between men of different rank in English society, but changes there were. By the fourteenth century, the formulaic, legal expression of relations, supposedly fixed in the common law, were taken, especially by the 'peasants' who revolted in 1381, to be anachronistic descriptions of real social relationships.[14] England was not at this time, if ever she had been, a society of fixed degree, wholly dependent on a fixed feudal mutuality of land tenure in return for customary services. Serfdom was, for the most part, dead; it was not economically viable. The social idyll of organically fixed groups, particularly in terms of fixed membership of such groups, was no more than an anachronistic and archaic legal and literary formula. If, as Gower and Langland complained, English society was increasingly dominated by low-born lawyers whose bread and butter were such fixed formulae, then the wider diffusion throughout society of their anachronistic legal theory ran counter to the rapid growth in social integration. Through intermarriage and the expansion of educational opportunities provided by legal apprenticeships and by the foundations of grammar schools, such professions were opened and extended. Literacy itself and the increased opportunities to obtain at least a functional and formulaic literacy, helped to increase social mobility in general.[15] It widened the membership of that group involved in local and national government and commerce. Just as Petrarch described it in Avignon, so too in England, literacy was on sale. Indeed, fourteenth-century society classified itself economically, according to tax brackets, far more frequently than in terms of socio-legal status and estates. Paradoxically then, more men were entering the professions that required that they should be literate at least in socially anachronistic legal formulae! Petrarch described what was an international situation:

> To these men (who are a great crowd in these days) letters are not the light of the mind and the delight of life but instruments for acquiring riches. Children are sent by their parents to study literature not as to an academy but as to a market place, at great expense to the family but with the hope of much greater financial return. So that it need be no occasion for surprise if they make a venal and avaricious use of an education which they have pursued for purposes of sale and on which they have based the sinful expectation of a usury not of a hundred per cent but of a thousand.[16]

We are interested to know how Englishmen who wished to be hired and socially advanced for their literate skills could come to the notice of some minor or major magnate in need of a court recorder, or of someone familiar with written formulae for commercial contracts, but it was important *that* such persons should know the formulae. A local householder, a Franklin as Chaucer describes him, who was also a pleader in court sessions and could take over responsibilities of local government, needed to be literate. Where did he learn the requisite formulae? In the local grammar school, followed perhaps by an apprenticeship in business or in a manorial court as part of some local lord's affinity, or in the Inns of Court in London. Or perhaps he went for a year or so to Oxford and studied business-letter-writing or conveyancing.[17]

The fourteenth century provides documents testifying to the founding of numerous grammar schools throughout the country to teach boys the rules of Latin grammar and some literature.[18] Reading, song and grammar as set out in a late Roman grammar text, the *De arte grammatica* of Donatus, were prerequisites for proceeding to the city grammar school and thence, perhaps, to the priesthood, or perhaps thereafter receiving a grammar scholarship and on to an Oxford or Cambridge college or to a cathedral school of higher studies. Or perhaps a boy was snatched, as it was feared, by the Franciscans and caught up in their Order at fourteen years old, provided with board, free tuition in their *studia* and good libraries; it was complained that the friars bought up all the books in use in the arts faculty and elsewhere. Ordinary village boys who became choristers were taught song and grammar, and as at the secular college of Ottery St Mary with a school for canons, a grammar master was appointed to teach the public as well as the choristers. Priests were more and more frequently endowed by generous benefactors in various parts of the country to teach local scholars and anyone desirous of learning grammar. There was no stipulation, and not even an expectation, that those with Latin skills would thereafter necessarily become priests.

Nor were they guaranteed places at Oxford or Cambridge (at this time the colleges were post-graduate halls and undergraduates lived in lodgings), but those whose careers led them into minor orders and the arts faculties at either of the two universities found that their grammar studies were not at an end. They went further than Donatus and heard lectures on text-books of Priscian, another Roman grammar master. They were required to be more than 'pragmatic' readers, and indeed were 'cultivated' to some degree, like Chaucer's Clerk, who preferred to read Aristotle in Latin than to dress well or eat heartily. At university, although not within the degree course, grammar and dictamen, and the art of formal letter-writing, were taught, as was instruction in business methods. These were taught in Latin, sometimes in French, and we only begin to hear of English as a language of professional discourse in mid-century when John of Cornwall, an Oxford grammar master, was said to be teaching Latin grammar in English. There were complaints that students were forgetting or never learning sufficient French and they were consequently ill-prepared for travel abroad, that is, were of no use as potential ambassadors or royal representatives – at Avignon where the papacy was lodged for most of the century, for instance. This is of further interest when we recall that of Chaucer's thirty-two pilgrims in the *Canterbury Tales*, at least thirteen of them were professional travellers or travellers by taste. England was a mobile society, socially mobile and on the move – for commerce or war abroad.[19]

We have most information about the provisions made for those wishing and able to continue their studies in the higher faculties of theology and law at the universities.[20] Scholars were supported by their towns, their families and their friends, and hoped, upon the attainment of their degrees, for preferment in the Church or in some civil-service post. By the end of the century and despite the plague in 1348–9 and its decimation of a generation, there were more of the *sublimes et literati* – those who held prize benefices in the Church, were non-resident pluralists but were often in London or at the papal Court, or seeking and attaining bishoprics and the more powerful positions within the ecclesiastical hierarchy. We shall have more to say about them later. There were also many more of what we might call the pastoral clergy, some relatively well educated, certainly literate after an arts degree at university, and living like Langland of the C text

of *Piers Plowman*, in London, married, teaching and saying a paternoster in the city's chantries. In fact, the increase in numbers of those
seeking the limited posts within the Church became such a problem
that the volume of complaints became a deafening roar – first, that
there were too many absentee foreigners provided by the papacy to
English livings, and secondly that too many of the clergy were
'illiterate' as well as London-, Avignon-, or Rome-runners, not interested in their 'cures of souls' and their parishioners. It is doubtful
if on the whole the clergy *were* less literate than previously,[21] and it is
not always clear what is meant by the slanderous references to
illiteracy. Was it to their lack of skills in Latin, or Anglo-Norman, or
English? Chaucer's poor Parson of the town, holy in thought and deed,
is described as learned: 'He was also a lerned man, a clerk, / That
Cristes gospel trewely wolde preche . . .' (General Prologue, 478–81).
The Summoner knows a formulaic Latin only out of memorized
decrees, but of his friend the Pardoner, 'the geldyng', Chaucer says:
'He was in chirche a noble ecclesiaste. / Wel koude he rede a lessoun
or a storie, / But alderbest he song an offertorie' (General Prologue,
708–10). There seem to have been more such men unable to live on
the slender livings provided by parish churches with fixed incomes that
did not keep pace with inflation. Some London churches were ration-
alized and those lucky enough to receive a place made do with the
collections from more than one parish.[22]

Or perhaps, like the proverbially poor scholar, they earned additional
money by copying manuscripts for stationers, who hired out books and
paid for sections of the most popular legal and theological texts to be
copied *pecia* by *pecia*.[23] The London book trade, from the mid-century,
flourished as a bespoke trade, it seems, largely through the requests of
a literate *haute bourgeoisie* of the city, who wanted romances and
saints' lives, pious and edifying after-hours entertainment, which they
would themselves read, closeted away (as Chaucer describes himself,
after the day spent in the customs' accounts office), or have read aloud
to them.

To get some idea of the Latin snippets one read and was asked
to imitate at an early stage of education, one need only look at
the medieval school-books like the anthology known as the *Liber
Catonianus* (Cato) that categorized *bons mots*, and moral *exempla*
from Seneca, Cicero, Boethius, Horace, Ovid and Virgil, and asked
school-boys to imitate the 'sentence' *and* the form. And some of these
authors were available in French translations in case one needed a bit
of help. Works like Ovid's *Metamorphoses* were translated, commented
on and allegorized. And one could hear quotes and commentaries on

exempla taken from classical Latin works in sermons, interspersed with English prose and verse that served as translations of the Latin quote. The Franciscan collection, the *Fasciculus Morum*,[24] a relatively early fourteenth-century Latin *summa* of vices and virtues, discussed these in ways that were useful for preachers addressing lay people. A moralized 'picture', an abstraction, would be allegorized, stories drawn from the Bible or from classical fable and history would be told, and English verses would be reiterations, in metre, of the Latin text. The bulk of the English verses collected in the *Fasciculus Morum* is the result of translation from Latin, something that is particularly evident in the case of verses that summarize formulations like the Creed or aspects of confession that are meant to be memorized. Here we have quotes or paraphrases from Seneca's *Declamationes*, from Valerius Maximus' collection of *Facta et dicta memorabilia*, that comprise, when offered in English, renderings of a fairly comprehensive collection of meditative commonplaces in English verse. Many of these are repeated and translations improved in a later preacher's handbook, that by John of Grimestone, prepared in the 1370s.[25] Once again, the frequency with which one confronted Latin formulae, in sermons, in school text-books and in business formularies, and the increasing practice of committing to memory such *exempla*, looking them up in handbooks and rendering the text into a memorable English, provides more evidence of the expanding practice of developing the English language as a written translation exercise, whereby theological, pastoral and moral subtleties discovered a *corresponding* rather than a wholly new language in the vernacular. Standard Latin prose and verse appear in many different Middle English versions indicating, as with the commonplaces of the English verse in the *Fasciculus Morum*, that many people could and did translate or paraphrase the Latin moral *sententiae* of the *auctores*, be they in origin pagan or Christian.

With snippets from Ovid and Virgil as school texts to be imitated by the novice grammarian and the practice of collecting formal rhetorical letters in books of high rhetorical examples to be copied (*Liber Epistolaris*), it is clear that the formularies edited by Salter, giving examples of the *ars dictaminis*, are yet further evidence that grammar, dictamen and rhetorical arts were taken seriously in the Oxford of the fourteenth century.[26] Here was one more means of edging one's way up the civil-service ladder, being successful in commerce, or earning a living as a notary public, serving the Crown, the nobility or Church officials in ambassadorial or legal capacities. Chaucer and Gower, like Boccaccio, wrote at least some of their works with merchants, lawyers (civil and canon) and civil servants, as well as royal patrons, in mind. In England these groups would have more than a fleeting familiarity with Latin formulae – legal, moral or commercial – if we can use Mr John Lydford's Memorandum book, recently edited, as an example.[27] He had the book compiled from the documents he required as a busy, middle-ranking canon lawyer of the West Country, active during the 1370s as a proctor for various English causes at Avignon. Here we see entries with 'good versions' of documents he needed, collected from the last forty years of the century, with marginal references to particularly eloquent bits he wished to imitate.[28]

In other words, the venerable medieval Latin tradition of Seneca, Cicero, Valerius, Ovid, appearing in grammar and rhetoric text-books, in mythological encyclopedias, in confessional handbooks and preaching-aids, in formularies of all sorts, was used by all manner of Englishmen and helped to serve the development of English as a status language. And it did this with increasing ease, in part by confronting the consultant of a florilegium of, for example, *exempla* drawn from the classics, with useful alphabetical indices and organized tables of contents – methods of categorizing a vast quantity of Latin snippets and stories to be employed by clerics and laymen alike, who could read for edification and delight, and who were bent on sermonizing, moralizing and edifying their contemporaries.[29]

Ovid's *Metamorphoses* itself, so familiar to the Middle Ages, served as a model of a skilful *compilatio* of around fifty stories linked and woven into a continuous narrative. The work is a florilegium of myths, ancient and 'modern', suited to the encyclopedic compendial prefer-ences of sermon-writers of the thirteenth and fourteenth centuries. The *Metamorphoses* comprises stories classifiable as burlesque, romance, debate and rhetorical genre-painting, and Ovid presents the stories literally, in a pseudo-naive manner that appealed to the literal-minded treatment of Bible stories by some medieval preachers, as well as to the subtle mind of Chaucer.[30] There are strong affinities between the shape of the *Metamorphoses*, the construction of other similar long, episodic, narrative poems in Italian, and the *Canterbury Tales*. Indeed, some near contemporaries, scribes or editors, interpreted the *Canterbury Tales* – and Chaucer may have seen them himself – as a *compilatio* of myths and moral *exempla*, ancient and modern, woven together in a continuous narrative whose art resides in skilful transitions.

To note that it is not only the content but also the form of long, narrative, classical poems like Virgil's *Aeneid* and Ovid's *Meta-morphoses* that served Chaucer as structural models, is to focus our attention on the ways in which sources available to a preacher, entertainer, poet, or theological and political commentator, would be used in fourteenth-century England, both by the talented and by the untalented literate person. Chaucer, no more than lesser literary contemporaries, could not stand outside his linguistic environment. Latin, French and Italian literature, and especially the formal imitation required to produce a successful rhetoric according to the rules, influenced the shape of English verse and to some extent prose. The influence that the *English* language had on someone like Chaucer seems to have been more thematic than structural. Gower is an even better example, particularly in his *Vox Clamantis*, of someone 'composing' by means of the scissors-and-paste method; classical and medieval Latin snippets and citations glued together to suit an historically and socially current English theme – the complaint against the specifically enumerated corruptions of the times during Richard's unfortunate reign.[31]

Another extraordinary use of given Latin texts as foci from which the English verse radiates out in translation and commentary is *Piers Plowman*. Langland seems frequently to have begun an episode with a Latin, often Biblical, quote and, using the handbook aids and alphabetically arranged Biblical concordances of the later fourteenth-century English preacher, he 'divides' his Latin text by focusing on a word, finding other Latin texts with verbal parallels in his handbook, and through the use of English dramatizes and exemplifies his original 'theme'.[32] In other words, here too we see someone 'composing' in English, in a language without a strong or exalted literary tradition, by imposing an external organizing principle on the work by focusing on a given Latin text and, in effect, translating it, literally, then allegorically, and pushing his poem forwards didactically by finding a narrative transition from one Latin quote to the next, one episode as defined by the Latin sentence to the next.

To say that a great deal of English poetry of the fourteenth century shows strong affinities with the sermon, merely points out in the first instance how the secular world was viewed then as manifesting the spiritual. From the standpoint of compositional methods, many people writing either in the didactic or the lyric mode in English were using pious, homiletic, devotional or ecclesiastical, Biblical Latin models. Even the Middle English romance has close affinities with the pious saint's life.[33] But Chaucer, it has often been noted, while indeed familiar with preachers' confessional manuals – the most complete was that by Bromyard, the *Summa Praedicantium* – used it extensively only in the *Parson's Tale*. For a religious society, although its theology was in a state of confusion as we will see, England produced what seems to be a paradox in that its greatest poet wrote remarkably unreligious matter. Kean has noted at the same time how Chaucer's dependence is on an intimate knowledge of a few seminal books from which he draws inspiration and whole passages,[34] indeed from which he virtually translates, and these are all late Roman classics – Boethius, Seneca, Macrobius, something from Virgil, Ovid, Statius – and he is thence dependent on French and Italian literature, particularly the latter, where there is a notable classical element. Is this classicizing, but none the less medieval, impulse only or primarily exemplified in England by Chaucer? For an answer we must turn now to that classicizing group of English friars in the earlier part of the century whom Beryl Smalley has revealed and elucidated.[35] Thereafter we can see the surprising extent to which many of the formal theological issues of the century inspired or reflected similar discussion in philosophical circles where classical Latin literature was drawn upon as corroborative source and inspiration.

If one looks at early fourteenth-century English commentaries on the Bible written by Franciscans and Dominicans, one finds oneself surrounded by ancient gods and heroes, by the thorny philosophical questions of Fate and Fortune, personal responsibility and free will. Mixed in with allegorized Biblical history would be the story of Troy and of Brutus, the classical 'founder' of Britain. Geoffrey of Monmouth, the monastic 'historian', had already related the story of how Brutus the Trojan had conquered giants inhabiting Britain and thereafter ruled the isle. The English had a personal stake in the *Aeneid*, and Arthur was an heroic descendant of Brutus. On the continent the matter of Troy had been set down in the thirteenth century by Guido delle Colonne, and Chrétien de Troyes' *Erec* speaks of the scenes from the *Aeneid* embroidered on a saddle. If one looks at English universal chronicles where Great Britain is discussed, say that of the Benedictine Ranulf of Chester, the *Polychronicon* (mid fourteenth-century), one confronts a self-confessed 'compiler' of quotes from Virgil and Horace, a not unusual defence of the scissors-and-paste method of presenting fact, legend and myth. One also meets an explicit statement that all genres of source-material, like the Anglo-Norman *Roman de Brut* (by Wace), Benoit's *Roman de Troie*, Alexander romances, the Bible and extracts from classical history, taken together, enable Englishmen to know their own history. The pagan fables particularly related to Troy were to be found in confessors' manuals like the *Manuel des Pechiez*, translated into English as *Handlyng Synne* by Mannyng, so that antiquity came to Englishmen, as Smalley says, as 'just part of the ancient record'.[36] But then there appears a rather extraordinary 'group' of men with a quite elaborate familiarity with classical history, philosophy and fable, and the abilities to employ the stories and the subleties of meaning found in the Latin classics. These men do not seem to have what one might refer to dismissively as a typically florilegial acquaintance with classical texts. The Dominican Nicholas Trevet, the Biblical scholar and classicist, appears as one of the first with such interests, and he was engaged by Pope John XXII, resident at Avignon (1316–34), to comment on Livy. Classical studies were coming into fashion in Avignon, at least by the second decade of the century as we shall see, and Senecan tragedies were also requested of Trevet in some simplified form. Not only were this Oxford Dominican's commentaries the 'rage' in Avignon and in early fourteenth-century Italy, but Petrarch himself read them. Similarly Trevet, like Petrarch, read Augustine with the view that this Church Father was better understood against his pagan and classical Latin background. Thomas Waleys and John Ridevall, two other Oxford Dominicans, surpassed Trevet and 'invented' the classicizing Biblical commentary. Ridevall converted the fifth-century *Mythologiae* of Fulgentius into a preacher's handbook; *Fulgentius Metaforalis*. Waleys taught in Italy and then became chaplain to a Dominican cardinal at Avignon. Other Englishmen with ecclesiastical connections, not all friars, but all highly educated and employed in a variety of ambassadorial or proctorial capacities in Avignon, carried the torch for classical studies further, wrote according to the strict rules of rhetorical dictamen, collected formularies of high-Latin letters, collected books, praised Sallust, Cicero, Boethius, Macrobius, Lactantius and Martianus Capella, wished they could read Greek, and wrote biographies of ancient sages with excerpts from their writings. The Bishop of Durham, Richard de Bury, a great patron of the classics, of book-collecting and of classicizing scholars, gathered round his table distinguished scholars, most of whom shared his interests and had been to Avignon. De Bury himself had met Petrarch in Avignon and had apparently created a favourable impression on the Italian. Patronized by de Bury were the Mertonian, theologian and 'calculator' Thomas Bradwardine, future Archbishop of Canterbury; Robert Holcot, the well-known Dominican Biblical commentator whose *Liber Moralitates* and commentaries on the sapiential Biblical books were mines of classical allusion and reference; Richard FitzRalph, the antimendicant future Archbishop of Armagh; Walter Burley, the influential logician and theologian who wrote a *De Vita et Moribus Philosophorum*; Richard Kilmington, Dean of St Paul's – all doctors in theology; Richard Byntworth, a civil lawyer who later became Bishop of London; Walter Seagrave, later

Bishop of Chichester; and the canonist John Aston. Here was a
miscellaneous group of the *sublimes et literati*, who had risen in the
royal service and/or the Church, and/or the universities, all with a
penchant for the Latin classical authors in versions that were more
than gleanings from excerpt-filled encyclopedic grammar-books or
preaching-*summas*. Did this incipient 'humanism', if that is what it
was, thereafter die in England, insular conditions dominating and
cutting Britain off from early 'humanist', continental, philosophical,
literary and political trends? Was Richard de Bury's *Philobiblon*
(1344), which is a rhetorical treatise on the love of books and the
ancient authors, no more than a one-off exercise in dictamen? He, like
Petrarch, argued that one could not understand the Church Fathers or
the Bible without the classical poets. In his commentary on the
Wisdom literature of the Bible, Holcot referred to Boethius and
Hermes Trismegistus (as did Bradwardine in his *De Causa Dei*); Holcot
goes on to cite Agamemnon, Ulysses and Hercules as heroes who
laboured for glory and virtue with God's help (Lectio 120). Was this
merely a flashy and élitist mimicry of Italian and Avignon classicizers,
which would not be repeated or taken up by a later English generation? Are there conscious parallels between Holcot's book of moral
'pictures' (the *Moralitates* of 1334), Petrarch's *Trionfi* and then
Chaucer's *House of Fame*? Do we paint an accurate picture of a
generation of English classicists, especially those in de Bury's circle, if
we say they were wholly dependent on a pseudo-classical library
circulating largely by means of scriptural lecture commentaries[37] and
that they were drawing on the classics in a medieval and moralizing
way that Petrarch had left behind? To what extent, and in what sense,
is it true that Petrarch's classicizing is one of the earliest examples of
what would flower as 'true' Renaissance humanism but that the
English version is a misconceived imitation that cannot escape the
Middle Ages?

If we look to the library left to Merton College by the book-
collecting bishop William Reed, we have evidence that in 1374 there
still were English clerics who read widely and provided a college library
with many of the texts that had interested the early friar 'humanist
movement'.[38] And these 'classics' were not snippets, found florilegium-
style in Biblical commentaries, but the whole works of Macrobius,
Boethius, 'books on Scipio', Odes of Horace, Martianus Capella and a
Legenda Jerosolimita (Josephus' history), in addition to those standard
medieval authors who wrote encyclopedic works, like Alain de l'Isle,
Peter de Riga, Gregory the Great, Albertus Magnus, Bede, and
Augustine, and who drew on classical legend and heroes. Reed had

these books categorized and classified for the library, and all the books just mentioned were either used or cited by Chaucer.

If we turn to one of Chaucer's early works, the *House of Fame*, where he seems to be at an experimental stage, thematically and stylistically, we find him familiar with Virgil's *Aeneid*; this familiarity may have been no more than with the synoptic presentations already available and exploited in the various moralized and categorized versions of Ovid's *Metamorphoses*, especially Book XIV. But where Chaucer extends his narrative beyond his source, as in Dido's complaint, he none the less finds inspiration in some version of *Aeneid*, IV. The expansion of Dido's sorrow may have explicit affinities with the venerable medieval genre known as the *complainte d'amour*, but Dido's lament is also what Virgil focused on. The *House of Fame*, the *Parliament of Fowls*, the *Knight's Tale*, the *Troilus and Criseyde*, all develop classically ornamented and inspired themes, and Chaucer often shows a distinct sense of the past combined with a sense of the eternality of human dilemmas. It has nevertheless been said that his classically inspired Nature and Venus, like his Virgil, are firmly medieval.[39] If his iconography, his scientific lore and his themes of interlocking Love, Fame and Fortune, providence and free will, 'the affairs of love and the vicissitudes of fame' are to be considered traditionally medieval (as Professor Bennett indicated), we must ask ourselves whether it is necessary to adjust our perspectives accordingly when we look at the use of similar classical texts and themes in trecento Italy. We are confronted again with the age-old problem of justifying the criteria we invoke when we speak of English medievalism and Italian early humanism. There may well have been more than the usually noted affinities between Dante's, Boccaccio's and Petrarch's reliance on the Latin classics, and Chaucer's. Trecento Italy may have been much closer to fourteenth-century England in sharing certain attitudes towards politics, rhetoric, Latin classical history and philosophical concerns. And their common ground according to recent evidence, quite literally may have been that geographical meeting-point of Europe, sustained for nearly a century, where religious sentiments, politics, economic policies, the Latin language and the vernaculars of the north met the south: Avignon.[40]

When Clement V chose a place for his papal coronation in 1305, this former Archbishop of Bordeaux, and compliant vassal of Edward I, chose Vienne in the Dauphiné, on the main road to Italy. Gradually he traversed the south-west of France and established his papal Court at Avignon, across the river from France in the Comtat-Venaissin.

Throughout the fourteenth century there were numerous major and minor official and unofficial English contacts with Avignon, through proctors – who were somewhere between solicitors and advocates – diplomatic envoys, cardinals and ecclesiastics of various levels confirming or requesting benefices and involving themselves in the highly complex legalities that linked the pope with Church property and dignities at home and abroad. Bishops-elect went to Avignon to confirm their elections, as did abbots-elect of English monastic houses. It was once thought that fourteenth-century Avignon was 'not a good place' for the English because only a relatively small number of English *curiales* could be calculated to have resided there. Today there is counter evidence to show that throughout the century and until the Schism of 1377–8 and well beyond, the English Crown and the episcopal hierarchy displayed a remarkably well-planned strategy in the papal curia and this strategy extended beyond resident curialists to unofficials visitors, proctorial representatives, frequent diplomatic embassies and a persuasive policy carried out on behalf of English interests by the college of cardinals.[41] It is most striking, given our interest in Englishmen familiar with rhetorical and formulaic Latin and with high-style, 'humanist' letter-writing, that it was in the 'audience of causes' of the papal palace that Englishmen and their friends were most prominent. This was the department of the curia that had most to say about papal provisions, who got them, where and when. This 'audience of causes' was known by 1336 as the *rota* (from the round table or room in which decisions were made) and it was the supreme judicial organ of the curia. Among the papal auditors, Englishmen who were doctors of canon law, and who then returned beneficed to England as bishops, are some of the major influential episcopal names, along with their less distinguished contemporaries, that one can call up for the century. And among the foreign friends of English causes at Avignon the name of the auditor M. Raymond Subirani, friend and correspondent of Petrarch, looms large. Richard de Bury mentions him in his *Liber Epistolaris*. Another papal auditor, one M. Bertrandus de Mediolano, papal chaplain, served as an executor for papal provisions to English benefices and heard English cases at the curia; he was pensioned by the English Crown and described in English documents as an advocate for English causes in the curia. If I can be brief without oversimplifying such matters, I can summarize by saying that the most important position at the papal curia at the end of the fourteenth–early-fifteenth century was called 'abbreviator' of the papal chancery. In the early fourteenth century the corresponding post was 'auditor of causes of the apostolic palace'. The way up was via the

notariate and writerships of the chancery.[42] These posts were dominated by English canon lawyers.

I have already noted in passing that the early friar 'humanists' had
intellectual and ecclesiastical links with Avignon, but English scholars
in general, theologians in particular, were also drawn to Avignon as an
intellectual centre with patronage. Bradwardine, Lutterel, Ockham,
Waleys and FitzRalph were there for a host of different reasons; later
in the century English students of law were registered at the university
in Avignon. The chapel of angels and archangels in Avignon cathedral
was the work of an English stonemason, one Hugh Wilfrid. On an
almost daily and mundane level, there was a steady stream of Englishmen making their way to Avignon to seek absolution in reserved cases
and to defend legal rights in court cases.[43] The number of resident
Englishmen at least by 1331 was sufficient, informally, for there to be
an English boarding-house run by one Peter Miller.[44]

It is frequently noted that the early humanists in Italy were civil
lawyers and notaries. It was just such Englishmen, familiar with civil
and canon law, who were sent out from England to act under notarial
commissions as proctors. Either they were sent *ad hoc* to represent
English principals in specific cases, or they were in semi-permanent
residence at the curia and were paid salaries to look after any English
business that might arise. Such men's contacts were varied; many of
them were multi-lingual, certainly in contact with French and Italian
political and cultural developments. There were also Italians like
Andreas Sapiti, a citizen of Florence who served as proctor at the curia
for numerous high-ranking English ecclesiastics as well as for continental bishops. He resided in Avignon but travelled to England
several times from 1313 to the 1330s. Edward II described him as
'clericus et familiaris', gave him a Crown pension, and supported and
extended Sapiti's family's interests in England.[45] Numerous resident
Dominicans represented the English Crown at Avignon but it is not
clear precisely what their status was: proctor, envoy, messenger?
Generally then, the frequency and magnitude of importance of
embassies were far greater than has been previously suggested, and the
rewards of English benefices for Englishmen and Italians who served
as abbreviators in the papal chancery, and formulated the king's
petitions, were extensive. The high proportion of foreign cardinals
with English pensions along with foreign absentee pluralists who were
awarded English livings caused violent responses in England throughout the 1342–78 period, and this is linked with the increasing number
of educated Englishmen who desired papal provisions at home.
Although there were only two English cardinals during the Avignon

stay of the papacy, when Simon Langham, the Benedictine, was
selected in 1368 he was able to provide significant contacts and
financially rewarding posts for a generation of *sublimes et literati* in
the legal or ecclesiastical hierarchy.

Testimonies of the Court and city of Avignon, usually unflattering,
are frequently cited from six traditional sources: the letters of St
Catherine of Siena, the *epistolario* of Salutati, the *Epistolae de Rebus
Familiaribus* of Petrarch and his *Sine Nomine* letters, the *Revelations*
of St Brigitte and the *Florentine History* of the Villani. But there is
also a vast quantity of correspondence and legal data written to and
from Avignon by Englishmen with duties at the curia. This is not the
place to begin an examination of the English experience of Avignon,
but what Petrarch saw was also seen and commented on by learned
Englishmen. Englishmen experienced the 'early humanism' and the
patronage of high art, rhetoric, classical history and book-collecting,
especially on the part of three popes: John XXII, Clement VI and
Gregory XI.[46] It is insufficient to say, then, that the English classicizing
impulse was insular, brief and abortive, limited to Franciscans and
Dominicans, and then to de Bury's little group of the earlier part of the
century. But more work must be done here to enable us to specify the
nature of the continuing contact with Avignon classicizers with whom
England had to be in constant touch, if she was to maintain her
interests in the legal and ultimately financial sphere of Church–state
international relations.

Pope Urban V (1362–70) was able to fulfil the long-desired transfer of
the basic papal library from Rome to Avignon, but he was adding to
what some of the scholarly French popes had already collected.
John XXII (1316–34) collected papal decretals, Bibles, the works of
relatively contemporary theologians, and patristic authors, as would
be expected of a lawyer–pope involved in considerable theological and
legal controversy. But he also collected geometric and arithmetical
works, and the *Declamationes* of Seneca and his *Tragedies*, bought the
encyclopedic Valerius Maximus and sponsored Trevet's editions and
commentaries on Livy. Robert of Naples, who spent time in Avignon
at that period, returned to his Neapolitan Court in 1335 to promote
the classical Latinate literature of the *ars dictaminis* that had excited
him at the curia, at the expense of the Italian vernacular.[47] But at
Avignon this was only the beginning. The papacy enforced its right
of spoliation and absorbed the libraries of clerics who died: the
inventory of 1353 counted 1389 books and by 1369 there were over
2000. Petrarch commented that only as John XXII grew older and

busier did he find little time to read his books and so was grateful for possessing the summarizing (and medieval) florilegia of excerpts from the classics, for which he composed tables of contents.

Clement VI (1342–52), with a successful scholastic career in theology at the University of Paris behind him, was not only involved in political battles with Louis of Bavaria, the papally unconsecrated Holy Roman Emperor who had also engaged John XXII: Clement, like his predecessors, was actively involved in the traditional medieval *regnum–sacerdotium* controversy. But he was also a lover of high Latin rhetoric and famed for his eloquence in his own preaching. His private chambers were painted with scenes of hunting and fishing; he was a lover of luxury not seen before to this extent in Avignon; he doubled the size of the pontifical palace and brought in international artists. 'Our predecessors did not know how to be pope', he is reported to have said. He inspired Petrarch to search for Cicero manuscripts, and Petrarch requested of him the loan of an exemplar of Pliny. His expenditures exhausted the papal treasury but no one present in Avignon during his pontificate could escape the fact that this pontiff had transformed the atmosphere of his Court into a secular, even 'humanist' centre of culture. These were the years of Petrarch's crisis, about which he was to write in the *Secretum* and during which he observed that literacy was being sold in the market-place. In dialogue with Augustine, Petrarch resolved to forsake his excessive concern for love, fame and glory.

If Clement VI prepared an atmosphere where the Latin classics were valued and imitated, Gregory XI (1370–8) was even more important in continuing the love of classical Latin and the company of books. He mourned Petrarch's death, had all his works copied for his own library, was an avid book-collector and, like the later Petrarch, tried not to ignore scholastic authors but showed their relationship with the virtues of Roman antiquity. Chaucer was negotiating with Bernabò Visconti for Edward III at the same time that Gregory XI was in contact with Visconti; the pope's concern, however, was with the defeat of the tyrant of Milan. Papal negotiations established a truce with the Visconti in 1375. Gregory XI was also actively involved in promoting an Anglo-French conciliation during that phase of the Hundred Years War when England was doing none too well. Planning year after year to return to Rome, he procrastinated until it was too late. At his death the Great Schism broke, when two popes were elected, and France and England were further divided by their opposing loyalties. England supported the Italian, Urban VI. But proctorial activity at the curia was, on England's behalf, intensified if anything.

This cursory summary of England's contacts with an Avignon that was seething with international literary, legal and theological currents is an attempt to highlight certain characteristics of the England that Chaucer, our courtier, M.P., customs official, ambassador to Italy (and to Avignon?), who wrote poetry after hours, could not but reflect in his writing. Furthermore, in 1378 Urban VI, whom England supported against France, was elected pope. Formerly he was Bartholomew Prignano, the Archbishop of Bari and a Neapolitan. Boccaccio had only recently died, but his memory would be alive amongst Florentines and Neapolitans. It was Urban VI's policy to have the young Richard II marry Anne, the daughter of the Holy Roman Emperor, Charles IV of Bohemia. He was successful in 1382.

We can focus on England–Avignon contacts even more specifically by asking what would a middle-range ecclesiastical English lawyer be doing at Avignon during the 1370s, that period when Chaucer was a continental traveller on the king's business? A rapid review of John Lydford's career (as we can see something of it in his Memorandum Book) can tell us something here. First, Lydford's book contains a variety of documents concerned with Bishop William Wykeham's commissions: others apply to the archdeacon's court of Oxford, and to the Oxford chancellor; some refer to episcopal consistories of Hereford, Winchester and Exeter, along with a good deal of information about the papal court. Lydford was an advocate in the court of Canterbury, a canon lawyer of William Wykeham's circle and acted for the Arundel family in Avignon but, perhaps most important, from his Oxford days, he became part of William Courtenay's circle. Courtenay, the future Archbishop of Canterbury and hammer of Wyclif, recommended Lydford to the notice of the English cardinal Simon Langham, himself a former Archbishop of Canterbury, now resident in Avignon, 'whose advice and help were frequently sought by English suitors at the papal court in this period'.[48] Lydford was probably Courtenay's proctor.

Now the Avignon registers of Pope Gregory XI for the year 1375–6 have serious gaps, but episcopal registers and the Memorandum Book itself give us information of Lydford's activity as proctor for a variety of important English ecclesiastics. During his Avignon stay he may have made (or renewed) an acquaintance with the book-collecting Adam Easton, Langham's secretary; at any rate he had access to documents relating to Easton's early life and had them copied into his book. He certainly was either associated with or had access to records of a vast amount of Avignon business from 1370 to 1376. His Avignon stay advanced his prestige and fortunes, for Lydford acquired further benefices and valuable contacts upon his return home: in 1377 he was appointed William Wykeham's official. He was associated with the papal and legal intricacies involved in Wykeham's foundation of New College, Oxford. He was appointed an assessor at the Blackfriar's council that sat in judgement on Wyclif's doctrines in 1382 and condemned them. His Memorandum Book collects a variety of defences and appeals to Rome on the part of Wyclifite supporters and preserves replies of others accused of heretical Lollard preaching. Why he would have such a private collection remains unclear, especially when there are so few public records concerning heresy in England. What does seem clear is that Lydford was known for drafting documents according to the appropriate canon-law *forma* and with considerable eloquence. His own preoccupation with Lollard documents seems entirely legal; otherwise he was involved, as is to be expected, with the legal and financial intricacies of benefices. In sum, he was regarded as an expert in the drafting of appeals to Avignon and Rome, and the Memorandum Book has several comments concerning his own drafting or that of others, with a marginal 'bona littera' or 'forma bona', in appreciation.

By the time Lydford was in Avignon, Petrarch had departed for the courts of benevolent tyrants in northern Italy. Lydford would be more in touch with current theological controversies than would the ageing Italian poet. And the papacy was quick to see the dangers of a Wyclif, the rising star of English theological and political circles, ostensibly because his eucharistic theology was radical.[49] In fact, Gregory XI, our 'humanist' and materialist, saw that, not unlike Cola di Rienzo, Wyclif was arguing that the only hope for a renaissance of the Church was a renaissance of the state.[50] He advocated the material dispossession of the Church and argued, from his Oxford scholarly position, that the origins of public power were in *dominium*: state-maintained property. The present Church had sacrificed its spiritual power by having become a thrall to its material possessions.

Now this, one might think, was a remarkably political stance for a theologian to take; indeed Wyclif was politically sponsored by John of Gaunt during the dotage of Edward III and the chaotic minority of young Richard. But there was, throughout the fourteenth century, a curious practical and secular strain in English theology and it was in many respects closely linked with the philosophical concerns of a revived Boethius, a Seneca, a Cicero, whose texts were anthologized and translated and read by the increasing number of the literate. One can only enumerate the century's theological and philosophical concerns here:[51] the role of Fate, Fortune, providence, the individual's

free will in directing his own life, the ability of man to cope with the
utter contingency of the natural and apparently supernatural world
and, perhaps most succinctly, the concern for the individual's moral
autonomy and his ability to be virtuous from his own nature, to 'do
what was in him' (*facere quod in se est*) and earn salvation. Some of
the English theologians who were most involved in defending various
shades of the 'modern' theology were followers of the Franciscan
William of Ockham, an Oxford logician and theologian concerned
with the strict logic of ordinary and spiritual language. He believed it
necessary that theologians should argue with the precision of logic or
they would fall into error. By the 1320s Ockham had been called to
account for his views at Avignon by John XXII. There he met the
radical members of his order and was induced to spend the rest of his
life writing political tracts against the current papacy's understanding
of its powers and its view of the Church universal. He was patronized
as a publicist by Louis of Bavaria, for whom he developed his ideas on
the relation of powers in Church and state.

But it was his logical method and his emphasis on the role of man's
and God's will that set something of the tone for subsequent English
theology. Those who took some of his ideas further were labelled by
a group of neo-Augustinian theologians as semi-Pelagians: it was
thought that too much emphasis was being placed on man's ability to
will his own salvation and his own virtuousness. God's powers were
seen to be limited in an unacceptable way. The main neo-Augustinian
position was mounted by Thomas Bradwardine, the future Archbishop
of Canterbury (d. 1349). The 'modern' semi-Pelagians were perhaps
best represented by the Dominican Robert Holcot in his Wisdom
commentaries. Their writings, scholastic and scholarly in the first
instance, were epitomized and summarized, and circulated outside
university circles. Both sides of this controversy drew on the classical
authors as never before to justify their claims. And it must be pointed
out, if the names do not already strike one's memory, that these two
extreme theological views were held by men who were members
of de Bury's classicizing circle, men familiar with Avignon when
Petrarch was there.

One of the major questions with practical consequences that was
asked in scholarly circles was that if the world was not absolutely
determined by God or Fate or providence, and was as utterly contingent as supposed, how was it possible to teach and establish a fixed
ethical order to guide men's lives? Questions about the world were
being framed in the language of possibility rather than certainty.
Linked with what is technically called the logical nominalism of

Ockham and his followers, for whom reality could only be asserted of discrete individuals (this man, not 'mankind' as a general concept, was real), was the logically necessary, political and ethical conclusion: society was nothing but the sum of discrete, responsible, autonomous individuals, and all one could do was to hope that if one did one's best, did what was in one, the appropriate reward would be forthcoming. The Church sacraments seemed to recede into the background; men wondered if a heathen who lived as well as he could would receive salvation as soon as any Christian, and by Wyclif's time, there was a movement to provide a vernacular Bible for literate Christians so that they could know all that was necessary to salvation by confronting God's word directly. *Piers Plowman,* in its three versions, served a generation or more of Englishmen and women, literate in some Latin and English, with a pilgrimage through the thicket of theological possibilities and variant orthodoxies. It ends with a quest after salvation rather than with an assured answer as to how to be saved. Chaucer responded in a different way, although he was aware and said he was, of the altercations in the schools that involved Bishop Bradwardine and the distinction between the necessary and the contingent. He saw the problems of individual responsibility, Fortune and man's free will, as issues that had confronted men of antiquity as well; the Boethian dilemma, Troilus' dilemma, was now the ancient *and* Christian problem conflated in the context of a pious but overwhelmingly lay culture, his own and the one he absorbed from his sources.

Contemporary French poets called Chaucer a moral philosopher. In the fifteenth century he would still be referred to as 'the noble philosophical poet'. Like Petrarch, Chaucer's inclination was to value philosophy for its contribution to the strengthening of human virtue. But was Chaucer still medieval in his understanding of the lessons to be learnt from ancient philosophy whilst Petrarch moved in the humanist and Renaissance direction? It has recently been argued that Petrarch's suspicion regarding dialectical scholastic methods and school theology was in fact based on a rather scanty knowledge of that theology and philosophy of the schools.[52] Trinkaus implies that Petrarch's humanism is less a reaction to the contemporary scene than a bypass of it. Chaucer's philosophical and classicizing poetry, medieval though it may have been, was not a bypass of contemporary issues but, as Kean has argued, an urbane and eclectic response to them.[53] This brings me back to some of the questions raised earlier about the criteria we use to label Chaucer 'medieval' and Petrarch 'early humanist' – and thereby create a north–south divide between

the fourteenth century and the Trecento. Trinkaus has noticed that
Petrarch's citations of pre-Socratics, sophists and others very often
show his knowledge to have been no greater than what was currently
available to numerous erudites of the medieval and clerical stamp.
He could not read Greek, and despite his admiration for Plato his
acquaintance with his doctrines came from Augustine, Cicero and
Macrobius. He displayed the same medieval taste for encyclopedic
epitomes of the classics and the compilations of rhetorical *loci
communes* that English contemporaries did. And like those whom we
dismiss as northern, insular medievals Petrarch preferred 'our Latin
writers, Cicero, Seneca, Horace', because he was more concerned
with rhetoric than with philosophy.[54] His interest in Plato, following Augustine's lead, was to show the Platonic compatibility with
Christianity. And perhaps Trinkaus' most interesting insight about
Petrarch, which we can draw on as a parallel with Chaucer's 'philosophical' purposes, concerns Petrarch's attempt to show that man's
moral autonomy was not only a pagan position, opposed to Christianity; Ciceronian and Senecan human autonomy was a position that
was analogous with the role of the individual in the Christian doctrines
of grace and justification. In his later years, Petrarch indicated his
disenchantment with Cola di Rienzo's failure to revive a Roman
republic. And after the spiritual crisis that made of him a disciple of
Augustine, Petrarch argued for a position that was more in line
with Bradwardine's neo-Augustinianism, the position of *sola gratia*,
whereby man's virtuousness is not in his own hands but under God's
or Fortune's or providence's auspices.[55] Chaucer's parallel Boethian
themes – the role of fame and Fortune, personal (in)decision and free
will – because they are not so explicitly in line with *sola gratia*,
appear far more secular, if not tragic and unresolved. Perhaps Chaucer
can be said to be using his Latin, French and Italian sources to provide
a lay readership with the many facets of irresolution and contingency
made so prominent by the English tradition of 'modern' semi-Pelagian
theologians. He need not have gone to Oxford to study this theology
to be familiar with these themes for, as Langland noted, high-born men
who were not ecclesiastics sat at table and discussed all manner of
theological and philosophical subtleties. There was already a literature
that simplified these themes for the literate.[56]

Lastly, Petrarch's interest in rhetoric was, ultimately, an interest in
lay Christian sermonizing. He thought of himself as a *poeta theo-
logicus*.[57] Chaucer seems, from his poetry at any rate, to have been
temperamentally humbler. Aware of high rhetoric, he appears to have
accepted the lay poetic vocation as one that included the role of the

moral counsellor (as did Petrarch and Gower). But he never took himself as seriously as did Petrarch. In the *House of Fame*, that most 'humanist' of his attempts to deal with Glory, Fame, Fortune and Love, his concern for simple, direct speech to relay one's 'sentence' allowed him one of the funniest parodies and conscious rejections of the high seriousness of the *ars dictaminis*, the early humanist rhetoric. After the eagle has explained the physics of speech as motion in air, he says:

> Telle me this now feythfully,
> Have y not preved thus symply,
> Withoute any subtilite
> Of speche, or gret prolixite
> Of termes of philosophie,
> Of figures of poetrie,
> Or colours of rhetorike?
> Pardee, hit oughte the to lyke!
> For hard langage and hard matere
> Ys encombrous for to here
> Attones, wost thou not wel this?
>   And y answered and seyde, 'Yis'.
>   (*House of Fame*, 853–64)

It has sometimes been suggested that Richard II, 'hardened to a tyrant's ways', was, by the end of the 1380s, more of a medieval monarch, even imperial in his attitudes,[58] than an England dominated by the Commons in Parliament could sustain. Gower and others came to see Richard in this way but Richard's models need not have been from the past: not only were there tyrannies in northern Italian cities, where Petrarch's art was patronized in a grand way, but Richard had married, in 1382, the daughter of Charles IV of Bohemia (d. 1378) and Anne could not have been ignorant of Cola di Rienzo's sojourn at her Bohemian Court. Cola was a learned jurist filled with ideas of the revival of classical republican Rome.[59] Furthermore, Anne's father had corresponded with Petrarch and was called on by the mature poet to revive Rome's political legacy in Cola di Rienzo's place, *replacing* the ancient republic with a revived *imperium Romanum*. In 1353 Petrarch had appealed to Charles to come to Italy and, like Caesar, restore the *imperium*.

In 1394–7, after Anne's death, Richard was negotiating to become King of the Romans, and he was corresponding with the Greek emperor, Manuel Palaeologus. Had Anne brought with her early humanist tastes of the Prague Court to such an extent that she influenced both her husband's foreign policy and also her poet?

Chaucer, an entertainer of Court women, known to be in frequent attendance on Queen Anne, would have sought to please his mistress with familiar, classical, Latin themes. Did Anne, at any rate, think England was barbaric and behind in 'humanist' studies? It was she, after all, who seems to have initiated marriage proposals with Richard on the advice of an Italian pope!

Among the characteristics that are frequently cited as evidence of a humanist movement is the development of the mirror-for-princes genre, the handbook of advice for monarchs or republics, brought, of course, to their *terminus* in the pair of treatises by the sixteenth-century Florentine Machiavelli: *The Prince* and *The Discourses*. There are supposedly no English equivalents. But a reading of the often undistinguished but plentiful complaint poetry of the latter half of the fourteenth century in England – which comprises the major literary 'tradition' in English one can cite before Chaucer: works like *Richard the Redeless, Mum and Sothsegger, Wynnere and Wastoure*, parts of *Piers Plowman*, the earlier *Simonie* and the anonymous complaint poetry of the MS Digby 102, all epitomized in Gower's *Vox Clamantis* and Lollard prose – leads us to another view.[60] Such works can be classified *thematically* as mirrors for princes. These are testimonies to the voice of a gentry and urban 'middle class' developing its own political, critical voice. And the logical end of such writings and the development of a political vocabulary of social and religious reform *in English* is the Lollard prose tract, mixing the religious with the political in a systematic way that had not been tried – in the vernacular – since Aelfric. Lollard vernacular preaching often penetrated the English hinterland but there was also definite support in the Court circle of Lollard knights and amongst the gentry and bourgeoisie, some of whom seem to have sponsored workshops for the production of a vernacular Bible. Ultimately, it was the piety, patronage and political astuteness of this urban bourgeoisie and gentry, united in the Commons, that dominated English life at the end of the century. They financed government policy, expanded the 'rule of law' through the legal profession, patronized the arts and developed English into a status language by the end of the century, and, if Gower is believed, it was they who removed one king – Richard – and made another – Henry, Duke of Lancaster, in 1399.

Notes

1 M. T. Clanchy, *From Memory to Written Record, England 1066–1307* (London, 1979); M. B. Parkes, 'The literacy of the laity' in D. Daiches and A. Thorlby

(eds.), *Literature and Western Civilization*, vol. II, 'The Medieval World' (London, 1973), pp. 555–77; Janet Coleman, *English Literature in History 1350–1400: Medieval Readers and Writers* (London, 1981), chapter 2, pp. 18–57.

2   Bot, unkind coward, wo was him [Philip of France] thare;
        When he sailed in the Swin it sowed him sare.
        Sare it tham smerted that ferd out of France;
        That lered Inglis men them a new daunce.
(Poem by Lawrence Minot, in T. Wright (ed.), *Political Poems and Songs* (London 1859), vol. I, p. 70). See also Coleman, *Medieval Readers and Writers*, pp. 71–8; V. H. Galbraith, 'Nationality and Language in Medieval England', *Transactions of the Royal Historical Society*, XXIII (1941), 113–28.

3 Eleanor C. Lodge and Gladys A. Thornton (eds.), *English Constitutional Documents 1307–1485* (Cambridge, 1935), chapter 7, 'The towns', pp. 375–419.

4 Coleman, *Medieval Readers and Writers*, p. 52; *Rotuli Parliamentorum* (Rolls of Parliament) ed. J. Strachey (London, 1767–83), vol. II, pp. 147, 158.

5 N. F. Blake, *The English Language in Medieval Literature* (London, 1977), pp. 11–33.

6 V. H. Galbraith (ed.), *The Anonimalle Chronicle, 1333 to 1381* (Manchester, 1927, repr. 1970), see the editor's introduction; John Barnie, *War in Medieval English Society: Social Values and the Hundred Years War 1337–1399* (London, 1974), p. 82.

7 Sir Goronwy Edwards, *The Second Century of the English Parliament, The Ford Lectures delivered in the University of Oxford 1960–1* (Oxford, 1979), ed. J. S. Roskell.

8 Edwards, *Second Century of Parliament*, p. 42.

9 J. G. Edwards, '"Justice" in Early English Parliaments', *Bulletin of the Institute of Historical Research*, XXVII (1954), repr. in E. B. Fryde and Edward Miller (eds.), *Historical Studies of the English Parliament*, vol. I (Cambridge, 1970), pp. 280–98; p. 297.

10 Taken from appendix B to Edwards, *Second Century of Parliament*, p. 81, in his translation.

11 A prominent proctor at the papal Court with an Oxford bachelor's degree in canon law, William Swan, Rochester clerk from Southfleet, was married and had a brother who was a London skinner. E. F. Jacob, 'To and from the Court of Rome in the early fifteenth century' in *Essays in Later Medieval History* (Manchester, 1968), p. 70.

12 Coleman, *Medieval Readers and Writers*, p. 162.

13 S. F. C. Milsom, *The Legal Framework of English Feudalism, The Maitland lectures given in 1972* (Cambridge, 1976).

14 Galbraith, Introduction to *The Anonimalle Chronicle*.

15 A developed discussion of this appears in Coleman, *Medieval Readers and Writers*, pp. 43–57.

16 F. Petrarca, *Prose*, ed. G. Martellotti and P. G. Ricci (Milan–Naples, 1955), p. 330, trans. in Charles Trinkaus, *The Poet as Philosopher, Petrarch and the Formation of Renaissance Consciousness* (New Haven, 1979), p. 72.

17 W. A. Pantin, 'A medieval treatise on letter-writing', *Bulletin of the John Rylands Library*, XIII (1929); H. G. Richardson, 'An Oxford teacher of the fifteenth century', *Bulletin of the John Rylands Library*, XXIII (1939); Coleman, *Medieval Readers and Writers*, pp. 22–65.

18 Nicholas Orme, *English Schools in the Middle Ages* (London, 1973), and *Education in the West of England, 1066–1548* (Exeter, 1976); J. A. W. Bennett, *Chaucer at Oxford and at Cambridge* (Oxford, 1974).

19 F. R. H. Du Boulay, 'The historical Chaucer' in D. Brewer (ed.), *Geoffrey Chaucer, Writers and Their Background* (London, 1974), pp. 33–57; p. 34.

20 Alan Cobban, *The King's Hall within the University of Cambridge in the Later Middle Ages* (Cambridge, 1969).

21 Alexander Murray, *Reason and Society in the Middle Ages* (Oxford, 1978), pp. 302–12.

22 Colin Platt, *The English Medieval Town* (London, 1976), pp. 168–70.

23 Graham Pollard, 'The *pecia* system in the medieval universities' in M. B. Parkes and A. G. Watson (eds.), *Medieval Scribes, Manuscripts and Libraries* (London, 1978); Coleman, *Medieval Readers and Writers*, p. 202.

24 Siegfried Wenzel, *Verses in Sermons, Fasciculus Morum and its Middle English Poems* (Cambridge, Mass., 1978).

25 Edward Wilson, *A Descriptive Index of the English Lyrics in John of Grimestone's Preaching Book* (Oxford, 1973).

26 Further discussion in Bennett, *Chaucer at Oxford and at Cambridge*, p. 82.

27 Dorothy M. Owen (ed.), *John Lydford's Book*, Devon and Cornwall Record Society, n.s., xx (London, 1974).

28 Other similar volumes compiled at much the same time (end of the fourteenth century), some by men known to and quoted by Lydford, are cited by Dorothy Owen, Introduction to *John Lydford's Book*, p. 4: British Museum MS Royal 9E viii, including Walkynton's *De vita et honestate*, fols. 122 and 128v, Ralph Tregrisiou's *De iuramento calumni*, fol. 131; John Schepeye's *De ordine cognitionum*, fol. 156 (Harley MS 862 (*Liber formularium*) – Ecclesiastical causes).

29 A discussion of organizing principles in preaching-handbooks, sermons and verse, is more extensively treated in Coleman, *Medieval Readers and Writers*, pp. 157–204.

30 L. P. Wilkinson, *Ovid Surveyed* (Cambridge, 1962), pp. 63–111; A. I. Doyle and M. B. Parkes, 'The production of copies of the *Canterbury Tales* and the *Confessio Amantis* in the early fifteenth century', in Parkes and Watson, *Medieval Scribes, Manuscripts and Libraries*, p. 190; also M. B. Parkes, 'The influence of the concepts of ordinatio and compilatio on the development of the book', in *Medieval Learning and Literature: Essays Presented to R. W. Hunt*, ed. J. J. G. Alexander and M. T. Gibson (Oxford, 1976), pp. 115–41.

31 Coleman, *Medieval Readers and Writers*, pp. 126–56, on Gower's complaint.

32 John Alford, 'The Role of the Quotations in *Piers Plowman*', *Speculum*, LII (1977), 80–99.

33 Dieter Mehl, *The Middle English Romances of the Thirteenth and Fourteenth Centuries* (London, 1968).

34 P. M. Kean, *Chaucer and the Making of English Poetry*, vol. I (London, 1972), p. 28.

35 Beryl Smalley, *English Friars and Antiquity in the Early Fourteenth Century* (Oxford, 1960).

36 *Ibid.* pp. 22–3.

37 *Ibid.* p. 306.

38 Bennett, *Chaucer at Oxford and at Cambridge*, pp. 67–8; F. M. Powicke, *The Medieval Books of Merton College* (Oxford, 1931).

39 J. A. W. Bennett, *Chaucer's Book of Fame, an exposition of 'the House of Fame'* (Oxford, 1968), pp. xi–xii.

40 G. Mollat, *The Popes at Avignon (1305–1378)*, trans. Janet Love (New York, 1963); B. Guillemain, *La politique bénéficiale du pape Benoît XII* (Paris, 1952) and *La cour pontificale d'Avignon: 1309–1376* (Paris, 1962). Also C. Vasoli, 'Les débuts de l'humanisme à l'Université de Paris', in (forthcoming) proceedings of a colloquium held at the Ecole Normale Supérieure, Paris, November 1981, *Preuve et Raisons au XIVe siècle – à l'université de Paris*, ed. Z. Kaluza.

41 J. Robert Wright, *The Church and the English Crown 1305–1334* (Toronto, 1980);

J. R. L. Highfield, 'The relations between the Church and the English Crown 1349–1378' (unpublished Oxford D. Phil thesis), cited frequently by Wright.

42 Jacob, 'To and from the Court of Rome', pp. 58–60.

43 Wright, *The Church and the English Crown*, pp. 103f.

44 *Ibid.* pp. 106–7.

45 *Ibid.* p. 112.

46 The following account is drawn from Guillemain, *La cour pontificale d'Avignon*.

47 E. F. Jacob, 'Middle Ages and Renaissance' in *Essays in the Conciliar Epoch*, 2nd edn. (Manchester, 1953), has the following to say about the nature of Robert's Latinity:
'Dr. Goertz's study (*König Robert von Neapel (1309–1343): seine Persönlichkeit und sein Verhältnis zum Humanismus* (Tübingen, 1910), especially p. 38) of the sermons of King Robert of Naples shows that interesting monarch not only citing Latin classics of the golden and silver ages with the freedom of a John of Salisbury, but taking the themes of his discourses from Sallust and Seneca independently of the influence of Petrarch. Those sermons, the discourses, be it noted, of a layman, are purely formal scholastic homilies of the most orthodox kind. This will not surprise any acquainted with the increasing classicism of the *Artes dictandi*. Moreover, the systematic elaboration of style in Italy had its parallel north of the Alps. The Bologna masters of Dictamen... had their spiritual progeny in England during the fourteenth and fifteenth centuries' (pp. 180–1).

48 *John Lydford's Book*, ed. Dorothy Owen, Introduction, p. 7. For Courtenay's letter to Langham on behalf of Lydford, see letter 177, p. 91.

49 A fuller discussion of the significance of Wyclif is in Coleman, *Medieval Readers and Writers*, pp. 204–31.

50 Some interesting remarks on Cola in Walter Ullmann, *Medieval Foundations of Renaissance Humanism* (London, 1977), pp. 137f; see also Hans Baron, 'The Evolution of Petrarch's Thought: reflections on the state of Petrarch studies' in *Bibliothéque d'Humanisme et Renaissance*, XXIV (1962), 7–41, reprinted in *From Petrarch to Leonardo Bruni* (Chicago, 1968), pp. 34–7.

51 Coleman, *Medieval Readers and Writers*, pp. 232–70. A more elaborate analysis of current English theology and its relation to vernacular poetry is in Janet Coleman, *Piers Plowman and the Moderni* (Rome, 1981).

52 Trinkaus, *The Poet as Philosopher*, p. 4; also Charles Trinkaus, *In Our Image and Likeness: Humanity and Divinity in Italian Humanist Thought* (2 vols., London, 1970).

53 Kean, *Chaucer and the Making of English Poetry*, vol. I, p. 43.

54 Trinkaus, *The Poet as Philosopher*, pp. 21–2.

55 *Ibid.* pp. 23–4.

56 Coleman, *Medieval Readers and Writers*, pp. 261–70, on 'non-scholastic literature'; also *Piers Plowman and the Moderni*, chapter 5: 'Fourteenth century non-scholastic literary themes'.

57 Trinkaus, *The Poet as Philosopher*, pp. 105–25.

58 Gervase Mathew, *The Court of Richard II* (London, 1968).

59 S. Harrison Thomson, 'Learning at the court of Charles IV', *Speculum*, XXV (1950); Baron, 'The Evolution of Petrarch's Thought', and Walter Ullmann, *Medieval Foundations*, pp. 137–9.

60 Coleman, *Medieval Readers and Writers*, chapter 3: 'The literature of social unrest'.

Anglo–Italian Contacts in the Fourteenth Century[1]

Medieval England was never an isolated western island, but one enmeshed in a network of communications stretching from Scandinavia to the Mediterranean, from Portugal to Russia, from Ireland to the Holy Land and even beyond. While her political and cultural traditions ensured a particularly close, if often hostile, relationship with France, connections with Flanders, Spain, Germany and Italy were also strong. Chaucer's pilgrims themselves illustrate the typical overseas experience of Englishmen at the time. His craftsmen and countrymen had not crossed the Channel, neither had his Serjeant-at-law, whose training would have been in the Inns of Court, far removed from the Italian centres of Roman law. His poor Parson, Monk, Doctor and Friar were also, it seems, untravelled. His Prioress was conscious of her French education, but it was wholly of English origin. The other seven were well-travelled. The Knight had been to Prussia and Russia, Turkey and Egypt, Spain and North Africa, as well as serving with his son, the Squire, in France and Flanders. The Merchant was particularly familiar with the Low Country trade, and the Shipman with Bordeaux, although he also knew the coasts from Gotland to Finisterre. The Pardoner was just back from the papal *curia*, the Clerk had been to Padua, and the Wife of Bath nearly equalled the adventures of the Knight with visits to Jerusalem, Santiago, Cologne and Rome.

England's Italian contacts were regular and longstanding, particularly through Church links with Rome, but also through political, intellectual, and commercial channels. English awareness of Italy came through both Englishmen (churchmen, pilgrims, envoys and mercenaries) returning from Italy, and Italians (merchants, envoys, churchmen) coming to England. The popular view of Italy came ultimately from the classical geographers, but was tempered by guidebooks and itineraries intended for the pilgrim, and added to by the reports of Italians and returning Englishmen. It was of a fertile and wealthy country, as John Larner describes above, and the life-style of the northern Italians in England, together with the rich cargoes of spices, of velvets, damasks and silks, of brocades powdered with gold, of exotica such as sugar-candy, ivory, monkeys and popinjays that Italians unloaded would simply enhance this view. Some visitors might remark on the run-down monuments of Rome, but all were impressed with the wealth of the northern cities.

Access to Italy after hundreds of years of contact was straight-forward. It was possible to go all the way by sea with the Genoese and Venetian trading-fleets, and, given good weather and the fact that these were liner not tramping services, the voyage need take no more than eight weeks. But the risks of adverse winds, wreck and piracy, and the well-attested cramped and smelly conditions of medieval ships made the quicker and more reliable land routes more attractive to all who could choose. The routes through France and Germany and over the Alps were well trodden by generations of travellers, and there was no difficulty about finding the way. A general route could be chosen from the pilgrim's itineraries, or from the advice of those who had already been, and immediate information was then available at the inns en route. The Alps naturally posed difficulties in winter, but local guides could keep travellers moving, as the writings of Buonaccorso Pitti and of the Spaniard, Pero Tafur, in the next century graphically describe.[2] Chaucer himself had to cross the Alps in winter when he left England for Italy on 1 December 1372.

A good, average speed for normal riders was something over 25 miles (40 km) a day, making Florence about 5 or 6 weeks away, and Rome a week longer. The payment dates for letters of exchange in the fifteenth century show merchant couriers to have kept up 35 miles (56 km) a day. Buonaccorso Pitti, when travelling as envoy, not uncommonly rode 40 miles (64 km) a day, and on occasion with urgent dispatches made nearly 100 miles (160 km) a day, but, as he remarked, this ruined the horses.[3] Any group with many pack-horses and walking members would be unlikely to do more than 20 miles (32km) a day. Actual itineraries show daily journeys to have varied considerably: Edmund Rose, going to Milan with Clarence's hounds in 1368, did anything between 12 and 52 miles (19 and 83 km) and travelling days were interspersed with rest days,[4] no doubt at particularly congenial stopping-places, or for the ill and tired.

Of particular concern to us is Chaucer's own exposure to things Italian before and after his own visits between 1 December 1372 and 23 May 1373 and again between 28 May and 19 September 1378, after which his work shows clear Italian influence. His career brought him into contact with Italy as with other foreign countries through a wide variety of channels, but the two of most immediate significance were the City of London and the Court, where he was most likely to meet those who knew Italy well and through which he was given his opportunities to go to Genoa, Florence and Milan.

In the City of London Chaucer would have been surrounded by Italians. They were particularly attracted to it, not only because it was a good market for the sale of their luxuries and a good distribution- and collecting-centre for most of the Midlands areas and the south of England, but also because it was so accessible from the even more important centre of Bruges. It was not, however, the main port for Italian shipping. The Genoese found the North Foreland too dangerous for their newly developed great carracks, and after experimenting with Bristol up to 1383, they settled on Southampton for their main shipping-centre and sent several ships a year.[5] When the Venetians returned to English ports they too used Southampton at first but with their more manoeuvrable galleys they found London accessible and returned there by the end of the fourteenth century. Although it con- sumed some of the Italian goods and distributed others westwards and northwards, for the Italians Southampton was more an outport of London, and cargoes unloaded there were sent overland or by coasters up to London, where the Genoese like other Italians kept their agents and warehouses.[6] Outside these two ports far fewer Italians were to be found. One Gaillard Tany of Florence was a burgess of Winchester in 1369 and Boniface de Castellato, a Lombard, took to agriculture at Chesterton in Cambridgeshire at about the same time;[7] Bernard Anton, the Florentine wool-broker, rode up to Hull for his clients.[8] Particularly few Italian merchants were found inland. The old familiarity with Italians inland was disappearing, as suspicion of aliens due to the Hundred Years War was growing. In Salisbury in 1379 Mark Lumbard of Venice was arrested as a spy and had to be bailed out by four London Italians, Peter Mark of Florence, Bartholomew Bosan of Lucca, Nicholas of Venice, and Peter Bragadyn of Venice;[9] and earlier in 1360 two Italians found wandering in York had been imprisoned because no one 'understood their idiom'.[10] However, despite this unfamiliarity and despite criticism of Italians in the Good Parliament in 1376, this was a relatively welcoming time for them in England and they received nothing like the verbal and physical abuse that they met in the 1430s and 1450s. Certainly the richest members of London's mercantile classes, Sir Nicholas Brembre, Sir John Philpot and Sir William Walworth, worked easily alongside Italians, and Brembre in particular offered help to merchants of Lucca, Bologna and Venice.[11]

Chaucer's own family background was a London mercantile one, and his official career immediately before writing *Troilus and Criseyde* and the *Canterbury Tales* took him back into the City as controller of wool-customs between 1374 and 1386, and more shortly as controller of petty custom. Since London was the busiest Italian centre in England, the Italian merchant community was an integral part of his working world, the more so since the only alien group to take part in the export of English wool by this time was the Italian.[12] As controller, Chaucer was expected to keep his roll in his own hand without a clerk or deputy, and so be present personally on the quay whenever wool consignments were weighed and customed. Since merchants needed cockets (customs certificates) to prove payment of duties, and since the controller on one hand and the customers on the other each kept half the cocket seal, a controller naturally came into personal contact with the merchants and their agents. Chaucer was of course allowed a deputy when he was absent on king's business and was allowed a permanent deputy shortly before he gave up the post, and it is worth noting that for quite long periods he did not have control of his half of the seal. When the king repaid loans from the customs income, his creditors often held half the cocket seal, more often than not (when it is specified) the controller's, thus making sure no possible income escaped their attention.[13] While he might become more negligent then, the controller should still have kept his roll, and in doing so he would come into contact with these creditors. In this way Chaucer would have come into contact not only with the Londoners, Lyons, Pyel and Walworth, but also the king's Florentine financiers, Matthew Cheyne (Cennini) and Walter de Bardes, member of the Bardi Company.[14]

With nothing resembling a census, the number of Italian merchants in London at any time is uncertain, but at least 69 Italians were active and present in London between 1365 and 1369. In the decade 1370–9, when Chaucer first took up his customs post, at least 102 names can be found, and in the decade 1380–9, 164. There were other Italians visiting Southampton, where the Genoese numbered possibly 64 over the 20 years and included members of the important families of Lomellini, Catanei and Centurione.[15] Italian galleys might allow crews of between 100 and 200 men ashore, although carracks needed fewer men, and the Italian presence in the small town of Southampton must at times have been overpowering. In London, where fewer ships called, crewmen would be more easily absorbed; moreover the Venetian Senate, mindful of the troubles of 1319, instructed galley patrons not to let crews ashore in London for fear of tavern brawls,[16] but it seems doubtful that such instructions could be easily enforced. However, it is not these Italians with whom Chaucer came into contact but the merchants themselves.

The merchants in London were all northerners and mainly from Florence and Lucca. Between 1370 and 1379 the Florentines numbered 33, Lucchese 21, Lombards 18 (and possibly 27), Genoese 9, Milanese and Pistoians 3 each, Venetians 2, and there was one from Bologna. An Italian of Crete visited once, and the naturalized Donat brothers came from Siena. Between 1380 and 1389 the balance shifted because of Florentine troubles and the Genoese resurgence, but there were still 22 Florentines, 16 Lucchese and 24 Lombards, together with 38 Genoese, 5 Bolognese, 4 Venetians, 3 Milanese, 3 Pistoians and one each from Siena and Asti. A further 45 Italians were recorded shipping in the customs account for 1389, the majority of them on the Venetian galley of Nicholas Belyn and unidentified by town name.

That the Florentine and Lucchese merchants should be the main groups Chaucer was likely to meet is not surprising.[17] Their companies had long histories of financial and commercial activities in England and they had weathered the bankruptcies of the 1340s and the Black Death quite well. They remained papal bankers and thus major European bankers, and the Florentine textile industry, moving as Villani showed towards better-quality cloth,[18] continued to demand good-quality English wool. The setting-up of the English wool monopoly at Calais had not been a major problem, as the Lombard wool interest had been acknowledged by the immediate appointment of four Lombard brokers there,[19] and some Italians anyway preferred to buy from an overseas Staple when alien export duties rose in England. Edward III had willingly granted licences to bypass the Staple, and this privilege was made permanent in the statute of 1378: Italian wool destined for the Mediterranean could go direct from England by sea.[20] Since the Florentines had no state fleet, nor many private Florentine ships except those of the exiled Alberti company, they used Genoese, Venetian or Iberian ships as available.

The Florentines had been able to rely on papal support and Edward III received several papal letters urging swift justice for Florentines whose agents or goods had been arrested, but these papal links turned sour for the Florentines in the War of the Eight Saints in 1376, and Dr Holmes has shown the ensuing disruption. The interruption in England was however quite short: on 30 January 1377 Edward III took all Florentines into his protection so that legally they traded 'to the King's profit'.[21] Peter Mark, a representative of the Alberti company, who had complained that he had had to flee from England after fourteen years there,[22] was certainly back by November 1378 and stayed on until at least 1389.[23]

Genoese links with England developed rather differently. Initial exchanges were made through the Champagne fairs rather than by Genoese visits to England, but direct contact increased after the opening of the sea route to Flanders pioneered by Majorcans and Genoese in the 1270s, and by the reign of Edward II a Genoese such as Antonio Pessagno could reach great heights in royal finance.[24] However the Genoese were not competing with the Florentines for the world of finance but looking for outlets for their alum from Asia Minor and their sweet wines and olive oil. It was the bulk of these cargoes that led them to abandon galleys in favour of the great carrack. Political problems bedevilled relations with the outbreak of the Hundred Years War, since Genoa inclined to the side of her near neighbour France and in 1338 helped the French in the burning of Southampton. However Genoa's commercial prosperity demanded reasonable relations with England, not only for the English market (which could anyway be reached through Flanders) but for the dangers of sailing past English coasts, as the celebrated cases of seizures in 1370 and 1374 showed so well. The treaty made in 1347, but not well kept, was renewed in 1371, probably prompted by the seizures of 1370.[25] Genoese ambassadors were present in England between Michaelmas 1370 and Easter 1371, and again between September 1371 and January 1372, and at least sixteen merchants played safe by buying English safe-conducts in October 1371 and 1372.[26] It was in the aftermath of these negotiations that Chaucer was sent to Genoa to certify clarifications of the terms and discuss what Genoese shipping-needs were in English ports. Edward III never managed to persuade the Genoese to help formally against France, but in 1373 individual Genoese did make arrangements to enter his service.[27] The attempt to make Southampton a formal Genoese staple, a move against the interest of the Londoners, failed in 1378 with the assassination of the Genoese ambassador, but the Flemish civil war and the decline of the Flemish cloth industry began to push the Genoese more heavily into England after 1379 anyway, and the Anglo-French truce of 1388 eased relations further. These moves are reflected in the growing numbers of Genoese in London between 1380 and 1389, and of ships at Southampton. Nonetheless Flanders remained the greater magnet, and the Genoese were happy to be wooed back with extensive privileges in 1395.[28]

Direct Venetian links were more fragile. State fleets came north from 1314, but avoided English ports after the assaults of 1319. The Venetians refused to respond to Edward III's requests for help against the Genoese in 1340, being unwilling to risk their expensive galleys in another's war. Since their cargoes were mainly of light-weight, expensive luxuries they could even afford to give up northern voyages altogether if Channel sailing became too dangerous and to return entirely to using the land routes to Bruges, since high profits on the luxuries sent north could offset lower profits on wool and cloth sent south. That the land routes were competitive with expensive galleys is indicated by the Venetian regulations protecting galley profits by adding a heavy tax on wool sent overland when galleys were available.[29] Like the Genoese they were hit by Flemish problems and in 1384 sent the first state ships to England since 1319, and thereafter generally one and later two came each year, at first to Southampton and then to London.[30]

Even if politics and piracy were troublesome to the Italian merchants, none would dream of giving up northern trade. It had become an essential part of their worldwide commercial and banking network. This meant that if at times the Italian shipping stayed away from England it was still to be found at Sluys, and Italian goods could be found on Flemish quays. In the tunnage and poundage account of 1389 for London, while a single Venetian galley brought goods worth £2500, Florentine, Lucchese and Genoese merchants on a medley of Low Country and English shipping imported goods worth over £11,000, most of them of Mediterranean origin trans-shipped at Sluys.[31] English merchants fetched Italian goods from there too. Clearly the Englishman's experience of Italians did not end with those in London, but took in other places where he traded.

Within London the Italians were well integrated into City life.[32] They traded, leased houses, brought up families, lent money, acted as brokers, recovered debts, acted as witnesses and sureties for Italians and Englishmen, sat on juries to hear cases according to law merchant, stored valuables in their safe-rooms, held royal offices, supplied luxuries for the royal household and went abroad for the king. They sued and were sued in English courts and were imprisoned in English prisons. The most spectacular accusations were made against Nicholas Sardouche of Lucca, active in England at least from 1364 to his murder in 1370 and first arrested for forcing up the price of silk in London. Further accusations followed of smuggling goods worth £6000, forestalling goods worth £4000 and exporting bullion worth 4000 marks a year. Sardouche had to pay a fine of £200 for his pardon.[33] At the other end of the scale was the case whereby James de Dyne, Lombard, had John Rothwell, London whitetawyer, committed to Newgate jail for snatching James' beaver hat from his head in 1365. Particularly troublesome to a merchant was the theft from Lodowic Gentyl of Genoa in 1376: before dinner on 26 November his purse containing his seal and letters was cut from his girdle as he crossed Westminster

Bridge. Immediately at 2 p.m. he hurried to the Mayor to register the loss so that all deeds sealed with his seal from that day should be void.[34]

In the London circles in which Chaucer moved it would have been easy to find Italians resident in London from their youth, settled and naturalized. Half a dozen families or more would have been of recent Italian extraction. John Donat of Siena received a royal grant to enjoy the liberties of London in 1358 because he had been there since youth and married his wife, Amy, there. He joined a London company and at his death in 1393 left a son, Nicholas, only just under age, to carry on his business. John is often mentioned in London records dealing with Englishmen and Italians, and no doubt the Italians found him a very useful contact, and used him as mainpernor and arbitrator in disputes. He himself appointed a Sienese attorney in 1391.[35] His brother Nicholas was also a London citizen by 1369; Nicholas' wife, Elizabeth, was a member of the London Stode family. Nicholas continued to travel to Lombardy, where he drew up his will. At his death in 1373 he left an infant daughter who died the following year; some of his tenements were then taken over by his brother John.[36]

The work of Dr Beardwood and Professor Thrupp has indicated similar families; those of Batholomew Myne of Florence; Bartholomew Thomasyn of Lucca, whose son Nicholas was a skinner; John Adam of Lucca, who died in 1358 leaving four children; Nicholas William of Lucca who, with his brother Brunettus, dealt with the royal household and left a son, John William, who became a spicer; John Gouche, freeman and spicer, who was born in Florence but lived in London from his youth; James Beal of Lucca, who married the aunt and heiress of Sir John Plesshey.[37] The families who kept their trading links with Italians were no doubt bi-lingual and maintained an interest in family and public affairs in Tuscany. While there is no evidence that Chaucer knew any of them, in a city the size of London it is very likely that he and his family did.

Some of these Italians were men of wealth and influence, closely linked to Court as well as City. John de Mari of Genoa in the 1350s and Guy de Lucca in the 1360s were household suppliers and as such obtained special protection. Walter de Bardes is the best-known financier. He was made Master of the Mint in 1361, an important position and one reflecting the great reputation of the Florentines as moneyers (another Florentine was Master of the Calais Mint). Walter became a freeman of London in 1366 and continued to deal in wool and to act as surety for Italian merchants.[38] He strove to recover the debts of the old Bardi company but was also involved in new loans to the Crown. His loans between 1377 and 1389 amounted to £14,272, but even higher were those of Mathew Cheyne (Cennini) of Florence, broker in London by 1373, dealer in wool, helper of fellow-Italians, attorney for Catalans and Aragonese, active in London at least until 1395. Between 1377 and 1389 he lent £22,261. As Crown financiers, however. Italians were now of limited importance. Edward III and Richard II drew far more from the City of London and their nobility than from aliens. Dr Steel found the period 1377–89 to be the busiest for Italians, with loans of £45,800, some 30 per cent of the total loans raised, and Bardi and Cennini were by far the most important with their combined total of £36,500.[39]

A more important banking activity for the Italians now was in the area of foreign exchange. The Alberti, the Strozzi and the other major companies, but also smaller companies and individual merchants, supplied letters of exchange for churchmen going to the *curia*, pilgrims going to Rome, merchants and ambassadors travelling all over Europe. These activities brought people of all classes into direct contact with Italians, from Margaret, Queen of Scotland, who received money from Londoners at the hands of the Alberti and Strozzi at Avignon in 1372, to Robert of Wodhull, rector of Thurlowe Parva, who bought letters of exchange worth 40 marks from Simon Bochel of Lucca, later citizen of London, payable in Avignon in 1367. Sadly Robert died at Poitiers before reaching Avignon and his executors claimed the money back from Bochel in London.[40]

The Italians in London form an interesting and varied group. They range from the representatives of the great Florentine companies, through representatives of the less-well-known companies such as the Guinigi of Lucca and the Arigi of Bologna, to members of small family firms and individual merchants such as Simon Bochel and William Tedys. Some came for years, and some for months. Walter de Bardes was in London at least forty years (1351–91), Peter Mark of Florence over twenty (c. 1363–89). Mathew Cheyne was here between 1373 and 1395, Bernard Anton of Florence between 1371 and 1389, Thomas Serland of Lucca between 1365 and 1378. Lodowic Andree of Florence probably punctuated his time in England with travels abroad; he is recorded here in 1371–4 but not again until 1386 and 1389. Others perhaps did the same, although some of those who appear infrequently in English records may simply be keeping out of the way of English officialdom. Some certainly visited only briefly. Buonaccorso Pitti was in London just a month when he arranged in 1390 for wool to be bought for him by Mariotto Ferrantini and Giovanni di Guerrieri de' Rossi.[41] Pitti offers an interesting light on Anglo-Italian contacts with his short stay. Here was a man of mercantile background and training who still actively traded but who spent much of his time in the Courts of northern Europe until in early middle age he returned to Florence to take his part in public life. His diary shows his interests to have been gambling and furnishing houses finely, but no doubt he had a passing cultural interest as befitted his station. He could impart up-to-date general information and gossip to Florentine compatriots, and other visitors could do the same.

This Anglo-Italian mercantile connection is provided almost entirely by Italians visiting England and hardly at all by English merchants visiting Italy. The men founding the English Hospices in Rome seem to be rarities, and not to have travelled back to England. Thomas Beaumond of London, who died in Lombardy before December 1380, either on that journey or another paid in Lombardy for scarlet silk bought earlier; and the petition of Walter Wilkyn, a London draper, for the return of woad, pepper and saffron worth £400 on a Genoese ship wrecked off Dorset indicates that he bought them in Genoa, but it is not clear if he went himself or employed Italian agents.[42]

The merchants' importance as cultural figures is difficult to assess. They were certainly distant from new Florentine developments, but many were from rich families with a tradition of civic culture. If French merchants in London had felt the need for entertainment and a cultural identity, which they expressed through the Feste de Pui in London, what more natural than that the Italians, much further from home, wealthy, literate, should have maintained interest in their own literature and learning, albeit in a more private way? Perhaps the London representatives of the Bardi company even had a particular interest in the work of Boccaccio, once one of their junior representatives in Naples.

How well Chaucer came to know any of these Italians we shall never know. Presumably he talked long with John de Mari and either Jacob de Provan or his son Saladin on the way to Genoa. (It remains doubtful whether Jacob made the journey then, as ten days after being named in the embassy he was appointed lieutenant to the Genoese galleys preparing, for once, to help Edward III in his wars, and there is no payment to him for his expenses.) Surviving customs accounts give us the names of twenty-nine Italians Chaucer certainly met trading through London in 1380–1 and 1384–5 as they were wool-exporters for whom he sealed cockets at the custom house.[43] Between 1381 and 1386, too, he would have had several occasions to meet Mathew Cheyne of Florence, who had repayments from the king of over £8000 secured on the customs income. He certainly held half the cocket seal for repayments of £5350 and possibly for all £8000. He would have been present over several months at a stretch: the £2500 to be raised from £1 on the sack of wool from February 1382 would have had to come from over one quarter of London's wool exports that year. He still held the cocket in August 1382 and either again or still in September 1383.[44] How friendly Chaucer ever became with these Italians and what he might have discussed with them will never be known, but certainly once his curiosity in things Italian had been aroused it would have been very easy for him to sustain his interest in London.

Chaucer's attachment to the Ulster household and then the royal household brought him a whole new range of contacts through the diplomacy and Court life of the time and gave him all his opportunities for travel to France, Navarre and, probably, Spain, as well as to Italy. Diplomatic exchanges with France, Spain and the *curia* at Avignon were more frequent than with Italy throughout the period, but the interlinking relationships of the pope, the Italian cities, France and England, besides the mutual interest in trade, made some diplomatic activity inevitable.

In his French wars Edward III wooed Venetians and Genoese for naval support, or at least an undertaking not to support France, and England was also always willing to sympathize with moves to limit the aggrandizement of France in Italy. In his wars in defence of the papal states the pope wanted English help in men and money, usually against Milan. The English, however, were less than obliging in deed: in 1361 the pope obtained money but no men and in 1372 he had extreme difficulty in obtaining even the money, but this was due more to England's unwillingness to see bullion leave England in papal taxes than to love of Milan.[45] In 1396–7 it looked for a few weeks as if Richard II, to please his new French father-in-law, might support him in alliance with the pope and Florence against Milan, but nothing came of the move.[46] Indeed England had no direct reason to fight Milan and saw her rather as a rich catch for a younger son. Edward had been very willing to accept the handsome dowry in cash and land that Visconti offered for a royal marriage. This marriage may have given Chaucer his first opportunity to go to Italy, but there is not a shred of evidence for that, and he had already left the Ulster household. The marriage certainly did give an occasion for many English nobles and gentlemen and their retinues to visit Italy, and perhaps some acquired a taste for Italian styles, as appears to have happened with Humphrey Bohun, Earl of Hereford, who led the negotiations in 1366 and whose family's manuscripts show evidence of Italian painting-styles. In 1367 knights in Lionel's retinue were putting their affairs in

order for a journey expected to involve absences of at least a year, and
the arrangements for Lionel's crossing the Channel included the hire
of enough shipping to carry 457 men and 1280 horses. Lionel's early
death prevented any permanent link, but his company stayed in Italy
holding the dower lands for a year from October 1368 in case there
should have been a posthumous heir. Their leader, Sir Edward
Despenser, stayed even longer.[47] Further marriages were mooted: for
Richard II in 1378–9, and for Derby in 1397–8 before his fall from
grace. Derby's visit to Milan on his return from Jerusalem in 1393–4
had clearly impressed Lucia, Visconti's sister-in-law, but Visconti had
no wish to be linked with a penniless exile, and Lucia, with regret, but
unable to foresee Derby's successful usurpation of the English throne,
sensibly married a German instead.[48] These contacts produced a
numerically strong group of men in courtly circles who had spent some
time in Italy, and it is likely that Bohun was not the only one to
become interested in the Italian elements of European civilization.

Military links with Italy were moderately strong too. The French
Earl of Bedford, husband of Edward III's daughter Isabella, was with
the papal army against Milan in 1370; Sir Richard Musard served the
Duke of Savoy from 1361 but temporarily joined Lionel in 1368; and
the best-known soldier of them all is undoubtedly Sir John Hawkwood,
who fought in Italy from 1362 to his death in 1394, and whom
Chaucer met when he went to Milan to negotiate in 1378. There were
besides several hundreds of English mercenaries in Italy and over a
hundred are known by name. Although they made Italians aware of
England it is extremely unlikely that they provided any useful cultural
channel between Italy and England. Hawkwood clearly had important
friends and contacts, but most soldiers were much humbler in status.
Probably few returned to England. Where careers can be traced, they
are found to have settled in Italy, as did William Gold, citizen of
Venice, or to have died on active service.[49] It is however possible that
Richard Dany, one of the King's armourers in the Tower of London in
1380, 'who has lived in Lombardy and there learned the mistery of
making breastplates',[50] first went with the mercenary companies and
was one of the few to return.

There had been enough diplomatic and soldierly contact, perhaps
enhanced by Chaucer's own writings, and certainly confirmed by the
desire to travel to Rome or to Jerusalem by way of Venice, to attract to
Italy some of the major figures in English politics at the end of the
century, some in exile, some not. Besides Derby with his entourage of
forty or fifty men, Archbishop Arundel and the exiled Duke of
Norfolk went south to Italy.

A further small group whom Chaucer may have met at Court were Italian doctors. The M. Peter de Florentia who was 'fisicus' to Edward III and Philippa in 1368 may have been Italian; M. John, son of M. Dominic de Markia de Ascoli, doctor of medicine, newly arrived in England, was given a licence to practise in 1385, and royal protection covered his men and servants, no doubt some of them Italians. In 1387 Antonio de Romanis of Naples was the physician accompanying Sir John Stanley, Robert de Vere's deputy, to Ireland, and reference is also made that year to the arrest of Brother Peter de Barulo alias M. Peter de Salernia, physician.[51] Perhaps with this group might be mentioned also Richard II's Venetian dancing-master of 1380, John Katerine.[52]

Beyond Chaucer's immediate circles of City and Court were the worlds of the Church and universities, both providing strong links with Italy. Not only was Chaucer likely to meet members of both in Court and civic life, but the Church and universities had moulded the intellectual world in which Chaucer had been educated and in which he wrote. Visits to Rome, the writings of the early Church Fathers and the works of classical Latin authors provided the oldest and strongest cultural links with Italy; they were by now so well integrated into European cultural life that they might be considered more a common European heritage than peculiarly Italian. Nonetheless, they meant that educated Englishmen were conversant with the history, the people and the places of classical and early medieval Italy, and even the uneducated would have heard some stories through the *exempla* of preachers.

Current religious contact with Italy remained strong despite the *curia*'s move to Avignon. English criticism of the Church in its 'Babylonian Captivity' might well increase (as it did all over Europe) and English relations with the *curia* might be strained during the French wars and with the passing of the Statutes of Provisors and Praemunire, but links could never be severed while England remained part of Christendom. At Avignon, moreover, although French popes and cardinals increased in numbers, the Italian element was still vigorous: Petrarch was honoured and Dante discussed. Moreover the popes recognized Rome as their base and strove to return, and England re-established direct contacts with a *curia* in Rome in 1378 at the beginning of the Great Schism.

Churchmen maintained contacts in many ways. The collection of papal taxes from England ensured a permanent establishment of a papal collector in London, closely connected with the Italian bankers for the transfer of money, and he kept a small household around him that included Italians. When Garnier was temporarily absent from London in 1374–5 he left affairs in the hands of M. Laurence de Nigris and his brother Angelo, together with the Florentine merchant Peter Mark. Laurence de Nigris spent some years in England; he was also proctor for Cardinal Orsini and he died in London in 1382, having appointed a merchant, Augustine Damasce of Lucca, his executor.[53] Italian proctors of a lowlier nature included those of the Hospital of St James of Altopassu in the diocese of Lucca, which held an English establishment at Thurlow in Suffolk from 1291.[54] Proctors for Italians holding English benefices were, however, more often Englishmen. The whole practice of papal provision to benefices did not bring many Italians into England, since many benefices so provided went to Englishmen and of the Italian-held benefices, mostly of the middle rank, few occasioned a visit, let alone the settlement of an Italian in England. The practice did on the other hand promote many English visits to the *curia*.

Papal nuncios were sometimes sent to organize clerical subsidies from England, or to mediate between England and France, but not all were Italians, and not all came to England: they might meet English ambassadors on neutral ground, as they did in Bruges in 1374. Even when they came to England, their visits might be short: Damian Catanei, knight of Genoa, stayed from January to April in 1391 and again from October 1391 to March 1393, but Pileus, Archbishop of Ravenna, was in England less than a month.[55]

Much more important numerically than these few Italians coming to England were the Englishmen who visited the *curia*, where they found not only a judicial and administrative centre but also a lively intellectual one, concerned not only with theology and canon law but also with classical learning. There were generally two or three permanent English curial officials to expedite administration concerning England; there were a few English cardinals; there were Englishmen sent to represent their Orders in Avignon and Rome. A few Englishmen stayed the rest of their lives at the *curia* and did not return to England to preach and teach, but they might still influence English thought. Adam Easton, who became conversant with Dante's work, corresponded regularly with his Order in England and left his books to his home monastery at Norwich;[56] similarly Simon Langham, once Abbot of Westminster, Chancellor of England and Archbishop of Canterbury, when he was made cardinal in 1368, spent the rest of his life at Avignon but bequeathed his books to Westminster in 1376.[57] Many others did return home: Richard de Bury, Bishop of Durham, who met Petrarch on one of his visits either in 1330 or 1333,[58] Ralph fitz Alan, later Bishop of Armagh, Thomas Brunton, once a curial official, made Bishop of Rochester in 1373 – all returned home.[59] Intellectual contacts were of course perfectly possible without physical contact. Bury had already shown an ability to collect Italian examples in his letter collection compiled about 1325, possibly obtaining them through the king's proctor; the Dominican, Nicholas Trevet, who was asked by letter by Cardinal Nicholas de Prato for a commentary on Seneca's *Tragedies* and possibly for a Livy commentary by the pope,[60] had worked in Oxford and Paris, in Avignon and in Italy, where his work was also known.

English clergy at the *curia* formed a far larger group than these relatively few scholars and included all ranks from archbishops to the lowliest parsons, taking all sorts of lawsuits to Rome or Avignon. Such journeys should have been made only with licence after the passing of the Statute of Praemunire, but recorded pardons show some men storming indignantly off without permission to forestall their opponents. Some indication of the scale of this contact is found after the tightening of regulations in 1389; 82 visits to Rome 'to obtain benefices' are recorded at the end of that year, and a peak of 116 in January 1390. Parks suggested overall perhaps fifty Englishmen a year went to the *curia* outside these extraordinary years.[61] Those with complex cases would stay a while, but many parish clergy and minor prebendaries with limited money and a precise objective might stay a short time. All would come into contact with the curial officials, with other petitioners and with preachers at the *curia*; how many of them found the atmosphere stimulating and took opportunities to discuss, dispute and read we do not know. Many, in any case, when they returned to England were in no position to make great impact on intellectual circles beyond the most localized.

Many of the Englishmen attracted to Italy were pilgrims to Rome, and their visits continued despite the removal of the papacy to Avignon. Their numbers are usually difficult to assess, since the only ones to leave much trace were the richest, who needed to leave attorneys to supervise affairs, and who paid to have these appointments enrolled on public records. The declared Jubilee of 1350 provides one firm point. Edward III first forbade participation and then licenced it, and licences were issued for 191 pilgrims with 186 servants. In 1362 John Shepherd, the English rosary dealer in Rome, and his associates thought it worth setting up an English Hospice; in 1390 the exchange rolls suggest possibly 300 pilgrims; and in 1396 it was worth opening another Hospice.[62] Some pilgrims saw more of Italy by going on to Jerusalem, a journey that by the later fourteenth century almost always took them to Venice to embark on the regular galley-sailings for Jaffa, unless, like the Earl of Derby, they could persuade the Venetian Senate to provide a special vessel.[63] Not all pilgrims of course returned to England with travellers' tales: Thomas Cheyne esquire died abroad, and his executors claimed back from Nicholas de Luk' of Florence the 'trussyng cofre' deposited with him for safe-keeping in London.[64] Perhaps Cheyne obtained his letters of exchange and up-to-date travelling information from the same source. The intellectual curiosity of the pilgrims and their opportunities for fulfilling it varied widely. Although a man like Derby could enjoy discussions with the mighty and collect books, it is unlikely that many could do likewise.

A vigorous channel for Anglo-Italian exchanges might have been through the Friar's Orders, which, with their emphasis on teaching and preaching and with their international network of schools and meetings of General Chapters, should have kept England and the continent in close touch. Their impact for Chaucer, however, was probably more limited than at first appears. Nicholas Havely shows below that Chaucer, unlike Boccaccio, had no known links with individual friars, although he would have met some in the circles in which he moved. Specifically Italian contacts through the friars are anyway fewer than might be expected. Some Italian friars were to be found in Chaucer's London: men such as Raphael de Lucca of the Hermits of St Augustine in 1363, and Anthony de Veneciis and Benedict de Arecio of the Friars Minor in 1378;[65] and certainly some English friars travelled to Italy: three Franciscans travelled to Perugia in 1323 and one went on to Bologna the following year;[66] Thomas Waleys, the Dominican, lectured at Bologna in the late 1320s and was replaced by another Englishman in 1331.[67] But General Chapters and lecturing appointments probably took more English friars to France, where the Franciscan and Dominican emphasis lay.

Numbers travelling abroad were relatively small, given the international aspects of the Orders. Many English friars remained in England all their lives, like most of the secular churchmen. Of a score of Yorkshire mendicants who were scholars at Oxford in the fourteenth century only five had been abroad, three to France and two to Italy.[68] Of the seven classicizing friars examined by Dr Smalley three never went abroad and two made only short visits. Analyses of the Dominicans and Franciscans in England show a surprisingly low number of foreign friars, especially for the later fourteenth century, although records are far from complete. Emden's list of 5250 Dominicans ordained in England shows only 280 identifiable foreigners and only 10 per cent of those were here between 1350 and 1399. Few were Italians.[69] Similarly Moorman's collection of 3000 Franciscans includes only 200 foreigners, of which 50 were Italians, over the whole medieval period. Like Emden, he found the foreign element particularly low in the late fourteenth century. At the schools at Oxford and Cambridge he found some attempt to comply with ordinances stipulating a continental lecturer every third year, but Italian lecturers were few. However, of six continental Franciscan students at Oxford two were Italian, and of eleven continental visitors known in the provinces for the fourteenth century six were Italian.[70]

Contacts there were, however, even if fewer than might be expected, and the friars were in fairly influential positions at the universities and at Court. Aston's analyses of Oxford and Cambridge alumni show friars accounting for many of the foreign students there.[71] The Dominicans were well established as royal confessors, and the Austin Friars, Geoffrey Hardeby and John Erghome, were welcomed at the Courts of Edward III and the Black Prince.[72] But the friars' libraries, where they are known as in the case of Erghome, while showing wide intellectual interests including an interest in the classics, do not indicate an interest in newer continental developments. Dr Smalley showed clearly the extent and limitations of the friars' interests for the generation before Chaucer, and they do not seem to have changed. While the English friars she examined tried to combine their classical and theological studies, they were in no way moving towards early humanism. Moreover the English Franciscans and Dominicans had their strongest links with France, where they would find less encouragement for the new classical studies or the mixing of classics and theology. Only the Austin Friars had lively Italian links, which Gwynn illuminated by noting their university contacts, their General Chapter meetings in Italy, their commentaries on the classics, their Order's friendship for Petrarch and Boccaccio, and the fact that the Italian magnet was strong enough to attract Willam Flete to permanent settlement there.

It is likely that Chaucer met friars who had been to Italy or had heard Italian masters, and that some were active and lively scholars, but they were unlikely to encourage his study of new Italian developments. As Dr Smalley concluded, the exciting developments there were taking place not within the Church but within the city societies of lawyers, notaries, politicians and merchants. Nonetheless she emphasized that the friars did help to educate Chaucer's audience and familiarize them with classical stories and people.[73] Their scholarly textual work also made serious study of Latin authors easier, and works such as Nicholas Trevet's, mentioned above, were appreciated all over Europe.

Despite much speculation, there is no evidence of Chaucer's formal schooling, but the suggestion that he studied at either university is now discounted. This does not mean that he was out of touch with university life, as he counted university-trained men among his associates, but the English universities were unlikely to introduce him to new Italian developments. It seems that the Oxford of Wyclif's time was still unacquainted with the work of Dante. Aston's analyses mentioned above established the later fourteenth century as the low point of exchanges between English and continental universities. This is mostly due to trouble in French exchanges during the Hundred Years War, but there is no evidence that other nations moved to fill the French gap. Specifically Italian contact remained low and was far outstripped by German contacts even in the fifteenth-century boom in interest in Italian movements. For the whole period to 1500, only 259 of the 15,000 recorded Oxford names were continental and only 74 were Italian; at Cambridge out of 7000 recorded names only 74 were continental and of those only 24 were Italian. The evidence for Englishmen at Italian universities, compiled by Parks, suggests a greater movement in the other direction: but of some 250 Englishmen at Italian universities between 1200 and 1499 only 28 are recorded for 1350–1400, 19 of them at Bologna.[74] The university teaching at this time was unlikely to have introduced scholars to the new Italian writings, although individuals might have developed their own interest. English universities still emphasized theology and philosophy, where the new excitement for scholars were Oxford's new advances in areas much discussed on the continent but very distinct from, and in some ways inimical to, Italy's vernacular and early-humanist literary developments. Petrarch himself recorded dislike of the cold logic of the English schoolmen. On the other hand, as John Larner points out above, in Italian universities the vocational studies of law and medicine remained supreme and university influence on the new movements was limited, although beginning to increase with the appointment of Boccaccio to lecture on Dante at Florence.

Numbers of course have a limited meaning in intellectual history, and cultural contact does not rely on university exchanges, nor even on direct Anglo-Italian contacts. Avignon and Paris could well act as disseminating centres for English and Italian works, private meetings of scholars could take place anywhere, correspondence was frequent and books were easily transported. There is no dearth of evidence for English book-collectors, from churchmen such as Bury, Easton,

Erghome and Langham to laymen such as the sons and grandsons of Edward III. Richard II's library was large, and the Duke of Gloucester left ninety-five books at his death in 1397.[75] The interest of other men is shown by wills, from Sir Bartholomew Bacon, who left one romance to his wife, to Sir William Walworth, one of Chaucer's city associates, who left nine religious books and law-books worth £100.[76] Many of these lay collections were unadventurous: collections of professional law-books, service-books, religious works, and well-known and well-tried romances, but some of these last provided a firm background for Chaucer's work, as the Troy stories did for *Troilus and Criseyde*.

There is little evidence for a mass, speculative, international book trade in England until the last quarter of the fifteenth century, when the customs accounts show mass imports through the Low Countries and from Venice.[77] It was easy enough, however, for churchmen, ambassadors and all sorts of travellers to bring back books bought abroad or received abroad as gifts, or to receive them as gifts in England. Indeed this continued to happen in the early years of the printed book, when the Dean of Salisbury bought a standard canon-law-book in Hamburg in 1465, and John Shirwood bought a copy of Cicero's *Orations* in Rome in 1474.[78] Handwritten books would not have been available in such profusion as printed books, but Bonvesin della Riva's description of Milan in 1288 as a city supporting over forty copyists making a livelihood although it had no university[79] indicates that some sort of ready supply was for sale, and a sojourn of a very few weeks would certainly provide enough time to commission plain texts. Scholars might also send for texts, and it is quite possible that books were brought to England by Italian merchants as a commercial venture despite the lack of information in the customs accounts. Although manuscripts would have fallen into the category of miscellaneous goods dutiable at 3d. in the pound value, merchants might well bring in one or two as personal property. Some of these they might have kept among the Italian colony in London, but it would have been easy enough to sell them, make presents of them, or have further copies made.

Purchases and gifts of more elaborate illuminated texts no doubt contributed to the appreciation of Italian styles and painting-techniques in the later fourteenth century. English manuscripts from London and Durham, and English wall-paintings adopt Italianate styles, and, while some larger Italian paintings clearly were in England (such as the 'table of six pieces of Lombardy' mentioned in Hugh Payntour's will in 1361), and some English painters apparently went to Italy,[80] it is likely that the English became acquainted with these styles

through more easily portable manuscripts. Whether the Italianate
style came direct from Italy or through Avignon, its adoption attests
once more to the international aspects of England's Court life.

Chaucer lived in a society where international contacts were a
commonplace of commercial, diplomatic, religious and intellectual life.
Links with France, Flanders and Spain were strong in his age, but
many Englishmen in his circle would also have been to Italy, or have
friends and relatives who had been there, or would know Italians in
England. Italy was only five to six weeks away on well-trodden roads.
Englishmen who had visited Italy probably numbered hundreds at any
one time: perhaps a hundred pilgrims and clerics went each year, a
handful of churchmen had been curial officials (in Rome again after
1378), tens of friars and men who had been to Italian universities were
back in England, half a dozen nobles had been there as ambassadors,
and among the aristocracy and gentlemen were the 457 who had
accompanied Lionel in 1368. The Italian colony in London was
numbered in scores, mostly merchants but with a scattering of churchmen, friars and doctors. A few hundreds in a population of perhaps
$2\frac{1}{2}$ million may not seem significant, but concentrated as they were
in the smaller populations of London, Court and Church they become
so.

How many of these Italians Chaucer knew really well, what he
discussed with them and learnt from them we cannot know. Nor do
we know where and when he learnt Italian, nor even how well he
spoke it; Latin and French were still the languages of diplomacy and
customs administration. We do not know how or where he got hold
of Italian books, nor even exactly where he went in Italy apart from
Genoa, Florence and Milan. What is clear is that he lived in circles
which knew Italy reasonably well, and which would prepare him
competently for his journeys to what John Larner shows to have been
a very complex country. Possibly they prepared him for Italy's new
literature and developments, but it is unlikely that they could have
introduced him to these fully. Without his own visits, made by chance
at a particularly fruitful time, it is doubtful if his consciousness of
Italy would have hardened, nor would his writings have contained
such ample and explicit references to Italian writers and their work.

Notes

1 I acknowledge with thanks the help of a grant from the British Academy,
  which enabled me to work in the Public Record Office for parts of this paper.
2 For a general view of travel to Italy see G. B. Parks, *The English Traveler to*

Italy, vol. I, 'The Middle Ages (to 1525)' (Rome, 1954), chapters 5 and 11; G. Brucker (ed.), 'The Diary of Buonaccorso Pitti', in *Two Memoirs of Renaissance Florence* (New York, 1967), p. 56; M. Letts (ed.), *Pero Tafur: Travels and Adventures* (London, 1926), pp. 182–3.

3 Brucker, 'Diary of Pitti', p. 49.

4 Parks, *English Traveler*, pp. 517–19.

5 Public Record Office (hereafter P.R.O.) E122/137/19, 138/11, 138/16, 138/20, 138/22: four in 1371–2, six in 1383–4, ten in 1387–8, six in 1391–2, five in 1395–6.

6 For Italian activity in Southampton see A. A. Ruddock, *Italian Merchants and Shipping in Southampton 1270–1600*, Southampton Record Series, I (Southampton, 1951).

7 *Calendar of Patent Rolls* (hereafter C.P.R.) 1367–70, pp. 251, 274.

8 *Calendar of Select Pleas and Memoranda of the City of London preserved among the Archives of the Corporation of the City of London at the Guildhall* (hereafter C.P.M. *London*) A.D. 1381–1412, ed. A. H. Thomas (Cambridge, 1932), pp. 130–1.

9 C.P.R. 1377–81, p. 294; Senobo Martyn of Florence also went to Salisbury for wool in 1373 (*Calendar of Miscellaneous Inquisitions*, III, p. 355).

10 *Calendar of Close Rolls* (hereafter C.C.R.) 1354–60, p. 608.

11 For brief descriptions of these men's careers see R. Bird, *The Turbulent London of Richard II* (London, 1949).

12 In 1380–1 and 1384–5 while Chaucer was controller they exported over 15 per cent and nearly 14 per cent respectively (P.R.O. E122/71/4, 71/9). Some comment on their activity will be found in T. H. Lloyd, *The English Wool Trade in the Middle Ages* (Cambridge, 1977), pp. 248–50, 255–6.

13 The cocket seal may have been out of Chaucer's hands for over half the twelve years of his appointment.

14 C.P.R. 1381–5, pp. 102, 154; ibid. 1385–9, p. 150.

15 The main sources are C.C.R., C.P.R., C.P.M. *London, Calendar of Letter-Books preserved among the Archives of the Corporation of the City of London*, Books G and H, ed. R. R. Sharpe (London, 1905–7) (hereafter *Letter-Books*), and P.R.O. E122 (K. R. Customs Accounts). Italian names are left as they appear in English records.

16 *Calendar of State Papers, Venice*, I, no. 96.

17 A good survey of Florentine activity in England is provided by G. A. Holmes, 'Florentine merchants in England, 1346–1436', *Economic History Review*, series II, 13 (1960–1); see also his *The Good Parliament* (Oxford, 1975), pp. 79–90, 118–26.

18 Giovanni Villani, *Cronica*, lib. XI, cap. xciv, trans. in R. S. Lopez and I. W. Raymond (eds.), *Medieval Trade in the Mediterranean World* (London, 1955), pp. 71–4.

19 T. Rymer, *Foedera, Conventiones, Litterae* . . . (4 vols., London, 1816–69), III, ii, 769.

20 *Statutes of the Realm* (11 vols., London, 1810–28), 2 Richard II, stat. 1, c. 3.

21 C.C.R. 1374–7, pp. 422, 478; Rymer, *Foedera*, III, ii, 1071.

22 Holmes, *Good Parliament*, p. 126.

23 C.P.R. 1377–81, p. 283; P.R.O. E122/71/13.

24 Ruddock, *Italian Merchants*, pp. 19–22, 24.

25 Rymer, *Foedera*, III, ii, 909–10, 931–2.

26 Ibid. 894, 906–7, 922–3, 932, 963.

27 Ibid. 965, 970, 994; C.P.R. 1370–4, p. 255; *Calendar of Plea and Memoranda Rolls*

preserved among the Archives of the Corporation of the City of London at the Guildhall (hereafter *C.P.M. London*), A.D. *1364-1381*, ed. A. H. Thomas (Cambridge, 1929), pp. 184-5.

28 Ruddock, *Italian Merchants*, pp. 52-4.

29 *Calendar of State Papers, Venice*, I, nos. 21, 23, 34, 37 for example.

30 *Ibid.* nos. 96-8, 102, 104-6, 109 for example.

31 P.R.O. E122/71/13. A whole fleet of great and small ships loaded with goods of Italians, Londoners, Hansards and others, was driven ashore and wrecked in 1370 (*C.P.R.* 1367-70, pp. 469-70).

32 For much information on their London lives see Holmes, 'Florentine merchants'; A. Beardwood, *Alien Merchants in England 1350 to 1377*, Medieval Academy of America Publications, VIII (Cambridge, Mass., 1931); *C.P.M. London; Letter-Books.*

33 Beardwood, *Alien Merchants*, pp. 81-4; *C.P.R.* 1367-70, p. 279; *Letter-Book G*, pp. 236-7, 247-8.

34 *C.P.M. London 1364-81*, pp. 21, 231.

35 *Ibid.* pp. 39, 110, 130-1, 254-5, 278; *ibid.* 1381-1412, pp. 174, 185; Beardwood, *Alien Merchants*, p. 197; *Letter-book H*, pp. 26-7, 32-3, 124, 382; S. Thrupp, *The Merchant Class of Medieval London* (*1300-1500*) (Chicago, 1948), p. 220, n. 48.

36 Beardwood, *Alien Merchants*, p. 197; *C.P.M. London 1364-81*, p. 158; *Letter-Book H*, pp. 26-7, 32-3.

37 Beardwood, *Alien Merchants*, chapter 4; Thrupp, *Merchant Class*, pp. 220-1.

38 Beardwood, *Alien Merchants, passim; C.P.M. London 1364-81*, p. 76; *ibid.* 1381-1412, pp. 26-8, 75, 82-3, 122; and many references in *C.C.R.* and *C.P.R.*

39 A. Steel, *The Receipt of the Exchequer, 1377-1485* (Cambridge, 1954), pp. 125-48. After 1389 the Italian share dropped to under 2 per cent.

40 Rymer, *Foedera*, III, ii, 948; *C.P.M. London 1364-81*, p. 77.

41 Brucker, 'Diary of Pitti', p. 45.

42 *C.P.M. London 1381-1412*, p. 37; *C.P.R.* 1385-9, p. 552.

43 P.R.O. E122/71/4, 9; the twenty-nine included at least seven Florentines, five Lucchese, three Venetians, two Genoese, two from Pistoia and one from Bologna.

44 *C.P.R.* 1381-5, pp. 102, 154, 307-8; full details of the loans secured on the customs are to be found in M. M. Crow and C. C. Olson (eds.), *Chaucer Life-Records* (Oxford, 1966), pp. 179-80 and table 2.

45 Papal relations are dealt with by W. E. Lunt, *Financial Relations of the Papacy with England*, vol. II, '*1327-1534*', Medieval Academy of America Publications, LXXIV (Cambridge, Mass., 1962), and W. Pantin, *The English Church in the Fourteenth Century* (Cambridge, 1955).

46 D. M. Bueno de Mesquita, 'The foreign policy of Richard II in 1397: some Italian letters', *English Historical Review*, LIV (1941), 628-37.

47 Rymer, *Foedera*, III, ii, 797, 817, 827,-8, 842-5; Parks, *English Traveler*, pp. 383-4.

48 *Ibid.* pp. 289-90; for Lucia's comments see *Calendar of State Papers, Milan*, no. 2.

49 Parks, *English Traveler*, pp. 384-95.

50 *C.P.R.* 1377-81, p. 458.

51 *Ibid.* 1367-70, p. 103; *ibid.* 1381-5, p. 531; *ibid.* 1385-9, pp. 232, 324.

52 J. Harvey, *The Plantagenets* (London, 1959), p. 155 note.

53 Holmes, *Good Parliament*, pp. 85-6; *C.P.M. London 1381-1412*, p. 37.

54 *C.P.R.* 1364-7, pp. 218, 374; *ibid.* 1381-5, p. 224; R. M. Clay, *The Medieval Hospitals of England* (London, 1909), pp. 209, 322.

55 Lunt, *Financial Relations*, vol. II, pp. 668-76, 683-5.

56 Pantin, *English Church*, chapter 8.

57 R. Widmore, *An History of the Church of St Peter, Westminster* (London, 1791), appendix, p. 189.

58 N. Denholm-Young, 'Richard de Bury (1287–1345) and the *Liber Epistolaris*', in *Collected Papers* (Cardiff, 1969).

59 Pantin, *English Church*, chapter 8.

60 B. Smalley, *English Friars and Antiquity in the Early Fourteenth Century* (Oxford, 1960), p. 60.

61 Parks, *English Traveler*, pp. 344–8.

62 *Ibid*. pp. 345, 355–60.

63 For the development of the Venetian route see M. M. Newett, *Canon Pietro Casola's pilgrimage to Jerusalem in the year 1494* (Manchester, 1907).

64 C.P.M. London 1381–1412, p. 103.

65 *Letter-Book* G, p. 151; C.C.R. 1377–81, p. 528.

66 D. Knowles, *The Religious Orders in England*, vol. I (Cambridge, 1962), pp. 246–7.

67 Smalley, *English Friars*, chapter 7.

68 I thank Mr John Taylor for this information.

69 A. B. Emden, *A Survey of Dominicans in England, based on the ordination lists in episcopal registers (1269 to 1538)* (Rome, 1967), pp. 22–5.

70 J. R. H. Moorman, 'The foreign element among the English Franciscans', *English Historical Review*, LXII (1947), 289–303.

71 T. H. Aston, 'Oxford's medieval alumni', *Past and Present*, LXXIV (1977); T. H. Aston, G. D. Duncan, T. A. R. Evans, 'The medieval alumni of the University of Cambridge', *Past and Present*, LXXXVI (1980).

72 A. O. Gwynn, *The English Austin Friars in the time of Wyclif* (Oxford, 1940), chapters 7 and 8.

73 Smalley, *English Friars*, p. 307.

74 Parks, *English Traveler*, pp. 621–40.

75 *Calendar of Miscellaneous Inquisitions*, VI, no. 372; Viscount Dillon and W. H. St. John Hope, 'Inventory of the goods and chattels belonging to Thomas, Duke of Gloucester...', *The Archaeological Journal*, LIV (second series IV) (1897), 287–308.

76 Thrupp, *Merchant Class*, pp. 161–3, 248.

77 N. Kerling, 'Caxton and the trade in printed books', *The Book Collector*, IV (1955).

78 E. Armstrong, 'English purchases of printed books from the Continent, 1465–1526', *English Historical Review*, XCIV (1979).

79 Bonvesin della Riva, 'On the marvels of the City of Milan', trans. in Lopez and Raymond, *Medieval Trade*, pp. 61–9.

80 M. Rickert, *Painting in Britain in the Middle Ages* (London, 1954), chapter 7, nn. 15, 17.

Chaucer, Dante and Boccaccio[1]

The great events of history, cultural as well as political, have a way of happening unheralded and unregarded. When, some time in 1372, the English Chancery issued a warrant for a commission to one Galfridus Chaucer, 'scutifer domini regis', and others, to treat with the Genoese concerning the choice of a particular English seaport for the use of Genoese merchants, no one concerned, not even Chaucer himself, could have had the slightest notion that the said warrant was to be the first strand in a complex mesh of literary and cultural affiliations between Italy and England, and that it would affect the whole course and tone of English literature. Chaucer himself, as the warrant indicates, was not primarily a man of letters, but a civil servant. The books he most often consulted were books 'of reckonings' – the account-books that the Eagle alludes to in his *House of Fame* (653). And even when writing verse he kept an eye on costs. One of the differences between his Knight's account of the great theatre in which Arcite and Palamon tourneyed, and Boccaccio's depiction of it in *Il Teseida* is that in Chaucer Duke Theseus provides food and wages for the craftsmen who built it, and pays 'largely of gold a fother' for the statue of Mars, whilst the painter who decorated the statue of Diana lays out 'many a florin' on the tinctures. Chaucer's day-to-day life as Clerk of the King's works was spent in making just such payments to English workmen and English artists.

Chaucer began life as a vintner's son. The first foreigners he met would be those merchants or bankers of whom Wendy Childs speaks in her essay. Amongst them were the Heyrons, Italian pepperers. During all the time that he was in royal service, the king's moneyer was Walter de Bardi, scion of a great Florentine mercantile family. When he left for Genoa he was accompanied by two Italian merchants who had evidently long been resident in England: Jacop de Provano and Giovanni de Mari. The Provanos were bankers to Edward III. We may surmise that Chaucer picked up some Italian from them or similar acquaintances before he ever set foot in Italy. Genoese merchants are

mentioned in a writ directed to the sheriffs of London in 1371;
Genoese ships regularly put into Southampton.[2] By 1377 (and probably
earlier) not only Genoese but citizens of Siena, Venice, Lucca and
Milan were to be found in London: they were commonly called 'galley
men', and then or later occupied a quay near the Tower and lived in
the parish of All Hallows, Barking. A royal warrant speaks of the
Genoese as 'nos bien aimez les compagnons de Gene demoraunz en
nostre citee de Loundres'. In the same month that Chaucer left for
Genoa, Francesco de Mari and some thirty Genoese crossbowmen were
enlisted to serve in a new royal galley.[3]

Again, as controller of customs in the seventies Chaucer worked in
the Pool of London; and the three merchants from Lucca who in 1377
were fined £10 for undervaluing the goods they were importing,[4] were
but a few of the many such traders who used the port, and whose talk
would keep Chaucer's Italian in good repair. There is nothing to
suggest, however, that they traded in manuscripts; and nothing to
suggest that Chaucer had read a single Italian poem before he went
to Genoa.

Why from Genoa he proceeded to Florence before returning to
England in May 1373 we shall probably never know. Possibly he went
in Provano's company or at his suggestion. Provano came from
Cavignano, 20 miles (32 km) from Saluzzo, the 'Saluces' of the *Clerk's
Tale* – whither Chaucer may have accompanied him *en route* to
Genoa. And a notarial certificate dated Florence 18 December 1371
records an agreement between Provano and Antonio de Flischo and
Marco de Grimaldis, who had promised to provide eight or ten vessels
for the service of Edward III. Chaucer or Provano or both of them may
well have gone to Florence in connection with this agreement.

Certain it is that he stayed in North Italy long enough to taste the
rapture of an Italian spring – rapture that was to lend warmth to his
renderings of the May-time scenes that he found in Boccaccio's *Teseida*
as in his *Filostrato*. It is almost equally certain that he stayed in
Florence long enough to learn something of its greatest poet. It must
have been at this very time that some Florentines were proposing to
establish a chair for the exposition of the *Commedia*. Before Boccaccio
was chosen to fill it Chaucer had returned home. But the news that
Dante was to be lectured on as if he were one of the great medieval
auctores – an authority such as Aristotle or Aquinas – must have
spread abroad. Nothing could give a greater fillip to a vernacular
poet – a layman to boot, like Dante – who was just embarking on
the study of the *Comedy*. Not even Virgil or Ovid or Statius had as
yet been paid such honour. Boccaccio's name, then, was probably

associated with Dante's even before Chaucer left Italy in 1373. By the time of his second visit, in 1378, the author of the *commedia umana* that we know as the *Decameron* was dead, and so was Petrarch, his more renowned friend. It was Petrarch whose fame spread first, and furthest. Chaucer's Oxford scholar (who correctly calls him *Petrak*, from Petracco) knows that he was '*lauriat* poete': the ceremony on the Capitol in 1341, when he was given the laurel crown as 'the reward of genius', to the sound of pipes and trumpets, had made *Laureatus* Petrarch's peculiar epithet and brought him lasting *réclame*. This Oxford man, who (significantly) names Petrarch as a worthy 'clerk', claims to have learnt his tale of Griselda at Padua. That Chaucer ever got as far as Padua we cannot prove; but Oxford clerks certainly did, and Chaucer probably knew that they did; not to mention friars sent by their Paduan convent to Oxford, and *vice versa*. By the same token, the Oxford clerk's claim that Petrarch

> Enlumyned al Ytaille of poetrie
> As Lynyan dide of philosophie
> Or lawe, or oother art particuler
> (Prologue to *The Clerk's Tale*, 33–5)

bespeaks Chaucer's awareness of Oxford associations with the famous law school of Bologna, where Giovanni da Legnano held the chair of law, and whither several Oxford graduates (and friars) resorted.[5]

It is to such intermediaries rather than to French acquaintance or French translations that Chaucer would owe his awareness of Petrarch's fame, or Boccaccio's. I believe that the first specific French reference to Petrarch he is likely to have known is that in Philippe de Mézières' letter to Richard II – referring him to the very tale of Griselda that Chaucer translated.[6] The French translation of *Il Filostrato*, which he probably knew, makes no mention of the Italian author; nor does the (later) French version of *Il Teseida*, which even today is known chiefly because of the splendour of the fifteenth-century miniatures in the Vienna manuscript.

If Chaucer himself nowhere names the author of these two poems it is perhaps because the name *Boccaccio* is less easily anglicized than *Petracco*. Later writers, from Lydgate in the fifteenth to Douglas in the sixteenth century, made it *Bochas*, following the French model (and they knew him as the author of the *Genealogia Deorum*, not of the vernacular works). That the manuscripts of Boccaccio's works known to Chaucer bore the author's name is doubtful; and it is still more doubtful whether the titles *Teseida* or *Filostrato* would be at once intelligible to his patrons, or his audience; both, after all, display

Boccaccio's new-found classical learning, which they did not share. The only clear proof that Chaucer himself identified the author of both poems is in one of his characteristically covert jokes. In the *Teseida* Arcita at one point assumes the name Penteo, modelled on the classical Pentheus – just as 'Filostrato' Italianizes *philostratos, Teseida* suggests a pseudo-Greek Theseida, and the Decameron 'dekaemeron'. But when Chaucer comes to translate the relevant stanza he ignores this detail of Arcita's disguise. Only later does the English poet allude to this change of name – in the monologue that Arcite's rival overhears; and then he calls himself not *Penteo* but *Philostrate*:

> 'But ther as I was wont to highte Arcite
> Now highte I Philostrate, noght worth a mite'
>   (*Knight's Tale*, 1557–8)

Chaucer seized the opportunity to indicate that *his* Arcite's plight, and disposition, resembled that of the hero of *Il Filostrato*, namely Troilo: Arcite is a disguised prince laid low, like Troilus, by Love – and Fortune. Whether many English readers could have interpreted 'Philostrate' or seen the joke-cum-compliment implied when referring to a hero of Boccaccio's epic by the title of his verse romance is another matter. Like the names Palemone, Arcita and Panfilo (another name that Chaucer drops altogether from his version of *Teseida*) 'Filostrato' does occur in the *Decameron*; but it is still doubtful whether even Chaucer himself knew that work.

The couplet I have just quoted indicates, *inter alia*, that Chaucer knew (and had perhaps translated) *Il Filostrato* before he made his rendering of *Il Teseida*. But the discovery of the one may well have sent him forthwith to the other. Modern editors of the *Knight's Tale* tend to ignore the first book of the *Teseida* and to imply that Chaucer did so too; whilst modern readers (if any) of the Italian work are likely to see it as an unusually *avant-garde* presentation of the cause of 'Women's Lib', as espoused by Hippolyta's Amazons, resolved to die for *libertà* (I, 35). I, however, believe that Chaucer read every word of the Italian epic, beginning with the address to Fiammetta – in which he would find the figure of the plough that he introduces at the beginning of *his* version: 'Only the plough that has many aids can properly furrow the ground' says Boccaccio to his Fiammetta;

> I have, god wot, a large felde to ere,
> And wake ben the oxen in my plowgh
>   (886–7)

says Chaucer's knightly narrator at the outset of *his* tale. What would strike Chaucer in Boccaccio's opening stanzas is that Teseo was faced with just such a situation as his royal master – or his Italian acquaintance – might face. 'In the Scythian Kingdom the ports were watched' – says *Teseida*, I, 12 – 'so that no vessel could enter without peril': it was the complaints of Greek seamen that led Teseo to undertake his Amazonian expedition (st. 13). The description of the naval preparations, the watch for a favourable wind (st. 13), the voyage to Byzantium (st. 41), the landings by ladders joining galley ('galee': st. 80) to shore (st. 56) – all this detail in the opening book would appeal to the Chaucer who had recently crossed the Channel and was acquainted with Genoese galleymen; just as the details of Teseo's siege-works would remind him of similar English operations in the French wars. What to us seems remote would to him seem contemporary, and induce him to read on. But if, as is likely, Chaucer was steeped in Dante before he read a line of Boccaccio, another feature of the opening stanzas would strike him still more forcibly – namely, their Dantesque allusions.

Of Boccaccio's admiration for Dante his *Esposizioni*, his *Vita di Dante*, his gift of the *Comedy* to Petrarch are proof enough. But as John Addington Symonds, the first notable English historian of the Italian Renaissance, was constrained to remark, the *Life* betrays an astonishing want of sympathy with Dante's character: 'He transforms the *Vita Nuova* into a model of sentiment. Beatrice becomes one of the beauties of his own prose fiction.' 'The founder of Renascence Art', concluded Symonds, 'was incapable of comprehending the real character of the man he deified.' I doubt whether Symonds read through the *Teseida* or registered the dependence on passages in the *Comedy* that it (and the *Filostrato*) continually show. It was left for Professor Whitfield, in his Barlow lectures for 1959, to instance what he called Boccaccio's haphazard insertion of fragments from Dante and the nonchalant reversal of Dante's values in the *Filocolo* and, most palpably, in the *Filostrato*.[7] Whether or not Chaucer recognized the Dantean source of the figures that Boccaccio filched ineptly in Book II, st. 80, Book IV, sts. 27 and 85 of the *Filostrato*, he had no qualms about translating them. But he refrained from adopting Criseida's 'non odi tu la pietà del suo pianto?' (*Filostrato*, II, 72) with its indecorous echo of *Par.*, II, 106, or Pandaro's 'Che'l perder tempo a chi più sa più spiace' (*Filostrato*, II, 135) – a tasteless reminiscence of *Purg.*, III, 78.

As regards *Il Teseida*, Whitfield merely remarked on two phrases taken from the *Vita Nuova*. But most of the Dantesque passages in that epic derive from the *Commedia*. And too often they bear out Symonds' strictures on Boccaccio's poetic judgement. An early example is Hippolyta's appeal to her followers in Book I, 32, with its Dantean anaphora;

> 'Non risparmiate, qui, donne, il valore,
> non risparmiate l'armi, non l'ardire,
> non risparmiate il morire ad onore;
> considerate ciò che può seguire
> dell'esser vigorose o con timore . . .'

('Do not stint now your strength, my women; do not spare weapons, nor your boldness; do not avoid an honourable death. Think of what will follow from your bravery or your weakness . . .')

This is the very tone and language of Ulysses in *Inferno*, XXVI (118–20):

> 'Considerate la vostra semenza:
> fatti non foste a viver come bruti
> ma per seguir virtute e conoscenza':

('Consider your origin: you were not created to live like brutes, but to follow virtue and knowledge')

the tone, the language – but surely devalued by the new context.[8]

Literary history abounds in examples of poets whose idolatry expresses itself either in such indecorous adaptations or in multiplying effects used with greater economy by their masters. Giles Fletcher's *Purple Island* is more Spenserian than Spenser, Lydgate drank rather too deep in Chaucer, English poets of the fifties outdylaned Dylan Thomas. I would not claim that Chaucer always sensed the inappropriateness of Boccaccio's Danteisms. But he rarely adopts those that betray blatant disregard of Dante's intent. Whether he comprehended 'the real character' of 'the grete poete of Ytaille', his supreme gift of economy and precision, is discussed by Piero Boitani in 'What Dante Meant to Chaucer'.

I hasten to show that it is not my purpose to denigrate Boccaccio. Many a stanza shows that his responses were as fine as Chaucer's. Thus, when he evokes the spring morning on which Palemone and Arcita first catch sight of Emilia, he deftly adapts a notable image from the opening of *Purgatorio*:

> Febo, salendo con li suoi cavalli,
> del ciel teneva l'umile animale,
> ch' Europa portò sanza intervalli
> là dove il nome suo dimora aguale:
> e con lui insieme graziosi stalli
> Venus facea de' passi con che sale,

per che il cielo rideva tutto quanto
d'Amon, ch'n Pisce dimorava intanto.

(*Teseida*, III, 5)

(Rising with his horses, Phoebus beheld that lowly beast of the sky, which, without halting, bore Europa to the place where her name still survives. And, together with him, Venus made fair the steps by which she rises. The entire sky rejoiced then with Ammon, who meanwhile was in Pisces.)

The derivation from Dante is as unmistakable as Dante's poetic astronomy is unmatchable:

Lo bel pianeta che d'amar conforta
faceva tutto rider l'oriente,
velando i Pesci ch'erano in sua scorta.

(*Purg.*, I, 19–21)

(The fair planet which warms people to love was making the whole East to laugh, veiling the Fishes that were in her train.)

Boccaccio's stanza is in his best formal style, and if we are collating *Il Teseida* with Chaucer's version of it we may feel momentarily disappointed that Chaucer – who elsewhere readily accepts Boccaccio's astrological settings – should have apparently ignored this passage. But in his disposition of the tale the crucial scenes – the lovers' first glimpses of Emily, their chance meeting in the grove, the climactic tourney – are each carefully calendared: each taking place on a morning of early May, such as Chaucer would have delighted in during his first stay in Italy. And if we turn to the second of these scenes we find that Chaucer has there reorganized, reduced, and conflated three incidents that in the *Teseida* are distinct and separate, and at the same time accommodated the Dantean figure of the laughing sky, and in a totally new context.

(i) In the first of these incidents Arcita, *alias* Penteo, waking to the dawn chorus, prays to Venus and to Phoebus:

Allor, sentendo cantar Filomena
che si fa lieta del morto Tereo
si drizza . . . . .
        laüda Penteo
la man di Giove d'ogni grazia piena[9]
. . . .
poi ad Emilia il suo pensier voltava,
vedendo Citerea che si levava

. . . .
e gli augelletti, del giorno contenti,
davan, cantando in su' rami, dolcezza

. . . .

> E quando aveva gran pezza ascoltato,
> mirava inver lo cielo e sì dicea:
> 'O chiaro Febo, per cui luminato
> è tutto il mondo, e tu piacente dea...'
>
> (IV, 73–5)

(Then, hearing Philomela sing rejoicingly over the death of Tereus, Pentheus rose... and praised the great and wondrous handiwork of Jupiter, full of grace... Then, as he watched Cytherea rise, his thoughts turned to Emily... The birds, delighting in the new day and singing in the boughs, spread sweetness in the air... After listening long, he looked up at the sky and spoke thus: 'O bright Phoebus, you who give light to the whole world, and you, fair goddess...')

Thus (says stanza 79) was Penteo wont to begin his day.

(ii) But one morning, waking in the grove to which he often resorted, he complained against Fortune – Chaucer would here remember his own Black Knight's complaint – and in terms reminiscent of *Inf.*, VII, 51ff, though uninformed by Virgil's explanation there of Fortuna's role under Providence:

> 'O misera Fortuna de' viventi,
> quanti dài moti spessi alle tue cose!
> Deh, come abbassi li sangui e le genti...'
>
> (*Teseida*, IV, 80)

('O Fortune cruel to mortals, how quickly you reverse your actions! Oh, how you abase families and peoples...')

It is this complaint that Panfilo, Palemone's servant, overhears, with dramatic results.

(iii) In the third passage (in Book V of *Teseida*) Palemone, having escaped from prison, makes for the grove, reaching it when

> la notte le stelle
> tutte mostrava ancora per lo cielo,
> e' l gran Chiron Aschiro avea con quelle
> che vanno seco il pianeto che'l gielo
> conforta...
>
> (*Teseida*, V, 29, and cf. *Purg.*, IX, 37)

(The night displayed all its stars in the sky, and the great Chiron Ascyros, together with the stars that accompany him, was in conjunction with the planet that strengthens the frost...)

But by the time that Palemone comes upon the sleeping Penteo day is at hand: 'e a cantar gli uccelli han cominciato...' (V, 37).

Chaucer's conflation of these three situations begins even before the dawn scene proper. His knightly narrator is also a commentator, who heightens expectation with a miniature proemium or preface in which he accommodates the theme of Fortune from *Teseida*, IV, 81 and endows it with the kinetic, destinal force that it has elsewhere in his Tale:

> Now wol I turne to Arcite agein
> That litel wiste how ny that was his care
> Til that *Fortune* had broght him in the snare.
>
> (1488–90)

Then come lines of liquid freshness that capture the clarity of dawn on a May morning, even if they also answer to the rhetoricians' prescription:[10]

> The bisy larke, messagere of day,
> Salueth in hir song the morwe gray
> And firy Phebus riseth up so bright
> That al the orient laugheth of the light . . .
>
> (1491–4)

The 'larke' has taken the place of Boccaccio's Philomena. There is no dawn chorus; but Chaucer's characteristic epithet 'bisy' – it occurs more than fifty times in the canon – makes up for it. His bright Phoebus is certainly the 'chiaro Febo' of *Teseida*, III, 5 and IV, 75. But in *Teseida* it is Venus who causes the sky to rejoice ('per che il cielo rideva'). Chaucer has not missed the Dantean echo; but he has transferred to Phoebus the figure of *rider* ('laugh'), which brings with it from *Purgatorio*, not from *Teseida*, the glimpse of the reddening eastern sky: 'faceva rider tutto l'oriente' becoming 'al the orient laugheth of the light': the first instance in English of 'orient' meaning a particular region of the sky, and the only instance in Chaucer. The transference of the figure from Venus to Phoebus produces a time-reference different from Dante's. Dante is describing the hour *before* sunrise (cf. *Purg.*, XXVII, 94–6); that is the hour when the lark will sing, as Chaucer will later note.[11] Chaucer is intent on the sun as it brightens the east and silvers the dew (638).

The sequence that in the *Teseida* occupies some fifty stanzas Chaucer has compressed into fifty lines. But the essential difference between the two passages is a kinetic difference. His Phoebus is mounting the sky, his lark will soar to sing at heaven's gate, his Arcite (but not Boccaccio's) rises forthwith, and, 'looking on the myrye day', mounts his fiery steed. So will his Emily (but not Boccaccio's) rise a year later to do her sacrifice.

> Up roos the sonne, and up roos Emelye.
>
> (2273)

The lines immediately following our scene in the *Knight's Tale* have
no precise equivalent in Boccaccio, for in *Teseida* it is Palemone who
approaches the grove on horseback, having procured horse and arms in
Athens. It is Chaucer who mounts Arcite 'on a courser, startlynge as
the fir' – just as he had mounted Aeneas, in the epitome of *Aeneid*, IV,
143–56 that makes up the Dido story in his *Legend of Good Women*:

> Upon a courser, stertlynge as the fyr,
> Sit Æneas, lik Phebus to devyse . . .
>
> (1204, 5)

The locution in the preceding line in the Tale: 'Remembringe on the
point of his desir' (1501), may give us pause. This phrase has no
equivalent in Boccaccio. But it has in Dante. In *Purgatorio*, XII Dante
describes the sculptured tombs of the proud:

> onde lì molte volte se ripiagne
> per la puntura della rimembranza,
> che solo a' pii dà delle calcagne –
>
> (19–21)

(Wherefore there many a time men weep for them, because of the point/
prick of remembrance, which only to the *pitiful* gives spur.)

Chaucer is pre-eminently the poet of 'pitee', and that tercet would
have its special appeal for him, regardless of the following depiction
of Nimrod, Pallas, Niobe, Holofernes, Cyrus, all of whom figure in his
own verse – one of them (Holofernes) in the Monk's catalogue that
includes the story of Ugolino from *Inf.*, XXXIII. Dante's figure of the
spurring 'dà delle calcagne' makes clear enough the sense of his
'puntura': when he next uses the figure he is terser:

> Io stava come quei che in sè represme
> la punta del disío:
>
> Par., XXII, 25–6)

(I stood as one repressing in himself the point of [his] desire.)

The hooks and eyes of Chaucer's poetic memory have caught up
'la puntura della rimembranza' and 'la punta del disío' and so
produced the line in which Arcite is presented as pricked by the bright-
ness of the May morning into remembering his desired Emily, whom
he had first seen on just such a morning.[12]

I take another example of similar enrichment. The machinery of the
Teseida, like that of the *Filostrato*, includes the invocations of Fortune
and her wheel that were fourteenth-century commonplaces. One of the
differences between the English and the Italian poet is that in the
Knight's Tale, as in the *Troilus*, they cease to be commonplace. And

again it is Chaucer's reading of Dante that accounts for the difference. Nowhere, for instance, does he follow Dante more closely than in the comment inserted at *Troilus*, v, 1541ff:

> Fortune, which that permutacioun
> Of thinges hath, as it is hire committed
> Thorugh purveyaunce and disposicioun
> Of heigh Jove, as regnes shal be flitted
> Fro folk in folk, or whan they shal ben smitted . . .

With which editors rightly compare *Inf.*, VII, 78–82: where Virgil says that God

> Ordinò general ministra e duce
> che *permutasse* a tempo li ben vani
> *Di gente in gente.*

It is the very passage from which Boccaccio filched phrases for Arcita's complaint in *Teseida*, IV, 80. But Chaucer went on to read the later tercets, which gave him not only the very term 'permutacioun' but also the concept of 'purveyaunce':

> Questa *provede*, giudica, e persegue
> suo regno, come il loro gli altri Dei . . .
> Le sue *permutazion* non hanno triegue.
>
> (86)

Even the phrase 'heigh Jove' in the verse from *Troilus* shows Chaucer following Dante, who distinguishes between 'Giove' the planet and 'sommo Giove' (*Inf.*, XXXI, 92; *Purg.*, VI, 118), the all-ruler of Christian thought, 'cause of all thing' as Chaucer will say at the close of the *Knight's Tale*.

That Chaucer pondered deeply Dante's Fortuna is not only evident from his further association of Providence with Fortune in his *Balades de Visage sans Peinture*, in which Fortune claims to be

> the execucion of the majeste
> that all *purveyeth* of his rightwysnesse,
>
> (66–7)

it is evident also from the *Knight's Tale*. In *Teseida*, v, 77 Boccaccio remarks on the chance that led Emilia to come upon Palemone and Arcita just as they were fighting their duel:

> Ma come noi veggiam venire in ora
> cosa che in mill'anni non avvene
> così avvenne veramente allora
> che Teseo con Emilia d'Attene
> uscir con molti in compagnia di fora;

(It happened then – as something which does not occur in a thousand years takes place in a moment before our eyes – that Theseus, together with Emily and many others, left Athens.)

When at the beginning of *Teseida*, VI Boccaccio displays Fortuna's role in shaping the lives of the two Thebans, he incongruously combines phrases from *Inferno*, VII with fatalistic sentiments that Chaucer, steeped in Boethian philosophy as he was, could never accept. Chaucer, when preparing for the scene of this surprise encounter of Theseus with the rivals, fuses the two passages in *Teseida*, V, 77 and VI, 1, separated though they are by 28 stanzas, but frames the resulting sequence in couplets of deeper resonance than anything in Boccaccio. Boccaccio's earlier flicker of allusion to Dante's Fortuna in *Teseida*, IV, 80 recalled to Chaucer their original context. He prefaces his rendering of *Teseida*, V, 77 by lines that represent the passage from the *Inferno* that he has already adapted in *Troilus*, V – yet does so without repetition or overlapping. His lines strike the true Dantean note:

> The destinee, *ministre general*
> That executeth in the world overal
> The purveiaunce, that God hath seyn biforn,
> So strong it is . . .
> > (*Knight's Tale*, 1663–6)

This is more than a literal version of *Inf.*, VII, 78ff: it shows understanding of Dante's purport and signals Chaucer's acceptance of Dante's Boethian view that what men call Fortune plays a part in divine providence. And Chaucer's narrator goes out of his way to emphasize this affirmation by adding:

> For certeinly oure appetites here,
> Be it of werre or pees or hate or love,
> Al is this reuled by the sighte above
> > (1670–2)

Boccaccio's Fortuna belongs to the pseudo-classical form of the romantic epic he is creating out of Statius. Chaucer has put the tale into the mouth of a Christian knight, and he changes the key accordingly. 'Al is this reuled by the sighte above' means that Providence (whose wisdom is transcendental: 'colui lo cui saver tutto transcende': *Inf.*, VII, 73) not only permits men to hate and fight each other but also disposes that they may be constrained to cease from fighting and hatred. The Theseus who stops the duel thus becomes an agent of this Providence, of the 'Firste Moevere', 'colui che tutto move' as Dante had put it in the first line of *Paradiso* (cf. *House of Fame*, 81), and as Theseus will put it in his peroration.

Even Chaucer's 'appetites' has a Dantean flavour.[13] Cf. 'l'appetito de mortali' (*Purg.*, XXII, 41), 'chè là, dove appetito non si torce' (*Par.*, XVI, 5), 'seguendo come bestie l'appetito' (*Purg.*, XXVI, 84). Ten lines later he will apply the term in a novel way to Theseus himself: 'huntyng is al his joye and appetite'; whilst at the end of *Troilus* he objurgates the 'wrecched worldes appetites' of those who, like Troilus, Arcite and Palemon, put their trust in the pagan divinities – 'Jove, Apollo, Mars and suche rascaille'.[14] Was he there thinking of Virgil's repudiation of the 'dei falsi e bugiardi' (*Inf.*, I, 22) – which Boccaccio echoes in both the *Filocolo* and the *Ninfale* – or of Beatrice's comment on planetary influences that led the world astray; 'sì che Giove / Mercurio e Marte a nominar trascorse' (*Par.*, IV, 63)? Certainly the authorial invocation of Fortune in *Troilus*, III, 617ff is completely consonant with Beatrice's doctrine, though not with Boccaccio's:

> But O Fortune, executrice of wierdes,
> O influences of these hevenes hye,
> Soth is that *under God* ye ben oure hierdes
> Though to us bestes ben the causes wrye . . .

There is only one other work of Chaucer's in which Fortune is so often or so memorably invoked, and that is in the *Monk's Tale*, where again he is drawing on both Dante and Boccaccio. The Ugolino story that he found in *Inferno*, XXXIII provides the most poignant scene of all the Monk's Tragedies of Fortune. And again it is Boccaccio who has unconsciously directed the Englishman back to his master. No less than thirteen of the Monk's 'ensamples trewe and olde' figure either in Boccaccio's *De Claris Mulieribus* (Zenobia is the notable name here) or in his *De Casibus Virorum Illustrium*, who include 'Ugolino, Pisarum comes'. When in the *Monk's Tale* Ugolino's gaoler shuts (i.e. nails up) the door of the tower the Count bursts into tears:

> therwith the teeris fillen from his eyen
>
> (2430)

These are the tears that provoke his three-year-old son to ask the unbearable, the unanswerable question:

> 'Fader, why do ye wepe?
> Whan wol the gaoler bring us oure potage?
> Is ther no morsel bred that ye do kepe?'
>
> (2432–4)

So much has Chaucer made of the phrase 'amplissimo fletu' in *De Casibus* and Dante's plain 'che hai?' – 'What's the matter?' There are no tears in Dante's scene. Rather, his Ugolino twice insists: 'io non piangeva' (XXXIII, 49), 'non lagrimai' (53).

Did a gloss on the *De Casibus* direct Chaucer to that canto? Or is it rather another case of prehensile Coleridgean memory? Piero Boitani may have provided an answer.[15] Meanwhile enough to note that it is Chaucer's Monk, not Dante, who comments:

> Allas, Fortune, it was great crueltee
> Swiche briddes for to putte in swich a cage!
> (2413-14)

And it is Chaucer's Ugelyn, not Dante's, who, biting his arms 'for wo' after the boy's death as in Dante he bites his hands 'per dolor' before it, cries out, just as Zenobia and the Theban widows of the *Knight's Tale* had done:

> 'Allas, Fortune, and weylawey,
> Thy false wheel my wo al may I wyte':
> (2445-6)

No such cry could sound in Dante's Hell.

I may seem to have wandered far from the *Teseida*. Yet not so very far. For Dante's immediate comment on the crime comes in a reproach to Pisa as a 'novella Tebe'. Whatever Chaucer knew of the circumstances, surely that dark allusion to the tragedy of Thebes would – here as elsewhere in the *Inferno* – strike an attentive ear. For it is the Thebes of the *Thebaid* that is in Dante's mind, the Thebes that in the *Teseida* as in the *Knight's Tale* provoked Theseus' just vengeance on its pitiless King Creon. By the same token, when Dante in the same canto proceeds to denounce the 'Genovesi' as 'uomini diversi d'ogni costume' (*Inf.*, XXXIII, 151-2) – 'men estranged from all good practices' – the Chaucer who had dealt with the Genoese and lived with them would not read the lines quite as detachedly as we do. He might have reason, by the time he wrote the *Monk's Tale*, to know that they were as avaricious on shore as they were brave at sea.

A slightly different instance of Chaucer's Dantean improvements on Boccaccio happens to occur in a passage in the *Knight's Tale* portraying the worship of another pagan divinity (Diana) and Emily's acceptance of the ineluctability of Fate – a theme that threads through Chaucer's tale and keeps it taut. No sooner has Emily finished her prayer to Diana than

> she saugh a sighte queinte:
> For right anon oon of the fires queynte
> And quiked again, and after that anon
> That oother fir was queint and al agon;

> And as it queinte it made a whistlinge
> As doon thise wete brondes in hir brennynge,
> And at the brondes ende outran anoon
> As it were blody dropes many oon;
>
> (2333–40)

The phenomenon had been similarly described in *Teseida*, VII, 91–2 –
except that whereas Boccaccio's Emilia prayed that Diana should
signify her decision by means of the altar-fire, Chaucer's Emily makes
no such plea. Chaucer's scene is thus unexpected, and the more
dramatic. But it owes its most vivid detail to Dante.

Boccaccio (who is here following in general Statius' *Thebaid*, XII,
39; cf. also Ovid, *Metamorphoses*, X, 277) describes the burning
brands of pine (st. 74) on the altar as looking like blood:

> E parean sangue gli accesi tizzoni,
> da' capi spenti tututti gemendo
> lagrime tai, che spegnieno i carboni.
>
> (VII, 92)

(The burning brands, whose extinguished heads dripped such tears as to
quench the coals, looked like blood.)

This figure evidently derives from the episode of Pier delle Vigne in
Inferno, XIII (and 'geme' in st. 91 also echoes *Inf.*, XXVI, 58). When
Dante plucks a branch from the trunk it cries out, and

> Come d'un stizzo verde, ch'arso sia
> dall'un de' capi, che dall'altro geme
> e cigola per vento che va via,
> sì della scheggia rotta usciva insieme
> parole e sangue . . .
>
> (XIII, 40–4)

(As a green brand, that is burning at one end, at the other drops and hisses
with the wind which is escaping – so from that broken splint words and
blood came forth together . . .)

Boccaccio has nothing about *wet* brands nor does he say that the drops
running out of them look like blood. It is Dante who specifies green
hissing wood, and at once conjures up an image familiar at every
fireside; which prompts Chaucer to appeal to that everyday experience
with an appropriate colloquial pronoun:

> As doon *thise* wete brondes in hir brennynge.

Boccaccio's Emilia takes it as a good omen. Chaucer's Emily is 'sore
agast' at the sight. Chaucer, picking up Boccaccio's verbal allusions to
the Pier episode, has read beyond the simile. His Emily behaves as

Dante had behaved: when Dante dropped the branch he 'stood like
one aghast': 'stetti come l'uom che teme' (XIII, 45). One might explain
this away as mere coincidence. But not if one reads to the end of that
canto. For there we find Dante and Virgil startled by another noise
('romor') –

> similmente a colui che venire
> sente il porco e la caccia alla sua posta
> ch'ode le bestie e le frasche stormire;
>
> (112–14)

(. . . like one who feels the boar and chase approaching to his stand, who
hears the beasts and the branches crashing.)

Boccaccio had appropriated this epic simile too; but he applies it
at the point where Palemone and Arcita meet in the theatre (Teseida,
VII, 106), and alters it to the extent of putting the hunter into a
Libyan forest and making the beast a lion. Chaucer (besides altering
Boccaccio's lines in other ways) had applied them to the earlier meeting
of the rivals in the grove, when he reproduced precisely Dante's
picture:

> Right as the hunters in the regne of Trace
> That standeth at the gappe with a spere
> Whan hunted is the leoun and the bere
> And hereth him come russhing in the greves
> And breketh bothe bowes and the leves . . .
>
> (1638–42)

Of all episodes in the Comedy that of Paolo and Francesca is the most
famous, and the line

> Amor, ch'al cor gentil ratto s'apprende
>
> (Inf., V, 100)

is the quintessence of fin amor as rendered in the dolce stil novo. It is
typical of Boccaccio that when he puts a variant of it into Palemone's
mouth in Teseida, III, 27 he gives it his own twist:

> 'Amor,
> ladro sottil di ciascun gentil core'.

It is typical of Chaucer that he omits that line and so that figure from
Palemon's speech, though he adopts the original Dantean phrase no
less than five times elsewhere (notably in Troilus, III, 4–5). In the
Knight's Tale he reserves it for a striking scene – owing almost nothing
to the Teseida – in which Emily and the ladies of the Court beseech
Theseus not to condemn to death the two rivals:

The queene anon, for verray womanhede,
Gan for to wepe, and so dide Emelye . . .
Grete pite was it, as it thoughte hem alle,
That ever such a chaunce sholde falle,
For gentil men they were, of gret estaat
And nothing but for love was this debaat.

· · ·

And alle crieden, bothe lesse and moore,
'Have mercy, lord, upon us wommen alle . . .'
Till at the last aslaked was his mood,
For *pitee* renneth soone in gentil herte . . .

(1748–61)

The scene itself, I say, owes little to Boccaccio. And Mario Praz has claimed that the change from Dante's 'Amor' to 'pitee' in that last line is wholly characteristic of Chaucer.[16] But the modulations are more complex than this suggests. First, Chaucer gives this tale to a 'parfit gentil knyght', in whose mouth these sentiments are particularly appropriate. Secondly, in the corresponding passage in *Teseida* the duke, having alluded to the *pietà* that had once been shown to *him*, assures the rivals that

'vincerà il fallo la mia gran pietate' –

('My great mercy will pardon your fault.') It is Chaucer who associates this mercy with 'gentilesse', developing the characterization merely hinted at in *Teseida* when Teseo meets the Theban widows (*Teseida*, II, 43) and is

da intima pietà nel cor trafitto.

Already at that point Chaucer had shown him as 'the gentil duk'. Here he develops the picture. Thirdly, Chaucer is presenting Theseus as a model prince whose Ire is always subject to Reason. Hence he amplifies Dante's phrase into thirty lines that both provide a gloss on 'pitee' and hark back to the beginning of the tale:

And eke his herte hadde compassioun
Of wommen, for they wepten evere in oon
And in his *gentil herte* he thoughte anoon,
And softe unto himself he seide 'Fy
Upon a lord that will have no mercy . . .'

(1770–4)

The passage establishes the code of the poem, indeed the code of the *Canterbury Tales* as a whole. Chaucer's Theseus (but not Boccaccio's) will himself glance back at it at the close of the tale, when adjuring Emily to

'Lat se now of youre wommanly pitee

(3083)

For gentil mercy oghte to passen ryght'

(3089)

Even so Chaucer's Parson, in the last of all the Tales, will pronounce
that there is no thing 'more covenable to a man of heigh estaat
than debonairetee [cf. *Troilus*, III, 4, 5] and *pitee*' (*Parson's Tale*, 466).
Mario Praz, in whose steps I stumblingly tread, when he noted
Chaucer's ready response to the human and the touching – as distinct
from the sublime – in Dante, spoke of Chaucer as a bourgeois poet.[17]
Yet his Knight is hardly a bourgeois knight and his duke Theseus is
far from a bourgeois duke.

That we owe to Dante this persistent concern of the Tales with
'gentilesse' is manifest from another passage in the Tales themselves.
For the 'vekke' in the *Wife of Bath's Tale* goes out of her way to appeal
to 'the wise poete of Florence/That highte Dant', departing from the
conventions of naturalistic narrative to cite his sentence, his *sententia*:

'Lo, in swych maner rym is Dantes tale:
"Ful selde up riseth by his branches smale
Prowesse of man, for God, of his goodnesse,
Wol that of *Hym* we clayme our gentilesse"'

(1127–30)

It has long been recognized that these lines render *Purg.*, VII, 121–3
(a passage followed by references to two English kings that would catch
Chaucer's eye):

Rade volte risurge per li rami
l'umana probitate: e questo vuole
quei che la dà, perchè da lui si chiami.[18]

Chaucer's 'prowesse', then, here means *probitas*, 'worth': and this
unusual sense is confirmed by his rendering of Boethius' *probitas* by
this same term (see e.g. *Boece*, IV, pr. 1, 118).

Whether Chaucer also had in mind the discussion of *gentilezza* in
Convivio, IV, 15 is discussed by Piero Boitani in the essay that follows
the present one. But whatever the sources of his sentiments the passage
reminds us that to consider merely Chaucer's manipulation of particular passages is to misconceive the effect of his Italian experience, which
opened up for him a whole new world of feeling and took him far
beyond the boundaries of French romance and *courtoisie*.

It gave him also a new apprehension of the classical world. He
always had a well-read man's familiarity with Ovid. But Boccaccio

brought him to a new valuation of Statius, and Dante brought him to a new view of Virgil. The transition was painless, because the *Teseida*, for all its classical frame and classical allusions, and its gloss *à la Servius* – a veritable encyclopedia, in which Chaucer foraged – for all this, it keeps the spirit and assumptions of the courtly romance. Indeed in some ways Chaucer makes of the *Teseida* (as he makes of the *Filostrato*) something *more* medieval, more *courtois*. Thus into Theseus' *teatro* (which Boccaccio's gloss suggests that *he* conceived of as a classical Colosseum) Chaucer inserts the historical temples of pagan divinities that are the very embodiments of late medieval art, astrology and sentiment; that take us back, indeed, to the *Roman de la Rose*.

If the Dantean impetus and inspiration was immeasurably the greater it was partly because he must have felt Dante as essentially *simpatico* not only as regards his views on Fortune, free will, gentilesse, but also as practising a poetic that allowed easy passage from high to low style and deemed nothing too common, no image too homely. The similes of both poets are arresting, not in their poeticness but in their plainness. I use the term 'inspiration' deliberately, because Dante himself uses it, and in a passage that Chaucer partly reproduced – the early lines of the *Paradiso* (I, 13–22):[19]

> O buon' Apollo, all'ultimo lavoro
> fammi del tuo valor sì fatto vaso . . .
> Entra nel petto mio, e spira tue
> sì come quando Marsia traesti
> della vagina delle membra sue . . .

(O good Apollo, for the crowning task, make me such vessel of your worth . . . Enter into my bosom, and breathe as when you drew Marsyas from out what sheathed his limbs . . .)

and compare *Par.*, II, 8–9:

> Minerva *spira*, e conducemi Apollo,
> e nove *Muse* mi dimostran l'Orse.

(Minerva breathes, Apollo guides me, and the nine Muses point the Bears out to me.)

The verve and vigour of Chaucer's invocation of Apollo at the beginning of his 'liber tertius', in the *House of Fame*, are signal proof of the real impulse that Dante provided: it was nothing less than an assurance that the 'art poetical' was its own justification.

His earlier prayer to the muses, at the beginning of the second book of that poem, likewise derives from Dante:

> And ye, me to endite and ryme
> Helpeth, that on Parnaso duelle
> Be Elicon, the clere welle.
> O Thought, that wrot al that I mette,
> And in the tresorye hyt shette
> Of my brayn, now shal men se
> Yf any vertu in the be,
> To tellen al my drem aryght.
> Now kythe thyn engyn and myght!
>   (509–17)

– where 'Thought' has the force of Dante's 'mente' in *Inf.*, II, 8 and 'engyn' represents the 'alto ingegno', of *Purg.*, XXIX, 37–46, the 'ingegni' of *Par.*, XVIII, 82. Again, at the beginning of Book II of the *Troilus*, where Chaucer invokes Clio ('domina eloquentiae', says a marginal gloss):

> Thou be my speed fro this forth, and my *Muse*,

the context makes it certain that Chaucer is remembering the opening of *Purgatorio*:

> O sante Muse, poiché vostro sono;
> e qui Calliopè alquanto surga ...
>   (*Purg.*, I, 8–9)

(O holy Muses, since I am yours, and here let Calliope rise ...)

Thus the muses take their places in English poetry for the first time. Their presence in Dante would prepare Chaucer for Boccaccio's frequent allusions to them,[20] which were doubtless due as often to Dante as to Statius. It is thanks to Chaucer's reading of the *Comedy* that English verse joins the main stream of European poetry, which does indeed rise on Helicon. What he did not find by way of fresh classical lore in Dante he would find in Boccaccio's *Genealogia Deorum* or in those glosses to the *Teseida* in which the Italian loves to display his learning.[21]

Certain it is that he was aware of the *Teseida*'s dependence on Statius' *Thebaid*: it may well have been the poet himself who put as epigraph to the *Knight's Tale* the quotation from *Thebaid*, XII, 519–20:

> Iamque domos patrias, Scithice post aspera gentis
> Prelia, laurigero ...

– a modest hint at the tale's respectable antecedents, as well as an intimation that the opening scene of the tale comes from the closing scene of the Latin epic. Chaucer could not have failed to note that Dante grants to 'Stazio il dolce poeta' a rank as high as Virgil's.

And in the *Troilus* (v, 1485–1500) he gives us a more concentrated Statius than Boccaccio ever does. Not content with that, he, or an early scribe, actually inserts at that point another prècis of the *Thebaid*, in twelve lines of Latin verse; whilst earlier (II, 100ff) his Criseyde had summarized 'the romance of Thebes' for Pandarus' benefit; that Chaucer in presenting that scene had in mind the *Thebaid* rather than the *Roman de Thèbes* is suggested by his insistence that it was 'in bookes twelve' (108). Not for nothing, not simply to follow a convention, did he beg his 'litel bok' of *Troilus* to

> Kis the steppes whereas thou seest pace
> Virgile, Ovide, Homer, Lucan, and *Stace*.
>
> (v, 1791–2)

But Virgil designedly comes first in that roll-call and it was surely Dante who made Chaucer read Virgil with fresh eyes. Introducing the Dido story in the *Legend of Good Women* (the English equivalent of Boccaccio's *De Claris Mulieribus*), he bursts into praise of him:

> Glory and honour, Virgil Mantoan,
> Be to thy name, and I shal, as I can,
> Folwe thy lantern as thou gost beforn
> How Eneas to Dido was forsworn:

Virgil 'Mantoan'. Doubtless *mantuanus* was an *epitheton perpetuum*. But Dante uses it in the form 'mantovano' no less than four times, and notably at Virgil's first appearance. Just fifty lines after the prayer to the muses in *Inferno*, II comes Beatrice's

> 'O anima cortese mantovana
> di cui la fama ancora nel mondo dura
> e durerà quanto 'l mondo lontana . . .'
>
> (58–60)

('O courteous Mantuan spirit, whose fame still lasts in the world, and will last as long as the world . . .')

Just forty lines after the next appeal to the muses (at the opening of *Purgatorio*) Cato confronts Dante and Virgil with his memorable question:

> 'Chi v'ha guidati? O chi vi fu *lucerna*,
> uscendo fuor della profonda notte . . .?'
>
> (I, 43–4)

('Who has guided you? Or who was a lamp unto you when you issued forth from the deep night . . .?')

That Dante meant this image of the lantern to apply to Virgil is admittedly doubtful: the context at which it recurs at I, 112 suggests a very different interpretation. But Chaucer evidently read it as addressed to Dante's *visible* guide: as did the greatest English (or rather Scottish) Virgilian, Gavin Douglas, who is clearly following Chaucer when he opens the Prologue to his *Eneydos* with the words:

> Laud, honour, praysingis, thankis infinyte,
> To the, and thy dulce ornat fressh endyte
> Maist reverend Virgil ...
> *Lantern*, lode stare, myrrour and a *per se* ...

That Douglas has Chaucer's eulogy in mind is certain from his reproof of Chaucer for accusing Aeneas of perjury,

> Sayand he followit Virgilles lantern toforn.

Douglas' reading of *Aeneid*, IV is more plausible than Chaucer's. But my present point is that as Chaucer accepted Dante's estimate of Virgil, so Douglas accepted Chaucer's. Henceforth the place of Virgil in the poetic pantheon was secure. Centuries later Tennyson – who knew the *Comedy* so well that if given any line from it he could continue reciting the passage – was doing precisely what Chaucer had done when he chose Dante's epithet for *his* salutation:

> I salute thee, Mantovano,
> I that loved thee since my days began,
> Wielder of the stateliest measure ever moulded by the lips of man.

Tennyson, of course, was neither the first nor the last to follow Chaucer's lead. Spenser, for example, had adapted that episode of Pier delle Vigne in the *Fairie Queene* (I, ii, 33). And the manuscript of the *Waste Land* shows how deep was the impression left by *Inferno*, XXIII on the young Eliot. We might have guessed this from his essay on *Dante* (1929), with its epigraph from *Vita Nuova*, implying that for him (as for Chaucer) to discover Dante was indeed to begin a new life. In that essay he had also singled out an earlier canto – *Inferno*, XV. For signs of its influence we have to look in his very last poem. The second movement of *Little Gidding* presents itself as an *Inferno* in miniature. His first jottings ran simply:

> Winter scene May
> Lyric Air water and demonic fire
> The Inferno[22]

And the manuscript draft of this second movement (where it is set out in tercets) adds to the question 'What, are you here?' the appellative, *Ser*, before 'Brunetto', clinching the likeness to *Inferno*, XV:

e chinando la mia alla sua faccia
risposi: 'Siete voi qui, ser Brunetto?'

(29–30)

(. . . and bending my face to his, I answered: 'Are you here, Ser Brunetto?')

In this unpublished draft the poet's *persona* is at this point somewhat crudely approximated to Dante's; and there are other details, later excised, deriving from the same canto. It is illuminating to read the two passages side by side, preferably in the Temple Classics edition of the *Inferno*, which Eliot used: he had the advantage of Chaucer, who had to make his own translation. I see the influence of that edition in his rendering of 'lo cotto aspetto' as 'the baked aspect', replacing his manuscript phrase 'these scorched brown features' – which itself follows the Temple Classics rendering of 'il viso abruciato' as 'the scorching of his visage'. And when Eliot's interlocutor says 'the wonder that I feel is easy' he echoes Brunetto's 'Qual maraviglia' ('What a wonder' in the Temple Classics) as he catches Dante by the skirt. Again the prose draft or 'undercoat' continues, after that bare phrase 'The Inferno':

They vanish, the individuals, and our feeling for them sinks into the flame which refines.

'Poi s'ascose nel foco che gli affina' runs the last line of *Purgatorio*, XXVI. ('Then he [Arnaut Daniel] hid himself in the fire which refines them'); whilst *Purg.*, VIII, 120 has 'l'amor che qui raffina'. Eliot's poetic memory acts like Chaucer's, enfolding phrases from diverse passages. Thus his outline concludes:

. . . those who have known purgatory here know it hereafter – so shall you learn when enveloped by the coils of the fiery wind, in which you must learn to *swim*.

There 'swim' recalls the *notare* of *Inf.*, XXI, 131; XVII, 115; XX, 119. It may also recall the figure for Guinizelli's disappearance as he points out Arnaut Daniel:

. . . disparve per lo foco,
come per l'acqua il pesce andando al fondo.
(Purg., XXVI, 134–5)

(. . . he vanished through the fire, like a fish going through the water to the bottom.)

Eliot, as his Dantean adaptations show, is *par excellence* the magpie poet. But as the influence of Dante on English verse has increased, that of Chaucer has declined. From Chaucer's poetry Eliot took but one phrase: his Prufrock is 'full of high sentence'; and even there the accent disguises the allusion to the clerk of Oxenford whose speech was 'short and quik and ful of hy sentence'.

Notes

1 This is the text of a lecture delivered at the Accademia Nazionale dei Lincei in Rome on 27 April 1976 and published in Quaderno no. 234 (1977) of the Accademia. It is reprinted here by permission of the President and Fellows of the Accademia. The text has been slightly altered by the Editor to adjust it to the needs of the present volume.

2 Colin Platt, *Medieval Southampton* (London, 1973), pp. 107, 153, 155. Cf. Iris Origo, *The Merchant of Prato* (London, 1957), pp. 84–5.

3 For the evidence see M. M. Crow and C. C. Olson (eds.), *Chaucer Life-Records* (Oxford, 1966), pp. 38–9.

4 *Ibid.* p. 196.

5 The names of some of them (e.g. Thos. Crochin, Philip de Beauchamp) and those of Oxford men who visit Padua (e.g. Wm. Falconer, Geoffrey Hardeby) can be found in Emden, *Biographical Register of the University of Oxford*; see also *s.nn.* Thos. Edwardston, John Ergam. Figino. Of course travellers to the papal *curia* at Avignon during the 'Babylonian Captivity', which coincided with Petrarch's residence there, pilgrims to Roman churches and messengers or clerical visitors to the *curia* at Rome after 1376 might also bring back literary news or gossip.

6 See now the edition of the letter by the late G. W. Coopland (Liverpool, 1975), pp. xxix and n. 53. The author of the *Ménagier de Paris* relied on Philippe's version of the tale. Philippe, who counted himself as Petrarch's 'special ami', described the tale as 'escripte par le solempnel docteur et souverain poete, maistre Francois Petrac', and based on 'la cronique autentique' – which suggests that he was unaware of the *Decameron* version.

7 J. H. Whitfield, 'Dante in Boccaccio', in *The Barlow Lectures on Dante, 1959* (Cambridge, 1960) (suppl. to *Italian Studies*, XV (1960)), pp. 16–32. See also J. H. Whitfield, 'Chaucer fra Dante e Boccaccio', in G. Galigani (ed.), *Il Boccaccio nella cultura inglese e anglo-americana* (Florence, 1974), pp. 137–53.

8 And see P. Boitani, *Chaucer and Boccaccio* (Oxford, 1977), pp. 117–26.

9 Cf. *Knight's Tale*, 3069: 'And thanken Jupiter of al his grace'.

10 *Nova Poetria*, 781ff.

11 *Knight's Tale*, 2209–12: another new time-reference, specified by Chaucer for astrological reasons. See my note in my edition of the Tale (London, 1954), pp. 135–6.

12 John Livingston Lowes fifty years ago taught us how to detect such seams of association in a well-read poet: showing how stanzas 61–2 of *Teseida*, VII called up for Chaucer *Inf.*, V, 58–9, and also yielded the list of lovers in *The Parliament of Fowls* ('Chaucer and Dante', *Modern Philólogy*, XIV (1917), 705–35). Several years later Mario Praz and I noted independently that Chaucer's use of 'revoke' in *Troilus*, III, 1118 (cf. *Teseida*, IX, 22) shows him adopting Boccaccio's 'rivocare' in the sense of 'restore to consciousness' and so points to his reordering of scenes in the *Filostrato* – for Boccaccio's Troilo does not swoon on meeting Criseida but on hearing that she is to be exchanged for Antenor; see *Medium Aevum*, XXII (1953), 114, and Praz, *The Flaming Heart* (New York, 1958), p. 36.

13 The only comparable example cited in the O.E.D. is earlier: Wyclif, Ezek. XXI, 16. But 'Wyclif' has merely taken over the Vulgate 'appetitus'.

14 *Troilus*, V, 1850–3. There is a verbal equivalent in *Filostrato*, VIII, 29 ('appetito rio' – 'evil appetite'), but Chaucer radically altered the application of most lines in that stanza and omitted others.

15 See P. Boitani, 'The *Monk's Tale*: Dante and Boccaccio', *Medium Aevum*, XLV (1976), 50–69.

16 Praz, *Flaming Heart*, p. 56.

17 But I find that this phrase may have been inserted by his translator.

18 Compare the similar figure in *Purg.*, XIV, I 100–3.

19 This is further examined in Piero Boitani's two essays below.

20 E.g. *Teseida*, XII, 52, 84.

21 Not to mention the many contrived similes in *Teseida*: e.g. IX, 31, where Arcita's chariot is compared with the one 'Rome made to honour Scipio', and to Phaethon's, from which he fell into the Po; or the antiquarian allusions, e.g. VII, 10, 'arenarii'; 114, 'decurione'; IX, 34; XI, 68.

22 For a fuller account of these notes and drafts see my article 'Little Gidding: a poem of Pentecost', now in J. A. W. Bennett, *The Humane Medievalist and Other Essays in English Literature and Learning*, ed. P. Boitani (Rome, 1982), pp. 305–25.

What Dante Meant to Chaucer

When Geoffrey Chaucer was born, Dante had been dead some twenty years, and fifty had passed by the time Chaucer came to Italy in 1372–3. By that time several commentaries on the *Divine Comedy* had already appeared, Boccaccio was about to lecture publicly on the poem, and the polemical misunderstanding between Boccaccio and Petrarch concerning the importance of Dante's work had been cleared up in an exchange of letters more than ten years earlier.

Dante was not Chaucer's contemporary: his status in Italy was that of a classic – a poet to venerate or to ignore, but impossible to imitate. Dante was a man of the thirteenth century: he was thirty-five when the new century began and his lyric poetry, his philosophical ideas and his political ideals had all been formed in the world of Guinizelli and Cavalcanti, of Albert the Great, Thomas Aquinas, Bonaventure, Siger of Brabant, of Frederick II and the struggle between Guelphs and Ghibellines. John Larner has shown in the first essay of this volume how Italian culture changed between the time of Dante and that of Boccaccio, and there is no need to expatiate further on the theme. But in discussing Chaucer's relationship to Dante, we must not forget the chronological (and geographical) distance that separates them. We must not forget, for instance, that the Court in which Chaucer lived was for Dante no more than a concept, an aspiration (*De Vulgari Eloquentia*, I, xviii, 5).

Dante and Chaucer did, however, share a vast common culture, though each placed a different emphasis on different facets of this common heritage. They both loved the classics, in particular Virgil and Statius; they were both steeped in medieval philosophy and literature; they were both interested in science. There are important parallels in their formative years as poets and men: both started as love poets; for both the *Roman de la Rose* seems to have had a fundamental, though different, importance;[1] for both the reading of Boethius was a key experience. But if we are to understand the nature of Chaucer's response to Dante we must bear in mind that, although Chaucer did

not have access to all Dante's works, the fourth Tractate of the
Convivio and the *Divine Comedy* alone would have been enough to
show him one novel aspect of Dante's personality – his 'terrible
seriousness',[2] his self-consciousness, self-exegesis and self-affirmation.[3]

What, precisely, was Chaucer's response to Dante? What, in Eliot's
phrase, did Dante mean to Chaucer? The risk one runs in evoking
Eliot in this context is, I think, worth taking. Chaucer's relationship to
Dante is still mysterious, puzzling and elusive. It is difficult to pinpoint
Dante's influence on him. There are of course many Dantean reminiscences and adaptations in Chaucer's works – even if the number is not
as large as the 250 sometimes alleged; it is clear that Chaucer knew the
Divine Comedy well – perhaps better than Eliot, who had to have a
translation beside the text; it is obvious that Chaucer admired Dante,
thought about his poetry and was fascinated by it.

But it is helpful to employ Eliot's ideas when talking about
Chaucer's debt to Dante. Hitherto critics have been chiefly concerned
to discover and assess what Eliot would call Chaucer's *imitation* of
Dante. Thus Schless divided Chaucer's indebtedness into two major
categories: 'on the one hand, the many shorter images borrowed for
their verbal and dramatic force; on the other, the few direct adaptations and translations made for purposes of their content'.[4] Both Praz
and Schless sharpened and refined this kind of source-study by employing in practice and setting forth in theory the principle of 'transformation' 'in tone and purpose', which for instance makes Chaucer
'carefully shift the emphasis away from the concentrated terror of
Dante's description to the sympathetic, one might almost say sentimental, description of the death of Hugelino's children' in the *Monk's
Tale*.[5] In his books on the *Parliament of Fowls* and on the *House of
Fame* J. A. W. Bennett was to follow this method and bring it to
perfection, while in his essay in the present volume he goes still
further. He shows how Chaucer's 'poetic memory' is as prehensile
as Eliot's and how Chaucer is just as much a 'magpie' poet as
Eliot.[6]

This helps us to see a first significant likeness between the two
English poets, but it is still within the boundary of 'imitation'.[7]
Eliot himself indicated what he did *not* mean by a poet's important
debt to Dante:

I think I have already made clear, however, that the important debt to
Dante does not lie in a poet's borrowings, or adaptations from Dante; nor is
it one of those debts which are incurred only at a particular stage in
another poet's development. Nor is it found in those passages in which one
has taken him as a model. The important debt does not occur in relation to

the number of places in one's writings to which a critic can point a finger, and say, here and there he wrote something which he could not have written unless he had had Dante in mind. Nor do I wish to speak now of any debt which one may owe to the thought of Dante, to his view of life, or to the philosophy and theology which give shape and content to the Divine Comedy. That is another, though by no means unrelated question.[8]

He went on to point out the three lessons that as a poet 'one learns, and goes on learning', from Dante – the lessons of craft, of speech and of exploration of sensibility (or 'width of emotional range').

It is then in this context that I intend to look at Chaucer's Dante – both as a master of craft, of speech, of emotion and as a source of verbal imitation. The two aspects, I should hasten to add, are never separate. In both cases, moreover, Chaucer works a continuous counterpoint to Dante's text, first drawing close to him and using some of his words or images and then distancing himself so that Dantean echoes are only half-heard.

I   The Poet of Heaven and Hell

Clearly Chaucer recognized Dante as the poet of Hell. He implies this when, towards the end of his summary of the *Aeneid* in the first Book of the *House of Fame*, he refers his readers back to Virgil, Claudian and Dante for descriptions of 'every turment ... in helle' (445). And he confirms it later in the *Friar's Tale* when he has the fiend tell the summoner that he will soon know by his own experience that hell-lore which Virgil and Dante knew so well (1519–20).

The first point to notice is that Dante's name (mentioned more often in Chaucer's works than Statius') is here associated with that of Virgil, the greatest poet of antiquity known to the Middle Ages, Dante's master of the 'beautiful style', his guide through Hell and Purgatory in the *Divine Comedy*, and the creator of that Aeneas who visited Hell before Dante. In Chaucer's eyes, Dante possesses a dignity equal to that of Virgil, but – and this is our first example of his 'counterpoint' – he is not quite the equal of Claudian who, though associated with the Italian poet in the first Book, is singled out in the third Book of the *House of Fame* as the man who *par excellence* 'bar up al the fame of helle'. From that hall where the great writers of the past, standing on pillars of different materials, 'bear up' the fame of the various 'materes' of poetry, Dante is absent. But all those writers (with the possible exception of the mysterious Lollius) are not vernacular poets, and Dante had himself excluded vernacular (and Christian) poets from the 'goodly school' of Limbo in *Inferno*, IV. Chaucer's first response to

Dante as a model of poetry is therefore ambiguous. Perhaps he did not know quite what to make of a poet who was an expert not only on Hell but on Purgatory and Paradise as well.

Be that as it may, it is evident that in the rest of the *House of Fame* Chaucer drew much more from Dante's *Purgatorio* and *Paradiso* than from his *Inferno*. The eagle, as is well known, comes from *Purgatorio*, IX, with a reminiscence from *Paradiso*, I and perhaps a hint from *Paradiso*, XVIII–XIX. The Invocation to Apollo in Book III derives from *Paradiso*, I. The flight through the air in Book II is itself an echo, among other things, of Dante's ascent through the heavens in the *Paradiso*.

There are here two strictly linked aspects of Chaucer's response to Dante, which we can explore with some profit, following Eliot's example. First, there is the widening of the scope of poetry that takes place in the *House of Fame* if we compare it to the *Book of the Duchess*. Chaucer is now prepared to sing not only of love, but also of all aspects of the natural, animal and human world. The tidings of war, peace, marriages, fair winds and tempests fill the House of Rumour in Book III (1956–76). They are considered by Chaucer as potential material for poetry – they are actually narrated by Dante throughout the *Divine Comedy*. Moreover, that 'poetical physics' which the eagle expounds in Book II of the *House of Fame* is one of Dante's favourite topics. Dante's wide interest in the world of nature and man influences Chaucer, and prompts him to look for new grounds and at the same time to follow in the steps of Boethius and Alain de Lille (both in fact mentioned during the flight), who were already part of his philosophical and poetical culture.[9]

On the other hand it is quite clear that Chaucer's Dantean eagle, however transformed, fulfils that function of guide which Dante had assigned to Virgil and Beatrice. Following the precedent of Dante himself in his meeting with Beatrice on the summit of mount Purgatory, the poetic persona in the *House of Fame* is familiarly addressed by the eagle as 'Geffrey' – the only time that name occurs in Chaucer's works. Compare:

> Dante, perché Virgilio se ne vada ...
> quando mi volsi al suon del nome mio,
> che di necessità qui si registra ...
>   (*Purg.*, XXX, 55–63)

(Dante, although Virgil has left ... when I turned at the sound of my name, which of necessity is recorded here ...)

And:

And called me tho by my name . . .
'Geffrey, thou wost ryght wel this . . .'

(II, 558,729)

That 'Geffrey' is here an ironical echo of Dante is confirmed by another deliberately distorted reminiscence. Frightened by the prospect of his flight in spite of the eagle's reassurances, Geoffrey begins to wonder whether Jupiter is going to 'stellify' him and thinks:

I neyther am Ennok, ne Elye,
Ne Romulus, ne Ganymede . . .

(II, 588–9)

which of course transforms Dante's protestation to Virgil at the beginning of his journey: 'I am neither Aeneas nor Paul' (*Inf.*, II, 32). Here two points are interesting. The first is that Chaucer, though changing Aeneas and Paul into Romulus, Ganymede, Enoch and Elijah, does keep Dante's frame of reference (two of his characters are from classical mythology, like Aeneas, two from Scripture, like Paul), but adapts it to his own needs. He is not on a journey to Hell, like Aeneas, but to the heavens, like Romulus, Ganymede, Enoch and Elijah. That Paul, however, is in the back of Chaucer's mind is clear from what Geoffrey says later on (980–2):

'Y wot wel y am here;
But wher in body or in gost
I not, ywys; but God, thou wost!'

which echoes Paul's words in the Second Epistle to the Corinthians (XII.2), a passage that Dante recalls at the beginning of his *Paradiso* (I, 4–6). The second point is that the eagle's answer to Geoffrey is very different from Virgil's to Dante. To Dante's worried protestations Virgil had opposed Beatrice's mission and her saving love. To Geoffrey the eagle replies first with Virgil's words to Dante (600–4, and cf. *Inf.*, II, 49–51), but then with a reference to Jupiter's pity and his command to bring the poet – 'in som recompensacion / Of labour and devocion' to the god of Love – to the House of Fame, where he will find plenty of tidings of 'Loves folk'.

Beatrice's love ('amor mi mosse' – 'love moved me') is also a reflection and a part of that Love which is God ('l'amor che move il sole e l'altre stelle' – 'The love that moves the sun and the other stars'). Chaucer replaces this with the god of Love – Cupid, the son of Venus. In view of his play with *Inferno*, II I would say that this is not purely casual. Indeed, this is an indication not only of what Chaucer wants to do in the *House of Fame*, but also of what he thinks of his relationship to Dante as a poet.

Chaucer's journey in the *House of Fame* is, then, not a journey to
Hell (though the 'eryd lond' of I, 485 might be a reminiscence of the
'landa' and the 'rena arida e spessa' of *Inf.*, XIV, 8, 13), not Aeneas'
journey (though Aeneas is the hero of Book I), nor, more significantly,
is it a journey towards Heaven, towards Love, towards God, towards
the beatific vision.[10] At precisely the moment when Geoffrey thinks of
Boethius and of thought that can 'passen everych element' with the
feathers of Philosophy, when he wonders with St Paul whether he is in
the body or out of the body – at the point, that is, when he seems to be
on the threshold of Heaven, on the verge of the beatific vision – his
guide interrupts him with his deflating 'Lat be thy fantasye.' Geoffrey
is denied the 'trasumanar', the passing beyond humanity that Dante
undergoes in *Paradiso*, I.

He recognizes full well his limitations as a poet because he has
grasped what Dante is doing with *his* poetry and his 'art poetical'.
For one of Chaucer's most important meditations in the *House of
Fame* is precisely this: what are his art and his stance as a poet?
When, in the 'Domus Dedaly', the 'Laboryntus' of Rumour, Chaucer
hears and sees the 'tidings' of all natural, animal and human phenomena, which are but 'the poet's raw material', he is careful not to
include any potential, super-human, transcendental object of poetry.
When, asked if he has come to have fame, Geoffrey answers (III,
1873–82),

> 'Nay, for sothe, frend,' quod y;
> 'I cam noght hyder, graunt mercy,
> For no such cause, by my hed!
> Sufficeth me, as I were ded,
> That no wight have my name in honde.
> I wot myself best how y stonde;
> For what I drye, or what I thynke,
> I wil myselven al hyt drynke,
> Certeyn, for the more part,
> As fer forth as I kan myn art,'

he seems to be answering Dante, who has his ancestor Cacciaguida tell
him explicitly:

> Non vo' però ch'a' tuoi vicini invidie,
>   poscia che s'infutura la tua vita
>   vie più là che 'l punir di lor perfidie...
> Questo tuo grido farà come vento,
>   che le più alte cime più percuote;
>   e ciò non fa d'onor poco argomento.
>   (*Par.*, XVII, 97–9, 133–5)

('But I would not have you envious of your fellows, for your life shall know a future far beyond the punishment of their treacheries . . . Your cry shall be like the wind, which strikes most violently on the highest summits; and this is no small reason for honour.')

When, echoing *Inferno*, II, Chaucer invokes his 'Thought', he goes so far as to say, with Dante, that men shall now see if there is 'any vertu' in this Thought. Later he invokes Apollo and, echoing *Paradiso*, I, he asks the 'devyne vertu' to help him show what is 'marked in his head'. He hastens to add,

> Loo, that is for to menen this,
> The Hous of Fame for to descryve –
> (III, 1104–5)

Not, that is, Heaven, nor, for that matter, Hell.

In view of this, it would perhaps be worth asking ourselves what Chaucer's invocations in the *House of Fame* mean, when compared to Dante's. Dante introduces three main invocations, at the beginning of each canticle. The first is directed to the muses, his own 'alto ingegno' and 'mente' (*Inf.*, II, 7–9); the second to the 'holy muses' and in particular Calliope, with 'ingegno' again to the fore (*Purg.*, I, 1–12); the third to Apollo, with 'mente' in a key position (*Par.*, I, 10–33) and with the addition that the poet's journey is now guided by the nine muses, Apollo himself and Minerva (*Par.*, II, 8–9). It is clear that there is a crescendo in Dante's invocations: the muses (inspiration), the poet's own native talent and inventiveness ('ingegno') and his memory ('mente') are enough for the *Inferno*. Inspiration still guides him in the *Purgatorio*, but here the poet appeals in particular to Calliope, the muse of epic or sumblime poetry. Finally, in the *Paradiso* inspiration is shown to be necessary but insufficient (I, 16–18) and memory finds it difficult to follow the intellect as it draws closer to God. The poet will need Apollo – divine inspiration – and Minerva – the 'wisdom' that comes from God.[11]

Chaucer keeps Dante's progression. His first invocation, to the god of sleep (I, 66–9; 77–80), is in keeping with the dream setting of his poem as a whole, and the Dantean reminiscence in the prayer to God that accompanies the invocation ('he that mover ys of all', cf. *Par.*, I, 1) anticipates the direction that Chaucer's mind will take later. Chaucer underlines, then, that his is only a dream, and not a journey presented as if made in the flesh and culminating with a vision of God such as Dante's.[12] In Book II, where Chaucer is thematically and even iconographically closer to Dante, his invocation is to the muses and his own Thought, but with the addition of Venus (II, 518–28). In Book III, finally, where the poet will have to describe the Houses of Fame and Rumour – a task as high as Virgil's and Ovid's poems from which part of the imagery is taken – Chaucer appeals to Apollo, 'devyne vertu', 'god of science and lyght' (III, 1091–109).

We may note in passing some other interesting features of Chaucer's counterpoint to Dante and, by implication, of the way he conceives himself and Dante as poets. The first is Chaucer's addition of Venus in his invocation in Book II, otherwise derived from *Inferno*, II. It is already strange that the goddess – and planet – of love should be invoked at the beginning of a Book that, in spite of the eagle's promises, will not speak of love (whereas it would have been appropriate in Book I and will be appropriate in Book III of *Troilus*). But there is perhaps in this invocation a deeper sense – an acknowledgement of Chaucer's debt to love as the primary muse of his poetry, as the nucleus of his inspiration and culture, and as the original impulse that sends him now on the journey to the House of Fame. This is confirmed by the eagle's statement that the journey is Jupiter's 'recompensacion' for the poet's past 'labour and devocion' to Love. By asking Venus' favour before adapting Dante's invocation, Chaucer furthermore points to a difference between himself and the Dante of the *Comedy*. Dante, who had himself sung the 'dolci rime d'amor' (and Chaucer would have known this if he had already read *Convivio*, IV) is now, at the beginning of the *Inferno*, aided by love, by that very same woman whom he 'loved so much', Beatrice. But Beatrice is the 'loda di Dio vera' ('true praise of God') and her love is now transfigured and divine. And Chaucer could not have failed to understand this in reading *Inferno*, II. By adding Venus (derived from the *Teseida*), Chaucer indicates that his choice is and will remain 'secular'.

Chaucer makes another slight change in his invocation in Book II. In translating Dante's 'mente' (memory) he uses the word 'Thought' and makes 'ingegno' ('now kythe thyn engyn and myght') a part of it. Chaucer's Thought, as the context makes clear, must mean 'memory'. And yet Chaucer knew that 'man hath sapiences three, / Memorie, engyn, and intellect also' (*Second Nun's Tale*, 338–9, and cf. *Parson's Tale*, 452) and that 'engyn' could not be a part of memory. Moreover, later in Book II, 973 Chaucer uses 'thought' to translate Boethius' 'mens' (*De Consolatione*, IV, m. 1, 3, and cf. *Boece*, IV, m. 1) – certainly not 'memory'. Finally, in this very invocation Chaucer uses 'brayn' (525) for Dante's 'mente' (*Par.*, I, 11). Now, either Chaucer did not know precisely what 'mente' and 'mens' meant, and was not yet aware of the distinction between memory, 'engyn' and intellect, or else 'Thought' must be understood not only as 'power to remember' but as 'mental power', 'mind' – a more comprehensive concept, of which 'engyn' could be a part. If this is so – and the translation from Boethius seems to confirm it[13] – Chaucer is here underlining not so much the 'remembrance' on which he will rely later (in the *Legend*) as the importance of 'thought' in poetic activity, while considering native talent and inventiveness ('ingegno' – 'engyn') as slightly less central than Dante does – and in this he is characteristically more humble, and perhaps paying an indirect compliment to Dante himself, the poet of Thought and 'engyn' *par excellence*.

The absence in the *House of Fame* of an invocation to the muse of epic or sublime poetry, Calliope (Dante's special muse in the *Purgatorio*, as Chaucer's in the *Troilus*, III, 45), is also significant, particularly in view of the fact that Chaucer takes special care to mention her in Book III as 'the myghty Muse' who sings 'hevenyssh melodye of songes' and as being together with her sisters (she is singled out among them as in *Purg.*, I, 8–9) the muse 'of Fame'. Again, there is a reason for this other than a purely structural one (if Chaucer had had no other Book to preface, he could have inserted Calliope in the Proem to Book II): it is, I think, Chaucer's intention to make clear a difference of tone and purpose (there will be no sublime poetry, no 'maistrye' in the *House of Fame*), yet also to indicate his fascination with precisely that 'resurrection' of the 'morta poesì' of which Dante speaks at the beginning of the *Purgatorio*, and which Chaucer will himself celebrate shortly afterwards with the description of Fame's great hall, where the poets stand.

The invocation in Book III is again intriguing. Here Chaucer leaves out the muses and Minerva from *Paradiso*, II, but keeps Apollo from *Paradiso*, I, specifying, however, that he is 'god of science and lyght', a phrase notably absent in Dante. Dante's Apollo is not simply the pagan god, the leader of the nine muses, but the 'father', the '*divina virtù*', the giver of 'valor' to the 'vas electionis' ('Chosen Vessel'), in short the Holy Ghost that breathes ('spira') and enters the prophet's breast.[14] Chaucer faithfully keeps 'devyne vertu' and asks the god to enter his breast (not to breathe forth), but by adding 'god of science and lyght' he once more limits the scope of Dante's invocation and makes his own intention clear. We would have no way of knowing whether Chaucer was surprised by Dante's daring fusion of the pagan god and divine inspiration if it were not for those words, which make it certain that Apollo, however 'devyne' a 'vertu', remains a god of science (knowledge and wisdom) and light only (not, significantly, of poetry and prophecy, the two most important of his domains), and not the God of the 'beato regno'. The expression is, moreover, gratuitous in the context of Book III, which does not deal specifically with either knowledge (which is treated in Book II) or light. We cannot of course draw any definitive conclusion, for Book III breaks off suddenly at the end of a line. That Dante's poetic stature is on Chaucer's mind in these lines, however, is suggested by another hint. When Chaucer, following *Paradiso*, I, tells Apollo that if he helps him he will go 'unto the nexte laure' he sees, he humbly adds that he will kiss it. Yet Dante, much more ambitiously, had proclaimed that he would be *crowned* with laurel leaves, a wish which he was to express again in the *Paradiso* (XXV, 7–9) and which never came true. For Chaucer, Dante never was the 'lauriat poete'; that honour was reserved for Petrarch.[15] But Dante (like Boccaccio in the *Teseida*) had claimed the laurel crown, and Chaucer, whether or not he knew that he never received it, was aware that 'the grete poete of Ytaille' could rightly claim it, whereas he decided that to kiss Apollo's tree was honour enough for himself.

The *House of Fame* seems to be haunted by the shadow of Dante. It is with a great mystery that the poem breaks off, with the appearance of one who 'semed for to be / A man of gret auctorite'. Whoever this might be, there can be little doubt that the two lines that introduce him are reminiscent of that passage in *Inferno*, IV where Dante, who has already joined Homer, Horace, Ovid, Lucan and Virgil in the 'bella scuola' of Limbo, comes 'to the foot of a Noble Castle' and enters it through seven gates. Here, 'in a meadow of fresh verdure' ('in prato di fresca verdura'), within the walls of a castle that looks like the archetype of the Castle of Fame, Dante sees many 'people with eyes slow and grave',

> di grande autorità ne' lor sembianti.[16]
> (*Inf.*, IV, 113)

Between the Proem to Book II and the Invocation in Book III of the *House of Fame* Chaucer thus comes to understand the limits of his 'vertu' and his 'art', measuring them against Dante's achievements. He humbly refuses, in what is certainly, but perhaps only partly, a formula, to 'show craft' and 'art poetical'. His eagle prefers the language 'withoute any subtilite / Of speche, or gret prolixite / Of termes of philosophie, / Of figures of poetrie, / Or colours of rhetorike'. He has learnt the great lesson, as Eliot would put it, of Dante's craft, and he chooses for himself not the 'hard langage' and 'hard matere' of Dante's Virgil and Dante's Beatrice, but the 'lyght', 'agreable' rhyme, the 'palpable . . . skiles' with which to speak 'lewedly to a lewed man'. Not 'poema sacro al quale ha posto mano e cielo e terra' (*Par.*, XXV,

1–2), but feelings, experience and thought that he will 'drink' all by himself: this will be Chaucer's poetry, *as fer forth as he kan his art* (1879–82). And again, there is here a significant counterpoint to Dante, for the sense of suffering and meditation ('sì che m'ha fatto per più anni macro' – 'which has made me lean through many a year': *Par.*, xxv, 3) and the consciousness of the personal responsibility of the poet are the great lessons of Dante. Chaucer, who now 'knows his art', shuts out the sacred and prophetic nature of Dante's most exalted poetry.

He seems to confirm this choice later in his career, for in the Prologue to the *Legend of Good Women*, he opens his discussion of the value of authority and experience with a reference to the joys of Heaven and the pains of Hell:

> A thousand sythes have I herd men telle
> That there is joye in hevene and peyne in helle,
> And I acorde wel that it be so;
> But natheles, this wot I wel also,
> That there ne is non that dwelleth in this contre,
> That eyther hath in helle or hevene ybe,
> Ne may of it non other weyes witen,
> But as he hath herd seyd or founde it writen;
> For by assay there may no man it preve.
>
> (G 1–9)

It seems almost certain that these lines contain an allusion to Dante. Chaucer knew there was no one in his country who had been to Hell or to Heaven, but he also knew that Dante (whom he mentions by name and from whom he quotes later in this same prologue, G 335–6)[17] had been – in fiction, at least – to both places and had described their 'peyne' and 'joye'. Furthermore, the Englishman who wishes to learn the 'ways' to Heaven and Hell can, Chaucer says, find them either in oral tradition or in books. And Dante was for Chaucer, as we have seen, the great expert on Hell together with Claudian and Virgil. However – one more instance of counterpoint – Chaucer repeats in the *Legend* the choice he had made in the *House of Fame*. When, a few lines later in the Prologue, he declares that we must have recourse to books, 'yeven credence' 'to the doctryne of these olde wyse' and believe the 'olde aproved storyes', he gives a list of subjects for these stories which, though shorter than the one in the *House of Fame*, leaves out once again any superhuman and supernatural phenomena, that is any description of those infernal pains and heavenly joys with which, after all, he had himself opened his discussion.

This choice not to enter the 'segrete cose', the secret things of the

other world, is made once more in Chaucer's works, by the Knight of
the *Canterbury Tales*. When, in his Tale, he comes to Arcite's death,
he refuses to follow Boccaccio's *Teseida* and describe the ascent of
Arcite's soul to the eighth sphere and its ultimate destination (*Teseida*,
XI, 1–3), commenting instead:

> His spirit chaunged hous and wente ther,
> As I cam nevere, I kan nat tellen wher.
> Therfore I stynte, I nam no divinistre;
> Of soules fynde I nat in this registre,
> Ne me ne list thilke opinions to telle
> Of hem, though that they writen wher they dwelle.
>   (2809–14)

This is not a sneer at Boccaccio and perhaps, more generally, at Dante,
but an indication of a philosophical and narrative choice. What the
Knight is saying is that he refuses to speak of the destiny of Arcite's
soul after death because he himself has no experience of the 'undis-
covered country, from whose bourn no traveller returns', and he does
not regard it as part of his theme. Those who write of where souls dwell
express only 'opinions'. The Knight, then, is more sceptical than the
Chaucer of the Prologue to the *Legend*, who was prepared to believe
'wel more thyng than men han seyn with ye!' The Knight's choice is,
however, consistent with his narrative, steeped in the pagan world:
in this context it would be extremely difficult to indicate with
precision where Arcite's soul should dwell after death. Boccaccio, in
fact, refrains from specifying this, and perhaps only Dante could risk
doing so – could risk, that is, facing the theological intricacies and
dangers involved in the problem of the salvation of the heathens.

So far, we have followed one main line of Chaucer's relationship to
Dante – a line which brings to light the importance that Dante's
example has for Chaucer's definition of his own aims, province, scope
and stand as a poet, and which implicitly reveals Chaucer's consideration of Dante. In the *House of Fame*, the *Friar's Tale*, the *Legend of
Good Women* and the *Knight's Tale* Dante is for Chaucer the poet of
Hell and Heaven, the poet of the muses, of Thought, of 'engyn', of
science and light. Chaucer is willing to explore, with Dante, the full
range of possibilities offered to poetry by the world of man and of
nature. At one point, he seems to be prepared, with Dante, to go
further. But he checks himself. It is difficult, in view of the consistency
of his position in this respect, not to conclude that Chaucer's refusal to
find his own 'register of souls' is a deliberate choice of poetics and
philosophy prompted by his reaction to Dante.

Chaucer did, however, find a 'register of souls' in his *Troilus*. The very passage on the ascent of Arcite's soul which he read in Book XI of the *Teseida*, and which the Knight omits in his adaptation of Boccaccio's poem, appears (or had appeared) at the end of Book V of *Troilus* (1807–27). The story of Troilus is a story of love and death that, as Barry Windeatt will show later in this volume, imitates and amplifies Boccaccio's *Filostrato*; and Troilus' soul has no more reason to ascend to the eighth sphere and proceed to an unknown destination than Arcite in the *Knight's Tale*. But the Narrator of *Troilus* is different from the Knight. In the last stanzas of his poem he wants to bring his audience of 'yonge, fresshe folkes' from Troilus' love – now his 'blynde lust' – to God's love (V, 1842–8); he wants to bring them and himself from the 'corsed olde rites' of the pagans to an invocation of divine mercy (V, 1860–2); he wants to bring himself and his audience from 'the forme of olde clerkis speche / In poetrie' to Christian poetry, to the poetry of God (V, 1863–9). And he pays Dante the supreme homage of identifying him as the poet of the greatest mysteries – the Trinity, God's infinity, the Virgin Birth. For the first three magnificent lines, and the very last one of the final stanza of *Troilus* imitate Dante's *Paradiso*:

> Thow oon, and two, and thre, eterne on lyve,
> That regnest ay in thre, and two, and oon,
> Uncircumscript, and al maist circumscrive . . .

> Quell'uno e due e tre che sempre vive
> e regna sempre in tre e 'n due e 'n uno,
> non circunscritto, e tutto circunscrive . . .
> 　　　　　　　　　　　(*Par.*, XIV, 28–30)

> For love of mayde and moder thyn benigne.

> Vergine madre, figlia del tuo figlio . . .
> 　　　　　　　　　　　(*Par.*, XXXIII, 1)

That the *Troilus*, modelled on a work by Boccaccio that is full of Dantean images, is Chaucer's most serious effort to create his own equivalent of the *Divine Comedy* (and of the *Teseida*) is, I think, more than an impression. Chaucer uses in the *Troilus* all the devices at his disposal to construct a 'great' poem: he creates a Narrator and an audience, exploits French and Italian lyric and Boethian philosophy, invents the languages of Pandarus, Troilus and Criseyde, mingles interior monologue and dialogue, comic invention, melodrama, philosophical meditation. He invokes God, the muses, Venus and the furies, uses classical mythology, natural and astronomical images, deals in one text with Boccaccio, Petrarch and Dante.[18] He recreates that 'multiplicity of styles' which is Dante's notable characteristic but which is absent in the *Filostrato*.[19] Following Dante, he asks at the beginning of Book III, the most exacting of the entire work, for the help of Calliope, the muse of sublime poetry. Adapting Dante, he proclaims at the beginning of the 'purgatorial' Book II that he will now sail 'owt of thise blake wawes' (and cf. *Purg.*, I, 1–3). Following Statius (*Thebaid*, I, 41, 59), he invokes Clio, muse of history (II, 8–9), and, with an eye on Dante's *Inferno*, Tisiphone, one of the furies (I, 6–11). In other words, he deliberately presents the first three Books of *Troilus* as respectively the Hell, Purgatory and Paradise of the lover. Like Dante, he shows a particular concern for his vernacular, English, and for the changes language undergoes with time (II, 22–8; V, 1793–9).[20]

And like Dante, Chaucer knows what doing all this means: his 'litel book' must 'subgit be to alle poesye', must kiss the steps of 'Virgile, Ovide, Omer, Lucan, and Stace', must, in other words, be the modest 'sesto tra cotanto senno' ('sixth amidst such wisdom'). Like Dante, Chaucer cuts across centuries of literature to go straight back to the great examples of classical poetry.[21] It is not by chance that he calls the *Troilus* a 'tragedye', however 'litel' he proclaims it to be. Tragedy it is because of Fortune's operations and Troilus' death; unlike Dante's 'Comedy', it has what Dante would call a 'foul and horrible' end. Stylistically it may be classed as a 'tragedy', for it uses at appropriate points the 'high' style of Virgil's 'alta tragedìa' (*Inf.*, XX, 113).

Is it by pure chance that Chaucer prays God to give him 'myght to make in som *comedye*' just before he concludes his poem with the solemn and inspired words of that *Comedy* which was later to be called *Divine*? Chaucer may have intended to write such a comedy as he seems to express a desire to do here, at the end of *Troilus*. And perhaps this comedy was to be a collection of stories told by people on a pilgrimage and Chaucer was to appear in it as the pilgrim listening to stories – as Dante had heard stories in his pilgrimage through the other world.[22] Robin Kirkpatrick will attempt an answer to these questions in his essay on the *Decameron* and the *Canterbury Tales* later in this collection. But if Chaucer had this desire to write that kind of comedy while composing *Troilus* – and the last stanzas with their thrust towards God, the whole poem with its stylistic features, seem to confirm this – then he must have known that the *Divine Comedy* is not just the story of Paolo and Francesca.[23]

For, after all, *Troilus* is the story of a passionate love, which inevitably 'repairs' in 'gentil hertes', a love that 'a nullo amato amar perdona' (Pandarus paraphrases this with his 'love for love is skilful

guerdonynge': II, 392), a love – a 'blynde lust' – that inevitably leads
to death:

> Amor condusse noi a una morte
> (*Inf.*, V, 106)

> Swich fyn hath, lo, this Troilus for love!
> (V, 1828)

Such love could never become the Love that moves Beatrice, the sun
and the other stars. And Chaucer knew it. In Troilus' hymn 'O Love,
O Charite' he puts in his hero's mouth two lines (II, 1262–3) straight
out of Bernard's prayer to the Virgin in *Paradiso*, XXXIII (14–15).
But whilst Troilus' much greater song to the universal power of love at
the end of Book III makes use of Boethius, he does not adapt – although
the context would amply justify it – Dante's last line,

> l'amor che move 'l sole e l'altre stelle.

Troilus' love and death are recalled in the *Parliament of Fowls*
(291–4), another poem where Chaucer finds a 'register of souls' – this
time in the *Somnium Scipionis*:

> Thanne axede he if folk that here been dede
> Han lyf and dwellynge in another place.
> And Affrican seyde, 'Ye, withouten drede.'
> (50–2)

Chaucer is ready at once with his counterpoint, for he is not going to
describe either Hell or Heaven – or rather his Heaven is the 'Galaxye'.
And the failing day and dark night are not going to prepare him for
the 'war of the journey and of the pity' that Dante is ready to bear at
the beginning of *Inferno*, II (from which lines 85–6 of the *Parliament*
are drawn), but will simply deprive Chaucer of his book. This book,
the *Somnium Scipionis*, is for Chaucer the volume he has perused 'so
wel', with the same love and attention that Dante devoted to Virgil's
work (109–10, and cf. *Inf.*, I, 83–4). And it at once becomes apparent
that Chaucer is here playing with the first three cantos of *Inferno*
with the consummate skill of a man who has learnt his lesson from
Dante. Scipio himself becomes, then, a Dantean Virgil, and the gate
that gives access to the park bears a double inscription modelled on
that of the door of Dante's Hell. Like Virgil with Dante, Scipio takes
the dreamer's hand in his (169–70, and cf. *Inf.*, III, 19–20). And
Chaucer finally enters the 'segrete cose'.

That these should be other than a Dantean Hell or Heaven, that the
guide should disappear, that the poetic invocation should once more be

to Venus, we ought by now to expect from Chaucer. What is perhaps unexpected is that Scipio disappears at precisely the point Virgil does in the *Comedy*, and that the 'secret things' Chaucer's persona enters are at first like Dante's Earthly Paradise, the place of which 'those who in ancient times sang (*anticamente poetaro*) of the golden age and its happy state perhaps dreamed on Parnassus' (*Purg.*, XXVIII, 139–41).[24] Chaucer, who is dreaming not on Parnassus but in his bed, chooses however not the ancient poets, but Dante, a compliment not to be underestimated. But it is a sign of mature and confident artistry that Chaucer can now behave towards Dante with the same freedom with which Dante himself dealt with Virgil and the others who 'anticamente poetaro'. The description of the park and, later, that of the birds' parliament are fully Chaucerian and the poet now masters that 'craft' which is 'so long to lerne'.

II   The Wise Poet

Chaucer's reading in Dante's *Convivio* is even more problematic than his reading in the *Divine Comedy*. We know that he read and used Tractate IV and the *canzone* that prefaces it, *Le dolci rime d'amor*, but there is so far no conclusive evidence that he knew the first three Tractates.[25] Again, what could Chaucer's reaction have been to a work that discusses such weighty problems as the importance of the vernacular vis-à-vis Latin, the four senses of literary writings, the Heavens and angelic hierarchies, science and philosophy, love and the soul, or, to consider only Tractate IV, nobility, the history and authority of the Roman Empire, the history of philosophy and the authority of Aristotle, the eleven moral virtues, human happiness and perfection, the four ages of man and their characteristics? The *Convivio*, though unfinished, was a book in which a mind as alert as Chaucer's could find points of departure, hints on subjects that deeply interested him such as fame (I, iii, 6–11), freedom of the will and divine foreknowledge (III, xii, 8–9), authority (IV, vi, 4–7), courtesy, allegory, Fortune (IV, xi, 6–9), heavenly influence, Nature, pity, rhetoric and many others. It was a work in which Chaucer could not fail to notice Dante's technical abilities, his strong logical bent, the sudden explosions of concrete images, the burning fire of philosophical enthusiasm, the enormous range of culture – some of which Chaucer shared. It was a work, finally, where a man who died a mere fifty years earlier had written in his mother tongue a sort of spiritual autobiography and commented extensively on his own lyrics as if they were books of the Bible, the *Sentences* of Peter Lombard, or Virgil's

Aeneid. Nor was it necessary for Chaucer to know the whole *Convivio* in order to realize all this: Tractate IV was in itself 'God's plenty'.

Once more, Chaucer sensibly chose to deal with such a heavenly pantagruelic banquet in an oblique and comparatively circumscribed fashion. His use of the *Convivio* is not different in kind from his recollections of the *Comedy*. When the Wife of Bath decides to tell a story to prove her point about 'maistrie' in marriage, she has her heroine, the 'olde wyf', show also what true 'gentilesse' is. To do this – as J. A. W. Bennett writes in his essay in this volume – she quotes from the *Comedy* (*Purg.*, VII, 121–3; cf. *Wife of Bath's Tale*, 1127–30). But the discussion preceding and following this quotation (1109–64) is inspired by the *Convivio*, as Lowes demonstrated, specifically by the *canzone* called *Le dolci rime d'amor* and Tractate IV, which takes the form of a commentary on the poem, although Chaucer must also have borne in mind the relevant sections of the *Roman de la Rose* and of Boethius' *De Consolatione*.

'Gentilesse' is a concept central to Chaucer's interests; the problems of man's nobility, wealth and 'moral vertu' are discussed in works as diverse as the *Parliament of Fowls*, the *Franklin's Tale* (with an echo of Dante's discussion, 686–94) and the *Wife of Bath's Tale*; they affect the *Squire's Tale* and the *Clerk's Tale* (see 1570–8) and enter *Troilus*, the *Knight's Tale* and even the *Parson's Tale*. It is not the purpose of this essay to illustrate this. What interests us here is the place Dante occupies in Chaucer's consideration of 'gentilesse'. Chaucer used Dante's discussion in the *Convivio* once more, in his 'moral balade' *Gentilesse*. He could not have failed to notice with particular interest the opening lines of Dante's *canzone*:

> Le dolci rime d'amor ch'i solia
> cercar ne' miei pensieri,
> convien ch'io lasci . . .
>   E poi che tempo mi par d'aspettare,
> diporrò giù lo mio soave stile,
> ch'i' ho tenuto nel trattar d'amore;
> e dirò del valore,
> per lo qual veramente omo è gentile,
> con rima aspr'e sottile . . .
>
>   (1–14)

(The sweet love-poetry I was accustomed to seek out in my thoughts I must now forsake . . . And so, since it now seems a time for waiting, I will lay down that sweet style of mine which I held to in writing of love, and I will speak instead in harsh and subtle rhymes concerning the quality by which man is truly noble . . . (Text and translation by K. Foster and P. Boyde, *Dante's Lyric Poetry*, vol. I (Oxford, 1967), pp. 128–31).)

Nor could he fail to notice that if Dante was here abandoning his 'songes' and 'dytees' 'in reverence of Love', he was also setting aside the study of metaphysics (IV, i, 8–9, 11) to devote himself to an eminently moral problem. Dante was in fact turning to the poetry of that moral *virtus*, of that *rectitudo* which he theorized as one of the 'capital matters' worthiest of being treated by illustrious writers, and as his own particular province in Italian literature (*De Vulgari Eloquentia*, II, ii, 7–9).

It is tempting – and not unreasonable, in view of the direct relationship – to see *Gentilesse* as Chaucer's version of Dante's great moral *canzone*. And it is tempting to think that Dante's example might have prompted Chaucer to confront moral and philosophical themes in such poems as *Fortune* (where Dantean echoes are present), *Truth* and *Lak of Stedfastnesse*. In this sense Dante's *canzone* would have helped Chaucer to see that subjects that had been treated by Boethius and Jean de Meun (and the choice of which would be acceptable to 'moral Gower' and 'philosophical Strode'), could be dealt with in a concentrated poetic composition. Whether or not it is pure coincidence, Chaucer's intonation does at times have a vigour and a firmness comparable to Dante's:

> Forth, pilgrim, forth! Forth, beste, out of thy stal!
> Know thy contree, look up, thank God of al;
> Hold the heye wey, and lat thy gost thee lede . . .
> (*Truth*, 18–20)

Nor is it totally impossible that Dante's continuing concern with politics and the state of civilization – its decadence and moral corruption – could have encouraged Chaucer to deal with these themes in works such as *Lak of Stedfastnesse* or even *Melibee*.

What is certain is that at least once, in the *Legend of Good Women*, when Chaucer wants to quote an authority on matters of morality, and political and Court affairs, he resorts to Dante, to the speech of that model of a courtier–politician–poet who 'held both keys of the heart' of Frederick II, Pier delle Vigne, in a canto of *Inferno* that, as J. A. W. Bennett has shown in his essay, he knew well:

> Envie ys lavendere of the court alway,
> For she ne parteth, neither nyght ne day,
> Out of the hous of Cesar; thus seith Dante . . .
> (Prologue F 358–60 and cf. *Inf.*, XIII, 64–6)

Alceste is here using Dante's sentence as if it were a maxim and considering Dante himself as the repository of moral wisdom. It is a conception of him that the Wife of Bath and her 'olde wyf' share when, before quoting *Purgatorio*, VII and drawing on the *Convivio*, they say:

> Wel kan the *wise poete* of Florence,
> That highte Dant, speken in this sentence.
>
> (1125–6)

III   The Great Poet

Not only Dante's wisdom, but his *craft* continued to inspire Chaucer. Eliot noted that the section of *Little Gidding* where he tried to imitate not only Dante's 'content', but also his style – 'an approximation to the *terza rima* without rhyming' – cost him 'far more time and trouble and vexation than any passage of the same length' that he had ever written.[26] Whether Chaucer had the same feeling after writing sections II and III of his *Complaint to his Lady*, where he tried to reproduce *terza rima* (with rhyming), we do not know. But Chaucer never tried it again – not even when for, as far as we know, the first and only time of his career he actually imitated Dante for more than a couple of lines, in his adaptation of the Ugolino story in the *Monk's Tale*.

Praz, Spencer and Schless have compared the Dantean and Chaucerian versions of that story in well-known essays, and I have myself given a stylistic analysis of the two episodes in an article where I tried to set Chaucer's adaptation within the general context of the relationship of the *Monk's Tale* to all its Italian sources.[27] There is therefore no need to enter into a comparative discussion here. It will be sufficient to recall its general results. Chaucer 'translates' only five lines of Dante's canto, but sets them in a different context. The structure, the register, the imagery, the semantic level, the setting, the theme of the two versions are very different. Dante's horror becomes pathos, indirect poetry becomes detailed account and direct, 'prosaic', oral narrative. Chaucer's Hugelyn has its greatness; the central stanzas of his version are a noble poetic achievement. But the way this intensity is reached is totally different from Dante's. The Monk's Hugelyn is, in other words, a total *twisting* of Dante's text, and one that cannot but have been deliberate.

The first question we should ask ourselves is, therefore, why did Chaucer choose this particular episode out of the many he could have found in the *Inferno*, let alone the *Purgatorio*? Both the episode of Ulysses in Canto XXVI and that of Pier delle Vigne in Canto XIII of *Inferno* could have been fitted within the Fortune theme which dominates the *Monk's Tale* and to which the story of Ugolino is itself adapted. Ulysses was a mythological hero, one for whose legend the authorities of Virgil, Statius and Ovid could be recalled and one on whom Chaucer's friend, Gower, was writing. The figure of Pier delle Vigne was well known to Chaucer, who quoted several lines of *Inferno*, XIII in his works. Like Ugolino, Pier delle Vigne would, moreover, add yet one more *exemplum* to that collection of Biblical, classical, Italianate and Mediterranean tragedies, that world of history which Chaucer – following Dante and anticipating the Elizabethans – tackles in the *Monk's Tale*. Of course, Ugolino was mentioned by Boccaccio in his *De Casibus*, and this made it easier for Chaucer to associate him with Fortune. But there must also have been a literary reason for Chaucer's choice of Ugolino. And this, I think, is to be found not only in the unforgettable passion that vibrates in Ugolino's story – the 'width of emotional range' that is displayed in the episode (hate, fury, despair, grief, nostalgia, impotence, paternal and filial love) – but, above all, in Dante's handling of the narrative.

In however oblique a way, Chaucer recognized this himself when he concluded his 'tragedie' with expressions of admiration which are more specific than the usual mentions of authorities we find in his works and which can be seen as the remarks of a literary critic:

> Of this tragedie it oghte ynough suffise;
> Whoso wol here it in a lenger wise,
> Redeth the grete poete of Ytaille
> That highte Dant, for he kan al devyse
> Fro point to point, nat o word wol he faille.
>
> (VII, 2458–62)

Here, Chaucer refers his readers back to Dante's version. But the actual narrative of Ugolino in *Inferno*, XXXIII is only four lines longer than the Monk's (fifty-four versus fifty, the comment on Fortune and the lines quoted above not being narrative) – a difference hardly worth special mention. The Monk must therefore be conceived of as thinking of those sections of the Dantean episode which are not part of the 'tragedie', the narrative as such, but which constitute the indispensable background and corollary of Dante's story: the description of the two sinners, Ruggieri and Ugolino, and Dante's question at the end of Canto XXXII, Ugolino's raising his mouth and his introductory words at the beginning of Canto XXXIII, his return to the savage repast at the end of his story, and Dante's invective against Pisa that follows on its heels. Dante 'kan *al* devyse', and Chaucer recognizes the strong structural unity of the whole episode and the poetic coherence and fitness of background, narrative and invective.

The next thing the Monk says is that Dante 'kan al devyse /

Fro point to point', that is, in detail and from beginning to end. One's mind turns immediately to the Narrator's words in *Troilus*:[28]

> But now, paraunter, som man wayten wolde
> That every word, or soonde, or look, or cheere
> Of Troilus that I rehercen sholde,
> In al this while unto his lady deere.
> I trowe it were a long thyng for to here;
> Or of what wight that stant in swich disjoynte,
> His wordes alle, or every look, to poynte.
>
> For sothe, I have naught herd it don er this
> In story non, ne no man here, I wene . . .
>
> (III, 491–9)

Dante, then, is doing in the Ugolino episode precisely what the Narrator of *Troilus* had never heard done in any story – he is 'pointing' Ugolino's 'wordes alle' and 'every look', all those iterated, accumulated images of light, space, silence and mouth which dominate in *Inferno*, XXXIII and which Chaucer eliminates from his version, keeping only – and amplifying – those of hunger, grief and tears. But it is Chaucer who 'points' other details, mainly factual ones, that are totally absent in Dante: the location of the Mew, the 'fals suggestioun', the lack of 'mete and drynke', the 'potage', the 'morsel breed'. Nor does Dante's Ugolino tell his story from beginning to end. It is a characteristic of Dante's narratives that they start *in medias res*, and Ugolino's is no exception. He starts his story in the Mew, and only afterwards recounts in an indirect fashion, through his dream, how he was put in prison. Chaucer follows the same pattern (2407–22), but by eliminating the dream, with the temporal distortions this involves in Dante's text (it explains the past and anticipates the future), he establishes a cause–effect connection between two moments of the action and straightens out the narrative sequence (2415–19). He does the same by explaining clearly, before the main development of the tragedy, that Ugolino had no food (2420–2) – a detail notably absent in Dante's treatment.

It would seem, then, that Chaucer's comments on Dante's *dispositio* are at least partly off the mark, or that he is not aware of what takes place in Ugolino's narrative. We can, however, exclude the latter hypothesis, because Chaucer changes precisely those features of the sequence which in Dante's version contrast with his remark, 'fro point to point'. My impression is that Chaucer recognizes the overall fitness, consequentiality and unrepeatable cohesion of Dante's narrative: 'for he kan *al* devyse / Fro point to point'.

This different economy, this narrative omnipotence, this verbal, poetic infallibility, Chaucer acknowledges without hesitating:

> for he kan al devyse
> Fro point to point, *nat o word wol he faille.*

– because, to use Eliot's curiously similar phrase, 'no poet convinces one more completely that the word he has used is the word he wanted, and that no other will do'.[29] When directly confronted by an entire piece of Dantean invention, Chaucer cannot but recognize that Dante is 'the *grete poete* of Ytaille'.[30]

Chaucer, however, never went back on his decision not to follow the great poet of Italy in his journey into the afterlife, a journey made 'per modo tutto fuor del moderno uso'. Whether or not the 'viage' to Canterbury should also be considered 'the wey ... Of thilke glorious pilgrymage / That highte Jerusalem celestial', as the Parson would wish, the fact is that it is a pilgrimage well within 'modern usage'. Chaucer twice uses Bernard's prayer to the Virgin in *Paradiso*, XXXIII, in the Prologues to the *Prioress' Tale* and the *Second Nun's Tale*. The *Invocacio ad Mariam* was appropriate at the outset of two pious legends told by two women of religion, and Dante provided a beautifully elaborate *elogium* and *supplicatio*. It is interesting, then, to notice that the Prioress seems to paraphrase Dante in much the same way as Geoffrey in the *House of Fame*. At the end of her *Invocacio*, she declares that her 'konnyng is so wayk' that, in order to celebrate Mary's power, she has to pray her to 'guide' her 'song'. In her humility and inexpressibility formula, the Prioress inserts a phrase curiously reminiscent of one of Dante's tercets in that very Canto XXXIII of *Paradiso* from which Chaucer had drawn in the preceding stanza:

> But as a child of twelf month oold, or lesse,
> That kan unnethes any word expresse,
> Right so fare I ...
>
> (484–6)

> Omai sarà più corta mia favella,
>   pur a quel ch'io ricordo, che d'un fante
>   che bagni ancor la lingua alla mammella.
>
> (106–8)

(Now my speech shall fall shorter, even of what I can remember, than an infant's who still bathes his tongue at the breast.)

Immediately afterwards, though, Dante goes on to describe nothing less than the Trinity, whilst the Prioress tells her story of the little child martyr.

We are, then, back at the beginning of our search: Chaucer is aware of Dante as the supreme poet of Heaven and Hell and knows he cannot follow his path. He had one opportunity to become himself such a poet when, in the *Parson's Tale*, he described at some length the 'horrible peynes of helle', which ought to move a man to contrition (157–230), and, much more shortly, the 'endelees blisse of hevene', which is 'the fruyt of penaunce' (1076–80), at the very end of the Parson's and of all the *Canterbury Tales*. The Parson's concern, however, is not with fable or poetry but with 'sentence' alone. Decorum would forbid Chaucer to make the *Parson's Tale* a vehicle for Dantean verse.

Notes

1 Assuming, of course, that the *Fiore* was written by Dante. And see G. Contini, 'La questione del Fiore', *Cultura e Scuola*, XIII–XIV (1965), 768–73; s.v. 'Fiore' in *Enciclopedia Dantesca*, vol. II (Rome, 1970), pp. 895–901; 'Un nodo della cultura medievale: la serie *Roman de la Rose* – *Fiore* – *Divina Commedia*' now in *Un'Idea di Dante* (Turin, 1976), pp. 245–83.

2 G. Contini in the Introduction to his Dante Alighieri, *Rime* (Turin, 1965 edn.), p. x.

3 P. V. Mengaldo in the Introduction to his edition of *De Vulgari Eloquentia* (Padua, 1968), p. viii, expresses much more clearly the ideas I am paraphrasing here.

4 H. Schless, 'Transformations: Chaucer's Use of Italian' in D. S. Brewer (ed.), *Geoffrey Chaucer*, Writers and Their Background (London, 1974), p. 218. As the present volume goes to press, Pilgrim Books (Norman, Oklahoma) announce the publication in 1983 of H. Schless, *Dante and Chaucer*, which I have not been able to consult.

5 Schless, 'Transformations', p. 220. Schless refers to T. H. Spencer, 'The Story of Ugolino in Dante and Chaucer', *Speculum*, IX (1934), 295–301; but M. Praz's essay 'Chaucer and the Great Italian Writers of the Trecento' appeared in *The Monthly Criterion* in 1927.

6 *Pace* Schless, 'Chaucer and Dante' in D. Bethurum (ed.), *Critical Approaches to Medieval Literature: Papers from the English Institute* (New York–London, 1960), pp. 134–54.

7 Needless to say, the type of Eliot's 'imitation' of Dante is different from Chaucer's. Chaucer did not use lines or passages in Dante 'in the attempt to reproduce, or rather to arouse in the reader's mind the memory, of some Dantesque scene, and thus establish a relationship between the medieval inferno and modern life'. Chaucer's imitation of Dante was thoroughly medieval, but it was, nevertheless, 'imitation' as contrasted to what Eliot meant by 'important debt to Dante'.

8 T. S. Eliot, 'What Dante Means to Me', in *To Criticize the Critic* (New York, 1965), p. 132. The quotation in n. 7 above comes from p. 128 of the same essay.

9 On these aspects see J. A. W. Bennett, *Chaucer's Book of Fame* (Oxford, 1968), chapter 2; and my *English Medieval Narrative in the Thirteenth and Fourteenth Centuries* (Cambridge, 1982), chapter 6, 1.

10 This argument has been developed, though with a different emphasis, by M. Praz (now in *The Flaming Heart* (New York, 1973 edn.), pp. 52–4), to whom I am

indebted for some of the ideas here and in my later paragraphs on the *Legend* and the *Knight's Tale* in this section.

11 G. Padoan, s.v. 'Apollo' in *Enciclopedia Dantesca* (Rome, 1970), vol. I, p. 318; and s.v. 'Minerva' in *Enciclopedia Dantesca*, vol. III (Rome, 1971), p. 959; also G. Stabile, 'Navigazione celeste e simbolismo lunare in "Paradiso" II', *Studi Medievali*, 3rd series, XXI, 1 (June 1980), 97–140.

12 G. Padoan, 'La "mirabile visione" di Dante e l'Epistola a Cangrande', now in *Il pio Enea, l'empio Ulisse* (Ravenna, 1977), pp. 30–63, maintains that Dante thought of his poem as the record of a 'true' and 'real' vision.

13 Moreover, in *Anelida*, 8 Chaucer translates Dante's 'mente' from *Par.*, I, 11 (conflating Boccaccio's 'voglia' from *Teseida*, I, 2, 1) as 'mynde'.

14 Padoan, s.v. 'Apollo'. In Alain de Lille's *Anticlaudianus*, which Chaucer mentions in the *House of Fame*, II, 986, the invocation before the description of Heaven in Book V has 'Celesti Muse *terrenus* cedet Apollo, Musa Ioui...' ('Earthly Apollo gives way to the heavenly Muse, the Muse to Jove'). The concept is the same as Dante's, but expressed by exactly opposite names. Both Dante and Chaucer could find Minerva as 'wisdom' invoked by Bernardus Silvestris at the beginning of his *Cosmographia* (I, 5–6), which Chaucer certainly knew (see *Man of Law's Tale*, 190–203), and Pallas invoked as 'rerum sapientia' by Martianus Capella (whom Chaucer mentions in *House of Fame*, II, 985), *De Nuptiis*, VI, 567ff (Teubner: Stuttgart, 1969, p. 285, 6ff). See also Boccaccio's *Genealogie*, V, iii, and II, ii.

15 Whether Chaucer knew that Albertino Mussato had been crowned (with ivy and myrtle) – the first poet since antiquity – on 3 December 1315, while Dante was still alive and probably musing on it (see Padoan, 'Dante di fronte all'umanesimo letterario', now in *Il pio Enea, l'empio Ulisse*, pp. 7–29 and particularly pp. 20–2) we shall never know.

16 Dante's Limbo is in many ways an ancestor of Boccaccio's picture of Glory's followers in the *Amorosa Visione* and of Petrarch's Triumph of Fame as well as of Chaucer's House. Ovid, Homer, Lucan, Virgil, Aeneas, Caesar and Orpheus appear both in Dante and Chaucer. Dante includes many other characters absent in Chaucer – Trojan and Roman heroes and heroines, Greek and Roman philosophers and scientists, Avicenna and Averroes. In answering Statius in *Purg.*, XXII, 100–14, Virgil adds further Greek and Roman poets (and heroines out of Statius' own works) and declares that their souls dwell in Limbo. With another significant Dantean reminiscence (cf. *Inf.*, III, 55–7), Chaucer describes the 'congregacioun of folk', that fills the House of Rumour (2038–40). Eliot was to use the same passage in *The Waste Land* (I, 62–3):

> ...so many,
> I had not thought death had undone so many

17 And whom, as J. A. W. Bennett has shown in his essay above, he imitates in speaking of Virgil at the beginning of the *Legend of Dido* (924–6). Another reminiscence is perhaps later, at the beginning of the *Legend of Ariadne* in Chaucer's address to the 'juge infernal, Mynos, of Crete kyng': cf. *Inf.*, V, 4ff (where Dante adapts and enlarges on *Aeneid*, VI, 432–3 and *Thebaid*, IV, 530), and Boccaccio's *Genealogie*, XI, xxvi. Another Dantean echo can be found in the Prologue F 285–9, where *Inf.*, III, 55–7 is recalled (see Praz, *Flaming Heart*, p. 31), a passage Eliot paraphrases in the *Waste Land*, I, 62–3 (and see 'What Dante Means to Me', p. 128). Are Love's words to Chaucer in the Prologue F 552–3 (absent in G), 'But er I goo, thus muche I wol the telle: / Ne shal no trewe lover come in helle' a deliberate counterpoint on *Inferno*, V, where, among the 'peccator carnali', Dante finds Cleopatra and Dido, whose stories Chaucer recounts in the *Legend*? The women of the *Legend* are 'goode wommen alle, / And trewe of love'.

18 For all this see my *English Medieval Narrative*, chapter 6, 2.

19 'Multiplicity of styles' is but a pale translation of G. Contini's 'plurilinguismo'.

See his 'Preliminari sulla lingua del Petrarca', now in *Varianti e altra linguistica* (Turin, 1970), pp. 169–92.

20 See Book I of Dante's *Convivio*, completely devoted to the defence of Italian. J. L. Lowes maintained ('Chaucer and Dante', *Modern Philology*, XIV (1917), 734–5) that *Troilus*, II, 22–5 was inspired by *Convivio*, I, v, 55–66 and II, xiv, 83–9, with the addition of Horace's *Ars Poetica*, 70–1. That Chaucer knew at least Book IV of the *Convivio* is certain. In *Troilus*, III, 5, Chaucer translates with 'in gentil hertes ay redy to repaire' a famous line of Guinizelli that Dante quotes in *Convivio*, IV, xx, 7.

21 See Padoan, 'Dante di fronte all'umanesimo letterario', pp. 17–18.

22 And see Praz, *Flaming Heart*, pp. 76–8.

23 Schless writes that for him 'the fact that Chaucer never made use of the Francesca story from *Inferno*, V is one of the most striking problems of the Chaucer–Dante relationship' ('Transformations', p. 220, n. 1). The only place where Chaucer could have accommodated a story of that length would have been the *Monk's Tale*, but the story of Paolo and Francesca could in no way be forced into the Fortune scheme of that Tale. The 'women' of the *Legend* are all classical characters. And furthermore, Chaucer deals with the theme of tragic love in *Troilus*.

24 For a close and illuminating study of the correspondences between *Parliament*, 169–210 and *Purgatorio*, XXVIII, see J. A. W. Bennett, *The Parlement of Foules. An Interpretation* (Oxford, 1957), pp. 76–8.

25 J. L. Lowes, 'Chaucer and Dante's *Convivio*', *Modern Philology*, XIII (1915–16), 19–33; and 'Chaucer and Dante' (see n. 20).

26 'What Dante Means to Me', pp. 128 and 129.

27 For Schless, Spencer and Praz see references in nn. 4 and 5 above. Praz's discussion of Ugolino was summarized later in *The Flaming Heart*, pp. 55–6. My article, 'The Monk's Tale: Dante and Boccaccio', appeared in *Medium Aevum*, XLV (1976), 50–69. See also my 'Lectura' on *Inferno*, XXXIII in *Cambridge Readings in Dante's 'Comedy'*, ed. Kenelm Foster and Patrick Boyde (Cambridge, 1981), and 'Ugolino e la Narrativa', *Studi Danteschi*, LIII (1981), 31–52.

28 On which see J. A. Burrow, *Ricardian Poetry* (London, 1971), pp. 69–78.

29 'What Dante Means to Me', p. 129.

30 'Grete poete' is also Lucan, and 'gret' is Homer (*House of Fame*, III, 1499 and 1466). Virgil is a 'lanterne' (*Legend*, 926), Ovid is 'noble' (*Merchant's Tale*, 2125), Petrarch 'lauriat' (Prologue to the *Clerk's Tale*, 31).

Chaucer and Boccaccio's Early Writings

Some time after September 1368, four years before making his first visit to Italy, Chaucer composed the Book of the Duchess for John of Gaunt. Within conventional bounds associated with the French dits amoreux, a poetic tradition that had developed from Guillaume de Lorris to Guillaume de Machaut, Chaucer offers his patron comfort for the loss of his wife. The assurance with which Chaucer brings the standards and procedures of French courtly verse into English is quite remarkable; the poetic texture of the Duchess is, understandably, somewhat uneven. At certain moments Chaucer is brilliantly success-ful in transposing the finest qualities of French courtly diction into English; other moments give rise to a language more strongly reminiscent of popular native romance, what C. S. Lewis has termed 'the old, bad manner'.[1] But even if his language occasionally fails him, Chaucer is continuously supported by the excellence of his narrative and dramatic structure: in creating a poetic dream-world in which the noble patron is seen to bring comfort and consolation to himself, Chaucer both imitates and improves upon the example of Machaut.[2] The Duchess eloquently suggests that during the years preceding its composition – years in which Machaut's great admirer and imitator, Froissart, was resident at the English Court – Chaucer was a diligent and sensitive student of French verse.

In the House of Fame, Chaucer's second dream-poem, Machaut yields to Dante as the English poet's chief mentor. This is not to say that the discovery of Dante rendered Machaut and his French forebears obsolete for Chaucer, or even that it pushed them into the background. The old theoretical division of Chaucer's career into French, Italian and English periods is now generally discredited: Chaucer was willing to learn and borrow cumulatively from all good authors throughout his career; his 'English period' begins with his first poem.[3] And the great Italian authors cannot be seen as standing aloof from French verse:[4] they inherit richly from the poets of twelfth-century France, and from the Roman de la Rose. The triumph of the Commedia as an extended vernacular narrative was made possible by the precedent of the *Rose* and by the labour of the Italian poets who employed it as a model. It is possible that Dante, if he was the author of *Il Fiore*, participated directly in this assimilative process.[5] He certainly learned much from Italy's first imitator of the *Rose*, Brunetto Latini. Brunetto composed his Italian *Tesoretto* (and his French encyclopedic *Trésor*) while in political exile in France, between 1260 and 1266. Brunetto's poem has obvious corespondences with many of the *dits amoreux* inspired by Guillaume's *Rose*, and points of correspondence with Chaucer's dream-poems, particularly the *House of Fame*. It is not perhaps so surprising that the *Tesoretto* and the Chaucerian dream-poems should have so much in common: both poets stand near the beginnings of their native poetic traditions, attempting to expand their capabilities by employing the French model as a vehicle for their particular sentimental, speculative and scientific interests. Both poets apply themselves to the task armed with a considerable knowledge of Latin literature, in which Boethius and Alanus de Insulis figure prominently, and both are familiar with the theory and practice of the rhetorical arts. Both poets, in employing verse forms resembling Guillaume's octosyllabic couplets, experience evident difficulty with their chosen medium.[6] Both the *Tesoretto* and the *House of Fame* end incomplete, at a point high above the earth, at a moment when the poet–narrator is about to receive illumination from a man of great authority.

The *Tesoretto* exerted considerable influence on Tuscan poets for the remainder of the thirteenth century;[7] and later writers, although they may not have held Brunetto's poem in such high regard, were generally willing to work within the poetic boundaries that it had mapped out. The *Amorosa Visione*, Boccaccio's first Florentine poem, is recognizably a descendant of Brunetto's pioneering effort. Frequently echoing the *Tesoretto*, the *Visione* continues and extends its basic artistic enterprise: French narrative models are adapted to Italian conditions and asked to support considerable didactic and erudite interests. The sheer weight of these interests cripples the effectiveness of Boccaccio's poem; the *Visione* is one of his least successful compositions. Yet it represents a crux both in Boccaccio's development and in the development of Italian verse: looking back to Brunetto's *Tesoretto*, it looks forward to Petrarch's *Trionfi*. Girolamo Claricio, the poem's sixteenth-century editor, clearly regarded the *Visione* as being imitative of Petrarch; he prefaced his 1521 edition with the promise of 'five Triumphs, namely the Triumph of Wisdom, of Fame, of Riches, of Love and of Fortune'.[8] However, it is now accepted that the *Visione* predates the *Trionfi*; not only did it bring Petrarch inspiration, but it also appears to have directed his attention to the *Roman de la Rose*, a work for which he exhibited pronounced distaste.[9] The episodic structure of the *Visione* has parallels with several of the *dits amoreux* that followed the *Rose*; its headstrong, faintly comical narrator and his semi-allegorical guide would not seem much out of place in a Machaut poem. The five 'triumphs' of which Claricio speaks are frescoes, discovered within the confines of a noble castle. The dreamer, goaded on by his didactic guide, observes them with varying degrees of fascination and indifference; he is evidently relieved to pass from the castle to a delightful garden, the *locus amoenus*, where he discovers companies of ladies (some dancing in a ring), Venus and Cupid and, finally, his beloved. The mood and movement of the poem express definite affiliations with French verse.

The *Visione* is overshadowed by the influential presence of a great poet: this poet is not Petrarch but Dante. Brunetto had discovered scholars and writers in the company of Virtue; Boccaccio discovers Dante as the central figure in the 'triumph' of Wisdom, surrounded by the great authors of antiquity.[10] Boccaccio delivers an extensive and emotional tribute to Dante; and his entire poem, in fifty cantos of *terza rima*, reflects his diligent study of the *Commedia*'s design and detail. Placing Dante among the great classical authors is an appropriate compliment, one that Dante was pleased to pay himself.[11] It reminds us that Dante's prescription for vernacular eloquence centred itself upon studious imitation of the *auctores*. Boccaccio follows Dante in bringing the heroes and iconographies of the ancient world into his vernacular verse: but whereas classical matter in the *Commedia* subserves the needs of the narrative, in the *Visione* it threatens to overwhelm it. Each of Boccaccio's five 'triumphs' is illustrated by figures culled from classical texts. Some figures are imaginatively treated, but imaginative movement within the poem is often clogged by their sheer weight of numbers. Boccaccio came to realize that his passion for Latin learning could not be fully accommodated within the confines of vernacular fiction: this realization – perhaps first formed in writing the *Visione* – ensured that the narrative of the *Decameron* could develop without encumbrance. Latin learning was saved for the Latin works.

The *Amorosa Visione* offers parallels with the *House of Fame* both in its general enterprise and in its specific engagements with particular literary models. Chaucer and Boccaccio, working within a dream-vision framework that owes much to French verse, struggle to come to terms with the example of Dante and with their relationship as vernacular poets to the *auctores*. Both poets have derived from Dante a heightened sense of the importance of vernacular eloquence: but this has infected them with qualities of artistic self-consciousness that are quite foreign to Dante. There are moments in the *Commedia* at which Dante draws attention to his specific task as poet. But such moments – for example, the invocations to the muses – are of characteristically brief duration and are perfectly integrated into the fabric of the poem. In Boccaccio's early writings, such moments are made to *stand out*; Dantean examples are habitually imitated, inflated and moved to more obviously prominent contexts. A similarly self-conscious 'poeticizing' process is at work in the *House of Fame*; this process is readily discernible without the aid of the rubrics – 'Proem', 'The Invocation', etc. – with which modern editors draw it to our attention. The *Visione* and the *House of Fame* compel the reader to acknowledge explicitly the poet's role in bridging the gap between form and content. In each of these poems, the protagonist is a *poet–narrator*, a term that could not be applied to the *Commedia's* author.

Chaucer was evidently not quite comfortable in his new role as poet. His 'Invocation' to Apollo in Book III begins as a studied imitation of *Paradiso*, I and ends in humorous self-deflation and with a blunt imperative (1091–109). A similar downhill progress characterizes the *Aeneid* translation in Book I (143–467): such a transformation (or deformation) of Virgil's text provides a wryly ironic commentary on Dante's notion of *translatio*.[12] Irony and ambiguity characterize Chaucer's attitude both towards his poetic identity and towards the chief allegorical figure of his poem, the lady Fame. Whereas Boccaccio's *Gloria* is, particularly for a poet, a thoroughly attractive female figure, Chaucer's Fame is by turns attractive and alarming, noble and grotesque. The English deity might be taken to represent a 'medievalization' of the 'Renaissance' concept of Fame. But, in the sequence of Boccaccio's 'triumphs', Fame is followed by her negative counterpart Fortune, who muddles all the bright promises of her predecessor. In both poems, Fame and Fortune are sister figures.[13]

From its opening canto, the *Visione* reveals close parallels in content and procedure with Chaucer's poem. Many of the figures appearing in Boccaccio's first two 'triumphs' are also celebrated in the *House of Fame*. In both poems, for example, Virgil (1481–5; V, 7–16) and Ovid (1486–92; V, 25–7) are accompanied by

> The grete poete, daun Lucan,
> And on hys shuldres bar up than,
> As high as that y myghte see,
> The fame of Julius and Pompe.
>
> (1499–1502)

A' quai Lucan seguitava, ne' cui
atti parea ch'ancora la battaglia
di Cesare narrasse e di colui,
Magno Pompeo chiamato . . .

(v, 19–22)

(Lucan followed them: it seemed, by his actions, that he was still narrating
the battle between Caesar and the man called Pompey the Great . . .)

It cannot easily be demonstrated that the *House of Fame* consciously
borrows from the *Amorosa Visione*.[14] But it is apparent that at critical
points in their respective careers, Chaucer and Boccaccio were drawing
upon similar literary means in grappling with remarkably similar
problems. To appreciate and account for these similarities more fully,
we must consider Boccaccio's formative years. Boccaccio grew from
boyhood to maturity at Naples.[15] His father moved there in 1327 as
joint representative of the Bardi, a Florentine banking-company.
Boccaccio soon joined him at the Florentine merchant colony at Naples,
only returning to Florence in the winter of 1340–1, when the Bardi
were in grave difficulties. The *Amorosa Visione* was written during the
following year: its multiplicity of interests summarizes Boccaccio's
complex Neapolitan education. Four major works date from Boccaccio's
years at Naples, including the *Filostrato* and *Teseida*, the Italian works
that Chaucer made most use of.

Boccaccio enjoyed Angevin Naples' most brilliant years: the city,
under Robert the Wise, offered what was arguably the richest complex
of social and cultural influences conceivable in medieval Europe.
Literary activity thrived at all levels of society, forming what might
be figured as a pyramid of influences for the young writer. King Robert
stood at the apex of this pyramid: following his return from Avignon
in 1324, he made consistent attempts to encourage Latin learning.
At his invitation, many important scholars visited or took up residence
at Naples. The most distinguished of these, Dionigi di Borgo San
Sepolcro, arrived in 1338. This Augustinian friar, a close friend of
Petrarch, allowed Boccaccio access to important works, some of which
he copied into his first literary scrap-book, the *Zibaldone Laurenziano*.
The fulsome glosses to the *Teseida*, which Boccaccio probably completed after returning to Florence, also testify to the intensification
that his interest in classical learning underwent during his last years at
Naples.

Robert's grandfather Charles, the first of the Neapolitan Angevins,
came to Naples in 1266. Charles was a passionate *littérateur*. He
exchanged *coblas* and set both his own verse and the verse of fellow-
poets to music.[16] He judged *jeux-partis*, and once participated in one

of these poetic duels against Perrin d'Angicourt. Jean de Meun, whom Charles had befriended and patronized while still in France, commended Charles and his adopted city in his continuation of the *Roman de la Rose*.[17] The Mantuan Sordello and other troubadors followed Charles to Naples; Adam de la Halle entered his service there around 1283. French culture consolidated its position under Charles II, who ruled from 1289 to 1309. A good many French texts were copied at Naples during this period, including a number of translations from Latin into French executed for Italian patrons, who were evidently anxious to be included within the ambit of French culture.[18] By the time Robert came to the throne, French culture was firmly implanted at Naples; and although Robert had little time for any vernacular literature, his subjects continued to enjoy French works, particularly romances, during his reign and long after. The French charm of Naples clearly affected Boccaccio: his early writings give women a prominence and sensual emphasis that was unknown at Florence; his concept of the *brigata*, first developed in the *Filocolo*, reflects his familiarity both with French courtly practices and with the writings of Andreas Capellanus; in the same work he even suggests, in a pleasant pastoral fantasy, that he was born in France.[19]

Two Italian vernaculars flourished in early fourteenth-century Naples. The first of these, the more highly developed as a literary instrument, was Tuscan. The *Commedia* enjoyed great popular fortune in the city and was drawn upon for sermons; Graziolo dei Bambagliuoli, one of the earliest commentators on the *Inferno*, arrived at the city in 1334. He was preceded, in 1330, by the poet acclaimed by Dante as the finest Italian love lyricist and praised by Petrarch more highly than any other poet of his generation. This was Cino da Pistoia, who taught law at the Neapolitan Studio while Boccaccio was a student there. Cino appears to have allowed Boccaccio privileged access to certain Dantean texts and to his own verse. But although Tuscan eloquence was powerfully represented at Naples, it did not meet with official approval. This was hardly surprising: the *Commedia* viewed Robert and his forebears in a most unfavourable light; Cino left Naples in high dudgeon after less than two years, wishing perdition on the city and its inhabitants in a tart little *canzone*;[20] and most of the satirical and political verse at Naples was written and performed by Tuscan poets. As an enthusiastic proponent of the Tuscan vernacular, Boccaccio would not have found favour with Robert: indeed, his writings would probably have proved particularly irksome to the Angevin monarch. In a statute dated 15 January 1335, Robert denounced the behaviour of young men, which he saw as absurdly mannered, influenced by some strange new fashion, 'ut in eis sit modus incertus, ritus varius, cultus diversus, et gestus ridicula distorsione spectandus . . .'[21]

He might well have been observing the *Filostrato's* young hero. A document from later in the same year expresses Robert's distaste for the practice and influence of popular verse most directly: it announces prosecution against the notary Jacobello Fusco, who had been courting a certain Neapolitan wife by standing under her window, 'cantando et cantari faciendo matinatas, et fidem conjugalem sollicitabat'.[22] The king proposes to act rigidly, 'per exemplum ceteri discant' ('so that others might learn by example'). The *Filostrato* and *Teseida*, with their manifold affinities to the popular compositions that Robert condemns, could hardly have met with official favour at the Angevin Court.

The second Italian vernacular at Naples, forming the broad popular base of our literary pyramid, was Neapolitan. Popular forms enjoyed a continuous development, multiplying in a stream of *cantilene, strambotti, mattinate, villanelle, canzonette*, religious songs and versions of French *fabliau*.[23] Boccaccio owed much to this teeming literary undercurrent, which he acknowledged in his *Epistola Napoletana*, a splendid piece of self-satire in the local dialect.[24] This was composed after Boccaccio had abandoned his apprenticeship as a merchant in favour of studying canon law. Although Boccaccio climbed steadily towards the Latin heights of Neapolitan culture during his later years in the city, he clearly did not renounce his affection for its humbler levels of activity.

Boccaccio's first major composition, the *Caccia di Diana*, gives early notice of his ability to absorb and transform a remarkable multiplicity of influences. In presenting a conflict between allegiances to Diana and to Venus, the *Caccia* echoes a long Latin tradition of literary debate; it also reveals points of correspondence with French *jeux-partis*. The poem, in eighteen cantos of *terza rima*, owes much to Dante and something to the *Cacce*, a popular, flexible Italian genre of uncertain origin which, in various verse forms, presents scenes of fighting, fishing and hunting. Written in the early 1330s, the *Caccia* parallels a number of closely contemporary French hunting-poems, such as Jehan Acart de Hesdin's *Prise amoreuse* and (especially) Raimon Vidal's *Chasse aux médisants*.[25] Of all Chaucer's works, the *Caccia di Diana* most resembles the *Book of the Duchess*: in each poem, scenes of hunting – passively observed by a love-struck narrator – serve as prelude to the impressive emergence of the poem's chief character.

Fundamentally, the complexes of Latin, French and native influences that help shape Chaucer's writings and Boccaccio's early writings are not dissimilar. The artistic enterprise of these writings presents some remarkable parallels. The variety of social experience that they reflect is comparatively broad: but the social sensibilities that they express are radically different. Whereas Chaucer penetrates the aristocratic circle and is able to comprehend and represent its values, Boccaccio is always an outsider: for him, it remains a realm of pure fantasy. Chaucer composed his first long piece to please an aristocratic patron, whose surrogate, the Black Knight, dominates the poem. Boccaccio wrote his first long poem to please himself: in its final canto, he himself emerges most forcefully as the poem's protagonist. Although the *Caccia* features a host of noble names, it cannot be regarded as a Court poem;[26] nor can any of Boccaccio's other Neapolitan works.

The *Filocolo*, the prose opus of high artistic pretensions and monumental length that stands at the centre of Boccaccio's Neapolitan period, offers more illuminating parallels with Chaucer's large-scale artistic designs than any other Italian work. It sees Boccaccio experimenting with the tension between lyric and narrative components, meditating on the relationship of the modern author to his classical forebears and (a parallel concern) on the relationship of Christendom to the ancient, pagan world. The task it initially proposes for itself – to restore an ancient legend to its former dignity by the exercise of *parole ornate*, 'embellished words' – is unfolded in the opening chapter. Boccaccio tells how he was smitten with love for Maria, natural daughter of King Robert; he subsequently discovers her in a convent church near Naples, engaged in playful and lively conversation with several of the nuns. He and his companion (or companions: 'alcuno compagno') are cordially received into this group and its conversation. Passing from topic to topic, they finally come to speak of Florio and of his love for Biancifiore. Boccaccio's lady laments the fact that 'the fame of the lovers has not been exalted by the verses of any poet, but left to the undiscriminating utterances of the ignorant'. Turning to Boccaccio, she requests him – by the love he bears her – to compose a little book, employing the vernacular ('un picciolo libretto volgarmente parlando'). As Boccaccio makes a gracious speech of acceptance, it is clear that his narration of the 'Fleur et Blanchefleur' legend is to be seen as issuing from the activity of a convivial gathering, a *brigata*, in which he is specifically identified as poet.

In opening his *Canterbury Tales*, Chaucer early establishes his poetic credentials by the sustained brilliance of his General Prologue's opening period. Having set his scene with such dazzling precision, he describes his own appearance on it with studied casualness:

> Bifil that in that seson on a day ...
>
> (I, 18)

This compares with the way in which Boccaccio first brings himself into the *Filocolo*'s action:

Avvenne che un giorno ... (I, i, 17).

(It happened that one day ...)

This formula is repeated as Boccaccio describes how he came to join the *brigata*, emphasizing the chance nature of this encounter:

... avvenne che un giorno, non so come, la fortuna mi balestrò in un santo tempio (I, i, 23).

(... it happened that one day, I don't know how, fortune propelled me into a holy temple.)

The Chaucerian equivalent of a *brigata* is a 'compaignye'; the meeting of the pilgrims in 'The Tabard' is similarly fortuitous:

> ... a compaignye,
> Of sondry folk, by aventure yfalle
> In felaweshipe ...
>
> (I, 24–6)

It might seem improbable to compare 'The Tabard' with the 'holy temple' in which Boccaccio finds himself: but both are convivial places in which religious and secular motivations are subtly combined; both gatherings have a holiday atmosphere about them; and both scenes see a mixture of the three social estates.[27]

Like Boccaccio, Chaucer tells how he was received into this social group; as in the Italian work, the social bond is sealed by conversation (I, 30–2). He goes on to tell how his opus, the *Canterbury Tales*, is called into being by the figure that the 'compaignye' is to recognize as its 'governour' (813) for the duration of its existence. The tales are to be told by the various members of the company; Chaucer draws attention to his specific responsibility as poet–reporter (I, 725–46). His pilgrimage then gets under way.

Boccaccio begins his story-telling with an account of a pilgrimage, that of Quinto Lelio Africano and his wife to Compostella. Like the Canterbury pilgrimage, this is undertaken as an act of thanksgiving. Lelio and his knights perish at the hands of the Saracens, but his wife survives to give birth to Biancifiore, who is successively the object of Florio's amatory pilgrimage and then his partner in completing the Christian pilgrimage with which the story opened.

The pilgrimage framework allows both Chaucer and Boccaccio

a generous range of imaginative movement and emphasis. Their travellers are (more or less) mindful that their journeying has a serious end in prospect: but considerable pleasure lies in the travelling, much of it through story-telling. Given this constant assurance that their pilgrims are moving, moment by moment, towards a religious goal, Chaucer and Boccaccio are able to exercise their skills as secular poets with considerable freedom. Yet they evidently did not assume that the pilgrimage context could provide unqualified license for their pleasure-giving activities. In the course of their pilgrimage, the two poets exploit every colour of rhetoric and trick of art at their disposal; approaching its termination, they lay aside all this to point us towards a further journey,

> thilke parfit glorious pilgrymage
> That highte Jerusalem celestial.
>
> (X, 50–1)

Both poets elect to round off their opus with a sermon in plain prose based on the seven deadly sins. Renunciation is the theme both of the *Parson's Tale* and of the deathbed sermon of Florio's father, King Felice (v, xcii, 4–24). Renunciation is expressed in the form as well as in the content of each discourse: the fluid and leisurely style of the earlier writing, characteristically coloured by extravagant astrological references and instances from the pagan world, yields to a drab, monotonous discourse that concentrates solely and systematically on the *unum necessarium* of Christian salvation. The brittle shell of *parole ornate* falls away, revealing the hard kernel of Christian truth that (the poets might argue) has been the essence of their discourse all along.[28] *Troilus and Criseyde* effects an analogous transition: starting out in the service of secular love, Chaucer ends as a servant of religious orthodoxy, claiming his opus to be consistent with Christian doctrine.

In the *Filocolo's* final chapter, Boccaccio presents us with a revised evaluation of his writing: it translates the 'true testimony' of Ilario, the priest who received Florio and company into the Christian religion (v, xcvii, 10). In *Troilus and Criseyde*, Chaucer also purports to be following the account of an ancient author, one 'Lollius'. Both Ilario and Lollius are (almost certainly) imaginary; their supposed existence allows each poet to take up a particular authorial posture: by affirming that his work incorporates the historical witness of an *auctor*, each suggests that his modern vernacular narrative is supported by a back-bone of ancient authority. Elsewhere in his final chapter, Boccaccio elaborates on this image of himself as engaged in *translatio*. He tentatively aligns his work with that of Virgil, Lucan, Statius, Ovid and Dante (v, xcvii, 4–6). Such an alignment associates the *Filocolo* with two of its most illustrious predecessors as extended vernacular narratives, the *Roman de la Rose* and the *Commedia*. Jean de Meun and Dante also accord themselves sixth place in a line of six writers, a line that stretches from pagan antiquity to the Christian present.[29] And Chaucer, towards the end of *Troilus*, was to offer a comparable estimate of his poetic achievement. The five poets commemorated by Chaucer are those who had been (quite literally) put on pedestals in the *House of Fame*.[30] In his earlier poem, Chaucer could only eye these great *auctores* in passing: by the end of *Troilus*, he senses that he has achieved enough to associate himself tentatively with them:

> Go, litel bok, go, litel myn tragedye ...
> And kis the steppes, where as thow seest pace
> Virgile, Ovide, Omer, Lucan, and Stace.
> (v, 1786; 1791–2)

Like Jean, Dante and Boccaccio before him, Chaucer takes sixth place in a series of six poets, completing a poetic fraternity that conjoins the pagan past and the Christian present. All four vernacular authors give differing expression to this common awareness of poetic continuity. However, certain features of the *Troilus* stanza place it closer to the *Filocolo* passage than to any of the others: its positioning at the end of the work; its form as a *congedo* or *envoy* addressed by the author to his opus; and the modesty of its appeal, which urges the work to recognize its own limitations. Its first line recalls the opening phrase of Boccaccio's final chapter, 'O piccolo mio libretto' ('O, my little book'); and Boccaccio's willing deference to the 'wisest of men', who may wish to amend the work in the light of 'their clear judgement' (v, xcvii, 8), is paralleled by Chaucer's deference to 'moral Gower' and 'philosophical Strode' (v, 1856–9).

The *Commedia* and the *Rose* exert a particularly important influence on Book IV of the *Filocolo*, the part of the work that Chaucer apparently made most use of. The first part of Book IV centres on the activities of a *brigata* that debates 'questions of love' (*questioni d'amore*) in a garden near Naples: the source most active here is the *Commedia*, particularly those cantos of the *Purgatorio* describing the Earthly Paradise. The second half of the Book tells how Florio penetrates the tower at Alexandria in which Biancifiore is imprisoned, and how he consummates his love: the dominant influence here is the *Rose*. It is in *Filocolo*, IV that Boccaccio amplifies and extends the scope of his source-story most decisively. In all other versions of the legend, the fact of Florio's conversion from paganism is mentioned only in passing and is of little significance to the narrative: in the *Filocolo* it assumes central importance. Honest perseverance and fidelity in love are presented as the noblest capabilities of the pagan world; and as the love of Florio and Biancifiore approaches fulfilment, it seems that such qualities might be premonitive of higher, Christian experience.

In *Filocolo*, IV, ix, 3, Florio and company are washed up at Naples, having sojourned briefly at Certaldo[31] and then survived a tempest; in all this, Florio's teacher Ascalion plays the guiding and assuring role of Dante's Virgil. At Naples, Florio impatiently awaits the arrival of spring; this comes with a splendid flourish of *parole ornate*, which, in its syntactic complexity, its employment of astrological imagery, its celebration of natural regeneration, its emphasis that such a time is propitious for pilgrimage and its final recognition of the local facts of the narrative action invites comparison with the opening period of the *Canterbury Tales*:

Ma essendo già Titan ricevuto nelle braccia di Castore e di Polluce, e la terra rivestita d'ornatissimi vestimenti, e ogni ramo nascoso dalle sue frondi, e gli uccelli, stati taciti nel noioso tempo, con dolci note riverberavano l'aere, e il cielo, che già ridendo a Filocolo il disiderato cammino promettea con ferma fede, avvenne che Filocolo una mattina, pieno di malinconia e tutto turbato nel viso, si levò dal notturno riposo (IV, xii, 1).

(But Titan being already received into the arms of Castor and of Pollux, and the earth reclothed in the most ornate clothes, and every bough hidden by its leaves; (and the birds – having been silent during the vexatious season – were making the air reverberate with sweet notes, and the sky (now laughing) was promising Filocolo in good faith the longed-for passage); it happened one morning that Filocolo, full of melancholy and with a thoroughly perturbed expression, arose from his nightly repose.[32])

The melancholy felt by Florio on account of his dream[33] is dispersed by sounds of singing and rejoicing. These issue from a garden, which contains a *brigata* of Neapolitan nobles. Florio and company are persuaded to join them; Ascalion is prevailed upon to choose a sovereign to govern the *brigata*. He chooses Fiammetta and crowns her with laurel as one 'full of grace' ('d'ogni grazia piena': IV, xviii, 2). This authoritative female figure is, in a differing symbolic guise, the king's daughter who has called the *Filocolo* into being (IV, xvi, 4–5). Like the *brigata* of the work's opening chapter, this gathering brings together worldly and religious motivations; it is Maria (alias Fiammetta) who holds the balance between them. Boccaccio concentrates attention upon her complex symbolic significance in an episode that forms – structurally, thematically and dramatically – the centrepiece of the *Filocolo's* garden parliament. The Neapolitan nobleman

Caleon, when asked to continue the sequence of *questioni* in the aristocratic circle, fails to respond because he is absorbed in contemplating the beauty of Fiammetta. He notices how light reflected from a fountain strikes her face, bathing the whole company in a roseate glow (IV, xliii, 1–2). He sings a *ballata* in praise of her beauty, in which Love (Amore) speaks as a spirit that has descended from the Third Heaven:

> Io son del terzo ciel cosa gentile . . . (IV, xliii, 10).

(I am a noble being from the third heaven . . .)

The Third Heaven is, in Dante's cosmology, that of Venus, a deity that was particularly important for Boccaccio in bringing together religious and worldly *mores*.[34] Caleon alerts the company to the way in which Fiammetta's eyes sparkle like morning stars ('come matutine stelle'), illuminating the whole gathering. Florio and his companions, turning their eyes on the queen, 'saw that which, to hear speak of, had seemed impossible to them' (IV, xliii, 15). On arriving at the garden, Florio had identified himself as a 'poor pilgrim of love': but this manifestation of love amazes him, passing beyond the bounds of his previous experience. In gazing upon the splendour ('splendore': IV, xliii, 2) of Fiammetta's countenance, Florio is seeing the reflection of divine truth. When Dante meets the eyes of Beatrice in *Purgatorio*, XXXI, he exclaims at the 'isplendor di viva luce etterna' (139) that is unveiled to him. The term 'splendore' is generally used by Dante for reflected light, particularly in describing 'that light which God is'.[35]

In the subsequent debate between Fiammetta and Caleon, Florio learns something of the relationship between the love that he has pursued and the love that Fiametta reflects. Caleon advances the claims of 'love for pleasure' ('amore per diletto'), clearly believing the forces of pre-Christian literature to be aligned with his cause: he employs a battery of classical *exempla* in demonstrating the power of Amore and claims that the 'holy verses' ('santi versi') of Ovid were written in this god's service (IV, xlv, 3–8). Fiammetta insists upon the absolute superiority of 'honest love' ('amore onesto') by which 'we merit becoming eternal possessors of the heavenly kingdoms' (IV, xliv, 5).

It is generally accepted that the fourth narrative in the *Filocolo*'s *questioni d'amore* sequence furnished the source of the *Franklin's Tale*.[36] The context in which Chaucer discovered this narrative also has an important bearing on our appreciation of Chaucer's Tale. Boccaccio's story forms part of the deliberations of a *brigata* that has brought together Christians and pagans sharing an interest in Love.

The world of this *brigata*, like that of Chaucer's Tale, is curiously suspended between Christian and pagan terms of reference. Its central episode gives rise to a debate concerning the relative merits of 'love for pleasure' and 'honest love', a debate that is absorbed into the dramatic action of the *Franklin's Tale*.

Several of the *Filocolo* story's broadest thematic oppositions survive within Chaucer's Tale: contrasts between the seasons of January and May, and between the *loci* of garden and temple, are fundamental to the structure of both narratives. Each writer skilfully adapts an Ovidian *exemplum* in comparing changes in the physical world – the gradual erosion of stone – with gradual changes in the human intelligence. In presenting scenes of magical transformation, both writers stress the importance of lunar motion, although their narratives develop in different directions from this common point of departure. The divergences here, in the common attempt to create a suggestively magical atmosphere, are characteristic: Boccaccio offers a lengthy and exotic *imitatio* of a *Metamorphoses* passage, whereas Chaucer (author of *A Treatise on the Astrolabe*) dazzles with a virtuoso display of technical vocabulary. The most radical differences between the two narratives stem from Chaucer's decision to bring his female protagonist to prominence. The brilliant stroke of connecting Dorigen's anxiety about her husband with the task she sets her aspiring lover brings an extra dimension of psychological complexity to Chaucer's Tale: in the *Filocolo*, the wife's request is nothing more than a piece of subtle malice, a 'sottile malizia'. Dorigen's large speculations on the nature of divine will lead us away from the more straightforward concerns of the *Filocolo* story and still further from the interests of the *Decameron* analogue. But such speculations, we should note, form an essential part of the Book in which the *Filocolo* story is contained. The question with which Chaucer's Franklin concludes his Tale ('Which was the mooste fre, as thynketh yow?') expects no answer, but it does recognize the story's origin as a *questione d'amore*.

The *brigata*'s central debate – between 'honest love' and 'love for pleasure' – continues within the mind of Florio at Alexandria. Having penetrated the tower, Florio creeps between the arms of his beloved while she is sleeping. He explores her inert body and takes pleasure ('diletto') in a manner reminiscent of the ultimate erotic exploration in the *Rose*. Her body remains unresponsive for a worrying length of time (IV, cxviii, 2–7); when Biancifiore finally awakes, the effect is of a metamorphosis marvellously realized, similar in feeling to the climax of the *Rose*'s Pygmalion story. Like Pygmalion, Florio is anxious to declare his honest intentions; he too calls upon

Hymen and Juno in wedding his beloved, arguing that he has not laboured so long and hard

'... per acquistare amica, ma per acquistare inseparabile sposa, la quale tu mi sarai. E fermamente, avanti che altro fra noi sia, col tuo medesimo anello ti sposerò, alla qual cosa Imineo e la santa Guinone e Venere, nostra dea, siano presenti' (IV, 120, 3).

('... to acquire a lover, but to acquire an inseparable spouse, which you will be to me. And sincerely, before anything else takes place between us, I will wed you with your own ring; and may Hymen and holy Juno and Venus, our goddess, be present at this.')

Florio and Biancifiore pledge themselves to each other kneeling before a statue of mysterious origin and complex symbolic significance: a sighted Cupid. The pupils in the eyes of this deity (which, we are reminded, is usually depicted as blind) are carbuncles, which keep the room as brightly illuminated as if it were flooded with sunlight (IV, lxxxv, 8). Boccaccio probably realized the dramatic and symbolic possibilities of the mythical, self-luminous gems in reading a celebrated passage of the *Rose* that occurs shortly before the Pygmalion story. This describes the Christian Earthly Paradise, the *biau parc*, which is illuminated by a carbuncle situated at the centre of the 'fountain of life' ('fonteine de vie': 20,491). In a lengthy passage, Jean expatiates upon the beauty and virtue of the stone, which, in his hands, is evidently a Trinitarian symbol: like Boccaccio, he emphasizes its sun-like power to banish darkness (20,526–9), its 'resplendeur', which corresponds to the Italian 'splendore'. In setting his carbuncles in the eyes of Cupid, Boccaccio is again attempting to unite pagan and Christian iconographies within a single figure: he wishes us to regard the union of his lovers as signifying something more than the culmination of *fine amour* and something less than Christian marriage. So it is that Florio's petitions to this Cupid are answered, at his marriage, by the appearance of an unlikely Trinity: Venus (Citerea); Hymen, crowned with olive (the tree that overhangs the 'fountain of life' in the *Rose* and brings forth 'the fruit of salvation'); and Diana, singing 'holy verses'.

Florio's apostrophe has its counterpart in *Troilus and Criseyde* as Troilus – at last united with his beloved – addresses himself to Cupid, Venus (Citherea) and Hymen (III, 1254–60). The employment of 'Charite' as a synonym for Cupid in this stanza ('O Love, O Charite!') both parallels Boccaccio's duplex figure and continues the intertwining of pagan and Christian terms of reference that is a recurring feature of Chaucer's third book, first evident in its opening lines:

O blisful light, of which the bemes clere
Adorneth al the thridde heven faire!

This address to Venus, combining Christian cosmology and classical iconography, is similar in effect to Caleon's song in *Filocolo*, IV, xliii. It is important to recognize that Chaucer and Boccaccio do not seek to fuse or integrate the beliefs and practices of Christian and pagan worlds; nor do they, like Jean de Meun, juxtapose them for an effect that is preponderantly ironic: rather, they seek to explore the uncertain space between them. (It was to further such an exploration, C. S. Lewis suggests, that Chaucer turned to Boethius.[38]) Within such a space, they reveal the high moral integrity of pagan protagonists struggling towards enlightenment. By the end of Book III, Troilus has come to the highest plateau[39] of human happiness conceivable within a pagan world,

> so heigh a place
> That thilke boundes may no blisse pace ...
> (III, 1271–2)

Such a place corresponds to the Italian *paradiso terrestre*: the hero, through his devoted pursuit of love, senses that he has come to the very threshold of revealed truth. The unhappy confusion of the early *Canticus* ('Al sterelees withinne a boot am I': I, 416) is dispersed: God, Troilus proclaims, has willed that Criseyde should be his 'steere' (III, 1290–2). Individual affection appears to mesh with universal order. At this point – that part of the *Troilus* in which Young noted the most numerous correspondences with the *Filocolo*[40] – the positions of Florio and Troilus are directly comparable. But whereas Florio goes on to complete his pilgrimage to truth, Troilus loses both his faith in Criseyde and his faith in God. The falling-off of Troilus moves Chaucer's narrative in a direction opposite to that of the *Rose*, the *Commedia* and the *Filocolo*: their common impetus towards the happy fulfilment of pilgrimage – a movement that the *Troilus* fully complies with in its first three books – is tragically frustrated. Chaucer's awkwardness and discomfiture in his last two books is painfully evident: he is working against the grain of an illustrious tradition.

The *Filocolo* presented Chaucer with a model for his *Troilus* on the grandest scale, demonstrating how a romance of French origin might be transformed and become an extended narrative in the tradition of the *Rose* and the *Commedia*. It demonstrated much else besides: for example, how especial qualities of pathos might be achieved by placing an intensely personal and inwardly-focused *planctus* beneath a mighty superstructure of mythological and astrological reference. Such lessons could not have been learned from the *Filostrato*. Boccaccio's more youthful work, being slender in structure and design, could not achieve the grand effects of the *Filocolo*: nor could it attain to its high moral seriousness. The cheerful sensual abandon with which its protagonists consummate their love contrasts radically with the solemn dignity of the equivalent scenes in the *Filocolo* and *Troilus and Criseyde*.

Guided by C. S. Lewis, English readers have supposed that the *Filostrato* casts off decorums essential to medieval literature as readily as Criseida casts off her shift.[41] The *Filostrato* certainly lacks gravity and artistic maturity: Boccaccio was little more than twenty when he wrote it. His poem may be better appreciated if considered in association with a literary tradition that, if peculiarly Italian, is thoroughly medieval: the *cantare*.

A *cantare* is a stanzaic narrative, composed in *ottava rima* (the verse form of the *Filostrato* and *Teseida*), publicly performed by a street-singer or *canterino*; full of formulaic tags and epithets, it is typically a fast-moving narrative with a strong story-line and little lyric elaboration. It meets a taste for spectacular combats and fantastic adventures, often in exotic settings with women of high sensual beauty and sharp sexual appetite. The authors of the *cantari* made much use of translations from French *lais*, *fabliaux* and romances, often expanding the most lively and engaging parts of the translation. They meet and encourage the fascination of a popular audience with the distant world of aristocratic manners. Of course, their realization of this world bears little relation to actual aristocratic practice, or to its representation in authentic courtly literature. The *canterini* employ the term *cortesia* ('courtesy') with great frequency and little precision: it might be discovered in a noble hero, or in his horse.[42] The *canterino* who attempts to imitate the social and psychological subtlety of the *Chastelaine de Vergi* gets into a terrible mess and is palpably embarrassed by the paucity of narrative action that his poem has to offer.[43] The *cantare* format was, however, adopted by writers of greater abilities: certain members of the *famiglia* of St Catherine of Siena effectively employed it in their apostolic work; one of the four versions of the Ovidian Pyramus and Thisbe legend exhibits considerable erudition.[44]

Although the *Filostrato* is influenced by a generous variety of sources, its fundamental affiliations with the *cantare* are readily apparent. The *Teseida*, heavily buttressed with erudite apparatus, energetically strives to turn itself into an instant vernacular classic: but it remains, at heart, a poem to be classed among the *cantari*.[45]

In spite of its epic pretensions, it fails to achieve the gravity of movement realized by Chaucer's *Knight's Tale*: its protagonists, like *cantare* characters, rush hurriedly from place to place as if transported by magic carpet. In the opening book – which Chaucer cuts almost entirely – the warfare waged between Teseo's men and the Amazon women has farcical qualities reminiscent of many *cantare* (and popular English romance) passages: Teseo mocks his 'sad little soldiers' ('cavalier dolenti') as they are haplessly deluged in pitch, oil and soap.[46] Ipolita, the Amazon commander, seems to be a close relative of the *cantare* warrior Madonna Lionessa.[47] Boccaccio's evocation of the adolescent Emilia, which has been acclaimed as a delightful 'renaissance miniature', is more appropriately to be seen as a perfection of the *cantare* descriptive manner.[48] Chaucer again passes over this passage. Where he does follow the Italian text, he supplants Boccaccio's casual and complacent *cortesia* with his own more urgent and profoundly-meditated 'courtasye'. Teseo, having come across the young knights locked in combat, is at first an admiring spectator: Theseus furiously intervenes, incensed that these knights should fight like wild animals,

> Withouten juge or oother officere,
> As it were in a lystes roially.
>
> (I, 1712–13)

No *cantare* can be firmly dated as being earlier than the *Filostrato*: it has even been suggested that the *Filostrato* originates the genre, although this is most improbable. At any event, when Chaucer first travelled to Italy in 1372 the *cantare* was firmly established in Tuscany: he might well have heard the *canterini*, perhaps at the Piazza San Martino in Florence, which was specially designated for their performances. But even if he had never heard a *cantare* text in performance, he would doubtless have recognized the popular elements in the *Filostrato* and *Teseida*: such elements were fundamental to the English metrical romances; and the language of such romances, we have noted, found a place for itself in Chaucer's earliest verse. It seems, then, that Chaucer's relation to English romance might be equated with that of Boccaccio to Italian *cantare*. Boccaccio later came to hold himself aloof from the *cantari*;[49] Chaucer has nothing good to say about the English romances: but each poet is, nevertheless, fundamentally indebted to his humble native tradition. And, in fact, both poets affectionately recognized their indebtedness. Boccaccio, following the ambitious congestion of the *Amorosa Visione*, wrote a final essay in the *cantare* form; and on this occasion, rather than encumbering it with extraneous erudite matter, he allowed it to realize its innate potential. The *Ninfale Fiesolano* is a *tour de force* of lucid and affective story-telling. Chaucer, within the framework of his great 'comedye', present himself as the narrator of *Sir Thopas*, a splendid parody of the English tail-rhyme romance. Through his adventures into European literature, Chaucer had passed far beyond the capabilities of such native resources; and yet his earliest work suggests that the English romances provided the first foundations of his style. In composing *Sir Thopas* Chaucer was certainly, albeit affectionately, 'biting the hand that fed him'.[50]

Chaucer would have recognized and appreciated Boccaccio's deep devotion to Dante, his conscious emulation of the *auctores*, his intelligent and adventurous use of iconography, his acquaintance with the *Rose*, French romance and the *dits amoreux*; he would have sympathized with Boccaccio's attempt to marry all this with more humble native resources. Chaucer shares Boccaccio's proud awareness of continuing and extending poetic enterprise, an enterprise that brings together Christian and pagan worlds and makes it possible to explore the uncertain space between them. Yet one abiding disparity in the achievement of these two medieval poets must be set against such extensive parallels. Chaucer, although of bourgeois origins, received a courtly education. Boccaccio, however, remained an outsider to the courtly world; his conception of *cortesia* is inevitably impoverished and debased. In Boccaccio's early writings, the popular appropriation of courtly vocabulary – a degenerative process bitterly observed by the aristocratic author of *Il Fiore* – is made absolute.[51] It was perhaps for this reason that Chaucer nowhere acknowledges Boccaccio by name.

Notes

1 C. S. Lewis, *The Allegory of Love* (Oxford, 1936), p. 164. Lewis considers the *Book of the Duchess*, 985–93.

2 In Machaut's *Fonteinne amoreuse*, written in 1360, the poet-narrator overhears a young lord (his patron) deliver a fifty-stanza complaint; having written it down, he later presents the lord with his own poem, meeting his demand for a suitable complaint.

3 See Wolfgang H. Clemen, trans. C. A. M. Sym, *Chaucer's Early Poetry* (London, 1963), p. 2.

4 See Charles Muscatine, *Chaucer and the French Tradition* (Berkeley–Los Angeles, 1957), pp. 5–6.

5 *Il Fiore* is an accomplished translation of the *Rose* in 232 sonnets, executed by a certain 'Ser Durante': see Boitani, 'What Dante Meant to Chaucer', p. 115 and n. 1.

6 The *Tesoretto* consists of couplets of seven-syllable lines, *settenari a rima baciata*. Unlike Jean de Meun, Brunetto and Chaucer experience difficulty in accom-

modating their erudite interests within short couplets. Brunetto complains aloud on several occasions and obviously yearns for the less restrictive medium of prose: see *Tesoretto* in Gianfranco Contini (ed.), *Poeti del Duecento*, vol. II (Milan–Naples, 1960), lines 411–26, 909–14, 1113–24, 2900–2. The experience of writing the *House of Fame* apparently convinced Chaucer of the need to lengthen his line and helped stimulate the experimentations of *Anelida and Arcite*.

7 Contini, *Poeti*, vol. II, p. 172.

8 See V. Branca (ed.), *Amorosa Visione*, p. 541.

9 See G. Billanovich, 'Dalla *Commedia* e dall '*Amorosa Visione* ai *Trionfi*', *Giornale Storico della Letteratura Italiana*, CXXIII (1946), 1–52.

10 *Tesoretto*, 1229–32; *Amorosa Visione*, IV, 7 – VI, 33.

11 See *Inf.*, IV, 70–147.

12 In *De Vulgari Eloquentia* (esp. II, i–v), Dante argues that the title of poet may be legitimately bestowed on vernacular writers, admits that the gulf dividing such writers from the Latin masters is considerable, but proposes that it may be spanned by sedulous imitation of great Latin writing. Vernacular writers may thereby infuse the learnedness of *gramatica* into their own diction.

Chaucer's translation begins as a tolerably close literal rendering, contracts to become a paraphrase, and then concentrates on the romance of Dido and Aeneas. Following a series of Ovidian *exempla*, the paraphrase is summarily concluded. Chaucer makes the claim for poetic originality (311–14) in the middle of Dido's wooden and melodramatic 'compleynt', a piece of writing that recalls the 'old, bad manner' of several passages in the *Book of the Duchess*.

13 Chaucer expressly states that Fame and Fortune are sisters (1546–8); Boccaccio suggests that these figures are closely related by discovering Fortune in a hall ('sala') that, he tells us, closely resembles the hall of Fame that he has just left (XXXI, 4–6). The Boethian and Virgilian texts employed by Chaucer in his description of Fame are drawn upon by Boccaccio for his figure of Fortune.

14 A case was first made out by E. Koeppel in 'Chauceriana', *Anglia*, XIV (1891–2), 233–8, 245–7 and by C. G. Child in 'Chaucer's *House of Fame* and Boccaccio's *Amorosa Visione*', *Modern Language Notes*, X (1895), 379–84, and first opposed by H. M. Cummings in *The Indebtedness of Chaucer's Works to the Italian Works of Boccaccio* (Cincinnati, 1916). In spite of the manifold weaknesses of Cummings' methods, decisively exposed by J. L. Lowes in 'The *Franklyn's Tale*, the *Teseide* and the *Filocolo*', *Modern Philology*, XV (1918), 689–728, his book has exerted a long and misleading influence.

15 On Boccaccio and Naples, see E. G. Léonard, *Boccace et Naples* (Paris, 1944); Vittore Branca, 'Giovanni Boccaccio: Profilo Biografico' in the Mondadori edition of *Tutte le Opere*, vol. I (Milan, 1967); Francesco Sabatini, *Napoli Angioina* (Naples, 1975); Nicholas Havely, *Chaucer's Boccaccio* (Cambridge, 1980), pp. 1–12.

16 Sabatini, *Napoli*, pp. 34–7; Aurelio Roncaglia, 'Per la storia dell'ottava rima', *Cultura Neolatina*, XXV (1965), 10–11.

17 *Le Roman de la Rose*, ed. Félix Lecoy (3 vols., Paris, 1975–9), 6601–734: this passage seems to have inspired the tribute to the Angevin dynasty with which the *Filocolo* opens. See also *Roman*, 18, 697–9.

18 Sabatini, *Napoli*, pp. 38–40.

19 *Filocolo*, V, viii. It is highly unlikely that Boccaccio was born in France.

20 CLXV in M. Marti (ed.), *Poeti del Dolce Stil Nuovo* (Florence, 1969).

21 '...so that they behave unstably, in various ways and diverse manners, adopting visibly absurd poses...' (M. Camera, *Annali delle Due Sicilie* (Naples, 1841–60), vol. II, pp. 411–12).

22 '...singing (and getting others to sing) morning-songs and urging her to break her marriage-vows...' (Camera, *Annali*, vol. II, p. 413).

23 See Antonio Altamura, *La letteratura dell'età angioina* (Naples, 1952), pp. 57ff.

24 *Epistola Napoletana* in N. Bruscoli (ed.), *Giovanni Boccaccio, Opere*, vol. V, Scrittori d'Italia, CLXXXII (Bari, 1940), pp. 157–8.

25 Both poems date from the 1330s. The *Chasse*, like the *Caccia*, features a considerable number of huntresses (with their dogs) who represent contemporary local noblewomen.

26 Boccaccio nowhere displays the discretion required of a Court poet. He names daughters of powerful and distinguished Neapolitan families only to tell us how his own (unnamed) lady outshines them all. The picture of Boccaccio as a 'professional entertainer' at the Court of King Robert developed by Gervase Mathew in *The Court of Richard II* (London–New York, 1968), pp. 1–6, is quite misleading.

27 The mixture of estates in the *Canterbury Tales* is obvious enough; in the *Filocolo's* first *brigata* we have a number of nuns, a king's daughter and a student of canon law (as Boccaccio identifies himself in I, i, 30), with 'alcuno compagno'.

28 This image of the nut and nutshell was a commonplace of medieval commentators: see Giorgio Padoan, 'Teseo "Figura Redemptoris" e il Cristianesimo di Stazio' in *Il pio Enea, l'empio Ulisse* (Ravenna, 1977), pp. 134–5.

29 In the *Roman de la Rose*, the God of Love laments Tibullus, Gallus, Catullus and Ovid (10,477–95), then treats of 'Guillaume de Loriz' who is to begin the *Rose* (10,496–534) and 'Johans Chopinel' who will complete it (10,535–644). Jean de Meun appears to have evolved this meditation on the continuity of poetic enterprise from Ovid, *Amores*, III, ix. Dante meditates similarly in *De Vulgari Eloquentia*, II, vi and in *Inferno*, IV joins Homer, Horace, Ovid, Lucan and Virgil as 'sesto fra cotanto senno' ('sixth among those high intelligences': IV, 102).

30 Claudian was also featured in the *House of Fame*, as a poet associated with Hell: see Boitani, 'What Dante Meant to Chaucer', p. 117

31 This is Boccaccio's *patria*. Boccaccio takes the opportunity to predict his own poetic powers (IV, i, 13) in terms adapted from Dante; he follows the *Rose* in positioning such a prophecy close to the exact midpoint of the work.

32 Florio adopts the alias of 'Filocolo' in III, lxxv, 4–6, offering a fantastic etymological analysis of the word's Greek origin.

33 Florio dreams of a marvellous gathering of some thirty birds (the varieties are individually described: IV, xiii). It may be that in reading this area of the *Filocolo*, Chaucer hit upon the idea of fusing a dream-vision of an assembly of birds with a parliament of courtiers.

34 The *ballata* owes much to Dante. On Venus, see Boccaccio's gloss to *Teseida*, VII, l, ed. Limentani, pp. 462–72.

35 *Purgatorio*, trans. and comment by John D. Sinclair (Oxford, 1971), pp. 414–15.

36 See W. F. Bryan and G. Dempster, *Sources and Analogues of Chaucer's Canterbury Tales* (Chicago, 1941), p. 377.

37 See *Filocolo*, IV, xxxi, 5; *Canterbury Tales*, V, 829–36; and see *Ars Amatoria*, I, 475–6; *Ex Ponto*, IV, 10, 5.

38 *The Discarded Image* (Cambridge, 1964), pp. 45–91.

39 It is intriguing to note that III, 1271 is the central line of the central stanza of Chaucer's poem: see Alastair Fowler, *Triumphal Forms* (Cambridge, 1970), p. 65.

40 Karl Young, *The Origin and Development of the Story of Troilus and Criseyde* (1908; repr. New York, 1968), pp. 139–81; summarized by Robinson, p. 824, note to *Troilus and Criseyde*, III, 512–1190.

41 C. S. Lewis, 'What Chaucer Really Did to *Il Filostrato*', in *Essays and Studies by Members of the English Association*, XVII (1932), 56–75; repr. in R. J. Schoeck and J. Taylor (eds.), *Chaucer Criticism*, vol. II (Notre Dame–London, 1961).

42 See *Febus-el-Forte*, V, 43 in Alberto Limentani, *Dal Roman de Palamedés ai Cantari di Febus-el-Forte* (Bologna, 1962); Boccaccio refers to this *cantare* in *Corbaccio*, ed. P. G. Ricci (Turin, 1977), p. 62. See also *Spagna* in N. Sapegno (ed.), *Poeti Minori del Trecento* (Milan–Naples, 1952), lines 309–24.

43 *La Donna del Vergiù* in Sapegno, *Poeti Minori*, pp. 824–42. Boccaccio refers to this *cantare* in *Decameron*, III, 10.

44 Giorgio Varanini, *Cantari Religiosi Senesi del Trecento* (Bari, 1965); *Cantare di Pirramo e di Tisbe* in Armando Balduino (ed.), *Cantari del Trecento* (Milan, 1970), pp. 131–45.

45 The twelve books of the *Teseida* are numbered among *cantari* concerned with Theban subjects in the *Cantare dei Cantari*, in which a *canterino* boasts of his repertoire. See Pio Rajna, 'Il Cantare dei Cantari e il Serventese del Maestro di tutte l'Arti', in *Zeitschrift für Romanische Philologie*, II (1878), 220–54, 419–37.

46 *Teseida*, I, lii, 61–5. The warfare described here has few epic qualities: it rather suggests the conditions prevailing in a squabble between two medieval Italian towns, and parallels a passage in *Febus-el-Forte* (III, 22). Boccaccio's battle descriptions are, compared with those of Chaucer and the best English romances, remarkably inept.

47 *Madonna Lionessa* in Sapegno, *Poeti Minori*, pp. 882–95. In *Teseida*, I, cxxx, Teseo, gazing upon Ipolita, remembers his rape of Elena: he recalls a past conquest even in conceiving of a future one. This must have struck Chaucer as a gross lapse of 'courtasye'.

48 See Vittore Branca, 'Nostalgie tardogotiche e gusto del fiabesco nella tradizione narrativa dei cantari' in *Studi di varia umanità in onore di Francesco Flora* (Milan, 1963), p. 96.

49 In his *Corbaccio*, which dates from around 1365, Boccaccio satirizes a widow's fondness for *cantare* stories: see Ricci (ed.), p. 62; and see p. 74, where he refers to the *cantare* of Florio and Biancifiore, which was one of the sources of the *Filocolo*.

50 D. S. Brewer, 'The Relationship of Chaucer to the English and European Traditions', in D. S. Brewer (ed.), *Chaucer and Chaucerians* (London, 1966), p. 4.

51 Alberto Limentani (*Teseida*, p. 241) observes that Boccaccio, even where striving to attain the refined values of courtly literature, invests his material with 'una pingue e borghese fiorentinità' ('a flabby and bourgeois Florentine quality').

Chaucer and the *Filostrato*

Hire face, lik of Paradys the ymage,
Was al ychaunged in another kynde.

(IV, 864–5)[1]

I

'Al ychaunged in another kynde . . .' All that is most significant, most
moving and most mysterious about Chaucer's *Troilus* distinguishes it
from the Italian trecento poem from which it springs, Boccaccio's
Il Filostrato.[2] Yet for all that transformation-through-translation by
which Chaucer creates his own *Troilus* out of *Filostrato*, the fourteenth-
centuryEnglish poem would not be as it is without the Italian poem,
nor as essentially English as it is, were it not also in so many places so
Italian.

To look at the *Filostrato* and Chaucer's *Troilus* side by side can
suggest the experience of watching over the English poet's shoulder as
he works. Yet in such a comparison there is often a danger of too much
emphasizing the most striking 'changes', whereas what comes through
more unobtrusively from the Italian also has its own effect in the
whole. In the *Troilus*, its Italian source has in important ways been
taken over and held within the English poem. Many large interpolations and some considerable omissions have been made, and where it
is followed more closely *Filostrato* has been pervasively rephrased and
subject to much rewriting. But however transformed in its overall
structure and overlaid in its detailed texture, the Italian original
nonetheless remains within the *Troilus* at its core. And since the
Filostrato has been so absorbed in the *Troilus* as well as changed,
comparison of the two can locate what is common to both poems, what
is distinctively Chaucer's, and also what is in *Troilus* because it
represents a response to the Italian.

Filostrato was probably written about 1335 when Boccaccio was
in his twenties.[3] It is among Boccaccio's earliest works, from his
Neapolitan period. Some fifty years later in the 1380s in London, the
middle-aged Chaucer, in his mid-forties and well advanced in his
development as a poet, took up the Italian work as the basis for his
own *Troilus*. At different stages in their lives as they were, the Italian
and English poets chose to represent very differently the role of the

poet in their works and his relation to his subject matter. This difference of approach offers a clue to the wider difference of aim and effect between the works. Whether or not it represents any auto-biographical reality, Boccaccio in his Proem presents the author of *Filostrato* (i.e. 'the one overwhelmed by love') as love-sick for his lady, who has left Naples. To convey to her his desolation in her absence and remind her to return, as well as to celebrate their earlier happiness, he decides to make a poem of the old story of Troilus and send it to the lady.[4] The lyrically sensual romance that results is thus presented as a projection of the author's own scarcely-veiled feelings and experience through the character of Troiolo.

No trace of Boccaccio's Proem remains in *Troilus*, and in effect Chaucer has reversed the character of the poet's persona, with implications for the character of the hero and the interpretation of his story. Gone is the poet's experience both in writing and in loving, both in his art and in his subject matter, to be replaced by that familiar Chaucerian narrator–character, the bookish outsider to love – what might be termed the Bumbleninny. Nor is the hero any longer com-parably experienced in parallel with the poet: just as the poet dramatizes his tentativeness, so in *Troilus* the hero becomes innocent and, before the events of the story occur, an outsider to love. These shifts in perspective by Chaucer are bold and radical strokes in the whole process by which the significance of Troilus and Criseyde's experience is changed in translation. But nothing is gained in under-standing what the English poem becomes by depreciating inaccurately what the Italian poem is, for within its own terms the *Filostrato* is a gracefully accomplished work, with a form much better judged to its subject than many of Boccaccio's other early works.

When they are compared, it soon becomes clear that for long stretches *Troilus* follows *Filostrato* so closely that Chaucer must have worked with a copy of the Italian in front of him as he created the draft of his poem:[5] so much of the outline of *Troilus* is in fact the outline of *Filostrato*. The distribution of narrative and dialogue into stanzas is identical in the two poems for substantial stretches: over and over again, the first line of Chaucer's stanzas is very closely rendered from the parallel Italian line, stanza by stanza.[6] In this way, *Filostrato* provides much of the dramatic 'script' of the two romances in terms of what the characters do: when they speak and how they react is still in *Troilus* often built around the model received from *Filostrato*. There is much syntactical closeness in such passages,[7] and also a very real and sustained lexical influence from Italian.[8] Through translation there is also transferred into the English of *Troilus* some of *Filostrato's* way of presenting the experiences and attitudes of the lovers, along with the Italian descriptions of amatory behaviour and of distress, which add their strong colour to *Troilus* and seem to represent (despite all the changes of emphasis and presentation) an unsubmergible legacy of Italian sensibility transferred into English.[9] And this is also very strikingly so at moments where Chaucer echoes Boccaccio, who is himself borrowing from the *cantari*[10] or from the *dolce stil novo*.[11]

Yet although there is this outward closeness of shape for many sequences of stanzas in the two poems – with many opening lines in common – within most stanzas Chaucer can soon be observed to move away from translation in the modern sense of rendering like with like, and will begin to re-express, add and replace in his re-creative and adaptive 'translacioun'. Chaucer himself uses for other purposes within his poem some terms that help towards defining and distinguishing the processes and layers in his translating. There seem to be three broad types of activity: of generally rendering yet re-expressing the original, of working in small additions of phrases and lines, and of larger interpolated passages. When Chaucer is working at the closest level of adopting yet adapting the source stanzas, he seems engaged in a 'paynted proces' (II, 424) of something that suggests the analogy of processes involved in painting or forms of printing and film: he overlays the existing structure with his own tones so that actions, sequences of events, are seen in a different light. But further to this, Chaucer most pervasively works in translation through small added touches and emphases, and it is perhaps to such small insertions that the poem refers when it apologizes for words that have been 'in eched for the beste' (III, 1329). Beyond this again, there are also much larger passages interpolated into the narrative flow of *Filostrato* but without counterpart in the Italian. One such addition (I, 218–66) concludes by self-deprecatingly referring to 'thing collateral' (I, 262), but the term is useful in suggesting how much influential material – important in the ways it alters the implications of Chaucer's account of Troilus and Criseyde – is held in relation to the narrative within the new sequence of the translated text, and thus comments upon the action.

A brief selection of specific instances of Chaucer's translating of *Filostrato* may serve to introduce some of the characteristic emphases that Chaucer's 'translacioun' brings, and represent the patterns of thematic translating that will concern us in the *Troilus*.

When Pandaro is urging Troiolo to forget Criseida he argues: 'And as I have often heard tell, a new passion always drives out the old' (4.49). But for Pandarus this instead becomes:

And ek, as writ Zanzis, that was ful wys,
'The newe love out chaceth ofte the olde' . . .
Swich fir, by proces, shal of kynde colde.

(IV, 414ff)

What is common knowledge, personally felt, by Pandaro in *Filostrato*
becomes a characteristic bookishness and an added concern with
change and development, with time and nature, in *Troilus*.

A little later Pandaro tells Troiolo 'Be brave' ('Sii valoroso': 4.75),
but in 'translation' Pandarus tells Troilus 'Thynk right as a knyght'
(IV, 617), and this is representative of added trends in Chaucer's
translating: his sustained tendency to paint over his source with a
colouring of 'medievalization' and 'ritualization' in terms of added
courtliness, feudalism, religion of love and concern for secrecy within
the lovers' medieval society.

Again, when Criseida faints she asks Troiolo, 'Who is taking me
from you and where am I going?' (4.116), which in *Troilus* becomes:
'O Jove, I deye, and mercy I beseche!' (IV, 1149), and this brief but
re-expressed English exclamation points to several patterns of emphasis
'in-eched' into Chaucer's translating: added classical allusion; added
reference to death. And when Troiolo urges Criseida to elope, her cry
of distressed impatience ('Oh me, – disse Criseida – tu m'uccidi':
4.157) becomes Criseyde's cry:

'O mercy, God, what lif is this?' quod she.
'Allas, ye sle me thus for verray tene!'

(IV, 1604–5)

What in *Filostrato* seems like personal irritation sounds in *Troilus* like
an exclamation on life itself.

In a poem like *Troilus*, created out of a process of response to another
text through adaptation and interpolation, the poem's character may
best be identified at the level at which it is initially created in the
detailed act of translating, for the way *Troilus* grows as a translated
text explains that variousness which distinguishes it from *Filostrato*
and makes it both more profound and more elusive of interpretation.

II

'Thow moost me first transmewen in a ston' (IV, 467) retorts Chaucer's
Troilus to the suggestion that he should change to another lady, and
Chaucer's translation of lines and stanzas from *Filostrato* is marked by
a much more vigorous and defined sense of the processes and developments within the responses of the characters.[12] This is often expressed

with a learnedness quite distinctive in its detailed texture from *Filostrato*, and characterizes the 'second eye' of a translator passing over and elaborating the outline of original narrative. Whereas the love-struck Troiolo simply goes about thinking of Criseida ('di Criseida sempre gia pensando': 1.42), in English this becomes a more distinctively defined process of inward reaction:

> His herte, which that is his brestes ye,
> Was ay on hire ...
>
> (I, 453–4)

Again, whereas all Troiolo feels in his breast is his lady's excellence (1.44), in Troilus this becomes a more curiously-represented inward process:

> N'yn him desir noon other fownes bredde
> But argumentes ...
> That she of him wolde han compassioun ...
>
> (I, 465–7)

What is simply felt ('sentito') in *Filostrato* becomes explored by Chaucer as a development by which desire breeds the offspring ('fownes') of Troilus's self-persuasions. Such an interest in conveying the force of reactions through more specialized or stylized definition is recurrent.

It seems that unusually figurative or specialized language is to be used in *Troilus*, even if it needs to be explained within the poem. When taking over the word 'ambage' from Italian (6.17), Chaucer adopts a term so unfamiliar to his audience that he must spend two further lines glossing what it means (v, 898–9). Again, where Pandaro simply urges Troiolo to keep the affair secret (3.9), Pandarus says:

> Yet eft I the beseche ...
> That privete go with us in this cas
>
> (III, 282–3)

but he must then immediately explain the figure ('That is to seyn, that thow us nevere wreye': III, 284). This is also true of much added classical allusion in *Troilus* which is embodied within its own gloss ('satiry and fawny more and lesse, / That halve goddes ben of wildernesse': IV, 1544–5). The elaborated surface of the Italian narrative as translated into English may need some explanation. Only the English Troilus attempts to persuade Criseyde to elope with him by a learned figure added to the argument from *Filostrato* ('And thynk that folie is, whan man may chese, / For accident his substaunce ay to lese ...': IV, 1504–5), but must then add 'I mene thus ...' (1506) and explain his plan in plain terms. Similarly, after a flurry of proverbs added to

Filostrato (IV, 927–31), Pandarus starts the next stanza 'I mene thus...' and explains what he actually means. The poem's self-conscious variety of styles and register alerts and enlists the reader to appraise the appropriateness of language used in a world – unlike that of *Filostrato* – where the reader can watch language being manipulated 'for the nones' (I, 561; IV, 428) and as a 'conceyte' (I, 996).

Where Troiolo confesses to Pandaro that

> me ha preso Amore
> per tua cugina
>
> (2.20)

Troilus instead says,

> Allas! of al my wo the welle,
> Thanne is my swete fo called Criseyde!
>
> (I, 873–4)

and this characterizes how Chaucer in translating paints over his original with the language of a more courtly love. A whole range of added allusion, 'in-eched' by Chaucer in translation, presents love as a specialized, essentially secret pursuit, love as feudal service, love as religious devotion. For C. S. Lewis, Chaucer in this was restoring for its own sake an accepted, codified form of expression and behaviour in love, yet the virulent attack on D. H. Lawrence and Marie Stopes, with which his article on *Troilus* ends, reveals Lewis' own bias towards seeing Chaucer as the 'corrector' of a writer such as 'wicked' Boccaccio who – like others in Lewis' own times – seemed to be subverting all accepted conventions of behaviour between the sexes. Yet the experience of reading suggests that Chaucer's great extension in translating of the rhetoric of courtly hyperbole in *Troilus* is designed rather to accentuate that divergence between the experience and the description of love which develops with the poem.

The different terms in which the characters address each other in *Filostrato* and *Troilus* reveal some of the distinctive differences in their attitudes to courtly feeling. The social disparity in *Filostrato* between the prince and the astrologer's daughter is less regarded in *Troilus*, for Chaucer adds that Calchas was 'a lord of gret auctorite' (I, 65) and only his Criseyde mixes with Troilus' family (III, 211–17). And Pandarus is made part of Priam's circle (V, 284; not in *Filostrato*), although he calls Troilus at once 'Myn alderlevest lord, and brother deere' (III, 239) instead of simply 'Amico car' (*Filostrato*, 3.5). When Criseida awakes from her faint she addresses Troiolo as 'Signor mio' (4.116), whereas Criseyde instead cries 'Help, Troilus!' (IV, 1150). But by contrast, when Troiolo, grieving over news of the exchange, addresses Criseida as 'o dolce bene' (4.36), Troilus addresses his Criseyde as 'O lady sovereigne' (IV, 316). And again, when Criseida recovers from her faint Troiolo calls her 'Dolce mio disiro' (4.124), whereas Troilus addresses her as 'Lady myn, Criseyde' (IV, 1214).

In brief, Chaucer's characters are brought closer together socially in their manners, but the English Troilus is distinguished through additions in translation by his concern to express his love for Criseyde in terms of his feudal service and obligation to her, as in a string of added touches in Chaucer's translation of Book I. Thus, Troiolo's doubt whether he loves a goddess or woman is allowed to come through from Italian into English, but Troilus then adds: 'as hire man I wol ay lyve and sterve' (I, 427). Next, Troiolo's idea of himself prostrated at Love's feet (1.39) becomes instead Troilus' feudal subjection to Criseyde ('For myn estat roial I here resigne / Into hire hond, and with ful humble chere / Bicome hir man, as to my lady dere': I, 432–4). In the following stanza, the fire of love enflames Troiolo, but Chaucer when translating sees the power of love not only enflaming but also enslaving the lover ('But held hym as his thral lowe in destresse, / And brende hym so . . .': I, 439–40). Again, shortly after, Troiolo sets himself to curing the wounds of love (1.44), but Troilus' effort is here translated into different emphases:

> And he to ben hire man, while he may dure.
> Lo, here his lif, and from the deth his cure!
> (468–9)

Just as the feudal language of love is 'in-eched' in translation, so too is a sense of the conventions of secrecy, and a use of the religious terminology of love. In translating, Chaucer transfers the narrative of events into a society in which privacy can only be obtained with more difficulty and maintained with more dissimulation, in part through the much increased role of Pandarus, a character made both practical yet bookish, steeped in the theory of literary love.[13] And in the greater anxiousness and greater innocence of their affair – with all its more 'literary' flavour – the English lovers are made to express what they see in their experience together less in terms of individual sexual fulfilment, present though this is, but in more hyperbolically generalized terms, often drawing on religious phrasing and associations.

By such added 'thickening' of reference and allusion worked into the original texture of *Filostrato*, Chaucer suggests how much more – for better or worse remains to discover – the English lovers see in their experience, and this extends to the ways that some scenes, and the characters' actions and gestures, are visualized by Chaucer in his

mind's eye as he comes to translate them.[14] When Pandaro agrees to
help in the affair, Troiolo kisses and embraces him (2.33), whereas

> ... Troilus gan doun on knees to falle,
> And Pandare in his armes hente faste ...
>
> (1044–5)

Chaucer evidently is not removing kissing as such, for when Troilus
welcomes Antenor to Troy only Chaucer mentions that he kisses him
(V, 77). It seems rather Chaucer's taste for a solemnizing of important
actions and decisions. Again, when Pandaro assures Troiolo of success
with Criseida, Troiolo embraces and kisses him (2.81), but Troilus here
instead: 'to Pandare he held up bothe his hondes' (II, 974), the gesture
of prayer and supplication. Continuing the pattern, Troiolo throws himself on Pandaro's neck with joy after the consummation (3.56), whereas
Troilus at this point: 'To Pandarus on knowes fil adown' (III, 1592).

This more solemn approach, ritualizing experience, suggests the
increasedly reflective cast of mind in the English characters. In conversation with Troiolo after the consummation, Pandaro is described
as happy ('lieto': 3.59), yet in translating Chaucer chooses to reverse
this completely ('And Pandarus ful sobrely hym herde ...': III, 1616)
and makes his Pandarus concerned, mindful of the future. Similarly,
Troiolo was simply pleased ('contento') when Pandaro agrees to help
win Criseida (2.29), while Chaucer describes Troilus: 'With sobre
chere, although his herte pleyde' (I, 1013). This more reflective air in
the English characters is sustained by the sighs and the grave glances
that Chaucer adds for them in translating the equivalent responses of
their Italian prototypes. Criseida reacts to her enforced departure from
Troy with haughty pride (5.6–9) while Chaucer notes instead: 'Ful
sorwfully she sighte, and seyde "allas!"' (V, 58). Only Chaucer's
Troilus sighs as he waits in vain for Criseyde (V, 1196–7), and where
Troiolo responds sharply to Criseida's letter from the camp Chaucer
simply comments 'and sorwfullich he sighte' (V, 1633). The responsiveness of the English characters is also suggested by Chaucer's stress on
their paleness at moments of distress (as at V, 86; IV, 379) yet –
characteristic of Chaucer's added texture in translating – this is often
enfolded within a sense of change and development ('And thus she lith
with hewes pale and grene, / That whilom fressh and fairest was to
sene': IV, 1154–5). Criseyde's dreadful paleness is movingly mentioned
in contrast to her former, peerless radiance (cf. IV, 740; V, 243), and
the added perspective of change between present and past compactly
conveys – as does Chaucer's greater sense of time more generally in the
poem – the range and extent of the English lovers' feelings.

Through his 'in-eched' additions and changes in translating, Chaucer shows a more consistent concern with time in *Troilus* in a way distinct from *Filostrato*. He is careful to note times and seasons where the Italian is less specific (so that 'venuto il vago tempo il quale / riveste i prati . . .' (1.18) becomes 'comen was the tyme / Of Aperil, whan clothed is the mede / With newe grene, of lusty Veer the pryme' (I, 155–7)). Such additions as the opening stanzas of Book V give the affair a different pace, insisting on its length ('Thries hadde . . . The snowes molte') and thus its durability. Chaucer's added references to the passage of time in astrological terms of the stars and constellations – that starry dimension so distinctive of *Troilus* and not of *Filostrato* – bring the English lovers' lives into relation with a wider world. But from this stems a deeper concern in *Troilus* with duration and endurance, the survival and measurement of human emotion and experience against time. Boccaccio's Troiolo loves Criseida more than his own life (1.55), but Troilus will love her 'while that my lyf may laste' (I, 536), and throughout Chaucer builds in assurances of lasting and enduring not so insisted on in *Filostrato* (as with Criseyde to Troilus: 'I was youre, and shal while I may dure': IV, 1680).

This feeling for endurance is also sustained by the more classical atmosphere Chaucer adds in translating *Filostrato*, for although Boccaccio says in his Proem that he sought out an ancient story ('rivolgere l'antiche storie') he is not concerned to create that detailed *mise-en-scène* of antiquity that he is in *Teseida*. By contrast, Chaucer encrusts his translation with added references to classical figures, which form part of his concern to intensify the sense of suffering endured by his Troilus and Criseyde: their feelings are associated with the torments of Oedipus (IV, 300), Myrrha (IV, 1139), Ascalaphus (V, 319), Scylla (V, 1110) and Progne (II, 64). They also invoke the classical gods in many added oaths (e.g. by 'Joves name in hevene' (I, 878), by 'blisful Venus' (I, 1014), by Minerva (II, 1062), by Juno (IV, 1116)). And it is very striking that every classical figure mentioned in the Boethian account of Orpheus' visit to the underworld in the final, twelfth metrum of the *Consolation*, Book III, is also mentioned somewhere in *Troilus* (Orpheus and Eurydice (IV, 791), Calliope (III, 45), Cerberus (I, 859), Ixion (V, 212), Tantalus (III, 593), Tityos (I, 786)). Through such patterns of addition in translation, Chaucer intensifies and deepens: the horizons of the poem now stretch further, both stretching backwards into a sense of a past that peoples the natural world of birds and stones and trees with unhappy histories of their metamorphosis, and also stretching into Hell where the lovers' feelings propel them, and where they feel themselves awaited beyond death (by Proserpina (IV, 473), by Minos (IV, 1188), by the Manes (V, 892)).

Indeed, the verse of *Troilus* is shot through with added reference to death, as to God and Fortune, part of that texture of emphases interwoven into close translation of *Filostrato* and sustained through Chaucer's more freely invented passages. An added alertness to death pervasively expresses the extremity, as also the endurance, of the characters' feelings. Only Chaucer imagines the instant of Troilus' enamourment as an inward death ('sodeynly hym thoughte he felte dyen, / Right with hire look, the spirit in his herte': I, 306–7), and makes the moment of confession to Pandarus an added experience of near-death in its intensity of feeling ('And wel neigh with the word for feere he deide': I, 875). Troiolo and Criseida are distressed to notice signs of dawn after the consummation, but in *Troilus* 'hem thoughte feelen dethis wownde' (III, 1697). That feelings are such as equal death is a recurrent added touch by Chaucer. When Pandaro arrives Criseida is in indescribable woe (4.99), whereas Criseyde is in woe 'So gret that it a deth was for to see' (IV, 856), and only the English Troilus feels the pangs of death when he must leave Criseyde (IV, 1692). It is Chaucer's Troilus who is moved by Criseyde's empty palace to feel 'Wel oughtestow to falle, and I to dye' (V, 545), and while Troiolo imagines people will notice his pallid appearance, Troilus also thinks they will foretell his death (V, 627). And it is only Chaucer's Criseyde who yearns for death in her misery in the Greek camp ('Wel may myn herte longe / After my deth . . .': V, 690–1).

In brief, Chaucer floods his translating with an alertness to death: death that the lovers feel; death until which and beyond they will endure. It is Troilus, not Troiolo, who commends himself 'To hire that to the deth me may comande' (I, 1057); it is Troilus, not Troiolo, who devotes himself to Criseyde 'Whos I am al, and shal, tyl that I deye' (III, 1607). Yet on some occasions where there does exist a real possibility of suicide in *Filostrato*, Chaucer does not allow these to survive into the *Troilus*. Thus, after Troiolo has had his bad dream of the boar he grabs a knife and tries to kill himself, but Pandaro struggles and overpowers the hero, and then talks sharply to him about not believing in dreams (7.33–9). When translating this, Chaucer retains Troilus' wish for death that precedes his suicide bid in *Filostrato* ('For thorugh my deth my wo shold han an ende . . .': V, 1273–4). But Chaucer then begins the next stanza with Pandarus' advice against dreams ('Pandare answerde and seyde, "Allas the while . . .!" ': 1275). In short, the real possibility of suicide disappears; instead Chaucer only leaves the hero's association of death with his feelings. Similarly, Chaucer omits altogether Troiolo's earlier declaration that if his lady wishes him dead

then he will kill himself (*Filostrato*, 1.56). While Chaucer so inter-
twines the characters' emotions with a sense of dying, and so under-
scores their sense of death as a fixed inevitability against which their
feelings can be measured and affirmed, he thus removes from *Filostrato*
some such moments as might enact and make real all the added
rhetoric of death in *Troilus*.

This is more generally true of how Chaucer modifies what he
receives from *Filostrato* as he translates: the lovers' expression of
feeling and aspiration is overpainted and 'in-eched' with much added
lustre and force, yet their disposition is made much more submissive
and passive. They hope and speak so much more, yet can act so much
less. The difference between the Italian and English heroes is seen
when the lovers discuss the exchange: Troiolo urges Criseida 'Let us
find means and cause that you do not go' (4.144), but Troilus says
instead:

> with humble, trewe, and pitous herte,
> A thousand tymes mercy I yow preye;
> So rueth on myn aspre peynes smerte,
> And doth somwhat as that I shal yow seye ...
> (IV, 1499–1502)

The English Troilus subjects himself utterly to his lady's will, and
such a passivity of outlook forms a large part of the distinctive shift
from *Filostrato* in the hero's cast of mind. Overwhelmed with love,
Troiolo tells Pandaro:

> vanne, e lascia
> qui me combatter colla mia ambascia (2.8)

but Troilus says:

> but be thow in gladnesse,
> And lat me sterve, unknowe, of my destresse.
> (I, 615–16)

Troiolo is to struggle ('combatter') alone with his anguish, while
Troilus is to die alone and undeclared. (The sharp antithesis here in
Troilus' imagination between Pandarus' happiness and his own
misery is characteristic of the extreme contrast of light and shadow
pervasively added in Chaucer's translating.) Again, whereas Troiolo
considers a thousand ways to make himself known to Criseida (1.49),
Troilus simply laments that *any* approach is impossible (I, 503–4).
The English hero's relationship to Pandarus is also more submissive, as
is reflected in Chaucer's version of his gratitude to his friend in

Book III. Troiolo here declares he can never repay Pandaro, who has brought him back from Hell to Paradise (3.16). But Troilus instead declares his unworthiness:

> al myghte I now for the
> A thousand tymes on a morwe sterve
>
> (388–9)

and he will serve Pandarus

> Right as thi sclave, whider so thow wende,
> For evere more, unto my lyves ende.
>
> (391–2)

This vehement commitment to perpetual bondage shows Chaucer working into the translation a self-enslaving passivity of outlook for his Troilus. The extremity of this and comparable language and feeling in the English translation – together with the wider range of reference – works by its very force to promote a sense that the experience of the lovers – so individual and domestic in *Filostrato* – is in *Troilus* now susceptible of a more-than-individual significance.

For Chaucer, 'translacioun' constantly involves a 'trans-valuation' of his original through such emendations and addition, which, by creating a different atmosphere of implications for the original pattern of events, effects a shift in the moral import of the source. In *Filostrato* Pandaro exclaims that if their friendship still pleases Troiolo he should reveal what cruel thing is causing him to die (2.4). But Pandarus invokes their friendship in more resounding terms ('if evere love or trouthe / Hath ben, or is, bitwixen the and me': I, 584–5) and the cruelty is not now what is slaying Troiolo but the cruelty that Troilus does Pandarus in not revealing his heart. In brief, Chaucer in translating deftly seizes on and turns around the original phrasing, so that the friends' dialogue is re-expressed with a keener sense of the depth of their relationship.

Again, when encouraging Troiolo with Criseida's excellence of character, Pandaro feels there is no matter so great that Criseida would not undertake it as much as any king (2.22), whereas in *Troilus* the comparison is turned even more to Criseyde's advantage ('In honour, to as fer as she may strecche, / A kynges herte semeth by hyrs a wrecche': I, 888–9). And while Pandaro feels the only obstacle may be Criseida's sense of honourable behaviour ('ella è più che altra donna onesta': 2.23), Pandarus turns this right round so that the very goodness of Criseyde must mean that she is among other things compassionate ('sith thy lady vertuous is al, / So foloweth it that there is som pitee / Amonges alle thise other in general': I, 898–900).

The original impetus of moral comment in the Italian is turned around in a way that serves to create higher expectations of the English characters. To Troiolo Criseida is the 'chiara luce che'l cor m'innamora' (1.43), but to Troilus Criseyde is 'Good goodly, to whom serve I and laboure' (I, 458). To Troiolo Criseida's demeanour evinces that feminine haughtiness that Boccaccio admired (1.27), while to Troilus

> the pure wise of hire mevynge
> Shewed wel that men myght in hire gesse
> Honour, estat, and wommanly noblesse.
>
> (285–7)

After the consummation Criseida was simply 'di Troiolo parlando nel suo core' (3.55), yet Criseyde

> Of Troilus gan in hire herte shette
> His worthynesse, his lust, his dedes wise,
> His gentilesse ...
>
> (III, 1549–51)

And later when Criseida pictures Troiolo's past acts to herself in the Greek camp (6.2), Criseyde instead

> wente ay purtrayinge
> Of Troilus the grete worthynesse.
>
> (V, 716–17)

This different awareness in Chaucer's characters of moral qualities and issues is shown by Chaucer's emendations to the expression of sensuality in *Filostrato*. Pandaro hopes for success with Criseida because all women are really amorous at heart (2.27), but his cynically reductive view of female sexuality becomes in *Troilus* a generalization about love and all mankind ('Was nevere man or womman ...': I, 977ff). For Criseyde, in the context of this, it is proper 'A worthi knyght to loven and cherice' (I, 986). Later, Pandaro says he has 'corrotto il petto sano' of Criseida and implanted there the love of Troiolo (3.6), but note how this process of 'corruption' is re-expressed in *Troilus*:

> For the have I my nece, of vices cleene,
> So fully maad thi gentilesse triste,
> That al shal ben right as thiselven liste.
>
> (III, 257–9)

For Chaucer 'gentilesse' imbues their relations: in *Filostrato* the lovers, although insatiable, make the most of their night together for sensual gratification (3.41), but note how in *Troilus* their night

> was byset in joie and bisynesse
> Of al that souneth into gentilesse . . .
>
> (III, 1413–14)

At such points the English lovers' sensual pleasure is subsumed within a greater virtuousness of behaviour. Chaucer's Troilus and Criseyde rightly or wrongly see more in their affair than sexual dalliance (Troiolo's praise of love – 'Lodato sia Amor' – becomes 'thanked be the heighe worthynesse / Of Love': III, 1609–10). The expectations are higher, indeed idealizing: the disappointment is keener and – within the reverberations of the added moral language – seems to offer itself for more general interpretation by the early audiences of Chaucer as 'The noble philosophical poete in Englissh'.[15]

Some of this expectation and idealization is expressed through the more frequent pattern of asseveration and acclamation that Chaucer adds in translating. Thus, after his near-suicide, Criseida exclaims plainly that she would not have lived on after Troiolo ('Io non sarei in vita stata mai': 4.126). But for Criseyde this becomes a much more solemn statement of intent:

> For, by that ilke Lord that made me,
> I nolde a forlong wey on lyve have be,
> After youre deth, to han ben crowned queene
> Of al the lond the sonne on shyneth sheene.
>
> (IV, 1236–9)

It is the distinctive tone of Troilus that intentions are more expansively expressed, and more poignancy results from a deeper sense of failure to fulfil the declarations and promises. Comparable strength of expectation lies behind the added language of acclamation, the epithets by which the characters address each other. Criseyde's acclamation of Troilus as 'Myn hertes lif, my trist, and my plesaunce' (III, 1422; replacing Criseida's 'O amor mio': 3.43) expresses how much she sees in their relationship. A little later, Troiolo feels Criseida, as his donna, gives him all his delight (3.44). But for Troilus this becomes an acclamation of Criseyde as

> My lady right, and of my wele or wo
> The welle and roote, O goodly myn, Criseyde.
>
> (III, 1472–3)

Similarly, when Criseida begs Troiolo to be faithful in her absence, she avoids calling him anything ('E priegoti . . .' 4.162), but Chaucer's Criseyde here addresses Troilus as 'Myn owene hertes sothfast suffisaunce' (IV, 1640). That the English lovers hail and describe each

other in such added terms reveals the very different way they view
their experiences from the lovers in *Filostrato*.

It is through some of the added oaths and declarations of Chaucer's
characters that the much increased sense of God, as also of Fortune,
enters the English poem. Through Chaucer's additions to their
dialogue the English characters show a sense that they are not alone
on the stage of the poem, but share their world with a supreme being.
The differing focus of *Troilus* from *Filostrato* appears when Troiolo
urges Pandaro, 'metti in effetto . . . il mio disio' (3.19) whereas Troilus
begs Pandarus:

> So, for the love of God, this grete emprise
> Perfourme it out . . .
>
> > (III, 416–17)

An instinctive prayerfulness distinguishes the English characters, so
that Troiolo's exclamation

> > Oh Dio,
> > troverò io tornato l'amor mio?
> >
> > > (5.48)

becomes

> . . . Now Lord me grace sende,
> That I may fynden . . .
> > Criseyde comen!
> >
> > > (V, 502–4)

Even where Chaucer is translating closely, a sense of God's working is
invoked in English where it is not mentioned in Italian: thus, Troiolo's
wish

> Ed or foss'io pur venuto al porto . . .
> Questo mi saria grazia
>
> > (1.54)

is turned into

> *God wold* I were aryved in the port . . .
> A, *Lord*, to me it were a gret comfort.
> > (I, 526–8)

Just before this, Troiolo's wish that, since he must love, he were
loved by one who loved him (1.53) becomes

> > . . . *God wolde*,
> Sith thow most loven *thorugh thi destine*,
> That thow beset were . . .
> > (I, 519–21)

and this too is characteristic of how Chaucer in translating casts the Italian narrative within a sharpened sense of Fortune. He achieves this with the whole range of emendations through translation, from enormous interpolation like Troilus' Predestination Soliloquy to rephrasing a translated line (as when Troiolo tells the letter he sends Criseida 'tu sarai beata' (2.107), which becomes: 'Lettre, a blisful destine / The shapyn is' (II, 1091–2)). Simple events, simple unhappiness in *Filostrato* are 'philosophized' in *Troilus* by added alertness to Fortune (as in various 'in-eched' passages in Book IV, e.g. 323ff, 386–92). Sometimes a hint in the Italian is expanded, as when Pandaro's flippant question to Criseida after the exchange agreement ('Cre' tu cozzar co' fati?': 4.98) is developed into Criseyde's solemn, three-stanza reflection (IV, 827–47). And while, as a whole, the theme of Fortune is evidently a subject more concerning the *Troilus* itself than the relation of *Troilus* to *Filostrato*, yet Chaucer's 'translation into' *Filostrato* of an awareness of Fortune – from the largest interpolation through many small 'in-eched' references down to rephrasing of a closely-followed stanza – exhibits that whole range of distinctive processes and effects that throughout Chaucer's translating absorb, adapt and extend the *Filostrato*.

III

But he that parted is in everi place
Is nowher hol . . .

                                                    (I, 960–1)

Chaucer's involvement with *Filostrato* is very close, but is all the rich detail of his response to his Italian original united to fulfil a larger purpose in the English poem? Chaucer innovates very freely and boldly at many junctures in the new poem he creates out of *Filostrato*, yet within that new work *Filostrato* not only goes on providing much underlying structure, but for long stretches is not really submerged and comes very near to the surface of Chaucer's poem, however much that surface has been modified by Chaucer's interstitial activity, interpolating and overlaying. It may well be asked whether strain and inconsistency stem from this, and whether Chaucer has fully integrated all he has borrowed and invented – or indeed whether he needed or aimed to do so.

In presenting the characters of his protagonists Chaucer has consequently chosen to intervene in their characterization, to add or develop emphasis here, to offset a feature there. Chaucer's 'in-eched' characters are now 'fuller' and experience a wider and deeper range of feeling than their Italian prototypes, but in translation they may have acquired more sides to their character than are always easy to see as a whole. Thus, the courtly lover Troilus also expresses his thoughts in tortuous philosophical argument, and Pandarus, the worldly-wise go-between, the fixer, sometimes feels all the literal force of the hyperboles and figures of love language. Even more with the characterization of Criseyde does that detailed variousness produced by the way the English poem has grown suggest the tantalizing complexity of her character in a way not present in *Filostrato*. Thus, when Pandaro tells Criseida that Troiolo is in love with her, Criseida grows pale, scarcely stops herself from weeping, and then reproaches Pandaro (2.47–8). But as Chaucer refashions this scene, his Criseyde in effect has two responses. After telling her she is loved by Troilus Pandarus rushes on pell-mell to urge his suit, and only after he has spoken for nine stanzas since first divulging the lover's name is Criseyde at last allowed a reaction ('Criseyde, which that herde hym in this wise, / Thoughte, "I shal felen what he meneth, ywis." / "Now, em," quod she, "what wolde ye devise? / What is youre reed I sholde don of this?"': II, 386–9). And it is only after Pandarus' further advice that Criseyde shows the reaction parallel to Criseida's in *Filostrato* ('And she began to breste a-wepe anoon, / And seyde, "Allas, for wo! Why nere I deed?"': II, 408–9). In brief, the elaborated and doubled reaction that Criseyde is given by Chaucer's translating makes her character distinctly more 'double': she is made first cautious and thoughtful and then emotional, both in the same sequence, and this instance must stand to represent the way that more widely in his poem Chaucer's emendation through translation will often complicate interpretation of his characters.

In this light it is intriguing to examine such pattern as emerges in what Chaucer chooses to omit from *Filostrato*, what he acts to prevent surviving into English. One pattern that does emerge is that Chaucer recurrently omits or modifies occasions on which the Italian characters for reasons of experience or worldly wisdom 'think better' of what they are doing. Chaucer's first major omission from *Filostrato* is to cut out the moment when Troiolo talks from his own experience of love (1.23–4). Similarly, Chaucer retains Troiolo's concern at what lovers will say of him ('Che si dirà di te?'; 'What wol now every lovere seyn of the?': I, 512), but Chaucer omits the Italian stanza in which Troiolo knows that other princes will reproach him for wasting time unworthily on love in times of war (1.52). For Chaucer reduces possible self-consciousness of what may be wrong in the affair. When Pandaro counsels Troiolo he explicitly admits the shamefulness of what they are proposing to do with Criseida (2.25–6), but Chaucer omits this from his version. Again, where Troiolo feels he will die of grief over the exchange, but in the next stanza (4.37) says that if the departure had been delayed he could have grown more used to it, this latter stanza does not survive in the *Troilus* (cf. IV, 322ff). And, comparably, Chaucer suppresses the stanza (4.59) where Troiolo declares that although love can never be driven out it may well slip away through process of time. Such an unidealistically pragmatic view of love is removed by Chaucer from his hero as if it never existed, and other 'inappropriate' lines and parts of stanzas are similarly phased out. In urging Troiolo to abduct Criseida, Pandaro argues it will always be possible to bring her back if things go wrong (4.73), but this would not fit with the sense of more absolute actions and consequences in *Troilus* and the loophole of possible return disappears from *Troilus*. Similarly, when Troilus and Criseyde discuss her departure Chaucer has omitted Criseida's argument (4.152–3) that if they could enjoy at will their present furtive passion it would soon be spent. This again is just that type of worldly wisdom which does not seem part of Chaucer's conception of his characters as he creates them through translation and which he acts to remove from *Filostrato* as he renders it.

For the relative innocence of Chaucer's lovers and of his narrator means that, unlike the sensual Troiolo and Criseida, Troilus and Criseyde are confronted by what is often new experience to them. Hence the recurrent added interest in English in learning through a sense of contraries and antitheses (e.g. I, 946ff),[16] for the experience of reading *Troilus* is a more open one than *Filostrato*, because more issues are raised while attitudes to them are modified through the progression of the poem. In this way many of the patterns of small-scale change in translation are stabilized and contribute to the poem's larger effect. All the added courtly language of loving has developed a different timbre by the poem's end, and the introduction of more passive dispositions in the lovers builds towards Chaucer's large 'philosophical' interpolations on man's freedom, which are thus not later attempts to graft philosophizing on to a romance but are anticipated in the detail of the narrative by Chaucer's changes through translation. And Chaucer's added concern with time in translating causes the reader to be within Troilus' passion in Book III, yet also live on to sense the difference between present and past, experience and reflection, feeling and thought, which is expressed through the change of plane at the English ending.[17]

The only passage of *Filostrato* that Chaucer uses outside the *Troilus* is his adaptation into an address to the daisy (*Legend of Good Women*, Prologue, F, 84–94) of Boccaccio's opening address to his lady as his muse (*Filostrato*, 1.2), which Chaucer suppressed at the start of the *Troilus*. It is fitting to close on this scrap of *Filostrato* that Chaucer carried forward into his next work, not only because it is there that Chaucer represents himself as punished for writing, among other things, the *Troilus*, but also because Chaucer's handling of the passage suggests much of his activity as a translator of *Filostrato*. Boccaccio feels himself guided by his 'tramontana stella' which becomes

> The hert in-with my sorwfull brest yow dredeth
> And loveth so sore that ye ben verrayly
> The maistresse of my wit, and nothing I.
>
> (86–8)

And while the lady is to Boccaccio Jove, Apollo and Muse, for Chaucer

> My word, my werk ys knyt so in youre bond
> That, as an harpe obeieth to the hond
> And maketh it soune after his fyngerynge,
> Ryght so . . .

is the poet guided by his 'lady sovereyne'. In brief, even though the original declares all inspiration comes *not* from the poet, Chaucer in 'translating' astutely re-expresses his source in proportion as he claims to stress his own lack of creativity. Some characteristic guises and emphases in Chaucer's translating are here: the sensitive and anxious solitariness of the poet (loving and dreading), the feeling for constraint and subjectedness, a knowing reverence for the feminine. It is by such added themes in translation that the sense of human love is 'al ychaunged' from *Filostrato*, and understood at last in the context 'of Paradys the ymage'.

Notes

1 Cf. *Filostrato*, 4.100:
> e la sua faccia fatta in paradiso,
> tututta si vedeva trasmutata . . .

2 Cf. C. S. Lewis, 'What Chaucer Really Did to Il Filostrato', *Essays and Studies by Members of the English Association*, XVII (1932), 56–75; S. B. Meech, *Design in Chaucer's Troilus* (Syracuse, N.Y., 1959); R. W. Frank, Jr, 'Troilus and Criseyde: The Art of Amplification', in *Medieval Literature and Folklore Studies in Honour of Francis Lee Utley* (New Brunswick, 1970), pp. 155–71; P. M. Kean, *Chaucer and the Making of English Poetry* (London, 1972), vol. I.

3 Cf. V. Branca, *Boccaccio: The Man and his Works* (New York, 1976), chapter 4; P. Ricci, 'Per la dedica e la datazione del Filostrato', *Studi sul Boccaccio*, I (1963), 333–47; N. R. Havely, *Chaucer's Boccaccio* (Cambridge, 1980). See also M. Gozzi, 'Sulle fonti del Filostrato', *Studi sul Boccaccio*, V (1968), 123–209.

4 Cf. R. P. apRoberts, 'Love in the *Filostrato*', *Chaucer Review*, VII (1972), 1–26.
J. Norton-Smith, *Geoffrey Chaucer* (London, 1974), would see the differences
between *Filostrato* and *Troilus* in the relation of the poet and the story
producing a different sense of structuring in the English poem: 'Unlike
Boccaccio's segmental, romance structure (compare Boccaccio's use of "*argo-
menti*"), *Troilus* has a scenic and dramatic plot structure which is altogether
more complex. Chaucer manages this by the use of climactic sequences which
no longer relate to a mainly lyrical excursus (dependent on the identification
of the *autore* with Troilo)' (p. 206).

5 Whether or not he also needed the colourless French crib of Beauvau (cf. R. A.
Pratt, 'Chaucer and *Le Roman de Troyle et de Criseida*', *Studies in Philology*,
LIII (1956), 509–39). For the English and Italian texts in parallel, cf. my edition
of *Troilus and Criseyde* (Longman, London and New York, 1984).

6 E.g. the sequence of closely parallel stanzas: *Troilus and Criseyde*, I, 456 (from
Filostrato, 1.43); I, 463 (1.44); I, 470 (1.45); I, 477 (1.46); I, 484 (1.47). The closeness with which Chaucer translates the first lines of Italian stanzas into the
first lines of his own stanzas is a recurrent feature of his translating of
Filostrato, of which the following instances are only a selection: 'Era pietoso
Ettòr di sua natura' (1.13), 'Now was this Ector pitous of nature' (I, 113); 'Tu
stai negli occhi suoi, signor verace, / sì come in loco degno a tua virtute'
(1.39), 'Ye stonden in hir eighen myghtily, / As in a place unto youre vertu
digne' (I, 428–9); 'Io vo' con teco patir queste pene' (2.5), 'I wol parten with
the al thi peyne' (I, 589); 'Amore, incontro al qual chi si difende' (2.7), 'Love,
ayeins the which whoso defendeth' (I, 603); 'Pandaro disioso di servire' (2.34),
'This Pandarus, tho desirous to serve' (I, 1058); 'Troiolo al domandare era
presente' (4.14), 'This Troilus was present...' (IV, 148); 'E pien d'angoscia...'
(4.15), 'And ful of angwissh...' (IV, 155); 'Grave m'è la partenza, Iddio il vede'
(4.105), 'Grevous to me, God woot, is for to twynne' (IV, 904); 'Ell'era fredda e
sanza sentimento' (4.119), 'She cold was, and withouten sentement' (IV, 1177);
'Troiolo in guisa d'una cortesia' (5.10), 'This Troilus, in wise of curteysie'
(V, 64).

7 Compare

>   Piacendo questa sotto il nero manto
>   oltre ad ogni altra a Troiol...
>   (1.30)

with

>   She, this in blak, likynge to Troilus
>   Over alle thing...
>   (I, 309–10)

or again:

>   Questo dicendo il vecchio sacerdote,
>   umile nel parlare e nell' aspetto,
>   sempre rigava di pianto le gote...
>   (4.12)

with

>   Tellyng his tale alwey, this olde greye,
>   Humble in his speche, and in his lokyng eke,
>   The salte teris...
>   ...ronnen down.
>   (IV, 127–30)

For the Italian model of Chaucer's lines see B. A. Windeatt, '"Most conservatyf
the soun": Chaucer's *Troilus* Metre', *Poetica* (Tokyo), VIII (1977), 44–60.

8 As with the following instances, although numerous other examples occur in
any stretch of Chaucer's translating: 'alquanto sdegnosetto' (1.28), 'somdel
deignous' (I, 290); 'argomentava...male avvisando' (1.35), 'argumented he.../
Ful unavysed' (I, 377–8); 'rimovieno' (1.45), 'meve' (I, 472); 't'ha qui guidato a

vedermi languire' (2.2), 'Hath gided the to sen me langwisshinge' (I, 569);
'prima agli alti effetti lieto ... movesti' (3.76), 'first to thilk effectes glade / ...
Comeveden' (III, 15–17); 'riveste' (3.12), 'Revesten' (III, 353); 'se mia vita etterna /
fosse come è mortal' (3.15), 'al were my lif eterne, / As I am mortal' (III,
375–6); 'tanto la noia la strinse del partire' (3.52), 'So soore gan his partyng
hire distreyne' (III, 1528); 'Tornato Troiol nel real palagio' (3.53), 'Retorned
to his real paleys soone' (III, 1534); 'ch'io sento nuovo, è d'altra qualitate' (3.62),
'But now I feele a newe qualitee' (III, 1654); 'redenzioni' (4.10), 'redempcioun'
(IV, 108); 'accusarla' (4.69), 'accusement' (IV, 556); 'turbar con violenta / rapina'
(4.68), 'to perturbe / With violence' (IV, 561–2); 'La fama velocissima, la
quale / il falso e'l vero ugualmente rapporta, / era volata con prestissime ale /
per tutta Troia' (4.78), 'The swifte Fame, which that false thynges / Egal
reporteth lik the thynges trewe, / Was thorughout Troie yfled with preste
wynges ...' (IV, 659–61); 'sia cosa molesta / a Troiolo' (4.102), 'dooth Troilus
moleste' (IV, 880); 'essi procedon da malinconia' (5.32), 'For they procede of thi
malencolie' (V, 360); 'figurava' (5.45), 'Refiguryng' (V, 473); 'quinci discese poi
a domandare' (6.12), 'Fro that demaunde he so descendeth down' (V, 859).

9 Cf. the expression of affection: III, 1352–3 (Filostrato, 3.36); III, 1359–60 (3.37);
   III, 1401–4 (3.40); III, 1522–3 (3.51); and of sorrow: IV, 246ff, 295ff, 337ff, 353ff, 708ff,
   736ff, 855ff, 1128–1246.

10 Cf. V. Branca, Il Cantare trecentesco e il Boccaccio del Filostrato e del Teseida
   (Florence, 1936).

11 Cf. Troilus and Criseyde, IV, 246 and 869 with Filostrato, 4.28, 100, and La Vita
   Nuova, XXXI and XXXIX.

12 For a fuller account, cf. Barry Windeatt, 'The "Paynted Proces": Italian to
   English in Chaucer's Troilus', English Miscellany, XXVI–XXVII (1977–8), 79–103.

13 Cf. further Barry Windeatt, '"Love that oughte ben secree" in Chaucer's
   Troilus', Chaucer Review, XIV (1979–80), 116–31.

14 Cf. further Barry Windeatt, 'Gesture in Chaucer', Medievalia et Humanistica,
   n.s. IX (1979), 143–61.

15 Thomas Usk, in The Testament of Love, in Chaucerian and Other Pieces, ed.
   W. W. Skeat (Oxford, 1897), p. 123.

16 It is characteristic of Chaucer in translating that Filostrato's expression of
   Criseida's pre-eminent beauty ('quanto la rosa la viola / di biltà vince ...': 1.19)
   becomes in Troilus a twofold comment, first in more bookish and then in more
   sharply antithetical terms:

   > Right as oure firste lettre is now an A,
   > In beaute first so stood she ...
   > Nas nevere yet seyn thyng to ben preysed derre,
   > Nor under cloude blak so bright a sterre
   >   (I, 171–5)

17 See further Barry Windeatt, 'The Text of the Troilus', in Essays on Troilus and
   Criseyde, ed. M. Salu (Cambridge, 1979), pp. 1–22; Barry Windeatt, 'Pace in
   Chaucer', Poetica (Tokyo), XIX (1983), 51–65; and my forthcoming study
   Chaucer as Translator.

Style, Iconography and Narrative: the Lesson of the *Teseida*

For the modern reader, Boccaccio's *Teseida* is decidedly one of his minor works and hardly anybody bothers to read it who is not concerned with the development of Boccaccio's early career as a poet or Chaucer's relationship to Italian culture. It was not always so. In the *Decameron* 'cornice', for instance, during a pause between story-telling, Dioneo and Fiammetta 'sing of Palamon and Arcite'. An indirect compliment by the author to himself, this passage seems nevertheless to indicate that the *Teseida* was considered a fashionable work by a fourteenth-century Florentine upper-class audience. Appreciation of the *Teseida* continued throughout the fifteenth and sixteenth centuries, in Italy (where it was usually called 'il Teseo') and all over Europe (it was even translated into Greek). The poets of the Italian Renaissance, Poliziano, Pulci, Boiardo and Ariosto knew and liked it, perhaps recognizing in it the forerunner of their own themes and metre. Certain it is that when, between 1587 and 1594, Torquato Tasso, the last of the great Renaissance writers, composed his *Discorsi sul Poema Eroico*, he kept the *Teseida* constantly in mind. He recalled it as the first example of an 'heroic poem' to sing of love as well as of arms in the Italian tongue – in that 'highest style' advocated for such subjects by Dante in the *De Vulgari Eloquentia*.[1] He praised Boccaccio's choice of *ottava rima*, subsequently confirmed by all major Italian poets down to Tasso himself.[2] And he admired Boccaccio's technique: examples of metaphors and similes from the *Teseida* illustrate Tasso's treatment of 'elocution' in the last three books of the *Discorsi*.[3]

Boccaccio would have certainly been grateful to Tasso for his appreciation of the *Teseida*. It was precisely to write an 'heroic poem' in Tasso's sense of the word that he had set about composing the *Teseida*. The idea was to fill that gap in Italian literature which Dante had pointed out in his *De Vulgari Eloquentia*, the absence, that is, of a poem about 'arms' in the vernacular.[4] And of course the idea was to be carried out by following the great classical models: Virgil (the

Teseida numbers exactly as many lines as the *Aeneid*), Lucan (the ascent of Arcite's soul in Book XI recalls Pompey's apotheosis in the *Pharsalia*), and above all Statius (the *Teseida* is inserted within the Theban cycle and the *Thebaid* is imitated and adapted throughout). Thus the title, *Teseida*, is modelled on the illustrious precedents of *Aeneid*, *Thebaid*, *Achilleid*; the first two books recount Theseus' wars against the Amazons and Creon of Thebes; and Book VI contains a long 'catalogue' of heroes present at the Athenian tournament. The same impulse can be seen in Petrarch, who devoted so much time and energy to the composition of his Latin epic, the *Africa*.

Yet a modern 'heroic poem' could not leave out one of the central themes of European literature, that of love. The experience of many vernacular romances from the twelfth century onwards, 'courtly' literature and the *cantari* had shown the way; nor were the great narratives of the classics, Virgil and Ovid, lacking in love episodes. In the *Teseida*, Boccaccio sought therefore to combine 'armorum probitas' and 'amoris accensio' (two of the themes singled out by Dante as worthy of being treated in the high style). Hence a double invocation, to Mars on the one hand, to Venus and Cupid on the other, at the beginning of the *Teseida* (I, iii); hence its subtitle, 'delle nozze d'Emilia'; hence the tragic love story that forms the core of the poem; hence all the echoes of the love literature (*Roman de la Rose*, the Italian *stilnovo*) that resound in the *Teseida*; hence the 'cornice' that frames it – the dedicatory letter to Fiammetta with Boccaccio's pretended autobiographical love drama, the end of the poem with its praise of the lady (XII, lxxxvi) and her giving it a title ('Risposta delle Muse': 5–13).

Boccaccio pursued his double aim in the *Teseida* with great enthusiasm and earnestness, if not with total success. In the first place he created – or reworked[5] – a plot that could not but appeal to a medieval and Renaissance audience, the story of two noble knights who fall in love with the same maiden, fight against each other for her and summon their friends for a tournament that, according to Duke Theseus' decree, will decide the issue – a plot that has both a tragic and a happy ending. For the knight who wins the tourney will have the lady, as Theseus decides. But on this specific occasion Arcite, the winner, who has prayed to Mars for victory, is injured by his horse after the battle and dies, whereas his enemy, Palamon, who has prayed to Venus for the lady, is defeated but survives and eventually marries the maiden, Emily.

It is, therefore, a plot that rests on a point of tragic irony and raises several interesting problems of justice, of the ethics of love and war, of man's response to the powers that rule his life. While often losing sight of the main thread of his story and thus diluting the compactness and consequentiality of his theme, Boccaccio orchestrates his poem in twelve orderly books (like the *Aeneid*), each preceded by an introductory sonnet, and each enriched by a variety of scenes designed to cover the whole spectrum of narrative poetry. Thus the first two books, though not strictly necessary to the main action, describe Theseus' wars against the Amazons and against Thebes, the sailings, the sieges, the bellicose speeches, the duels, the triumphs, the procession of the Argive women asking Theseus for vengeance against Creon. Then, in the third book, the love theme comes to the fore, with Arcite and Palamon glancing through the window at young Emily in the garden and rhapsodizing on their passion. In the fourth, Arcite's wanderings take us through Greece, and his love-longing inexorably draws him back to Athens. In the fifth, the two lovers meet and fight their duel. The coming of the princes occupies the whole of the sixth book. The seventh is dominated by the prayers to the gods and the description of the great temples of Mars and Venus, and of the theatre. In the eighth book the muse of war takes over again in the duels that make up the tournament. In the ninth we have Arcite's triumph and fall. The tenth lingers melodramatically on the great choral scene of Arcite's agony and death. Book XI is devoted to the solemn funeral and the temple where Arcite's ashes will rest. And finally, Book XII recounts Theseus' grand speech and the marriage of Palamon and Emily.

Characterization, too, is often vigorous: Arcite is a pensive, lyrical, melancholy, courteous figure; Palamon is more violent; Emily is a beautiful young maiden who would prefer to dedicate herself to Diana but begins to love Arcite when she sees him victorious; Theseus is the great duke, irate but also compassionate, just, wise, mindful of order and peace.

Nor are the great themes absent: not only love and war, but friendship and death, Fate and Fortune, the role of the gods – all form part, though at times in a confused manner, of the *Teseida*'s fabric. This fabric is enriched – though often discontinuously – by those stylistic devices which Tasso admired. Following the classics and Dante, Boccaccio invokes the muses, employs elaborate similes and images drawn from the worlds of nature, myth, history and astronomy, inserts geographical details, evokes ancient customs, interweaves the stories of Troy, of Thebes, of Theseus; creates indeed for his poem a time and a space within the time and space of classical mythology and poetry. He provides the *Teseida* with his own prose commentary –

linguistic, iconographical, allegorical – as if it were the *Thebaid* or the *Aeneid*.[6] He quotes and adapts from Virgil, Statius, Lucan, Ovid, the *Roman de la Rose*, Cino da Pistoia, Guido Cavalcanti, and above all Dante.

These ingredients are not always harmonized, but they nevertheless make of the *Teseida* a wholly new piece of narrative poetry, poised between classical epic and medieval romance (Boccaccio's own *Filostrato* being much more 'romantic'), a mine of *topoi*, images, erudite information, and a mixture of styles and themes – in short, a model of that type of narrative which was to enjoy so much favour in the Renaissance.

It is, then, hardly surprising that Chaucer used the *Teseida* throughout his career, from the *House of Fame*, to the *Anelida*, the *Parliament of Fowls*, the *Troilus*, the *Legend*, the *Knight's Tale* and the *Franklin's Tale*.[7] In fact, together with the *Divine Comedy*, Boethius' *Consolation* and the *Roman de la Rose*, the *Teseida* seems to be the book that most influenced Chaucer, that most stimulated him in his experiments as a narrative poet and a stylist.

Whatever reason Chaucer had for calling him 'Lollius', Boccaccio clearly had a place of honour in the Englishman's poetic pantheon, for Lollius is one of the writers who 'bear up' all the fame of the matter of Troy in Fame's great hall (*House of Fame*, III, 1468). Here, as in the *Troilus*, Chaucer obviously refers to the *Filostrato*, the most recent of Troy poems for a fourteenth-century man. Yet the only lines from Boccaccio in the *House of Fame* come from the *Teseida* and not from the *Filostrato*. The Proem to Book II contains a poetic invocation that both J. A. W. Bennett and I have examined in our essays earlier in this volume. What is interesting about this invocation is that its second part ('O Thought') derives from Dante's *Inferno*, while the first, to Venus and the muses, is clearly indebted to the *Teseida*.[8] In 'What Dante Meant to Chaucer' I pointed out that Chaucer's addition of Venus in his invocation 'indicates that his choice is and will remain "secular"'. The fact that Venus in the *House of Fame* derives from the *Teseida* would seem to confirm that idea. The theme of 'secular' love is common to Boccaccio and Chaucer, and Chaucer would have found in the *Teseida's* invocation a confirmation of the importance of love as primary poetic muse. Nor should we overlook the fact that, by drawing from the *Teseida* just before imitating the *Inferno*, Chaucer places Boccaccio on the same level as Dante. The muses of *House of Fame*, 520–2, are those of Dante's *Inferno* (II, 7) and of Boccaccio's *Teseida*.

Right from the time of the *House of Fame*, then, the *Teseida* is for Chaucer a model of high style and a bridge between Dante and himself. In the *House of Fame*, however, Chaucer is obviously looking for his own path in narrative poetry, or rather he is asking himself some basic questions about the origin, development and nature of narrative poetry. However much he celebrates Lollius, he is not ready to follow him. Venus and her temple, presented at the beginning of the poem, have nothing to do with the iconography displayed by Boccaccio in Book VII of the *Teseida*.[9]

Things begin to change with *Anelida and Arcite*. Here, the impact of the *Teseida* on Chaucer is mainly stylistic. In the first place, *ottava rima* is translated into rhyme royal stanzas, one of Chaucer's favoured narrative metres. Secondly, the impact of the *Teseida's* solemn, 'classical' style is such that Chaucer tries to reproduce it without substantial alterations:

> Mars, which that through his furious cours of ire,
> The olde wrathe of Juno to fulfille,
> Hath set the peples hertes bothe on fire
> Of Thebes and Grece, everich other to kille
> With blody speres, ne rested never stille,
> But throng now her, now ther, among hem bothe,
> That everych other slough, so were they wrothe.
> (*Anelida*, 50–6)

> Ma Marte, il quale i popoli lernei
> con furioso corso avea commossi
> sopra' Tebani, e' miseri trofei
> donati avea de' prencipi percossi
> più volte già, e de' Greci plebei
> ritenuti talvolta e tal riscossi,
> con asta sanguinosa fieramente
> trista avea fatta l'una e l'altra gente ...
> (*Teseida*, II, x)

But the *Anelida* is more than a stylistic mirror of the *Teseida*. It is also Chaucer's first attempt to combine a love poem and an epic, along the lines indicated by Boccaccio in the *Teseida*: it is the story, dominated by Mars, of Theseus' wars against the Amazons and Creon, of his triumph in Athens (the plot of the *Teseida's* first two books), and the story of Queen Anelida and false Arcite, a narrative of love and betrayal to be sung 'with pitous hert' ('con pietosa rima': *Teseida*, I, ii–iii). The epic inspiration soon fades away, and what is left is only Anelida's complaint against Arcite – the kind of 'Complaint' Chaucer writes on other occasions. *Anelida and Arcite* is thus a first, aborted, romance – narrative and lyric being just superimposed. Moreover, the *Teseida*, which in the *House of Fame* acted as a bridge between Dante and Chaucer, now becomes an important intermediary between Chaucer and Statius, the 'Tholosan' mentioned in the *House of Fame* just before Lollius – an intermediary, that is, between contemporary and classical poetry.

The *Anelida* is unfinished and we shall never know if, as R. A. Pratt said, Chaucer really 'found no attraction in the story of the *Teseida*' at this time.[10] But what is certain is that the poem breaks off suddenly with the poet's promise to describe the temple of Mars (355–7), for which Book VII of the *Teseida* (xxx–xxxviii) and its source, Book VII of the *Thebaid* (40–63), provide the model Chaucer seems to be looking for. This might indicate a willingness on Chaucer's part to return to the plot of the *Teseida*. It certainly shows that the iconography and decoration of Boccaccio's poem already appealed to Chaucer.

The next Chaucerian adaptation from the *Teseida* was in fact mainly iconographic: it was not the temple of Mars, as the *Anelida* had promised, but the temple of Venus, from the same Book VII of Boccaccio's poem. Sixteen stanzas of the *Parliament of Fowls* (183–294) are adapted from the *Teseida*. They constitute Chaucer's closest imitation of Boccaccio.[11]

The stanzas devoted by Boccaccio to the description of the temples of Mars and Venus (and the glosses that accompany it) are in many ways the centre of the *Teseida*. In them, Boccaccio offers the reader a pictorial (and, in the commentary, allegorical) explanation of two of the forces that dominate the action of the poem, pointing as well to the knot of tragic irony that determines the subsequent plot. Gentle Arcite, interpreting literally Theseus' decree, according to which the knight who wins the tourney will have Emily, prays to Mars, the god and planet of war, violence and wrath. Bellicose Palamon prays to Venus, goddess and planet of love and 'concupiscible appetite'. An agreement between the two gods will later give literal satisfaction to the two lovers: Arcite will have victory, but Palamon will obtain the lady. Boccaccio makes every effort to convey the importance of these stanzas and of the parallel commentary (VII, xxix–xxxviii and l–lxvi). In particular, he has recourse to no less an authority than Statius for the temple of Mars, and he re-creates *ex novo* the ancient iconography of the temple of Venus. For this, he draws on Claudian, Ovid, the *Roman de la Rose* and various other medieval works, but fuses all preceding elements into a whole that is fundamentally new. It is a triumph of fourteenth-century iconography – and one which in many ways points to the encyclopedic mythography of Boccaccio's own later *Genealogie* and which was to have an influence on Renaissance poets.

It is in itself significant that Chaucer should prefer this to the purely medieval descriptions that he had followed in the temple of Venus of the *House of Fame*. And yet it is also clear that Chaucer uses it precisely because he can find in it a whole system of cultural references familiar to him (the classics, the *Roman*, the medieval exegetes). This compromise between old and new is a fundamental feature of Chaucer's career as a poet and as an intellectual.

At the same time, Chaucer uses Boccaccio's passage to serve his own purposes. Boccaccio's Venus is a stratification of courtly love (represented by the personifications found in the *Roman*), sensual love (Priapus, the naked goddess), tragic love (the stories painted in the temple), and of the planet (the copper columns). Chaucer needed – and preserved – all this, but wanted also the kind of garden that would link Venus and Nature (the protagonist of the second section of the *Parliament*). Thus, with the help of Dante and of the last section of the *Roman*,[12] he added an Edenic park, which is a sublimated garden of Nature, expanding on Boccaccio's description, re-ordering his author's material, and omitting important details such as the 'amorini' of *Teseida*, VII, liii.

The *Teseida* is a starting-point, a tableau on which Chaucer elaborates. He lingers on colours, and subtly shifts the emphasis of the iconography itself. The careful catalogue of trees,[13] flowers, fishes, birds and animals suggests that this is a garden of Love that has much to do with Nature. The music, the climate, the timelessness of the place suggest that this is also a 'Park of Paradise'.[14] These two aspects are clearly absent in the *Teseida*.

In the *Parliament*, then, Chaucer shows the extent of his cultural indebtedness to the *Teseida* as well as his poetic maturity: he translates Boccaccio very closely and yet manages to adapt his source to his own needs. Finally, he improves on Boccaccio's text stylistically: though he is still obviously fascinated by *ottava rima*, he finds a rhythm of his own and introduces pictorial details that enliven the texture:

> Con la quale oltre andando, vide quello
> ad ogni vista soave e ameno,
> in guisa d'un giardin fronzuto e bello
> e di piante verdissime ripieno,
> d'erbette fresche e d'ogni fior novello,
> e fonti vide chiare vi surgeno,
> e intra l'altre piante onde abondava,
> mortine più che altro le sembiava.
>
> (*Teseida*, VII, li)

A gardyn saw I ful of blosmy bowes
Upon a ryver, in a grene mede,
There as swetnesse everemore inow is,
With floures white, blewe, yelwe, and rede,
And colde welle-stremes, nothyng dede,
That swymmen ful of smale fishes lighte,
With fynnes rede and skales sylver bryghte.
                              (Parliament, 183–9)

e lasciata da lei quiv'entro entrare,
il luogo vide oscur nel primo gire;
ma poca luce poscia per lo stare
vi prese, e vide lei nuda giacere
sopr'un gran letto assai bello a vedere.
                              (Teseida, VII, lxiv, 4–8)

Derk was that place, but afterward lightnesse
I saw a lyte, unnethe it myghte be lesse,
And on a bed of gold she lay to reste,
Til that the hote sonne gan to weste.
                              (Parliament, 263–6)

Two references to Lollius, at the beginning and end of the poem, frame the *Troilus* (I, 393–5 and V, 1653), indicating Chaucer's decision to enter the mainstream of European narrative with a Troy story.[15] The way he adapted and changed the *Filostrato*, his authority on this occasion, is the subject of Barry Windeatt's essay in this volume. But R. A. Pratt had already suggested, over thirty years ago, that 'the *Teseida* may have profoundly influenced the characterization, the atmosphere, and the entire tone of *Troilus and Criseyde*', and I myself have developed this argument.[16] Pratt showed that the 'contributions from the *Teseida* . . . include addresses to the gods (an invocation by the poet, and light and serious adjurations by his characters); lines intensifying the atmosphere of fatalism; and ideas and phraseology transferred from the description of Arcita's funeral and urn to Troilus' discussion of his own funeral and urn'. Moreover, we find in the *Troilus* four of the *Teseida's* 'heightened time descriptions', that is 'four decorative stanzas, more or less enriched with mythological allusion, each of which describes either the dawn, or spring'.[17] Here is an example:

The gold-ytressed Phebus heighe on-lofte
Thries hadde alle with his bemes clene
The snowes molte, and Zepherus as ofte
Ibrought ayeyn the tendre leves grene,
Syn that the sone of Ecuba the queene . . .
                              (Troilus, V, 8–12)

And compare:

> Il sole avea due volte dissolute
> le nevi en gli alti poggi, e altrettante
> Zeffiro aveva le frondi rendute
> e i be' fiori alle spogliate piante,
> poi che d'Attena s'eran dipartute . . .
>
> (*Teseida*, II, i, 1–5)

Here, Chaucer even ventures to embroider on his source, transforming Boccaccio's simple 'sole' into 'gold-ytressed Phebus'. This and such other passages are, however, not merely decorative. They are functional to Chaucer's construction of a 'dual time-scheme' in *Troilus*[18] and to his intention of writing a romance that mixes high and low styles – a 'little tragedy' as he himself will call it. The epic matter (Dante's and Boccaccio's 'arma') as such is deliberately left out, but the love story is treated as if it were worthy of the sublime style. And if the *Divine Comedy* provided Chaucer with the supreme example of how to write a poem in such a composite manner, and the *Filostrato* with a suitable plot, it was the *Teseida* that offered him a model of how one could achieve loftiness in a *narrative* poem in the vernacular.

The influence of Boccaccio's poem on the *Troilus* increases as Chaucer draws nearer the end of his story. The first line of Book V is borrowed from the *Teseida* (IX, i, 1) and followed in the second stanza by the heightened time description that I have quoted above. The *rapprochement* culminates at the very end of Chaucer's poem, when Troilus, like Boccaccio's Arcite, ascends to the eighth sphere and proceeds to an unknown destination dictated by Mercury (*Troilus*, 1807–27; *Teseida*, XI, i–iii).

The *Teseida*, then, is for Chaucer not only a stylistic model for poetic invocations, time descriptions, and mythological and astronomical references. It affects the whole conception of the *Troilus* – its protagonist's character, its philosophical ideas, its turning from earthly events to the world beyond death, that world which Dante had described in the poem whose words conclude Chaucer's poem. For the first line of Book V of *Troilus* is

> Aprochen gan the fatal destyne . . .

and this line, which echoes the *Teseida*, sums up Chaucer's discussion throughout the *Troilus* of the role that Fate and Fortune play in human affairs. Hints of this theme could be found in the *Filostrato* (for instance, IV, 30–1), and Chaucer was to widen and deepen this perspective with his knowledge of Boethius (and Dante), but again it was the *Teseida* that put a strong emphasis on Fate and Fortune as two of the forces that dominate its story of love and give it a tragic atmosphere.[19] Nor is it pure chance that Chaucer's Troilus sounds more lyrical, more passionate, more profound than his model in the *Filostrato*. Indeed, this Troilus is more like the gentle, suffering, pensive Arcite of the *Teseida* – a Troilus who sings, laments, mourns, meditates like Arcite, a Troilus, moreover, who shares Arcite's ascent and destination after death.[20]

In a sense, then, the greatest triumph of Lollius as an 'auctour' is that he should have inspired the final dichotomy of *Troilus*, the seemingly abrupt change from earthly tragedy to the higher 'laughter' of Troilus (v, 21), the opening-up of an infinite perspective that shifts the focus of the poem from human to divine. It is the *Teseida* that sends Chaucer back to Dante, Lucan and Cicero.

When Arcite returns in disguise to Athens he assumes the name of 'Penteo', but in the *Knight's Tale* Chaucer will replace this alias with 'Philostrate', the very title of that work by Lollius which was the source of the *Troilus*. This is a characteristically oblique way of acknowledging one's debt to the author of the work one is imitating. Equally oblique is Chaucer's actual use of the *Teseida* in the *Knight's Tale*.[21] Here, Boccaccio's poem is a direct source and a narrative model that Chaucer must engage with at all levels – structural, iconographic, stylistic. And there is no doubt that the experiments of the *Anelida*, the *Parliament* and *Troilus* have some bearing on the attitude with which Chaucer now approaches the *Teseida*.

The plot of the *Teseida* is essentially respected in the *Knight's Tale*, but its time-scheme and its *dispositio* altered at key points. The time-span of the Tale is much longer than that of the source (for instance, the space between Arcite's death and the wedding of Palamon and Emily is a few days in the *Teseida*, 'certein yeres' in the *Knight's Tale*), and thus adds to the plot's narrative credibility. By contrast, the tourney is much shorter in Chaucer, who thus makes it more dense and dramatic. A typically narrative time-scheme replaces Boccaccio's more theatrical conception of the story. At the same time, the structure and *dispositio* are adapted by Chaucer to produce greater symmetry and tension. The twelve books of the *Teseida* are reduced to four parts, the first and fourth of which follow Boccaccio's structural order; but Books IV, V, VI and VII of the *Teseida* are rearranged by Chaucer so as to build up symmetrical patterns, suspense and dramatic tension. Similarly, Chaucer's choice of agents from the *Teseida*, his four main choral scenes, the pattern of Theseus', Arcite's and Palamon's speeches are designed to achieve symmetry through formalization and the construction of a pattern of repetitions and allusions. Finally, the central dramatic artifice of the *Teseida* – the literal interpretation that Arcite gives to Theseus' words – is kept in the *Knight's Tale*, but Chaucer makes it more effective by adding those details of the temple of Mars which show how the tragedy of Arcite's death depends also on his blindness, his ignorance, his failing to see all the implications of the planetary god's power.

The Tale's characters owe their basic traits to the *Teseida*, but Chaucer changes the system and depth of Boccaccio's characterization. Hippolyta has no role, minor characters such as Pamphilus, Alimetus and Itmon are altogether eliminated, Emily loses all individual depth and becomes a pretext, a romance device, the 'fair unknown'. The differences between Arcite and Palamon as characters are pared down, but they are set in much stronger dramatic contrast. At the centre of the Tale stands the only rounded character, Theseus, both an ideal figure and a typically feudal lord, the practical philosopher and a man of flesh and blood. Compared to Boccaccio's, Chaucer's characters are dramatic forces rather than human beings. They are lonely figures, whose mentality is dominated by feudal values rather than courtly manners, and who are for that very reason much closer to contemporary reality. They are surrounded by orderly crowds or isolated in the midst of mass scenes. Ligurge and Emetreus – the only survivors of Boccaccio's twenty-two kings arriving for the tourney – are concentrated symbols of characteristic forces (Saturn and Mars), which are mirrored in their external appearances. They have the flat surface of figures painted with no sense of perspective, but they are charged with all the meaning that colour, in the symbolically minded Middle Ages, is capable of conferring. There is perhaps nothing more alien than this to Boccaccio's mentality.

The setting, the iconography, the philosophy of the *Knight's Tale* are certainly inspired by the *Teseida*. Like *Troilus*, the Tale is set in the world of the mythological past. Like the *Teseida*, it shows us gods, temples, a theatre and pseudo-classical details. Like *Troilus* and *Teseida*, it is dominated by Fate and Fortune. The May and dawn themes run through it as in Boccaccio's poem. Yet there is no doubt that the overall effect of the *Knight's Tale* in these respects is profoundly different from that produced by the *Teseida*. Boccaccio constantly aims to set up as coherent a mythological and epic background as possible – in many ways his is an archaeological reconstruction of the world of classical antiquity, whereas Chaucer is decidedly ambivalent in this matter. On the one hand, he drops most of the purely decorative mythology of his source (even those

heightened time descriptions he used in the *Troilus*); he astrologizes
the gods, drastically cuts the catalogue of the princes, changes the
architecture of the theatre, and modifies the appearance of the temples.
He maintains, after all, that 'there is no newe gise that it nas old'
(2125). Thus, Boccaccio's Evander bears a storied shield that clearly
aims at reproducing the *topos* of Achilles' shield (VI, xxxviii–xxxix
and glosses), whereas Chaucer's warriors carry a 'Pruce sheeld' (2122).
Boccaccio speaks of princes, whereas Chaucer has 'every wight that
loved chivalrye'. Boccaccio talks of Arcady, Crete, Aegyna and all the
provinces of classical Greece, whereas Chaucer's Knight exclaims:

> For if ther fille tomorwe swich a cas,
> Ye knowen wel that every lusty knight,
> That loveth paramours, and hath his might,
> Were it in Engelond, or elleswhere,
> They wolde, hir thankes, wilnen to be there...
>
> (2110–14)

On the other hand, Chaucer keeps apparently minor details like
laurel crowns or the funeral torch; he follows Boccaccio closely when
describing the 'rites of the paien wise'; he even improves on his source
by pointing out the nakedness of wrestlers – a detail closer to classical
reality than the Boccaccio of the *Teseida* ever came. And if he gives his
gods an astrological significance, dozens of instances of pagan lore
borrowed from the *Teseida* are to be found in the *Knight's Tale*, where
Chaucer introduces Mercury's appearance to Arcite, which has no
equivalent in Boccaccio's poem. The Knight points out ancient
customs, specifying four times: 'as was that time the gise'.

The *Teseida*, in short, has a mythological, iconographic, cultural
influence on the *Knight's Tale*. Chaucer has expanded and underlined
the pomp, the ceremony, the formality and the colour of, for instance,
the great choral scenes of his story (arrival of the princes, entrance of
the two parties into the theatre, Arcite's funeral), and has subtly
established more than one parallel between his world – the world of
contemporary England – and that of classical Athens. But this, again,
was suggested by the *Teseida*. In the end, the difference between the
two poems at this level is measured by a different degree of mimetic
emphasis.

Where Chaucer resolutely departs from Boccaccio's practice – and
from his own in the *Troilus* – is at the level of style. Boccaccio
maintains an even rhythm and a high register throughout the
Teseida, his narrative is often built by the characters' speeches, his use
of rhetorical figures is explicit, his descriptive passages are often abstract
and complicated. Chaucer eliminates precisely those elements which

would help him to keep up evenness and grandeur. Boccaccio's courtly exchanges become harsh quarrels or academic disputations, his almost operatic sense of drama is transformed: a convention of extreme emotion, a heightening of tension together with images of violence and darkness fill the *Knight's Tale* with sound and fury. The style of the Tale is mixed, even more so than in *Troilus*: sudden changes of intonation (like the famous 'therfore I stynte, I nam no divinistre' of lines 2809–15) are more noticeable here than in the wider canvas of *Troilus*. The use of rhetoric is very marked (and there is no doubt that the *Teseida* is at work here, too), the Tale is full of *correctio, repetitio, compar, contrarium*, and the *occupatio* describing Arcite's funeral occupies forty-five lines. Chaucer's similes, however, rely more on traditional associations, on *consuetudo* rather than *audacia* ('The crueel Ire, reed as any glede'). Moreover, one of the central features of the *Knight's Tale* is Chaucer's constant effort to create what looks like a system of repeated allusions culminating in one central image and then continuing throughout the Tale. Such is the series of hints, premonitions and prefigurations referring to Arcite's death – the 'colde deeth, with mouth gaping upright' in the temple of Mars, the 'maladies colde' of Saturn, the 'coold of deeth' that overcomes Arcite at the end. Such is the animal imagery that refers to Palamon, Arcite, Lygurge and Emetreus, but also to Theseus. This technique has no equivalent in the *Teseida*.

Chaucer is never abstract in his images. When Boccaccio, following Statius, describes the temple of Mars, he at first uses concrete words, but then shifts the emphasis onto increasingly abstract details culminating in the bas-reliefs adorning the temple. There is, by contrast, no process of abstraction in Chaucer's description of the temple. There is in fact a crescendo of concreteness, a mounting accumulation of terrible – immediately terrible – details. Perhaps if one compares the two following lines

> E con gli occulti ferri i tradimenti
> 　　　　　　(*Teseida*, VII, xxxiv, 1)

> The smylere with the knyf under the cloke
> 　　　　　　(*Knight's Tale*, 1999)

one sees the force of Jorge Luis Borges' remark that we have in these descriptions a passage from allegory to novel, from species to individuals, from realism to nominalism.[22]

The ultimate difference between *Teseida* and *Knight's Tale* is one of narrative method and imagination. Chaucer works essentially by association – he accumulates a series of details that allude to a wider dimension. Lygurge and Emetreus are not similar to Saturn and Mars; they represent Saturn and Mars in their appearance, dress and colours. It is the list of these details that gives us their significance. This method of internal association, by which images are juxtaposed to build up a coherent pattern of suggested meaning, has been called 'metonymic'. It is profoundly alien to Boccaccio, who superimposes an external significance on his descriptions: Mars is an allegory of irascible appetite. The epic similes of the *Teseida* are part of a tradition, but they also respond to Boccaccio's constant need for a term of comparison, for a relationship of similarity or contrast. His method is essentially 'metaphorical'.[23]

These differences reflect two diverse cultural formations, a different degree of poetic maturity, and diverging philosophical attitudes. Yet the *Teseida* became part of Chaucer's culture, a model by which he was inspired and against which he reacted when it came to decisive choices of style and meaning. In the *House of Fame* Chaucer seems to say that the muses dwell on Boccaccio's Parnassus. The stylistic experiment of the *Anelida*, the iconographic tableau of the *Parliament*, above all the two widely diverging routes of *Troilus* and *Knight's Tale* seem to indicate that Lollius really deserved to be celebrated in the Palace of Fame.

Notes

1 T. Tasso, *Discorsi sul Poema Eroico*, II, ed. E. Mazzali in T. Tasso, *Prose* (Milan–Naples, 1969), p. 551.

2 Tasso, *Discorsi*, VI, p. 724.

3 Tasso, *Discorsi*, IV, p. 641; V, p. 678; V, p. 680.

4 *Teseida*, XII, lxxxiv, 6–8, and cf. *De Vulgari Eloquentia*, II, ii, 10. In the first section of this essay I sum up the results of a fuller examination of the *Teseida* that I completed in my *Chaucer and Boccaccio* (Oxford, 1977), chapter 1 *et passim*. For a bibliography on the *Teseida*, see E. Esposito, *Boccacciana* (Ravenna, 1976). A translation of the poem was published in America almost a decade ago: *The Book of Theseus*, trans. B. M. McCoy (New York, 1974). Much more accurate and useful is N. Havely's *Chaucer's Boccaccio* (Cambridge and Totowa, N.J., 1980), which includes a complete translation of *Filostrato*, excerpts from *Teseida* and *Filocolo*, from Benoit's *Roman de Troie* and Guido delle Colonne's *Historia*, and a good Introduction and Bibliography.

5 For the sources of the *Teseida*, see my *Chaucer and Boccaccio*, pp. 41–5 and notes therein.

6 For Boccaccio's commentary and the problems it presents, see my *Chaucer and Boccaccio*, p. 6 and the whole of chapter 1; and R. Hollander, 'The Validity of Boccaccio's Self-Exegesis in His *Teseida*', *Medievalia et Humanistica*, n.s. VIII (1977), 163–83. Hollander had already made some of his observations in *Boccaccio's Two Venuses* (New York, 1977), pp. 53–65 and 184–92. We reached our conclusions independently and do not agree on some points.

7 I am following R. A. Pratt's scheme in his 'Chaucer's Use of the *Teseida*', *PMLA*, LXII (1947), 598–621. While I do not agree with everything Pratt said, I think it is only fair to acknowledge the debt that anyone dealing with the present subject must have to Pratt's article, whose lines of inquiry remain valid and are still followed here.

8 *House of Fame*, 518–22; *Teseida*, I, iii, 3 (for Venus) and Teseida, I, i, 1–5 (for the Muses). The detail of the Helicon as 'clere welle' derives from *Teseida*, XI, lxiii, 3–4, as was pointed out long ago by J. L. Lowes, 'Chaucer and Dante', *Modern Philology*, XIV (1917), 725. Boccaccio mentions the muses and Parnassus before his invocation to his lady (imitated by Chaucer in the Prologue to the *Legend of Good Women*, F 84–96) in *Filostrato*, I, 4; and Dante invokes them in *Inf.*, II, 7, a passage Chaucer uses in the lines immediately following these (*House of Fame*, 523–8).

9 See my 'Chaucer's Temples of Venus', *Studi Inglesi*, II (1975), 17–21.

10 Pratt, 'Chaucer's Use', p. 605. I am very much indebted to Pratt's discussion of *Teseida* and *Anelida*. The following are the correspondences between *Anelida* and *Teseida*: *Anelida*, 22–44, *Teseida*, II, xviii–xxii (and ultimately *Thebaid*, XII, 519–35); *Anelida*, 50–70, *Teseida*, II, x–xii and III, i.

11 See my 'Chaucer's Temples of Venus', which I am following in this section.

12 *Roman de la Rose* (ed. F. Lecoy (Paris, 1970), vol. III), 19,900–20,673. This is the speech of Genius on the 'parc du champ joli' contraposed to the Garden of Deduit and Love.

13 See my 'Chaucer and Lists of Trees', *Reading Medieval Studies*, II (1976), 28–44.

14 See J. A. W. Bennett, *The Parlement of Foules. An Interpretation* (Oxford, 1957), chapter 2; and my *English Medieval Narrative in the Thirteenth and Fourteenth Centuries* (Cambridge, 1982), chapter 6, 1.

15 The fact that the first reference seems to point not to Boccaccio but to Petrarch, whose sonnet 'S'Amor non è' (absent in the *Filostrato*) Chaucer immediately afterwards adapts (400–20), is one of those mysteries of Chaucerian studies I will not try to unravel. And see my Introduction above.

16 Pratt, 'Chaucer's Use', p. 612; Boitani, *English Medieval Narrative*, chapter 6, 2.

17 Pratt, 'Chaucer's Use', p. 609 and notes therein.

18 H. W. Sams, 'The Dual Time-Scheme in Chaucer's *Troilus*'; and D. C. Boughner, 'Elements of Epic Grandeur in the *Troilus*', both in R. J. Schoeck and J. Taylor (eds.), *Chaucer Criticism*, vol. II (Notre Dame–London, 1961), pp. 180–95.

19 On the role of Fate and Fortune in the *Teseida* see my *Chaucer and Boccaccio*, pp. 11–20.

20 See G. Velli, 'L'apoteosi di Arcita: ideologia e coscienza storica nel "Teseida"', now in his *Petrarca e Boccaccio* (Padua, 1979), pp. 122–55.

21 To this I have devoted most of my *Chaucer and Boccaccio*, which I follow here, in particular pp. 127–30, 76–8, 131–4, 82–7, 135–47, 148–64.

22 J. L. Borges, 'De las alegorías a las novelas' in his *Otras Inquisiciones* (Buenos Aires–Madrid, 1976 edn.), p. 156.

23 For metonymy and metaphor in this sense, see R. Jakobson and M. Halle, *Fundamentals of Language*, 2nd edn. (The Hague–Paris, 1971), pp. 90–6; and, for Chaucer, D. S. Brewer, *Chaucer*, 3rd edn. (London, 1973), pp. 208–10.

The Wake of the *Commedia*: Chaucer's *Canterbury Tales* and Boccaccio's *Decameron*

My principal concern in this essay will be to draw attention to the dissimilarities between the *Canterbury Tales* and the *Decameron*. There is no clear evidence that Chaucer ever used the *Decameron* as a source of material, and on examination his work reveals itself to be consistently different in character from Boccaccio's. However, on a number of general points the two works plainly are comparable; and the resemblances between them need to be considered if the originality and distinctiveness of each is to be duly recognized.

In the first place, the two authors are closely akin in their cultural origins and literary preparation. Both, of course, were deeply indebted to the French tradition. Indeed, given the interest that they both took in *fabliau* and romance, the influence of this tradition might seem to be paramount. Yet it needs to be emphasized – as the present volume is well-placed to do – that the literature of the Italian Trecento also exerted an influence upon the formation of the *Canterbury Tales* that was by no means unlike the influence it had upon the *Decameron*. The *Decameron* is firmly rooted in its native tradition, reflecting in particular Boccaccio's life-long study of Dante's *Comedy*. But Chaucer, too, revered Dante, as Piero Boitani has shown, and expressed his regard in such intelligent and subtle acts of 'translation' as we find in the *Monk's Tale*.

In view of the tradition from which they emerge, the second and most obvious resemblance between the two writers suddenly becomes problematical. If we couple Boccaccio and Chaucer at all, it is of course because they both produced collections of relatively short stories, written for the most part in a comic key. Yet the example of Dante's *Commedia* would have pointed to a wholly different development. In the *Commedia* Dante had demonstrated once and for all that vernacular poetry was capable both of sustained narrative and of philosophical rigour. And there is every reason to suppose that Boccaccio and Chaucer were responsive to this example. Each of them had a capacity for lengthy narrative.[1] Each was interested in philosophy and competent to write it; Chaucer translates Boethius and Boccaccio cites the *Consolatio* with considerable finesse in his *Esposizioni sopra le Comedia di Dante*.[2] Why, then, should each have devoted his best energies to a form that might reasonably have been regarded as trivial?

The question is one that Chaucer and Boccaccio would both have considered legitimate, as is evident from the apologies and retractions that punctuate their work. Chaucer ends the *Canterbury Tales* with a comprehensive repudiation of his former 'translaciouns and endytings of worldly vanitees' – but thanks God for allowing him to write the 'translacioun of Boece de Consolacione' – while Boccaccio, more pugnaciously, confronts those who 'will say that I have allowed myself too much licence in writing these stories'.

Boccaccio and Chaucer may, then, be alike in lineage and in the forms they employ. Viewed, however, in the light of the Italian Trecento they also share a common artistic and intellectual problem. And to see more precisely what this problem was we may turn to the work of the Italian author who, after Dante, was held in the highest esteem by Boccaccio and Chaucer – 'Fraunceys Petrak, the lauriat poete'. In Petrarch's case, the difficulties that beset the post-Dantean writer are presented with an unresolved, almost tragic acuteness.

At the heart of Petrarch's poetry in the *Rime Sparse* lies the problem of self-consciousness. From the moment in the introductory sonnet where Petrarch speaks of the shame he feels for his past error ('onde sovente / di me medesmo meco mi vergogno'), his verses record the continual oscillation between glory and guilt in his love for Laura and demonstrate his unfailing attention to the shifts of his own conscience. In its own way the *Commedia*, too, represents an act of self-investigation; at every point in the poem, the poet trains a critical eye upon his own shortcomings and successes as represented in the *personaggio*. Yet there is a marked difference between Dante's procedure and Petrarch's. Petrarch – as is clear, for instance, from *De sui ipsius et multorum ignorantia* – deliberately discarded a number of the principles that Dante had employed, and indeed celebrated, in the triumphant self-analysis of the *Commedia*. Petrarch 'did not adore Aristotle' or scholastic philosophy. And with the courage that declares him to be a precursor of humanistic thought, he rejects the technical ability that Dante acquired from this philosophy to analyse, clarify and focus the erring spirit upon a settled end.[3] The tragic result, however, is that consciousness itself becomes problematical, so that Petrarch can at times embrace the image of his own transformation into the insensible stone or laurel. To Dante such a transformation would have seemed fit only for an infernal punishment; the one change that he would admit is that which is wrought upon the spirit in purgation and beatitude.

In their moral preoccupations Chaucer and Boccaccio are closer to Petrarch than they are to Dante. Neither, of course, presents the problem of self-consciousness as directly as Petrarch does. Indeed, it is an important function of comedy and narrative in each case to keep the issue on a relatively impersonal plane. Yet the comedy in its simplest and most rumbustious aspect also amounts to a vindication – achieved without recourse to systematic thought – of the natural impulses that caused Petrarch such suffering and shame. Chaucer and Boccaccio also share a fascination with a particular type of figure – the hypocritical cleric – who provides a fictional and ironic expression for the central issues of Petrarch's dilemma. In Chaucer's Pardoner or Friar and almost any of Boccaccio's guileful priests, a picture emerges of the mysterious force of appetite and the convolutions of the human conscience; simultaneously, the schemes of pardon and redemption that the false clerics adapt to their own devices are – if not wholly discredited – at least called into question. In the *Commedia* not even the corruption of Pope Boniface VIII could detract from his power as pope to proclaim a Jubilee.

The self-consciousness of Petrarch in its moral aspect marks a considerable change in sensibility from the work of Dante.[4] But an even more striking indication of change is the acutely literary self-consciousness that inspires Petrarch's writings. It is one of the most important characteristics of the *Commedia* that no division should appear to exist between the literary and the moral life. Virgil and Beatrice are principles of the spiritual and intellectual life; equally the two figures are associated with modes of poetic procedure. Thus whether Dante is writing epic or love lyric, he seems confident that he is performing a valid moral task. In Petrarch this confidence has been lost. Laura, to be sure, can at times represent poetic glory just as she can represent celestial purpose. But in all her aspects she can prove delusive in a way that Beatrice never could, and, in poem after poem, Petrarch envisages the possibility that poetic glory may be as fallacious as secular love itself. The literary instinct has become autonomous, seeking a satisfaction that has no sanction in morality. (In the *Secretum*, Augustine can reprove Petrarch for his delirious devotion to the mere word, Laura.)

Among the manifestations of Petrarch's literary self-consciousness, there are two in particular that concern us as we approach Chaucer and Boccaccio. The first is his peculiarly strong sense of his own place within the traditions of vernacular love poetry. In, for instance, the seventieth poem in the *Rime Sparse* – the canzone 'Lasso me, ch'i' non so in qual parte pieghi' – Petrarch laments his present inability to speak freely of his love as once he could, and, as if to remedy his own inarticulateness, he begins each stanza with a quotation from a predecessor in the Romance tradition. Arnaut Daniel, Guido Cavalcanti, Cino da Pistoia and Dante are all cited, and the canzone ends with a direct quotation from an earlier poem in the *Rime Sparse* – number XXIII, 'Nel dolce tempo de la prima etade'. The sense is that, while Petrarch once had the right to associate himself with the great poets of the immediate past, he no longer commands the words that prove his title.

Canzone LXX is among the most tragic poems in Petrarch's collection. And the literary pathos that it expresses will surely be familiar to the twentieth-century reader: individual talent seeks a voice of its own; yet it relies upon the voices of the past, and, the greater the merit of past achievements, the greater the difficulty of finding an original voice. Thus on the one hand Petrarch acknowledges Dante in his quotation from 'Così nel mio parlar', on the other, he can say that he fears to be overwhelmed by the influence of Dante.[5] The prestige of Dante was as much a difficulty as a stimulus and resource.

The presence of Dante also lies behind the second difficulty that Petrarch faces. This is the problem of structure. In few things is Petrarch further from Dante and in few closer to Boccaccio and Chaucer than in the structure he has devised for the *Rime Sparse*. For the *Rime Sparse* possess nothing of the philosophical or narrative coherence we associate with the *Commedia*. The work, as the designation 'Rime Sparse' indicates, is a collection of fragments. It is none the less clear that Petrarch was concerned to achieve a sort of order within the collection – albeit of a different kind from the order of the *Commedia*. His continual revision of the text and disposition of his poems is evidence of this. And the result is a work that depends not upon narrative (even the obvious chronological order is never strictly observed), but upon a highly wrought tissue of verbal cross-references and echoes. In respect of theme, the poet is as likely to contradict as to advance the implications of one poem in the poem that immediately succeeds it. Yet as echo follows echo the ghost – or promise – of an order haunts the apparent fragments.

In Boccaccio's *Decameron*, the notion of order, in both its philosophical and its artistic aspects, enjoys an exceptional prominence, and in

organizing his work Boccaccio seems to have been influenced by the
Commedia far more consciously than Petrarch was. There can be no
doubt that he was a devoted reader of the work; the language of all
his vernacular writings is shot through with reminiscences – conscious
and unconscious – of Dante's poetry, while in two works that
immediately precede the composition of the *Decameron* – the *Amorosa
Visione* and the *Ameto* – Boccaccio, like Dante, depicts a process of
spiritual education and chooses a form that can only be described as a
free variation upon the form of the *Commedia*. All of this supports
the view, vigorously argued by Vittore Branca, that the *Decameron*
may be seen as an imitation of the *Commedia*.[6] The work is not
dissimilar in its surface structure, being composed, as the *Commedia*
is, of a hundred units. More importantly, the scope of the work is also
comparable in Branca's view to Dante's. The *Ameto* and the *Amorosa
Visione* are Dantean depictions of spiritual education, and so, we
might say, is the *Decameron*. The work proceeds from the misery of
the plague, evoked in the Introduction, through a portrayal of love and
intelligence in the behaviour of the *brigata*, to the moment when the
young people of the *brigata* return to a healthy and revitalized
Florence. Then, too, the stories told in the *Decameron* have clearly been
conceived to express the greatest possible variety in human behaviour,
from the depravity of Cepperello in the first tale to the saintliness of
Griselda in the last.

In outline at least the *Canterbury Tales* displays a similar deter-
mination to build a significant frame around the fragments of the tales
themselves. The General Prologue, in conjunction with the subsequent
prologues and epilogues, provides a structure of great imaginative
force; our reading of the work as a whole is governed by a process of
continual cross-reference between the authorial comments of the
General Prologue and the dramatically-conceived manifestations of
character in particular prologues and epilogues. Thematically, too, the
General Prologue expresses a precise understanding of how the
schemes of nature, society and devotion govern the lives of individual
beings. Pilgrimage is the expression of all three; as birds are moved in
their hearts to sing, so, when April comes, then 'longen folk to goon
on pilgrimages', and in these pilgrimages the social order is soon in
evidence. Then, within the framework of the pilgrimage, the tales
sketch an arc of spiritual movement that runs from the secular virtue
of the Knight to the religious virtue of the Parson.

So far, Boccaccio and Chaucer appear to have achieved a more explicit
and stable representation of order than Petrarch ever did. And this in

a sense is so. Yet the most striking similarity between the *Decameron* and the *Canterbury Tales* is that clarity of structure is counterpoised by an ambiguity as sharp as any that emerges from the *Rime Sparse*. The case of Boccaccio is especially telling. It is, for instance, an essential characteristic of Boccaccio's art that the story of Griselda – which would represent a triumphant conclusion if the *Decameron* followed a simple progression towards virtue – should be told by Dioneo, who throughout the *Decameron* has been responsible for the most licentious stories in the collection. I shall have more to say on this score in considering the Griselda story in relation to the *Clerk's Tale*. The figure of Dioneo himself, however, is of cardinal importance to the structure of the *Decameron*.

Throughout Boccaccio's collection, Dioneo is recognized as a principle of licensed anarchy. Thus when the *brigata* decide that the stories they tell should follow definite themes rather than be wholly *ad libitum*, Dioneo asks for a dispensation; though he admits the value of the 'ordine' which his companions will observe, he asks as a special favour ('di spezial grazia') that he should not be constrained to proceed 'secondo la proposta data' if he feels disinclined, but rather be allowed to speak as he himself pleases ('ma quale più di dire mi piacerà') (First Day, Conclusion, 12–13). Dioneo claims the right to respond to the promptings of his own wit, even to the point of subverting the order that his fellows have agreed upon. Yet he does this with the consent of his companions and cannot be considered a purely anarchic figure.

The tension between order and arbitrariness that is expressed in the figure of Dioneo is a central feature of Boccaccio's vision in the *Decameron*; in the framing images of the work and in the events of particular stories, the tolerance of established schemes is constantly tested against the claims of the unpredictable. The work begins with a portrayal of the wholly unexpected devastation that the plague wrought in Florence; and the emphasis here falls upon the dissolution of the established rituals and decencies of Florentine life 'which in large part ceased or were replaced by new forms' (Introduction, 33–5). Against this, however, the young people of the *brigata*, from their first appearance surrounded by the horrors of disease, display a vital instinct for orderly behaviour. Though others have found an excuse for vicious living in the disruption of the plague, the *brigata* are determined to 'avoid like death' these base examples and to live, at their country house, 'without transgressing in any respect the limit of reason' (Introduction, 52–75). Their first acts on arriving in the country involve the election of a ruler to regulate the day-to-day festivities. Every aspect of their behaviour is governed henceforth by conventions and ceremonies of their own devising, which maintain and enhance the social bond that the plague had threatened.

Though the order that the *brigata* creates is emphatically rational, it is not in any ordinary sense moral in character; it has, rather, a strongly aesthetic component – as is clear from the part that song, dance, and story-telling play in it – and depends upon the exercise of a free intelligence that can constantly discover and delight in new modes of conduct. In this respect, the impulses of the *brigata* at large are not at odds with those of Dioneo. His companions share with him an untrammelled flexibility of intelligence, and this same flexibility is the central feature both of theme and structure in the *Decameron*. The classic situation in a Boccaccian tale is one in which a man recovers his fortunes by an action which may be as unpredictable – or amoral – as the initial stroke of misfortune but which proves to have a perfect suitability to circumstance. For instance, when the merchant Landolfo – Second Day, iv – is ruined by a glut on the market of the goods in which he specializes he turns pirate to repair his fortunes. (It is not difficult to discern here in outline Machiavelli's opposition of 'virtù' and Fortune.)

A similar flexibility is reflected in the structure of the *Decameron* itself. At no point does Boccaccio offer or even seek the whole truth – which Dante is always confident he can find – even about the phenomena that the author is most interested in. Love, Nature, Fortune and Magnanimity are themes that are all proposed in the *Decameron*. Yet none is ever brought to a final definition. Love is shown in every aspect from coarse sexuality to charming sentimentality. The desire to be magnanimous may inspire the fabulous generosity of Saladin or Charlemagne, but also provokes the perversities of Mithradanes, Titus and Gisippus and the Marquis of Saluzzo. Even within the confines of a single story the definition of a notion may shift, as for instance, in the third tale of the Second Day: a young steward restores his wastrel masters to prosperity by his financial acumen and wards off further disaster when an English princess – against all the rules of social decorum – falls in love with him; the changes of Fortune in the first half of the story derive, not from the caprice of a metaphysical providence, but from the action of economic laws, and then, in the second half, are attributed to sexual attraction.

At the heart of the *Canterbury Tales* there is an ambiguity as suggestive as any we have seen in the *Decameron*. The guiding symbol of the work, the Canterbury journey, is itself inherently ambiguous; as a pilgrimage it may define the true goals of the human spirit, but another goal is the victory supper – the celebration of flesh and frivolity – in the Tabard on the return from St Thomas' shrine. Though the plan of the *Canterbury Tales* is not complete, the complexity of Chaucer's image could only have increased if we had witnessed the arrival at Canterbury and the return to Southwark. Even as it is, the image points to the highly charged contradictions at the centre of the work.

The most significant of these focus upon the figure of the Host. Not only does the Host remind us constantly of the ethos of the Tabard, but he is also allowed to question, in a far more radical way than Dioneo does, the principles upon which the work that contains him is constructed. For the Host is above all a plain speaker and the voice of commonsense. Yet the tales that the Host commissions – and undoubtedly enjoys – are works of highly literate fantasy that could well be presented as a folio of exercises in late medieval stylistics. The Host's presence, along with the effects of the prologues and epilogues, challenges the very literacy that has generated the work in which he appears.

I shall have more to say of the Host, especially since the implications of the figure are related to the literary incompetence of the Chaucer-persona, and to certain aspects of two sequences that I shall consider shortly – the *Wife of Bath's Tale* and Prologue, and the *Pardoner's Tale* and Prologue. It will already be clear, however, that the Host, as director of proceedings, is an appropriately disorderly guide to a group of individuals who have fallen together by 'cas or aventure'. And where in the *Decameron* a similarly random group quickly establishes a law for itself, the Host presides over a sequence that, while pretending to good order, is marked at every turn by the subversive or distracting impact of voices declaring their pleasure. So far from there being no Dioneo in the *Canterbury Tales*, it might be said that every speaker in the work is a Dioneo. So, at the end of the *Knight's Tale*, when the Host sensibly attempts to proceed by due degree to the Monk, he is stopped in his tracks by the drunken insistence of the Miller: 'For I wol speke, or elles go my wey' (Prologue to the *Miller's Tale*, i, 3133). This is the first of several such derangements proceeding from drunkenness or animosity. But disturbances can be created by far subtler tones; the incompetence of the pilgrim Chaucer, the cynical self-dramatization of the Merchant, the headlong indiscretion of the Canon's Yeoman all have an immediacy of appeal that outweighs the considerations of overall design.

As in the *Decameron*, so in the *Canterbury Tales* the contradictions of structure are compatible with the details of particular stories. In regard to the treatment of theme, Chaucer is no more interested in final statement than Boccaccio is, and juxtaposition – an effect frequently noticed in Chaucer's collection – is one indication of this. The *Miller's Tale* parodies the solemn interest that the Knight has taken in love and, in portraying the Carpenter's mystic dabblings, mocks the sea-deep questions of predestination. From the many views of marriage that the *Tales* present, no single or general notion of a good marriage prevails. (Unless it be the Franklin's. Yet the Franklin shows happiness to depend upon a coincidence of generous intentions that is so particular that it necessarily defeats generalization. Nor does his authority derive from argument or philosophy but from the geniality and persuasiveness of his presence.) Then again, when the Monk takes up the theme of tragedy, the seriousness that might attach to the subject is dissipated by the knowledge of the Monk that we carry from the General Prologue; no account of the mutability of man's life can be received with total gravity when voiced by a figure so singlemindedly devoted to pleasure as the Monk. An ironic response is inevitable.

Enough has been said to suggest that the notion of order itself and the structure that reflects it are as problematical in Chaucer as in Boccaccio. It will also be apparent that the two authors differ in their approach to the problem and in the solutions they project.

In Boccaccio's case, the short story, though admitting the possibility of fragmentation, is employed so as to place before the reader a pattern of constantly changing themes and experiences. This pattern simultaneously evades definition and calls into play the critical and interpretative powers of the reader, who, like the *brigata*, is invited to take pleasure in the moves and counter-moves of a sophisticated game. The ordinary experience of life is important primarily as the material for art; the anecdotes, gossip, legend and folk-tales of the Florence that the *brigata* left are transformed first into highly literate entertainments – and ultimately into the book that Boccaccio lays before us. Art – or craft – is shown to be as efficacious and essentially human as any normative exercise of moral reason or commonsense.

Chaucer offers us the reverse of this. The originality of the *Canterbury Tales* is best indicated by the prologues and epilogues that Chaucer wrote specifically for the work; and when the English reader complains that Boccaccio's story-tellers lack individuality, he mistakes the focus of Boccaccio's work, but accurately identifies the nature of the *Canterbury Tales*. Here, the short story, precisely in being fragmentary, is used to show how human individuality constantly evades confinement. The voices of Chaucer's pilgrims, so far from observing decorum, threaten the circumscription of literary art itself, and carry the reader back to the sphere of badinage and brouhaha that the narrators of the *Decameron* keep aristocratically at a distance. In the *Decameron*, the Host, the Wife of Bath, the Pardoner, even the pilgrim Chaucer would have been characters not players. But Chaucer's art is to show that art itself is not enough to comprehend the value of individuality. His work consistently requires of the reader a directness of response and a common humanity that together constitute an unsystematic but secure morality.

We have now to consider how the difference between Boccaccio and Chaucer is registered in the detail of their texts. In this regard a feature of central importance is the representation that each author offers of his own activities *as* an author. Both the *Decameron* and the *Canterbury Tales* contain passages that reflect the artistic self-consciousness of their creators. This is especially clear in Chaucer's case; indeed the Chaucerian persona may be seen as a comic but wonderfully sufficient remedy for the intellectual and artistic troubles that so beset Petrarch. Presenting himself – in Morton Bloomfield's words – as 'a bumbling creator', Chaucer admits the limits and relative unimportance of art; he abdicates any claim to the confusing laurel, but wins the right, by his modesty, to be looked upon with the 'objective love' that Petrarch could only crave without total conviction from God.[7] In Boccaccio we find nothing of this.

Boccaccio as author of the *Decameron* appears in three sequences of the work, in the Proem, the Epilogue and the remarkable Prologue to the Fourth Day. In all of these – though most notably in the Fourth-Day Prologue – Boccaccio sets himself to answer the criticisms, real or imagined, that the work has already begun to attract. One essential move in this defence is a claim for the dignity of his own enterprise. He draws attention to the labour that the composition of the work requires of him, suggesting, in terms that would not be out of place in Dante's *Paradiso*, that divine grace has aided him in bringing the work to its conclusion. In the closing lines he offers not a palinode but rather thanks to God that after so much labour ('sì lunga fatica') He should have brought the author to his desired end (29). Nothing could be less like the modest and self-critical retraction with which Chaucer ends his work. Nor do such passages strike one as depictions of a persona. Boccaccio here seems to be conducting a debate with himself and it is hard to repress the sense that he himself was foremost among his own detractors; he speaks as a nervous humanist, uncertain as to the standing of his literary work, yet convinced that his true worth will only be known to those who recognize the merit of his writings.

Thus far, Boccaccio has revealed a kinship rather with the Petrarch of the *Rime Sparse* than with Chaucer who in the Chaucer-persona – and also in his conception of the Host – allows literature itself to be called into question. There are, however, two further aspects of the defence, which do indicate a certain restriction of aim and point to the characteristics of the comic solution that Boccaccio found for the problems of self-consciousness.

The first of these is Boccaccio's insistence that the *Decameron* is intended as a pastime for lady readers who 'for most of their time are enclosed in the little circuit of their rooms' (Proem, 9–11). The work will not pretend to encompass the wide-ranging affairs of the 'real' or 'masculine' world. Even so Boccaccio is not self-deprecating. For one thing, it is entirely in the tradition of courtly love that the servant should offer the best of his labours to the lady; and it is significant that Boccaccio should justify his devotion to the 'carissime donne' by invoking the example of Guido Cavalcanti, Cino da Pistoia and Dante – three of the four poets whom Petrarch cites in the canzone 'Lasso me, ch'i' non so in qual parte pieghi' (Fourth Day, Prologue, 33). Yet, while recognizing the tradition, Boccaccio's attitude to the lady reader entails a notion of literature – and a view of readership – that extends and radically alters the implications of the tradition. In writing for the 'Donne ch'avete intelletto d'amore', the poet recognized that there was an absolute moral sanction for the fundamental activities of the human being, and sought in the light of that to bring the reader to a rational realization of his potentialities. Such a view involves a vindication of the movements of the human psyche. And it is this aspect of the *stil novo* that Boccaccio sets himself to develop.

In writing a work that is confessedly a pastime, Boccaccio plainly abandons the sphere of angelically certain principle, but allows himself consequently to focus – as Petrarch also does – upon the movements of human nature within the sphere of time. The lady, with time on her hands and confined within the circle of her room, displays precisely the possibilities that this restriction of aim reveals. Her confinement, in inverse proportion to her free time, will make her only the more aware of the fluctuating impulses and remote tonalities of mood that the human imagination can produce. So Boccaccio addresses himself to those who 'out of fearfulness and shame keep their love hidden in the delicate breast – and hidden love is far more vigorous than open love' (Proem, 10). There is a hint of decadence in this – more than a hint in that appalling picture of neurosis, the *Elegia di Madonna Fiammetta* – and clearly we are some distance here from the prevailingly open-air atmosphere of the *Canterbury Tales* with its four-square certainties of space, time and itinerary. But Boccaccio's concern at its healthiest is to create an inner space, liberating through literature the manifold possibilities of the human being. The reader, like the *brigata* – and like the witty and unfettered women who appear throughout the *Decameron* – is called upon to accept and cultivate free time.

The final point that concerns us in Boccaccio's view of his art is his critical sense of the medium that his narrative art employs – his view of language itself.[8] Boccaccio realized as profoundly as Dante the conventional and arbitrary character of human discourse. And in keeping with his sense of the purpose of literature, he stresses the infinite adaptability of language to the shifts of the mind's pleasure. Thus in the Epilogue he denies any inherent virtue to words, insisting that they are instruments to be used like any other as the mind desires (Conclusion, 13–14). This is the crucial point in Boccaccio's defence of such vulgarisms of diction as 'foro', 'caviglia', 'mortaio', 'pestello', 'salsiccia' and 'mortadello' ('hole', 'rod', 'mortar', 'pestle', 'dish' and 'stuffing'); words are utterly neutral and unmagical, the mind is their master: 'A corrupted mind never understood words aright' (Conclusion, 11). The richest statement of this theme occurs in the story that Boccaccio tells as part of his self-defence, in the Fourth-Day Prologue. The story tells of how Filippo Balducci, on the death of his wife, retires from the world to live a life of religious solitude. He is accompanied by his young son, whom he attempts to defend from all worldly vanities and attractions. But this attempt is a failure. The son, having to make an expedition to Florence for the necessities of life, is stirred by the beauty of the city and particularly by the beauty of its women. And nothing that his father can say will divert him from his innocent enthusiasm.

Thus far, the tale stands as a demonstration of the ineradicable claims of natural instinct; and Boccaccio emphasizes the prelapsarian sanity of the boy's response. But the fulcrum of the action is a linguistic one. The father – who is said to have taught the boy 'nothing but prayers and sacred discourse' (15) – pursues the same policy when he witnesses the boy's response; he twice attempts to evoke an absolute moral standard, insisting, as if to charm the mind of the boy with an incantation, that women are 'a bad thing' ('mala cosa') (21). But the boy resists, and demands to know the name of these 'things'. Balducci now attempts to conjure; they are, he says 'goslings', thinking, it

seems, that the designation itself is sufficient to divert his son's
attention. The son, however, remains as determined as ever – if these
are goslings then he wants one and will feed it – at which the father,
whose speech hitherto has been the speech of prayer and devotion, is
tragically reduced to the lewd play on words: you do not know where
such goslings peck.

Here then the rigidity of the father's mind is shattered by the flying
fragments of language. But his son demonstrates a healthy ability to
take and use, in pursuit of his natural ends, whatever word is offered
him. And in this respect he serves as a model for some of Boccaccio's
most characteristic heroes. When the young convert Alibech is told
that the sexual act is known as 'putting the devil back in Hell' she
innocently profits by the joke, freeing her own sexuality by a repeated
practice of the exercise while at the same time satisfying her religious
zeal (Third Day, x). In the great Cipolla story, Cipolla – Boccaccio's
Pardoner – finds that one false relic has been substituted for another
as he steps out before his congregation. But he is a 'natural Cicero',
and, as 'things' shift bewilderingly before his eyes, his words prove
equally agile; in an exuberant fantasy, he convinces the crowd that he
had meant all along to show them – not a feather from Gabriel's wing
– but a coal from the fire that roasted Saint Laurence; the audience is
made to inhabit the world that his words have prepared for them, not
the world of immutable objects (Sixth Day, x).

The verbal dexterity of a Cipolla or an Alibech constitutes an
essential feature of Boccaccio's comedy. Many of his finest creations,
notably Cepperello, are downright liars; nearly all are wits or racon-
teurs. But the seriousness of Boccaccio's position is best illustrated by
the story of Madonna Filippa (Sixth Day, vii). When charged on
pain of death with adultery, Filippa utters a well-timed witticism that
reveals to the court, precisely at the moment of their laughter, that
their statutes against adulterous women are unjust. The lady is freed,
and the statutes themselves are altered. In short, the law is revealed to
be no absolute construction but a system of human conventions – a
tissue of words – which can be and must be readjusted to meet the
impact of the new circumstances. Madonna Filippa is the typical
Boccaccian heroine, free in sensibility and appetite, and able to ensure
her freedom through the instrumentality of the witty word.

Turning to Chaucer, the first point to insist upon is that Chaucer does
provide in the course of the *Canterbury Tales* a consideration of
art and language that if less explicit than Boccaccio's is equally
penetrating. The 'Sir Thopas' sequence is, after all, what T. S. Eliot

called a highly 'conscious study in a worn-out poetic tradition', which demonstrates Chaucer's awareness of the novelty of his actual achievement in the *Canterbury Tales* and equally suggests his unwillingness, as an author, to stand upon his dignity; he is close to Boccaccio in the first respect, wholly different in the second. Likewise, in the Prologue to the *Man of Law's Tale*, Chaucer records his own achievements in the *Legend of Good Women*, but does not fail to qualify the reference with a comment on the 'lewedness' of his own metres and rhyming. In the same introduction the treatment of the Host also deserves attention:

> Oure Hooste saugh wel that the brighte sonne
> The ark of his artificial day hath ronne
> The ferthe part, and half an houre and moore,
> And though he were nat depe ystert in loore,
> He wiste it was the eightetethe day
> Of Aprill that is messager to May;
> And saugh wel that the shadwe of every tree
> Was as in lengthe the same quantitee
> That was the body erect that caused it.
>
> (1–9)

Here and throughout the subsequent twenty lines, Chaucer contrasts the language of high art and science with the normal perceptions that characterize the Host; the Host may not be 'depe ystert in loore', but 'quantitee' and 'cause' would hardly enter into his observation of the shadows. A certain mockery of art is admitted, which is entirely consistent with the unpretentiousness expressed in the Chaucer-persona. Yet the joke is not levelled here at a piece of pastiche, but at a highly competent – even Dantean – display of art and science. There is a sense that the various levels of language act one upon the other so as to reveal their mutual limits and the relativity of each.

Where Boccaccio in the Fourth-Day Prologue investigates the conventionality of language – the disjunction of language and stable fact – Chaucer in his treatment of the *Wife of Bath's Tale* and Prologue explores the interaction of two linguistic extremes, the word that pretends to final and fixed authority and the word that is born from the flow of experience. Thus the Prologue begins:

> Experience, though noon auctoritee
> Were in this world, is right ynogh for me
> To speke of wo that is in mariage.

But perhaps the Tale offers the most striking single indication of the theme. For it is here that Chaucer allows the loathly lady of his romance to cite Dante for her purpose. The discussion of nobility at lines 1109–38 is drawn from the chapters of Dante's *Convivio* in which the Italian poet, as Chaucer must have realized, proposes one of the most characteristic tenets of his philosophy, that man's nobility is a function of his essential rationality. What is more, Book IV of the *Convivio* itself includes, like the Wife of Bath's sequence, an investigation of the concept of authority;[9] Dante sets his face against the authority that the Emperor Frederick has falsely assumed in defining the nature of nobility, but does so to establish the grounds of true authority – in philosophical reason – rather than to deny its possibility. We need not suppose that Chaucer denies the possibility of authority. Yet there is in his attitude a benign ambivalence that allows him, in spite of his respect for Dante, to reduce Dante's argument to a move in the marriage game, or, more precisely to make an argument about intellectual dominance serve the turn of sexual mastery.

It should be emphasized that Chaucer's paraphrase of the *Convivio* shows great intelligence and skill. It is indeed one of the marks of Chaucer's approach to authority that his language often suggests a perfect sympathy for the material he translates; in the *Wife of Bath's Tale*, it is only the context of a passage that betrays his parodic intent, and in many cases, as in the *Canon's Yeoman's Tale*, Chaucer takes an evident pleasure in his own handling of technical terminology. Boccaccio also employs a considerable variety of styles and registers. Yet the element of parody – as, for instance, in Cepperello's parody of holy dying – is always sufficiently evident for the witty ear to appreciate its presence. Chaucer, on the other hand, seems often to enter momentarily into the mind and system of his author. His comedy, in the manipulation of context, may call all in doubt. Yet Chaucer seems to allow that there are pleasures not only in ambiguity but also in the well-considered telling of truths. The comedy of the Prologue to the *Wife of Bath's Tale* depends to a considerable extent upon its author's ability to keep in play simultaneously words that are striking in their clarity and words that are opaque with suggestions of undefined experience.

The Prologue divides into three phases. In the first, which ends at line 162 when the Wife is interrupted by the Pardoner, the Wife displays her mastery over the authority of Scripture itself; whatever verse she cites she can adapt its sense to her particular purposes. Text after text is smartly paraphrased and then either dismissed out of hand or dextrously perverted and misapplied. So virginity, she admits, may be great perfection, but when Christ counselled such perfections

> He spak to hem that wolde lyve parfitly;
> And lordynges, by youre leve, that am nat I.
>
> (111–12)

On the other hand, when God himself 'bad us for to wexe and multiplye' (28–9) the text may be considered a 'gentil' one that the Wife 'kan wel understonde', while the lustiness of the 'wyse kyng daun Salomon' excites her admiration and envy (35–8). Finally, the Wife is herself able to turn judicious scholar, and, concentrating wholly on the letter of the law, deny that there is any textual authority either for marriage or virginity:

> Wher can ye seye, in any manere age,
> That hye God defended mariage
> By expres word? I pray yow, telleth me.
> Or where comanded he virginitee?
>
> (59–62)

These lines illustrate the clarity of thought that can inform the Wife's words; she at times exercises Chaucer's own cogency of phrase, whether in the gospel directness of Christ's words to the Samaritan, 'And that ilke man that now hath thee / Is noght thyn housbonde', or the Apostle's careful discrimination: 'This is al and som, he heeld virginitee / Moore parfit than weddyng in freletee.' But the argument can also breed a rich suggestiveness of phrase, as when the Wife plays on the metphor of virginitee as 'breed of pure whete-seed':

> And lat us wyves hoten barly-breed
> And yet with barly-breed, Mark telle kan,
> Oure Lord Jhesu refresshed many a man.
>
> (144–6)

Likewise, the immediacy of the Wife's vocal gesture has an authority of its own quite distinct from force of argument. The vigour of rhythm in

> In wyfhod I wol use myn instrument
> As frely as my Makere hath it sent.
>
> (149–50)

overwhelms the reverence that the name and implication of God as 'my Makere' might arouse; while the speed with which she yokes argument to argument creates a fluidity of context in which no statement can stand firm.

In the second phase of the Prologue, which describes the first four marriages of the Wife, Chaucer goes even further in his study of the force of vocal gesture. For the victory that the Wife achieves over her husbands is accomplished not only by the well-timed wit of a Boccaccian heroine nor even by the skill in argument that she herself has already displayed, but purely by the bludgeoning volubility of her 'continueel murmur or grucchyng' (406). It is hardly too much to say that sheer noise replaces sense in the Wife's words. Indeed she can even admit the truth of any argument against herself without fear of riposte precisely because her instrument is sound rather than significance. Thus she can turn back upon her husband the points he might have used against her – and prove simultaneously their validity – without in the least weakening her own position:

> Thow seyst we wyves wol oure vices hide
> Til we be fast, and thanne we wol hem shew . . .
> But folk of wyves maken noon assay,
> Til they be wedded; olde dotard shrewe!
> And thanne, seistow, we wol our vices shewe.
>
> (282–92)

The husband – the 'olde barel-ful of lyes' – has, of course said nothing at all; Jankyn is the only articulate husband of the five and his drama is still to come. So the Wife's voice runs on, unqualified and unchecked, and it is a significant conclusion to the second section that she should finally be distracted by the flow of her words and lose the thread of her story:

> But now, sire, lat me see, what shal I seyn
> A ha! by God, I have my tale ageyn.
>
> (585–6)

At this moment the anarchic force of the Wife of Bath is fully realized. We have seen in the first section how she undermines the intellectual order of authoritative statement. Now she eludes even the subtler control of orderly narrative; in effect she proves herself to be an 'incompetent narrator'. Yet here experience plays its ace against authority. For by this time the sound of the Wife's voice has itself become an experience; like the 'drasty rhyming' of the 'Sir Thopas' tale it acts directly on the nerve of its audience and can only be met by a response as direct as the Host's response to the pilgrim-Chaucer. Noise, divorced from intelligent application, is something of recurrent interest to Chaucer, from the cacophony of the *Parlement of Foules* to the 'Tee Hee' of Alison in the *Miller's Tale*, and, frequently, as in the *Parlement*, it is noise that provides a counterpoint to Chaucer's most lucid writing. Noise is the ultimate ambiguity, asserting but not explaining the presence of a being beyond one's own.

In the Wife of Bath, then, Chaucer has conceived a character who attacks his own enterprise as the clerkly author of the *Canterbury Tales*. And the conflict is played out in the final section of the Prologue, where the Wife depicts her married life with Jankyn the clerk.

Until the climax of this section, it seems as if the Wife has met her match. On marriage Jankyn reveals his hitherto hidden vice; he is a male – and literate – shrew, who brings to bear upon the Wife the accumulated wisdom of the ages, ranging over the whole of history and literature from the Scriptures, to classical narrative, to sermons, to 'proverbes and olde sawes' for antifeminist arguments. The Wife responds with the strategy that hitherto she has employed with complete success. She remains a 'verray jangleresse'; she rejects confinement and roams the neighbourhood to gossip at every door. Nevertheless, the words of her husband still penetrate; she is made to recognize her vices and cannot tolerate being told of them. Indeed literary art comes close to defeating her entirely. When Jankyn arrives at the story of Pasiphae's perversity, she is so outraged as to be struck dumb for the only time in the whole account:

> Of Phasipha, that was the queene of Crete,
> For shrewednesse, hym thoght the tale swete;
> Fy! spek namoore – it is a grisly thyng –
> Of hire horrible lust and hir likyng.
>
> (733–6)

Plain nature rebels against the literary fantasies of 'Phasipha', 'Clitermystra' and Livia.

But literature throws the game away; for in the end literature itself becomes no more than sheer repetitive noise, and the Wife, 'whan I saugh that he wolde never fyne / To reden on this cursed book alnight' (788–9), in sheer irritation snatches five leaves from his book and knocks him back onto the open fire. But now Jankyn, transformed by anger and pain from the cold clerk he was, must meet the Wife with her own weapons of instinctive action; where earlier she was said to be as 'stibourn' as 'a leonesse' (637) Jankyn becomes a 'wood leoun' (794). With such weapons, however, he cannot win. He first strikes the blow that deafens her – and thus for the future effectively frees her from the torment of his unwelcome words. Then pity, dread and grief at what he has done well up in him; a wealth of natural emotion is released which the Wife can work upon in fashioning their subsequently 'blisful' marriage.

The crowning irony of the work – and a mark of its formal complexity – is to be observed in the manner in which the Wife consolidates her triumph. After all, she has learned something from the dreadful books of Jankyn – not their morality but the words that enable her to act a part. So, lying prostrate she delivers, as a stimulus to her husband's natural feelings, a superb parody of a tragic and magnanimous heroine:

'O! hastow slayn me, false theef?' I seyde,
'And for my land thus hastow mordered me?
Er I be deed, yet wol I kesse thee'.

(800–2)

In this lies the germ of that mastery over texts and words which the Wife displays in the opening section of the Prologue. But the conclusion also points to an alteration in styles between the three sections. Where the first is broadly discursive and the second broadly narrative, the third has many of the qualities of drama. The Wife may be an incompetent narrator, but as an actress, whose presence impinges directly on the audience, she is consummate.

The Wife appeared at first view to be a highly Boccaccian figure in whom Chaucer had depicted – as Boccaccio does in so many of his women – a liberation of the natural being. Her disruptive, or, so to say, Dionysiac, force is even greater than that of the aptly named Dioneo. Yet the differences in implication and treatment are as significant as the similarities. In the first place, while Boccaccio certainly does envisage a liberation of natural impulse, he sees true liberation as lying in a certain civilization of the natural being. From the *Ameto* to tales in the *Decameron* like that of Cimone, or the Prologue to the Fourth Day, Boccaccio shows the importance of intelligence – demonstrated in a flexible and sensitive appreciation of language – to the fulfilment of nature; his 'carissime donne' need fictions to pass their time, the wit of his heroine ensures that society acquiesces in their pleasure. Yet the Wife of Bath is not a wit. Though she speaks of wit as one of the attributes of womankind, her use of it is a challenge to art and refinements of language. Nature in her case is not expressed, as in Boccaccio, through the subtle modulations of a social organism, but in the 'stibourn' resistance that her individuality offers to any kind of control, coherence or mastery.

If the Wife is not herself a wit, then neither is Chaucer's art adapted to the representation of wit. Boccaccio's short stories focus upon moments of action – it is not surprising that the *Decameron* influenced the development of Italian theatre in the Renaissance;[10] and the most characteristic mode of action in the *Decameron* is one in which the witty word acts with the efficacy of a deed to transform the situation in which it is spoken; the story of Madonna Filippa is one illustration, others are the tales of Cisti the Baker, Guiglielmo Borsiere and the Donna di Guascogna (Sixth Day, ii; First Day, viii and ix). Conversely, there is an absence in Boccaccio of any detailed interest in the individual. His characters are 'bellissime donne', 'uomini molto savi'

or 'stoltissimi' or 'ricchissimi'; this is appropriate, since Boccaccio is
concerned with the formulae of relationships and their permutations,
of actions and results. But Chaucer's use of the monologue draws
attention away from the decisive word or action; we are concerned
with the continuum of the speaker's presence, not with the alteration
of circumstance. I say 'presence' and not 'character'. 'Character'
implies a configuration of attributes that are open to inspection and
analysis. In the Wife's case, however, we are faced with the irreducible
ambiguity of the individual being, expressed in the 'noise' she employs
so effectively. No generalization can contain her or explicate her
significance; she proceeds from and justifies the whole history of antifeminist literature, yet proves its incapacity to hold the particular
case.

At the end of every tale in the *Decameron*, Boccaccio outlines the
reactions of the *brigata*; the ladies blush at lasciviousness, as decorum demands, but also smile knowingly; some take the part of the
hero, others condemn him, some admire the telling of the tale, others
are more critical. Such reactions admit the ambiguities inherent in the
tales, but show that there is a pleasure in the text that orderly and
intelligent discussion can only enhance – and in this regard the
brigata represents the ideal readership of Boccaccio's work. But the
end of the Wife of Bath's Prologue is marked by the ribald inter-
ruptions of the Friar, and the drunken confusion of the Summoner's
voice, eager to tell a tale or two at the Friar's expense. The noise of the
Wife has provoked an inevitable but natural reaction of impatience.

The question is whether this reaction may be taken as a guide to
the responses of the reader of Chaucer's text itself. It cannot be wholly
reliable; the sense of the author's own achievement in creating the tale
must after all be allowed to modify our irritation. Yet as Morton
Bloomfield has suggested, there is a Chaucerian 'negative capability'
that requires us to appreciate to the full even the most unlikely objects
of admiration;[11] and certainly where Boccaccio invites an urbanely
aesthetic or good-humoured response, the response to which Chaucer's
text points will be natural, direct and in a certain sense confused. It is
a reaction of this sort that the Wife's tragic acting evokes from the
clerkly Jankyn. And, to speak more generally, it is noticeable that
wherever Chaucer presents an example of true tragedy – as in the
Ugolino story – 'pitee' is the emotion he expects to stimulate. The
defining feature of 'pitee' is that it should be a heart-felt appreciation
of the needs and sufferings of the individual, and while 'pitee' is not
the only response that Chaucer calls for, its importance in his work
underlines his concern with the ways in which one individual may

grasp the existence of another. This is in part a moral concern involving a particular conception of the functions of imagination and intellect. But the literary consequence is that Chaucer is not concerned with the creation of types or general models. Generalization is, of course, a tendency to which all kinds of writing are prone; anti-feminist literature is an extreme example, but few modern novels would be comprehensible unless we supposed that the characters they contain provided some general model of behaviour. Chaucer's art is to contradict this tendency, and to that extent it liberates the reader from one of the most usual forms of literary response.

We have seen something of this already in the Prologue to the *Wife of Bath's Tale*. But the Pardoner's sequence – which is as much concerned with language and art as the *Wife of Bath's Tale* is – offers further evidence, and underlines the distance between Chaucer and Boccaccio.

Unlike the Wife of Bath, the Pardoner is a highly competent narrator. His Prologue displays the pride he takes in his own technique, and the tale itself – were it not for its context – would entirely justify that pride. When considered as Chaucer's own creation, it is a technical *tour-de-force*, providing a comprehensive history of man's unhappiness while investigating, in a dramatic rather than narrative fashion, the consequences of sin in the particular case of the revellers. The combination of scope and intensity recalls Dante's handling of the canto form, and the moral issues that the tale proposes are also Dantean; as in the *Inferno*, greed and ill-will are shown to be the prime causes of man's misery. Sin is observed with a categorical clarity that in the *Canterbury Tales* can only be paralleled by the *Parson's Tale* – and predictably has no parallel at all in the *Decameron*.

Yet the Prologue serves to complicate this in a wholly un-Dantean fashion. For the categorical scheme is dubious precisely because we know it to be from the first the product only of technique. We also know that the Pardoner is insincere. It is, however, the very competence that the Pardoner boasts of – his malign 'bello stile' – that distracts attention from the spiritual content of the tale, making the audience most suspicious of those utterances which are most cogent and imaginatively attractive.

The exact converse appears in the Prologue to the *Parson's Tale* where the speaker, before he begins his account of sin and redemption, insists that he is 'nat textuele', allowing that his words must stand 'under correcioun / Of clerkes' (Prologue to the *Parson's Tale*, 55–60). But the Pardoner, far from admitting 'correcioun', is so sure of his ability to charm his audience that he finally tries out his standard

sales pitch recommending to them his spurious relics. Like Jankyn, he
here oversteps the mark and provokes the Host into a response that –
while it is so undesigning as to be gross – voices all the moral condemnation that the Pardoner has mocked: 'I wolde I hadde thy coillons
in myn hond' (952).

There is no space to consider in detail the construction of the
Pardoner's sequence. It is, however, important to note the consistent
dissimilarities between Chaucer's treatment of the Pardoner and
Boccaccio's treatment of figures such as Cepperello and Cipolla (First
Day, i; Sixth Day, x).

In all three cases, the point of departure is the same – the picture
of a hypocrite whose guileful words discredit the sacred forms of
speech he is skilled in. Yet the difference is that Cipolla and Cepperello
are notable for the lies they tell – their lies are imaginatively more
attractive than their natural voices – while the Pardoner, though he
is a liar, is shown in the act of telling the drunken truth about himself;
he himself insists that his audience should pay attention to his actual
self.

Throughout Boccaccio is concerned with the technique of his protagonists, concentrating less upon a character than upon an action or
process in which the virtuosity of the word substitutes a fictional
creation for apparently certain fact. Thus Cepperello, though resonantly presented as perhaps the 'worst man in the world' (15), in his
final confession recreates his own life entirely; by his skilful parody of
accounts of holy dying, he convinces his confessor, and through him,
the local congregation, that he is a man of the highest virtue, and is
venerated after his death as a saint. Cipolla effects a still more profound
recreation; to justify his production of 'coal from the fire that roasted
St Laurence' in place of the 'feather from Gabriel's wings' – a lump of
coal instead of a parrot's feather – Cipolla weaves around his audience
a world of purely linguistic reality that contains such poetic items as a
'few rays of the star that guided the Magi', the jawbone of Death, the
'holes from the Holy Cross' and the sound of bells from Solomons'
temple (45–6). These phrases illustrate the brilliance and sheer
creativity that Boccaccio allows to Cipolla, and there are comparable
moments in the Cepperello story. Indeed, in the *Decameron*, hypocrisy
has almost invariably a creative aspect; the shifts and convolutions of
the conscience serve to stimulate the tongue to new audacity.

There is no such creativity in the Pardoner, nor any such com-
plaisance in Chaucer's representation of him. From the first we know
all there is to know about him; he tells us himself and little space is
left for surprise or freshness. At every point attention is focused upon

the relentless and ultimately monotonous voice that proclaimed with absolute finality:

> Thus kan I preche agayn that same vice
> Which that I use, and that is avarice.
>
> (427–8)

In the Pardoner Chaucer has created a thoroughly Dantean figure. Throughout the *Inferno*, figures come before us who singlemindedly demand attention, even love, of the onlookers; and, as the gate of Hell declares, primal love itself was as active in creating Hell. But as love searches the souls of the damned it finds nothing that can refresh it or give it new life – in the way that the sight of Beatrice gave Dante new life – and Hell is the condition of final rejection. Thus far the case of the Pardoner is closely comparable.

Yet Dante in discovering the emptiness of sinful humanity is able to rely for comfort upon the eternal schemes of judgement that underlie Hell itself and are brought home to him by the words of Virgil. It is here that Chaucer is at odds. For Chaucer relies upon no eternal scheme of judgement in his assessment of the Pardoner but rather sets the virtuosity of the Pardoner against the unavoidable actualities of ordinary life and invites us to judge the man from our own experience of normality. Thus the background to the Pardoner's Prologue is the crushing poverty of the world in which the Pardoner himself operates. The diseases that spell disaster to crops and cattle are brought before us as the Pardoner boasts of what his relics can cure; and the Pardoner himself points to the economic pressures that determine his behaviour:

> For I wol preche and begge in sondry landes;
> I wol nat do no labour with myne handes,
> Ne make baskettes, and lyve thereby . . .
>
> (443–5)

But the Pardoner cannot conjure this reality away in the manner of Cipolla. And when he declares:

> I wol have moneie, wolle, chese, and whete,
> Al were it yeven of the povereste page,
> Or of the povereste wydwe in a village,
> Al sholde hir children sterve for famyne,
>
> (448–51)

an elemental decency rebels against the viciousness of his tone, as it does later in the Host's response. In depicting the world in which the Pardoner moves Chaucer has written with greater realism and sympathy than Boccaccio ever does – Cipolla's audience is characteristically 'a crowd of stupid bumpkins'. But precisely in Chaucer's

sense of the normal world, there lies a moral sensibility that may be
less systematic than Dante's but is no less penetrating. The Pardoner
is gripped as firmly by the realities of 'moneie, wolle, chese, and whete'
as Dante's traitors are by the eternal ice, and technique cannot save
him as it saves Cipolla from exposure.

At the outset I suggested that the *Decameron* and the *Canterbury
Tales* are both works in which serious moral questions were presented
and successfully resolved. The Pardoner's sequence – which is a
sustained portrayal of the 'smyler with the knyf under the cloke' –
demonstrates how sensitive Chaucer could be to malice and the
unreliability of human motive; the Pardoner's untrustworthy voice is
as much a parody of the frank human presence that the Wife of Bath
or the Franklin or the Knight put forth as Ugolino's bloodstained
mouth is a parody of Beatrice's smile. Boccaccio, though aware of the
unreliability of the mind, does not at any point present treachery with
comparable force. In his case, the emphasis falls upon the realization
of the constant changes of Fortune, of riches and love won and lost.
Chaucer, too, understands 'the drenchyng in the see so wan'.

However, it is not my purpose here to compare the gloomy Chaucer
and the often-neurotic Boccaccio, but to see, in conclusion, how the
tragic question as it runs through the comedies of each is answered by
the comic vision that characterizes each. In Boccaccio, the insecurity
of life reveals the possibility that all things may be taken – in a spirit
of 'virtù' – as the pawns and pieces in a delightful game. In Chaucer's
case, his sense of the utter dependence of man upon man, which is
reflected in his hatred of treason, leads to the careful, indeed loving
attention to the human individual that inspires his finest comedy. Two
representative examples must suffice, Boccaccio's story of the Three
Rings (First Day, iii), and Chaucer's *Nun's Priest's Tale*.

In Boccaccio's story, the magnanimous Saladin finds himself short
of funds and applies to the Jewish money-lender Melchisedech. But
Melchisedech is notably tight-fisted. And Saladin realizes that he will
have no success unless he exerts a certain pressure. So he attempts to
trap the Jew into an indiscretion by asking him to declare which of
the three great religions of the world, Hebrew, Muslim or Christian,
possesses the truth of God. Melchisedech then tells the famous story
of the three rings – a father who loved all of his three sons equally
but had only one precious ring to dispose of in his will, has two copies
made of the authentic ring. These are so perfect that his heirs are
unable to distinguish false from true; they know that a true ring
exists, but who possesses it they cannot tell. Saladin understands the
application of this story to his question, and is so delighted by the

story-teller's dexterity that he abandons his claim; the money-lender, in turn, impressed by Saladin's magnanimity, relents and allows him the loan that he requires. The conclusion emphasizes the continuing friendship and good will that obtained between the Jew and Muslim from this point onward.

But Melchisedech's story and the context in which it is cast deserves attention. The story itself provides a suggestive emblem of the dangers and intellectual difficulties that Boccaccio seems to have confronted. It acknowledges the profound enmity that can exist between races, and pictures how the shifts of economic necessity can forge the most unlikely bonds of kinship. Then, again, in its more metaphysical aspect, the story amounts to an admission of the relativity of truth. A truth exists that each of the great religions in its own way venerates; yet the identity of that truth can never be comprehended by any single system; one must live as though simultaneously one did and did not possess it. Finally, the image of the true and the counterfeit rings may easily be taken to suggest the arbitrary and instrumental nature of language – and to indicate Boccaccio's engagement with a problem that is also at the heart of Petrarch's linguistic procedure in the *Rime*. Just as Petrarch is never certain of the true substance of Laura – whether woman, or laurel, or breeze or gold – so the heirs of the ring can never be certain of the substance of their inheritance.

In the face, however, of all these difficulties – social, metaphysical and linguistic – the tale as a whole suggests that there are still resources we may draw upon. And these are resources that belong specifically to narrative fiction. Story-telling itself is here on display; for it is not the moral content of Melchisedech's tale that moves Saladin but the sheer skill and charm of the telling. The pleasures of fiction release the protagonists from the rooted enmity that the pursuit of 'racial' truth might have engendered, and the intelligence and good will that are involved in the enjoyment of the story foster a sympathy between man and man that zeal for the truth – whether in religion or in speech – would quickly have destroyed. It is precisely to ensure such sympathy that the *brigata* chose story-telling as their pastime; of all games, this is one into which no acrimony would enter, since 'as one person speaks, he gives pleasure to the whole company of his listeners' (Introduction, 111–12).

Fiction, then, sidesteps disaster and chooses a ground where human interest and intelligence can be allowed free play. So it is that the *brigata*, in the course of their stories, return at least four times to the figure of the accident-prone and stupid Calandrino. Even Calandrino, who in his coarseness, hamfistedness and idiocy is everything that the *brigata* are not, becomes, so to speak, a figure in a ritual of delight. Whatever the ambiguities of the human condition – and Calandrino displays them in abundance – it is possible to make 'play' with them – 'multiplicare la festa' (Ninth Day, ii, 1) – and tell the same story a 'thousand times over' without tedium (Ninth Day, v, 1). If the comedy enhances the relationship between teller and audience, then this itself, regardless of truth or morality, is a true achievement.

We spoke earlier of how the English reader of the *Decameron* may be disappointed by its relative lack of characterization; he will be no less disappointed by the absence of that most obvious of Chaucerian qualities – irony. There is certainly nothing in the *Decameron* to compare with the *Nun's Priest's Tale*, which is almost a case study in the many modes of irony.

The mainspring of the comedy within this tale is, of course, the Nun's Priest's handling of dramatic irony – of events foreseen by all but the protagonist – in his account of Chauntecleer's pride. But irony also operates in the relation between the tale and its larger context; the Nun's Priest's contribution is a deliberate and skilful parody of the tale that immediately precedes it – the *Monk's Tale*, with its catalogue of tragedies and stiff platitudes. Indeed, a full account of the *Nun's Priest's Tale* would examine the contrast between the intellectual dexterity of the Nun's Priest and the procedures of other clerics such as the Parson, the Clerk and certainly the Pardoner. Here, however, I must concentrate mainly upon the way in which the irony of the tale both admits and resolves the doubtfulness of systematic truth, since it is in this regard that the tale may be compared to Boccaccio's story of the Three Rings. In form the story is a moral fable. Yet at no point are we allowed to approach the moral sentence directly. Nor are any of the philosophical issues that the tale raises allowed to stand unqualified by irony; the discussion of dreams, physic and predestination are sound in local detail, but are rendered ludicrous by their context. At the same time, it is irony itself that provides an answer to the doubts it raises.

The especial characteristic of Chaucer's irony in this tale is that it invites the audience to look beyond the confines of philosophical statement – and even of fiction itself – so as to fix attention on the teller of the tale, estimating how the narrative detail may be related to the narrator. It is generally agreed that the *Nun's Priest's Tale* provides as much information about the speaker as the prologues and epilogues do. But in the Epilogue the Host offers a clear indication of what the readers' response should be. Sensing that the tale is something of a *roman-à-clef*, his reaction is to look with renewed attention upon the person of the Priest; an ironic intelligence allows him to see a parallel between Chauntecleer and the Priest himself – cock of the convent walk – and to declare with an appreciative gusto that is focused wholly upon the identity, or 'trouthe', of the person and not at all upon the truth of his words:

> See, whiche braunes hath this gentil preest,
> So gret a nekke, and swich a large breest!
> He loketh as a sperhauk with his yen:
> Him nedeth nat his colour for to dyen
> With brasile, ne with greyn of Portyngale.
> Now, sire, faire falle yow for youre tale!
>
> (3455–60)

An essential part of Boccaccio's comedy was the good-fellowship that the act of story-telling produced. And it is clear from the Host's response – as indeed from his professional character – that some of the stories of the *Canterbury Tales* are meant to produce a similar effect. Yet the effect is not identical. The Host's response demonstrates that the ground of his liking for the Nun's Priest is a fresh and generous acknowledgement of his individuality – he sees him 'anew' in precisely the way that we are never allowed to see the Pardoner anew – and the process by which this response is evoked involves not the playing of a mutually delightful game but the unfolding of a tune, carried on the voice of the individual, which the audience is invited to hear and learn. The Host thus answers the Priest in accents of irony that he has acquired from him; throughout his tale the function of the Priest's irony has been to liberate the particularity and precision of view that – as a final irony – the Host then levels at him.

Though the mock-heroics of the Chauntecleer story have been analysed too often to need close attention here, it should be said that there is no mockery in the *Nun's Priest's Tale* either of misapplied terminology or of the humble object to which it is attached. On the contrary, his irony is a device that allows an enhanced appreciation of the object and the language he applies to it. When Pertelote is described thus:

> Curteys she was, discreet and debonaire,
> And compaignable, and bar hyrself so faire,
> Syn thilke day that she was seven nyght old,
> That trewely she hath the herte in hoold
> Of Chauntecleer . . .
>
> (2871–5)

the reader is invited to take pleasure in the words themselves and the object itself in a way that neither an accurate application of terms nor

an accurate description would have allowed. The irony, drawing
attention to the discrepancy in the description, endows the reader with
the freedom to observe the artifice, and to enjoy both the language and
its object without any urgency of practical application. It is a similar
device, on a broader plane, that allows Chaucer to employ – without
commitment to system or finality of application – the terms of physic
and philosophy on the one hand, and on the other the actualities of
the farmyard. Even tragedy can be evoked with momentary gravity
precisely because we are freed by the context from an obsessive or
singleminded concentration upon the tragic; one is invited to give full
weight to the picture of human treachery and decay in the lines:

> And in the myddel of the dong they founde
> The dede man, that mordred was al newe.
>
> (3048–9)

for the context assures us that we shall not be entrammeled by the
significance of the lines or required to act upon them. Irony frees the
contemplative eye.

The same irony admits the limitations of art; and we might indeed
say that in the voice of the Nun's Priest there is a knowing combination of the voice of a literary sophisticate such as the Clerk of
Oxford and the voice of the Wife of Bath. While managing without
effort a whole repertoire of scholastic terminology, the Priest can
also share with the Wife an appreciation of the vigour and value of
extra-linguistic 'noise'. Thus the climax of the story lies not in the
action of the chase – though technically the handling of this is as
brilliant as in any Boccaccio story – but rather in the exuberance of
the incoherent 'Out! harrow and weylaway! / Ha! Ha! the fox'
(3380–1). In this regard, moreover, the central fiction – that in 'thilke
tyme ... beestes and briddes koude speke and synge' (2880–1) – is rich
in suggestion: is the discourse of the wise no more than the crowing
of a cock; is the crowing of the cock itself a form of wisdom? It is,
finally, this same sense of the limitations of linguistic arts that gives
to the voice of the Priest an authority in total contrast to the voice of
the Pardoner, so that the final lines of the tale are marked by what is
in effect a retraction, a retreat from technical brilliance:

> But ye that holden this tale a folye,
> As of a fox, or of a cok and hen,
> Taketh the moralite, goode men.
>
> (3438–40)

There is no reason to suppose that this recommendation is impractical.
To be sure, its authority does not depend upon the invocation of an

impersonal moral scheme, nor can we read it as a predictably moral conclusion to the fable. But the richness of the Priest's irony has itself won the good will of the Host, and the force of the narrator's utterance arises from the aura of good will that his voice and presence generate.

Having won the right to be heard, the Nun's Priest is able in conclusion to utter a benediction that points to truths that are higher than the truths of literature:

> Now, goode God, if that it be thy wille,
> As seith my lord, so make us alle goode men,
> And brynge us to his heighe blisse.   Amen.
>
> (3444–6)

But it is even more significant that the Priest should have begun his tale with a recognition of the value of day-to-day life and its essential poverty – the realm that the Pardoner so clearly despised. Thus among the many intensely beautiful lines in this tale, few are more so than the description of how the poor widow's table 'was served moost with whit and blak, / Milk and broun breed in which she found no lak, / Seynd bacoun, and somtym an ey or tweye' (2843–5). Here the Priest shows an appreciation, which Vermeer might have envied, for the order and particularity of domestic life; art draws attention to the simple contrasts of white and black in the widow's diet and enhances the sensuous apprehension of the scene. Equally it casts the tableau in an emblematic key. And the meaning of this emblem is that there is an order in the presences of bread and eggs, table and farmyard that renders literary sophistication either ridiculous – as it is in Chauntecleer – or, at best, a skilful but unassuming interpreter – as it is in the Priest and Chaucer. One can understand why Wordsworth was attracted to the tale. One can also see that Chaucer, in disclaiming the right as a poet to encompass order, resolves the doubts and discomfitures that the shadow of Dante had cast around his successors. The comic truth is that the self can never be satisfied with literature alone. Beyond literature there always lie the realities of bread and commonsense.

Notes

1 See David Wallace's essay on this subject above.
2 Especially in his discussion of the figure of Fortuna in *Inferno*, VII.
3 So in *De ignorantia*, he repeats a favourite maxim: 'Nimium altercando veritas amititur', and proceeds to argue that is better to love the good than know the true: 'Voluntatis siquidem obiectum, ut sapientibus placet, est bonitas; obiectum intellectus est veritas. Satius est autem bonum velle nosse.'

4 For a fuller account of these changes, see John Larner's essay in this volume.

5 Notably in the letter to Boccaccio in which Petrarch discourses at length on his own attitude to Dante, and insists that his decision not to collect volumes of Dante's writing arose, not from *invidia*, but from a certain wariness about the influence of Dante: 'Eidem tunc stilo deditus, vulgari eloquio ingenium exercebam; nichil rebar elegantius necdum altius aspirare dediceram, sed verebar ne si huius aut alterius dictis imbuerer, ut est etas illa flexibilis et miratrix omnium, vel invitus ac nesciens imitator evaderem' (*De Rebus Familiaribus*, XXI, XV, 11). On the relationship between Petrarch and Dante's writing, see M. Feo, 'Petrarca' in *Enciclopedia Dantesca*, vol. IV (Rome, 1973).

6 See *Boccaccio medievale* (Florence, 1956), chapter 1, esp. pp. 12 and 24.

7 Bloomfield, 'The Gloomy Chaucer' in *Veins of Humor*, ed. Harry Levin (Cambridge, Mass., 1972), pp. 67–8.

8 For a thorough examination of the view of language that emerges from Boccaccio's work, see G. Sinicropi, 'Il segno linguistico del *Decameron*', *Studi su Boccaccio*, IX (1975–6), 169–224. See also G. Almansi, *The Writer as Liar* (London, 1975).

9 See the canzone of *Convivio*, IV and caps. iii, x, xiv and xv.

10 Leo Salingar has shown this influence to be strongly present even in Shakespearian comedy; see his *Shakespeare and the Traditions of Comedy* (Cambridge, 1974).

11 'The Gloomy Chaucer', p. 68.

The Griselda Story in Boccaccio, Petrarch and Chaucer

The story of patient Griselda is one that exerted a considerable influence upon the imagination of writers in the late Middle Ages. In origin the story was no doubt a folk-tale of the Cupid and Psyche family.[1] The first extant version, however, is that which appears as the last tale in Boccaccio's *Decameron*. It was this version that Petrarch translated into Latin as *De Insigni Obedientia et Fide Uxoris* (1373/4). And from Petrarch's re-telling – which considerably expands and modifies Boccaccio's original – there stemmed a number of renderings in French, which follow Petrarch's text very closely, and finally Chaucer's *Clerk's Tale*. It is unlikely that Chaucer was acquainted with Boccaccio's version; as is clear from the Prologue to the *Clerk's Tale*, he regarded Petrarch as his primary source. But he did know at least one of the French translations. So, while the opening sections of the tale display a notable fidelity to Petrarch's text, as Chaucer proceeds it appears that he made increasing use of the French *Le livre Griseldis* as a guide in his translation of Petrarch's Latin, and at times chose to adopt the particular emphases and colouring that the anonymous French translator had given to the tale.[2]

Though the various versions of the Griselda story all have their own distinctive qualities, it is not difficult to explain in a general way the fascination of the Griselda figure. The literary image of the Lady had dominated the era immediately preceding that of Boccaccio, Petrarch and Chaucer – notably in the form of Dante's Beatrice – and throughout their careers all three authors were exceptionally responsive to the legends of women – be they 'good' or no better than they ought to be. The Griselda-figure herself offered the post-Dantean writer a number of opportunities to develop the significance of the Lady-image, and to modify according to his own lights the cultural implications of that image.

Like the ladies who were adored by the poets of the *stil novo*, Griselda – who is notable first for her constancy – could easily be taken as a model of moral perfection and stability in a world of vicious change. More profoundly, her other qualities of obedience and poverty could have had a particular resonance for any serious religious thinker. Certainly in the *Commedia* poverty and obedience are consistently shown to be essential features of all well-directed human conduct; Beatrice herself teaches Dante humility in the face of revealed authority, and the force of this lesson is evident in every part of the *Commedia*, whether in the deference that Dante the pilgrim shows to Virgil or in the joy that Piccarda expresses over the 'smallness' of her own being in relation to its Creator.

At the same time, the Griselda-figure points less to the intellectual absolutes of eternity than to the principles of conduct that are applicable in the sphere of time. In the long-drawn-out sufferings of Griselda, scanned and punctuated by the birth of children, there is a potentially very strong image of temporal sequence – which Chaucer, by virtue of his division of the story into 'acts', draws out more effectively than his predecessors. Equally the story is concerned not with an angelic lady but with a married woman. In some of the French versions and obviously in the *Clerk's Tale*, which is connected to the so-called Marriage group, Griselda is intended – if only in part and somewhat ironically – as a mirror for wives. This aspect of the tale would also have attracted the attention of Boccaccio and Petrarch; both writers touch in their humanist writings upon the theme of marriage. And usually the theme is allied to the notion that the intellectual must free himself from the entanglements of married life if he is to have leisure and peace for contemplation; it is thus connected to the strand of humanist antifeminism that runs through their work. Griselda would have been the perfect wife for a humanist – or antifeminist. Finally, the story has a strong romance aspect, in that it represents the victory of the individual will – expressed first in the Marquis' decision to marry 'beneath himself' – over the commonplace institutions and expectations of the social world. Boccaccio had pictured the disruptive power of love in the *Filocolo*, not to mention the *Decameron*. And Petrarch turns this motif to religious account, emphasizing the unpredictability of divine intention, which can send its grace 'even into the hovels of the poor' (p. 1316).

If the figure of Griselda is rich in imaginative possibilities, that of her husband the Marquis is no less so. However, the treatment of his behaviour seems to have presented something of a challenge to all three writers, and the most obvious differences between the three tales are to be found in the representation of his apparently cruel purposes. In a folk-tale or myth, the cruelty of the Marquis would have been easily seen as the caprice of a divinity. And this interpretation is not altogether absent, in a sophisticated and Christian aspect, from Petrarch's version. Petrarch, like Boccaccio and Chaucer, was acutely conscious of the complexity of human motive, as the *Rime Sparse*, along with writings such as the *Pardoner's Tale* and the Cepperello story, make plain. Neither Petrarch, Boccaccio nor Chaucer would have been unaware of the moral issues involved in the Griselda story, and each, in his own way, elicits from the interplay of the Marquis and Griselda a statement of his own moral position.

In Boccaccio's case, the difficulties of the Marquis' behaviour are given especial prominence and resolved with great vigour. As the teller of the tale insists in his introduction, the Marquis is guilty of 'matta bestialitade'. This is a striking beginning; for the theme of the day is the virtue of magnanimity and yet Boccaccio has, it seems, set himself to demonstrate that the apparent greatness of purpose on which the Marquis prides himself is nothing but a cloak for cruel whimsicality.[3] So we read, as Gualtieri takes it into his head to test Griselda: 'Ma poco appresso, entratogli un nuovo pensiero nell'animo, cioè di volere con lunga esperienza e con cose intollerabili provare la pazienza di lei ...' (But soon after this a strange idea entered his head – that is, to try her endurance by subjecting her to long-drawn sufferings and unbearable experiences). On the other hand, it is not impossible to argue that the true magnanimity that the Marquis seeks to display is after all displayed by the humble and socially ignoble Griselda. Yet a moral insight of this kind is more in keeping with Chaucer's treatment of the tale. And the prevailing sense in Boccaccio's version is that he has largely avoided moral conclusions, preferring to concentrate upon the peculiarity of behaviour and extremism of his two protagonists. Thus, Boccaccio's Griselda is a match for his Marquis in the inhuman passivity with which she meets her fate. This is particularly evident in the almost total silence that she maintains throughout the story. In Petrarch and Chaucer, Griselda is allowed to speak with some eloquence about her position. But Boccaccio time and again emphasizes the brevity of her responses. Which is the more striking in that throughout the *Decameron* Boccaccio's heroines have never been at a loss for words in their own defence, either the witty word of a Madonna Filippa or the tragically composed rhetoric of a Ghismonda. Though Griselda's silence has occasionally a hieratic quality to it, it is also, in the context of the whole *Decameron*, somewhat sinister and perverse.

The final effect of Boccaccio's story is one of ambiguity. If moral issues enter at all, they do so only to heighten our wonderment at the lengths to which the human being may be carried. It is not inappropriate that, alongside the moral issues, the refinements of consciousness that Boccaccio has apparently brought to bear upon the original folk-tale should also produce a sadistic lingering upon such details as the nakedness and degradation of Griselda. Such moments as these are out of keeping with Chaucer's version, though in elaborating Petrarch's text he does introduce ambiguities of his own. Petrarch himself, however, in his own version has been at pains to give his tale a definite moral direction.

Something of Petrarch's intention in translating the *Decameron* version emerges from the highly interesting epistles that were meant to accompany his text on its way to Boccaccio.[4] The story, Petrarch declares, is one in which he himself found delight. And his delight was of a kind that would be shared by any educated man; the story deserved re-telling in the monumental and, so to speak, 'public' form of Latin, for at one and the same time it stirred the emotions and satisfied the moral sense. It is not difficult to see that for the lover of Laura such a story would be especially valuable. Where Laura in the *Rime Sparse* had been as likely to signify doubt and lost days as much as peace, Griselda was an emblem of the constancy that human beings could achieve – and in this connection it is not irrelevant that Petrarch should picture himself writing the tale in a disquieting time of war-like uncertainties ('bellicis ... motibus inquietum': *Seniles*, XVII, 3). Where, moreover, in the *Rime Sparse*, tears and reason had often kept unhappy company as expressions of frustration and guilt, their union in contemplating Griselda could be expected to bear moral fruit.

Within the tale itself, the clearest indication of Petrarch's intentions are to be found in his handling of one of the few moral generalizations that Boccaccio introduces into his tale, and in his suggestion at the end of the tale of the possibility of an allegorical interpretation for the marriage of Griselda and Walter. In the last lines of Boccaccio's tale, we read that

anche nelle povere case piovono dal cielo de' divini spiriti, come nelle reali di quegli che sarien più degni di guardar porci che d'avere sopra uomini signoria

These lines are as satirical as they are solemn. But there is no breath of satire in Petrarch's Latin, which is used in the introduction to Griselda's first appearance:

sed ut pauperum quoque tuguria nonnunquam gratia celestis invisit, unica illi nata contigerat Griseldis nomine ... (p. 1316).

(... but as divine grace visits from time to time the hovels of the poor also, so he happened to have a daughter by name Griselda.)

If anything modifies the simple religious feeling of this, it is the slight sense that Petrarch – so sensitive to paradox – had appreciated the 'paradox' of God's concern for the poor. Chaucer, we may note, is at this point less conceptual than Petrarch, but hints more graphically at a direct analogy between Griselda's condition and that of Christ himself:

> But hye God somtyme senden kan
> His grace into a litel oxes stalle.
>
> (206–7)

On the second point, Petrarch suggests an interpretation that allows Griselda to represent the soul of man – tested but constant – while the Marquis becomes a figure for God himself. This reading, in returning the Marquis to the mythic sphere from whence he came, forestalls the disquiet we may feel over his behaviour. Chaucer, in his turn, translates the text almost entire. But his position on the Marquis is, as we shall see, by no means so easily defined. And indeed while the Clerk is allowed to recommend the lesson of constancy and humility to 'every wight in his degree' (1145), it is significant that before he proceeds to suggest any analogy between wife and soul and husband and God, he enters a concluding acknowledgement to Petrarch who 'writeth / This storie, which with heigh stile he enditeth'. The responsibility for the analogy seems to be transferred firmly to Petrarch.

Petrarch's position involves a considerable revision and expansion of Boccaccio's text, most evidently, of course, in the treatment of Valterius. These revisions, however, while justifying the Marquis, are by no means allegorical in character; it is here rather that Petrarch introduces a far more minute consideration of moral motive and social background than is to be expected from Boccaccio's somewhat anecdotal piece. Petrarch opens up, so to speak, a narrative space in the story that Chaucer, retaining most of Petrarch's additions, finds convenient for the exercise of his own skills and emphases. For instance, when Petrarch pictures the bachelor life of the Marquis, he does so in such a way as to contrast the spurious freedom of the chase, which Valterius enjoys, with the mature freedom that comes from submission to the legitimate yoke of marriage. Boccaccio allows his story-teller the cynical suggestion that the Marquis was to be considered very wise to avoid marriage. But when the counsellors in Petrarch's text advise

...collumque non liberum modo sed imperiosum legitimo subicias iugo
(p. 1314).

(...that you should bow your neck not only free but lordly to the lawful
yoke.)

they are playing dextrously upon a moral notion and a figure of
speech that will be familiar to any reader of the *Rime Sparse*;[5] the
notion of liberty and the paradox that expresses it are both highly
Petrarchan. Chaucer retains the figure, which is notable, because it
does not appear in *Le Livre Griseldis* and this itself indicates that in
the early sequences of the work Chaucer is making a particular effort
to render Petrarch's Latin exactly. At the same time, Chaucer's
version is expanded in an extremely interesting way. He writes:

> Boweth youre nekke under that blisful yok
> Of soverayntee, noght of servyse,
> Which that men clepe spousaille or wedlok.
>
> (113–15)

In slightly labouring Petrarch's point, Chaucer underlines the issues
of marriage and mastery that are to make the *Clerk's Tale* a fitting
contribution to the marriage-debate in the *Canterbury Tales*.

In the same speech of the counsellors, Petrarch establishes an
explicitly feudal background for the story and provides a good political
reason for marriage – the security of succession – and a meditation
upon the rapid passage of time. These lines are translated very
sensitively by Chaucer:

> And thogh youre grene youthe floure as yet
> In crepeth age alwey, as stille as stoon.
>
> (120–1)

But they have no place at all in Boccaccio, and are indicative of an
attention – not to graphic detail as in the *Clerk's Tale* – but to points
of thematic coherence that affect even Petrarch's treatment of the
mysterious Griselda. Thus when Griselda speaks – as she rarely does
in the *Decameron* – she does so in terms that draw attention to the
issue of the freedom of will that the counsellors first introduced:

'Et dixi' ait 'et repeto, nichil possum seu velle seu nolle nisi quod tu'
(p. 1326).

('I have said to you', she declared, 'and I repeat that I cannot wish or not
wish anything that you do not consent to.')

Then again, where Boccaccio pictures Griselda on her return to her
father's house, 'doing little services for him', Petrarch draws attention
to her peacefulness and inward calm 'quippe in mediis opibus inops

semper spiritu vixisset atque humilis'. Chaucer here provides another translation that is alert to the tense moral vision of the original and adds features of its own (again neither the quality of the translation nor the additions are due to the *Livre Griseldis*). Thus he translates:

> No wonder is, for in hire grete estaat
> Hire goost was evere in pleyn humylitee.
> No tendre mouth, noon herte delicaat,
> No pompe, no semblaunt of roialtee,
> But ful of pacient benyngnytee,
> Discreet and prideless, ay honurable,
> And to hire housbonde evere meke and stable.
>
> (925–31)

The exactitude of the opening lines is followed by a descant on the same themes and motifs, encouraged perhaps by the exigencies of a stanzaic form rather than prose, and for a moment this seems to be leading to a literary and sentimental indulgence that Petrarch – whose resonantly moral lines mark the end of a section – would not allow himself. But against this Chaucer ends his own section with the addition of a scriptural reference – to the Book of Job – which is far more explicitly Christian than Petrarch's conclusion (932).

Two final illustrations of Petrarch's treatment of Griselda must suffice. First, we note that she, like the Marquis, is given a political role; she does not limit herself to womanly matters but is a competent delegate in her husband's absence: 'sed ubi res posceret, publica etiam obibat officia, viro absente'. Boccaccio's Griselda breathes only a vague concern at this point for her husband's honour. And Chaucer, too, tends not to emphasize the public arena in which Petrarch's Griselda stands; *Le Livre Griseldis*, translating word for word, speaks of Griselda's concern for 'la chose publique' and the 'salut du bien commun publique', where Chaucer seems more concerned with her individual characteristics of judgement and equity. Secondly, and most characteristically, at the especially cruel moment when the Marquis invites Griselda to act as handmaiden to his new wife, Boccaccio's heroine replies with liturgical simplicity, 'Signor mio, io son presta e apparecchiata', but Petrarch's Griselda embraces the moral imperative with all the vigour of a Henry James heroine:

'Non libenter modo' inquit illa 'sed cupide et hoc et quecunque tibi placita sensero faciam semper, neque in hoc unquam fatigabor aut lentescam dum spiritus huius reliquie ulle supererunt' (p. 1334).

('I will always do this, not only willingly', she said, 'but eagerly – both this and whatever else may please you, nor shall I ever tire or fail in doing so while any remnant of my living spirit remains in me.')

Chaucer's alteration here is slight but significant; where Petrarch
(followed by the rather pedestrian French) emphasizes the unfailing
labour and service of Griselda under the 'legitimate yoke' of marriage,
Chaucer adds to this a concluding emphasis upon her love and
integrity, in short, upon her 'trouthe':[6]

> 'Nat oonly, lord, that I am glad,' quod she,
> 'To doon youre lust, but I desire also
> Yow for to serve and plese in my degree
> Withouten feynting, and shal evermo;
> Ne nevere, for no wele ne no wo,
> Ne shal the goost withinne myn herte stente
> To love yow best with al my trewe entente.'
>
> (967–73)

Some of the characteristics of Chaucer's version will already be
apparent. But before I attempt to define the general implications of
Chaucer's work, it needs to be emphasized how close Chaucer stays
in most respects to the text of Petrarch. It has frequently been remarked how minute and economical the alterations are and yet how
radical in their overall effect. At the same time, there is reason to
suppose that the work is the product of conscious scholarship and
'clerkly' devotion on its author's part – in which respect, the tale
would possess a peculiar suitability to its teller. A single example in
parallel text must serve here to illustrate the combination of fidelity
and freedom that distinguishes the translation. The passage describes
the moment at which the Marquis chooses Griselda (a choice that
Boccaccio treats very offhandedly; it is a passage in which the *Livre
Griseldis* suggests a detail of the scene but none of diction):

In hanc virgunculam Valterius
sepe illac transiens, quandoque
oculos non iuvenili lascivia sed
senili gravitate defixerat, et
virtutem eximiam supra sexum
supraque etatem, quam vulgi oculis
conditionis obscuritas abscondebat,
acri penetrat intuitu. Unde effectum
ut et uxorem habere, quod
nunquam ante voluerat, et simul
hanc unam nullamque aliam habere
disponeret.

Upon Grisilde, this povre creature,
Ful ofte sithe this markys sette his ye
As he on huntyng rood paraventure;
And whan it fil that he myghte hire
                              espye
He noght with wantown lookyng of
                              folye
His eyen caste on hire, but in sad
                              wyse
Upon hir chiere he wolde him ofte
                              avyse,

Commendynge in his herte hir
                       wommanhede,
And eek hir vertu, passynge any
                              wight

Of so yong age, as wel in chiere as
dede.
For thogh the peple have no greet
insight
In vertu, he considered ful right
Hir bountee, and disposed that he
wolde
Wedde hire oonly, if evere he wedde
sholde.

Instabat nuptiarum dies; unde
autem ventura sponsa esset, nemo
noverat, nemo non mirabatur . . .
(pp. 1316–18)

The day of weddyng cam, but no
wight kan
Telle what womman that it shoulde
be;
For which merveille wondred many
a man,
And seyden, whan they were in
privetee,
'Wol nat oure lord yet leve his
vanytee
Wol he nat wedde? allas; allas; the
while!
Why wole he thus hymself and us
bigile?'
(232–52)

Certain details are predictable here, notably the concrete reference to Walter's hunting (which Chaucer adopts from the French) and the original addition of the words spoken, suggestively enough, 'in privetee' by Walter's cautious subjects. Equally, the use of Griselda's Christian name contributes to the sense of identity and of identification that Chaucer seeks to arouse in his representation of the heroine. More subtle, however, is the handling of the notion of vision in the first two stanzas. In Petrarch this is a notion of some importance; his hero is credited with a mystic acuity of insight that contrasts with the crudity of the sensual eye – as Shakespeare has it, 'Love looks not with the eyes, but with the mind / And therefore is wing'd Cupid painted blind.' But Chaucer seems to have recognized this contrast and gone out of his way to preserve it. This is the more striking in that Chaucer's Marquis does not, overall, deserve to be credited with such a faculty as 'acer intuitus'. Nor is the translation as neat as some I have quoted earlier. The point, however, is that there is a distinct effort here to be faithful. Thus, these stanzas represent one of only three or four instances in the Tale of stanzaic enjambement, and it is this connection that brings into relief the contrast between the 'wanton lookyng of folye' and the inward 'commendynge' in the heart. This gentle and contemplative phrase renders something of Petrarch's 'acer intuitus'. But not all, and Chaucer then proceeds to add what is missing – even if a little clumsily – by his use of the phrase 'insight / In vertu'. The Marquis is – just – allowed the grasp of essential qualities that he has in Petrarch; one might add in the process, Chaucer has also managed to give an emphasis – which is far more characteristic of his own tale – to the inward wholeness and working integrity of Griselda, to her youth, her 'chiere', her deeds and 'hir bountee'.

Petrarch, in his revision of Boccaccio, produced a work of considerable intellectual coherence, but the very intelligence of the work – though often devoted to the service of narrative or emotional effect – detracts in the end from the imaginative suggestiveness of Boccaccio's version. In the *Clerk's Tale* we find a profundity of religious sentiment. Yet it is different in kind from the sentiment that inspires Petrarch's work and exactly suited to narrative treatment. For it is the very essence of Chaucer's Christian sensibility that it should express itself in particular interest in the fate of the individual. Chaucer is not concerned as Petrarch is with a discovery of the general patterns that govern humanity; indeed when Petrarch provides the allegorical instrument for deriving a general lesson from Griselda's story, Chaucer's translation is, as we have already seen, guarded and, as a whole, the conclusion of the tale is shot through with ironies. But Chaucer does hold firm to the value of 'pitee'.[7] And before considering how the narrative of the *Clerk's Tale* operates as a function of 'pitee', we may briefly consider a passage from a work which, if less successful than the *Clerk's Tale*, deals with similar issues and states them very clearly.

In the *Man of Law's Tale*, at the height of Dame Custance's sufferings, Chaucer writes:

> God liste to shew his wonderful myracle
> In hire, for we sholde seen his myghty werkis;
> Crist, which that is to every harm triacle,
> By certeine meenes ofte, as knowen clerkis,
> Dooth thyng fore certein ende that ful derke is
> To mannes wit, that for oure ignorance
> Ne konne noght knowe his prudent purveiance.
>   (477–83)

With a clarity of thought and cogency of phrase that would not discredit Dante, Chaucer here approaches the mystery of predestination. Discussions of this subject – which had moved to the centre of theological debate in Chaucer's time – recur throughout his writing;

indeed on this particular aspect of theology, Chaucer, is, if anything, more explicit and technical than Dante, who regards the mystery as logically impenetrable and tends therefore to express its reality, not in philosophical terms, but in resonant images like the image of his own predistined journey to God or Beatrice's absolute security in the sight of her Creator. Nonetheless, the train of Chaucer's thought in this stanza is closely comparable to the implications of Dante's imagery. Like Dante, he appreciates the essential poverty of the human condition. As creatures of the physical realm, we are inevitably stricken by the alterations of Fortune. Yet poverty itself, when properly understood, provides an answer to this condition. For poverty is a condition, not simply of the physical being or the pocket, but of reason and intellect itself, and the true act of self-knowledge – which is knowledge of man's position in God's scheme – is to recognize that the limitations of the human being are not a restraint but a definition of its nature. Thus Chaucer, like Dante in *Purg.*, III, 37–9, allows that men may comprehend the mere mechanics of God's action in the universe – 'clerkis' know the 'certeine meenes' by which God works – but they cannot rationally know the divine purpose, the 'certein ende that ful derke is / To mannes wit'. The most pregnant point, however, in both Dante and Chaucer is that while man in his human nature is constitutionally restricted, he is not helpless nor, as an individual, is he humiliated in the sight of God. For Chaucer in these lines comes close to a position that Dante only reaches at the height of the *Paradiso*: that God is in the end best understood, not through pure reason, but through a rational contemplation of the way in which he works upon his individual creatures. Thus in the Heaven of Justice, Dante is faced with the miracle of the redemption of two pagans, Ripheus and Trajan; he begins to question why they should be destined for salvation where all other pagans must be damned, and is sharply made to realize that, reasonable as this inquiry might seem, it is a presumptuous attempt upon divine counsel. Yet he does not remain without an answer. The salvation of Ripheus and Trajan, precisely as a miracle, as a wholly unique and unfathomable act of God, offers a sign for him to contemplate. Although Dante may know nothing in terms of reason of God's eternal counsel, he nonetheless has evidence in the fate of Ripheus and Trajan of God's intentions for the individual. Since God himself loved these two men, Dante will draw them closer to God in his own love of their miraculous sanctity.

It is a precisely similar point to which Chaucer directs us in speaking of how in Custance 'God liste to shew his wonderful myracle.' Here, too, the individual creature is the final word of God, and our natural response to tragic sufferings will itself be the answer to the tragic problem. For the 'pitee' that tragedy inspires is the emotional and imaginative due that one individual should properly pay to the sufferings of another. For all our ignorance of the 'certein ende', we emphatically *see* God's 'myghty werkis' in the destiny of his creatures. As Hopkins puts it:

> Mark, the mark is of man's make
> And the word of it sacrificed.
> But he scores it in scarlet himself on his own bespoken . . .
>   (*The Wreck of the Deutschland*, st. 22)

As soon as we return to the *Clerk's Tale* – a far more successful piece of narrative – it is clear that Chaucer's interest in Christian 'pitee' is consistent with some of his most characteristic talents as a poet and narrator. The word 'pitee' itself and its derivatives recur constantly in the story; indeed the Marquis' decision to marry at all is motivated by the 'pitee' he feels when the spokesman of his people comes before him with 'pitous cheere' (141–2). In keeping with this, the dominant stylistic effects of the tale – what Elizabeth Salter calls 'pathetic realism' and 'dramatic realism' – are designed to heighten the poignancy and emotional appeal of Griselda's predicament.[8] In, for instance, Griselda's encounter with the 'ugly sergeant' – which Salter and Severs have analysed in detail – Chaucer goes out of his way to underline the viciousness of the Marquis' agent as he steals Griselda's children from her:

> Suspecious was the diffame of this man,
> Suspect his face, suspect his word also;
> Suspect the tyme in which he this bigan.
> Allas! hire doghter that she loved so,
> She wende he wolde han slawen it right tho.
>   (540–4)

The first three lines follow the rhetoric of Petrarch rather than the simple description of the French, but do so with a rhythm of increasing menace, which finally produces the pathetic exclamation 'alas', which is not found in Petrarch. Here, as at many other points, Chaucer constructs an emotional drama that invites the direct participation of the audience. Petrarch's text by no means diminishes the emotion of the text, but there is little sense in his work that the direct responsiveness of 'pitee' may be a more valid response than rational consideration. Though he admits in the Marquis the virtue of 'acer intuitus', his own writing maintains a measured and reflective grasp on the broad pattern of moral and psychological issues that the story raises. Chaucer's text in contrast is in large part highly theatrical.

Yet the theatricality of the *Clerk's Tale* is only partial. And it is noticeable that the most graphic effects and the most vivid emotional reactions tend – at least until the final section of the work – to be associated with the Marquis rather than Griselda. In his picture of the Marquis, Chaucer increasingly distances himself from Petrarch's relatively sympathetic view and presents him in a critical and even melodramatic light; where Petrarch's Valterius, hearing how Griselda bore the abduction of her daughter, has to fight a vehement paternal emotion to continue with his scheme ('vehementer paterna animum pietas movit'), Chaucer's Walter 'somwhat ... hadde routhe in his manere' (579) – and no more than 'somwhat'. It is likewise the pomp and circumstance of Walter in his public position that naturally enough attracts Chaucer's descriptive interest. But Griselda is hardly described at all. We see nothing of her features, and only in the closing sequences of the tale are her emotions brought to the fore. The effect of this is particularly marked in a passage of Chaucer's devising that I quoted earlier. In the midst of the magnificent preparations for the marriage, the public are suddenly aware that there is no bride, and Chaucer pictures their mutterings about her absence. But this is only the first of a series of passages in which Griselda, so to speak, absents herself, and disappoints the gaudy expectations that readers of fiction entertain of a normal heroine. It is true that Griselda, if not described, has a good deal to say for herself. Yet she does not have the moral vehemence of Petrarch's Griselda; her words tend to be characterized by negatives, or to retreat – like a form of authorial retraction – into the undramatic sphere of liturgical language, 'Ye been oure lord, dooth with youre owene thyng / Right as yow list' (652–3). Then again, while, as Severs suggests, Griselda is shown to possess an active virtue, the action is of a kind that characteristically negates itself. Thus when she returns to her father's house, Petrarch emphasizes how unspoilt she is by her former prosperity, but Chaucer, with an anaphora on the negative, draws attention to the mystic blankness of her present conduct:

> Ne shewed she that hire was doon offence;
> Ne of hire heighe estaat no remembraunce
> Ne hadde she, as by hire contenance.
>
> (922–4)

Even when she is finally released from her sufferings, Chaucer adds details to the original that emphasize the incompatibility between her

characteristic reality and the sphere of theatrical gesture that her
husband inhabits:

> And she for wonder took of it no keep;
> She herde nat what thyng he to hire seyde;
> She ferde as she had sterte out of a sleep,
> Til she out of hire mazednesse abreyde.
>
> (1058–61)

To some degree, Chaucer has returned to the simple oppositions
that Boccaccio creates in his tale. Certainly when the narrator, with
growing impatience at Walter's conduct, exclaims:

> But as for me, I seye that yvele it sit
> To assaye a wyf whan that it is no nede
>
> (460–1)

he unconsciously echoes the similar disgust of Boccaccio's narrator,
Dioneo. There is, too, as I have suggested, a certain liturgical solemnity
to Griselda's utterances in Boccaccio as there is in Chaucer. Yet here
the resemblance ends; for there can be no doubt or ambiguity at all
about the function of Griselda's self-effacement in the *Clerk's Tale*.
Not only does it express Chaucer's moral concern with the true nature
of poverty, but it amounts to a test that Chaucer performs upon the
sharpness of the pitying eye; the eye of the reader is asked to penetrate
through the meretricious attractions of theatrical events and exercise
itself upon the still but ever-receding point of Griselda's person. Thus
in the story there are some – 'the sadde folk in that citee' – who can
do this and who reprove the light-headed reactions of those citizens
who are fascinated by the glamour of the Marquis' second – and, let
it be said, 'fictional' – wife:

> O stormy peple! unsad and evere untrewe!
> Ay undiscreet and chaungynge as a fane!
> Delitynge evere in rumbul that is newe . . .
>
> (995–7)

But a better guide to the force that Chaucer intended his story to have
is a figure of whom as yet I have said nothing at all, that of the
narrator, the Clerk himself.

The one aspect of the *Clerk's Tale* that is entirely original to Chaucer
is his conception of the Clerk and of the Clerk's own relationship to
the tale he tells. Thus, in a simple and extremely important way, the
narrator of Chaucer's tale is allowed to comment upon the action far
more vigorously than Petrarch or even Boccaccio's narrator does. When

the narrator at the outset criticizes the bachelor Marquis for lack of foresight (the very quality, ironically enough, that the Marquis might seem to arrogate to himself in his treatment of his wife), he establishes for himself a presence that is to be expressed in a sequence of similar interpolations. And the same attitude also seems to account for a number of innovations in the translation, such as the introduction of 'wikke' in the phrase: 'Among al this, after his wikke usage / This markys . . .' (785). Cumulatively, such modifications as these entirely alter the emphasis of Petrarch's text.

There is, however, a further, more complicated sense in which the Clerk's presence, as expressed particularly in the Prologue to the tale and its epilogues, radically affects our attitude to the tale itself. In brief, we cannot forget that the tale is told within the framework of the Canterbury game. Of course, Boccaccio's story too is set within the 'cornice' of the hundred tales; and, as Ann Middleton has recently shown, we cannot ignore the epistles that accompany Petrarch's version. But the implications of these 'contexts' for the reading of the work are quite different from those that Chaucer provides.

In Petrarch's case, his letters reveal his tale to be a deeply personal creation, expressing vividly the moral and cultural preoccupations of the great humanist. In translating Boccaccio's vernacular, he will prove himself even in his old age to be the friend, admirer and mentor of his also-aging disciple. More poignantly still, he can demonstrate by undertaking the labour at all that he is yet in command of his faculties. Boccaccio had written to suggest that he should save himself from the labour of further composition. But the translation will demonstrate that his emotional and linguistic capacities are undimmed. And here a touching identity arises between the heroine of the tale and the author himself; the constancy and endurance of Griselda is a model for Petrarch himself as he labours to the end at his chosen task.

As for Boccaccio, the position of the story in the *Decameron* serves only to enhance and justify its inherent ambiguities of tone. First, the teller is the scurrilous and mercurial Dioneo. This in itself is enough to subvert any moral authority that the story – as the last tale in the *Decameron* and as an *exemplum*, supposedly, of magnanimity – might be supposed to possess. Nor does Dioneo miss the opportunity to introduce innuendo into the tale alongside a spectrum of tones ranging from sentiment to cynicism. Finally when the tale is done, the *brigata* make no comment on the morality of the issues raised; some of the ladies take one side, others the opposite, and while it is said that they utter words of praise and condemnation, the phrasing suggests that the critique attaches to the effectiveness and tenor of the story, not to the conduct of its characters. So, fittingly, the *Decameron* ends with an intelligently affable debate in which moral principle bends to a refreshing exercise of critical sensibility.

But what, then, of Chaucer's case? In the first place, the Prologue is surprisingly literary in cast considering the seriousness of the religious issues that dominate the tale. The Host, with slightly mocking reverence for the professional 'deepness' of the scholar, invites him to tell a 'myrie tale', specifically banning the use of 'heigh style', with its 'termes, colours and figures' (16), which is used in addresses to kings. The Clerk accepts this commission. But here a certain subtlety enters. For if the Clerk is not going to speak in high rhetoric, he still finds room for literary conversation of his own, claiming acquaintance with 'Fraunceys Petrak, the lauriat poete/ . . . whos rethorike sweete / Enlumyned al Ytaille of poetrie' (31–3). Quietly and subtly he insists on the dignity of his profession. And with equal skill and quietness, he succeeds at one and the same time in criticizing Petrarch and celebrating his example. For while he allows that Petrarch's topological introduction to the Griselda is a 'thyng impertinent' (54), he nonetheless translates this example of 'heigh style' almost in its entirety, dividing it between a disclaimer and the actual beginning of his own story. The Host may be right to suspect that clerks are wordy, but he has been obliged by this Clerk's sleight of hand to attend to a swathe of rhetoric.

The canniness of the Clerk at first seems to have little to do with the morally frank narrator (and linguistically faithful translator) of the tale. Yet in the epilogue, he is to show himself a superbly confident and joyful ironist. And the Prologue in another aspect does indeed demonstrate how literary issues may merge with issues of morality that are close to those which the tale confronts. In itself the homage to Petrarch expresses something of the cultural solidarity – or constancy – that Petrarch himself sought to exemplify in his response to Boccaccio. Likewise, the Prologue contemplates the highly Petrarchan themes of glory and mutability, of the brevity of human achievement; Petrarch may have 'enlumyned al Ytaille' but he has now been extinguished 'as it were a twynklyng of an ye', 'he is now deed and nayled in his cheste', 'and alle shul we dye' (29 and 38). The moral stability of Griselda will be as welcome, it seems, to Chaucer's Clerk as it was to the lover of Laura.

In this regard, however, perhaps the most significant of the Clerk's attitudes at the meeting-point of literature and morality is his decision to conform – as substantially he does – to the Host's request for plain speech, preferring a *sermo humilis*, which is equally a 'volgare illustre', to the brilliance of Petrarch's Latin, or a style that 'men to kynges write'. The very humility of his choice reveals a cast of mind that would see itself reflected in Griselda; and indeed like Griselda the Clerk is scarcely visible till he is called to by the Host to play his part in the game. 'Sire Clerk of Oxenford', says the Host:

> Ye ryde as coy and stille as dooth a mayde
> Were newe spoused, sittynge at the bord.
>
> (1–3)

Moreover, it is not difficult to explain in similar terms the Clerk's antipathy to the Marquis. Not only is the Marquis' plan proud and flamboyant – a huntsman's plan – but it presumes to displace the providence of God in its 'assaying' and ordering of the destiny of Griselda's soul – as we learn from the *Man of Law's Tale* it is the function of clerks, not marquises, to know the working of God's will, and clerks know, too, that they cannot plumb the 'certein ende'. But as Griselda retains the mystic integrity of her being in the face of attempts not only to destroy but also to distract her with the trappings of her high position, so the Clerk, thrust onto an unaccustomed stage by the Host, still retains the integrity of his peculiarly subtle and sensitive being.

It is this being – at first hidden, 'coy' and barely visible – that bursts out triumphantly in the epilogues of the tale. Having told his tale the Clerk is ready to take on even the Wife of Bath, which he does, not with the predictable antifeminism of a clerk such as Jankyn but with a 'lusty herte, fresshe and grene' (1173) and with a generous irony that can mock and yet find amusement in even the senseless chatterings of a termagant; 'Grisilde is deed' he proclaims – as Petrarch is – therefore let wives follow 'Ekko, that holdeth no silence' (1189).

So the Clerk in the process of telling his tale has released his personality, as nearly all of his fellow-pilgrims do in the course of their tales. And as happens in nearly every other case, his reward is to be recognized for what he is by his fellows, and most especially the Host. Thus, though we might not have thought the tale the 'myrie' tale that the Host commissioned, the Host bestows the accolade of his approval on it – which is hardly the laurel crown that Petrarch desired but *is* a living recognition.

It is the sudden glory that the Clerk enjoys in the company of the Wife and Host that provides a pattern for our response to Griselda herself. She, too, after riding 'coyly' through the Marquis' fiction, has a sudden moment in which, to quote Hopkins again, the 'immortal diamond' of her self is revealed entire. This moment is that at which, not in obvious triumph but 'pitously wepynge' (1082) she trains her eye and emotion upon the sight of her children, who stand revealed as constant features not cancelled from her life. 'O which a pitous thyng it was to se', says the Clerk. And pity here, we might say, is 'instress', the ability to respond with all one's being to another being. The Clerk himself enjoys such attention at the conclusion of his tale. For those likewise who know how individuality is to be valued, the vision of Griselda's selfhood – evanescent but constant – will be a 'myrie' tale.

Notes

1 On this point and throughout, the present essay is much indebted to J. Burke Severs' exhaustive study *The Literary Relationships of Chaucer's Clerkes Tale*, Yale Studies in English, XCVI (New Haven, 1942).

2 The text of *Le Livre Griseldis* referred to here is to be found in Severs' volume, see n. 1; the text of Petrarch's *De Insigni Obedientia* to which I refer is contained in Petrarch's *Opere Latine*, ed. A. Bufano (Turin 1975), vol. II, pp. 1312–39.

3 Compare the self-deceit of Mitridanes in *Decameron*, X, iii, who contemplates murder in order to safeguard a reputation for magnanimity.

4 See *Seniles*, XVII, 3 and XVII, 4. On the importance of the epistles, see Anne Middleton's valuable study, 'The Clerk and His Tale: Some Literary Contexts' in *Studies in the Age of Chaucer*, vol. II (The University of Oklahoma, 1980), pp. 121–50.

5 As, for instance, in Canzone CCLXX: 'Amor, se vuo' ch'i' torni al giogo anticho'.

6 Cf. E. T. Donaldson, *Chaucer's Poetry* (New York, 1958), pp. 919–20.

7 See Mario Praz' discussion of 'pitee' in *The Flaming Heart* (New York, 1973 edn.), pp. 55–6.

8 See Elizabeth Salter's *Chaucer: The Knight's Tale and The Clerk's Tale*, Studies in English Literature, V (London, 1962).

Chaucer, Boccaccio and the Friars

'A frere wol entremette hym everemo'

'A friar will always be meddling' declares Chaucer's Summoner, as he responds with churlish chivalry to the Friar's criticism of the Prologue to the *Wife of Bath's Tale*. His and the Wife's subsequent comparisons of friars to flies around food, swirling specks of dust in the sunlight and swarms of bees all reinforce this impression of busy activity; and so also does the degree of space and prominence that both Chaucer and Boccaccio accord the mendicants in their work.

Friar Hubert's portrait is the longest of all those in the General Prologue, whilst – in his own right as a story-teller and through his *alter ego* Friar John in the *Summoner's Tale* – he makes a substantial contribution to the drama of the Canterbury pilgrimage. In eight of the *Decameron's* stories friars and their immediate associates have leading parts to play,[1] and they are also brought to the fore in the conclusion to the whole work. These appearances reflect mendicant 'meddling' in the imaginations of the two authors clearly enough, even if we take no account of the friar-like figures of, for example, Daun Russell the Nun's Priest's fox, or the potential misinterpreter of Chaucer's dream in the *House of Fame* (98), or the actual enemies of poetry that Boccaccio portrays in the *Genealogie Deorum* (XIV, v). And in view of this manifest concern it is not surprising that Boccaccio's Emilia should, at the start of her tale on the Eighth Day of the *Decameron*, specifically include friars among the clerics who plague the souls of her sex.

Given the prominence of the perch that the clergy in general occupied at the time, it is readily understandable that they should have presented what Boccaccio's Filostrato calls 'a sitting target' (*Decameron*, I, vii, 4) for critics and satirists of various backgrounds and persuasions. Of course neither Boccaccio's portrayal of clerics nor Chaucer's reflects a root-and-branch revolutionary or heretical attitude and such generalized criticism of the clergy as we find, for example, in Emilia's remarks (referred to above), in the tale of Abraham the Jew (*Decameron*, I, ii), or in the story of the priest's cloak (*Decameron*, VIII, ii, 3–5) seems to be, as R. Davidsohn puts it, 'confined within the framework of a family quarrel'.[2] Nonetheless it would be wrong to characterize either author's anticlericalism entirely in such limited terms – still less to view it simply as the product of cynically detached amusement.

Fourteenth-century anticlericalism was wide-ranging in its objects, as the portrayals of monks, nuns and priests in both the *Decameron* and the *Canterbury Tales* plainly show; whilst even the papacy was not exempt from violent criticism of the sort that is given voice, for example, by Dante throughout the *Comedy*, or in several of Petrarch's sonnets and letters.[3] And criticism of the friars was one of the most highly (if recently) developed of its forms.

Such criticism stemmed from various motives and origins, including some within the mendicant movement itself. The faction-ridden Franciscans were, as an Order, particularly given to reappraisal and self-criticism, as is evident from the pronouncements both of an established figure like Bonaventura in the later thirteenth century (see his *Opera*, VIII, 468–9) and those of radical and rebellious Spiritual Franciscans such as Jacopone da Todi in the early fourteenth. Outside the Orders themselves antifraternal hostility is apparent for example among those – such as the secular clergy and the university masters – who saw the friars as a challenge to their authority and a threat to their privileges and interests. Such hostility had been perhaps at its most active during the later thirteenth century, but it continued to erupt at times during the fourteenth – and the polemics of Guillaume de Saint-Amour, the leading opponent of the mendicants during the former period, provided an apocalyptic terminology that (as P. R. Szittya has shown) continued to influence the language of anti-fraternal exegesis, criticism and satire long after the time of the dispute that generated it.[4] In this latter form at least antifraternalism could be considered a 'family quarrel' or even 'a clerical form of anticlericalism'.[5]

As well as finding expression in the Latin treatises of Guillaume de Saint-Amour and his fourteenth-century followers (such as Jean de Pouilly and Richard FitzRalph), antifraternalism also took a variety of forms in vernacular literature. Friars may thus, for example, play a stereotyped role in *fabliau* farce and satirical verse;[6] or they may appear in a more insidious guise, as dealers in 'fables' and fraudulent fictions – as do Boccaccio's Frate Alberto and Chaucer's Friar Hubert (narrator of the *Friar's Tale*) and Friar John (the 'lymytour' and preacher in the *Summoner's Tale*). They may also be presented as examples of corruptible idealism (as in Dante's Guido da Montefeltro in *Inferno*, XXVII) or portrayed as images of intellectual arrogance

(as in Langland's 'doctour' in *Piers Plowman*, C–XV [XVI]). Or (drama-
tizing the apocalyptic terms of Guillaume de Saint-Amour's polemic)
they may even be identified with the harbingers of Antichrist in the
'last days' – as is the case at the end of *Piers Plowman*. In general,
therefore, the discrepancy between the activities of such *falsi fratres*
and the apostolic ideals that their founders observed can be said to
have concerned imaginative writers at a wide variety of levels. Hence,
when Friar John in the *Summoner's Tale* advertises himself (III,
1820–1) as one who is wont to

> ' . . . walke, and fisshe Cristen mennes soules,
>   To yelden Jhesu Crist his propre rente'

– Chaucer tersely demonstrates (through the allusion to Matt. IV.19)
the distance between Christ's purposes for his Apostles and the pred-
atory practices of this particular 'lymytour'.

Yet whether Chaucer knew it or not, the very gospel text that he
makes his Friar mouth here had also been ironically invoked by
several previous antifraternal writers. As early as 1247 one of the
friars' first critics, the chronicler Matthew Paris, had described them
as 'no longer fishers of men, but fishers for coins' (*Chronica Majora*,
IV, 635) – whilst a little later in the century the poet Rutebeuf
referred to the Dominicans in similar terms (*Des Jacobins*, 33–6). And
during the seventh story of the Third Day in the *Decameron* Boccaccio's Tedaldo degli Elisei warns his mistress of how friars like
fishermen casting nets gather up numbers of 'devout ladies, widows
and other foolish women and men' (35).

This allusive gibe of Tedaldo's offers an appropriate starting-point
for some exploration of Boccaccio's antifraternal attitudes and their
context. It forms part of the *Decameron*'s longest diatribe against the
friars, in the course of which the speaker, like other antifraternal
critics, contrasts contemporary mendicants with their 'worthy and
most holy predecessors', whilst levelling at them the traditional
charges of lust, avarice, gluttony and casuistry. Tedaldo, however, is
by no means an impartial or uncompromised witness. He has disguised himself first as a pilgrim and then as a confessor in order to
persuade Aldobrandino's wife to repent her failure to persist in
adultery with him. And, appropriately, it is only after deploying some
eloquent casuistry on his own behalf (30–2) that he identifies himself
for the first time as a friar. In thus adopting the very habit he decries
Tedaldo perhaps reflects the ambivalent attitude of an author who in
some measure owed his education and that of his audience to the
Orders that he satirized.

Indeed, the more closely we consider Boccaccio's intellectual milieu and the works that it nourished, the more complex does his relationship to these Orders come to appear. For example, during his years of scholarly and poetic apprenticeship at Naples he became acquainted with the Franciscan Paolino da Venezia (Bishop of Pozzuoli, 1324–44), whose *Chronologia Magna* greatly influenced the treatment of legend in the *Filocolo*;[7] and even more prominent among his mentors at that time was the Austin friar Dionigi da Borgo San Sepolcro, a classicist and astrologer who had taught at Paris and was a friend and correspondent of Petrarch. Like Petrarch, Boccaccio was also to develop close ties with the Austin Order, which had been established in Florence (at Santo Spirito) since the middle of the thirteenth century.[8] One of its members, Martino da Signa (d. 1387), became his spiritual director, executor of his will and inheritor of his library; and he was also the correspondent for whose benefit (in Letter XXIII) Boccaccio expounded the allegory of his *Bucolicum Carmen* poems. A younger friar of the same Order, Luigi Marsili (1342–94), acted as an intermediary between Boccaccio and Petrarch during their last years; and Boccaccio's will provided that if he were to die in Florence he should be buried in the Austins' church. Certain other mendicant Orders (notably the Franciscans) are on occasion identified or recognizable as objects of satire in the *Decameron*, but as Branca points out (*Decameron*, p. 1369, n. 2) the Austins never are. Moreover, during his years in Florence the poet also appears to have formed some associations with the Franciscans and the Dominicans whose *studia* at, respectively, Santa Croce and Santa Maria Novella had been of major importance to the city's intellectual life since the later part of the thirteenth century.[9] In such respects at least it is probably true to say that some of Boccaccio's best friends were friars.

Some considerable degree of sympathy for the mendicant (and especially Franciscan) ideal of poverty is also evident at points in his own work. A few years before the young Boccaccio's arrival in the kingdom King Robert of Naples had demonstrated support for the radical *Fraticelli* in their struggle against the revisions that Pope John XXII sought to impose upon the Franciscan Order. The treatise on poverty that was written by him (or at his command) in 1322 would doubtless have been known to Boccaccio and may even be echoed by, for example, Fiammetta's praise of contented poverty in Book IV of the *Filocolo*.[10] Moreover, by continuing to celebrate the virtues of poverty in works of his later Florentine years the poet also seems to be dissociating himself from the city's confident materialism.[11]

Boccaccio's praise of poverty tends, however, to give prominence to its Roman civic aspects,[12] and it thus takes a somewhat different turn from the attitudes that had been earlier voiced by the Spiritual Franciscan Jacopone da Todi in a number of his *laude* (especially XXXII, LIX and LX). Yet Jacopone's work should perhaps be taken into account as part of the broad context of Boccaccio's anticlericalism and antifraternalism. His *laude* could conceivably have struck a chord or two in the later writer not only through their concern with apostolic poverty but also by virtue of the vividness with which they portray a decadent religious Order (e.g. XXX), a worldly pope (e.g. LVIII) and – in particular – an arrogant learned friar (XXXI).

Dante's criticism of the clergy was more directly influential upon Boccaccio, and it often accommodates elements of Franciscan idealism.[13] Thus St Benedict, characterizing the decadence of his own Order in *Paradiso*, XXII, finds a ready comparison (88–90) in the betrayal of original principles on the part of St Francis' *convento*. Such concern is also evident of course in the representation of strife within the Franciscan Order itself (*Par.*, XII, 112–26) and in the somewhat briefer comments about worldliness among the Dominicans (*Par.*, XI, 124–32). And, with regard to the friars, it achieves perhaps its most poignant expression in the portrayal of Guido da Montefeltro the Romagnuol soldier–politician who became a Franciscan late in life, but was tempted back to his Machiavellian *coperte vie* in order to further the ambitions of the 'leader of the modern Pharisees', Pope Boniface VIII (*Inf.*, XXVII, 67–129). This particular tragedy dramatizes the precariousness of an individual's conversion, but it may also convey something of Dante's awareness (a prophetic awareness when we think of John XXII's dealings with the Franciscans) of the choices and dangers that were faced by the Order to which Guido belonged.

Boccaccio may well have been affected by such manifestations of Dante's concern for the state of the Church and the mendicant Orders, and he was directly influenced by the language of the *Comedy*'s anticlerical satire in at least one important instance: Beatrice's long denunciation of false preachers towards the end of *Paradiso* (XXIX, 94–126). Other writers with whose anticlericalism Boccaccio's might in some ways be compared are, as Branca suggests (*Decameron*, p. 1174), John of Salisbury in the twelfth century (*Policraticus*, VII),[14] the Franciscan chronicler Salimbene de Adam in the thirteenth, and Boccaccio's near-contemporary Franco Sacchetti (*c.* 1333–*c.* 1440). To these we might also add a contemporary of Dante's, the Sienese poet Bindo Bonichi (esp. sonnets XIX–XXI), and Boccaccio's Florentine friend, Antonio Pucci (*c.* 1310–88), who wrote a number of sonnets about the decadence of the various religious Orders within the city.[15]

The last three writers, especially, often represent friars in ways
that approach the lighter manner of some of the *Decameron* portrayals.
Yet, bearing in mind Boccaccio's indebtedness to certain individuals
and groups among the mendicant Orders – as well as his reverence
for Dante and his friendship with Petrarch – it becomes difficult to
regard his antifraternal satire as deriving solely or even mainly from
a spirit of light-hearted or cynical amusement. Tedaldo (in *Decameron*,
III, vii) is, as we have seen, a competitor with those very friars whose
vices he condemns – but his hypocrisy is also in some measure a tribute
to virtue, and in his references to the spirit of *contemptus mundi* that
was symbolized by the clothing of the original mendicants (34) there
are surely echoes of Boccaccio's sympathy with the ideals of Franciscan
poverty. Such echoes are more clearly resonant in Elissa's later out-
burst against fraternal luxury at the opening of her tale of Frate
Rinaldo (*Decameron*, VII, iii, 9–12), where God's justice is invoked
upon the mendicants in general – although the effect of her appeal is
complicated by the fact that the particular friar concerned in the
story escapes at the end with impunity.

More broadly speaking, an idealistic strain can be seen to coexist
with the vein of irony in Boccaccio's anticlericalism at other stages of
his career as a writer. Among his earlier works, the flippant remarks of
Pandaro concerning the hypocrisy of lecherous clerics (*Filostrato*, II,
135) can be set against the graver emphasis given to the avarice of
'modern Pharisees' in Canto XIV of the *Amorosa Visione*. Among
those which follow the *Decameron*, the sardonic characterization of
friars as consolers of widows in *Corbaccio* (ed. P. G. Ricci (Milan–
Naples, 1965), p. 538) is consonant with the tone of that work, yet
contrasts somewhat with the impassioned indignation visited on those
pharisaical figures (presumably friars) who are said in the *Genealogie*
to have denigrated poetry (XIV, v). In *De Mulieribus Claris* (XLV, 6–7)
Boccaccio's comments on the vain hopes of parents who put their
daughters in convents to pray for them recall the humour of, for
example, *Decameron*, III, i and IX, ii – but they nevertheless strike a
very different note from his condemnation of clerical avarice in the
Esposizioni on Dante's *Comedy*. Here, in his last major work, Boccaccio
voices the kind of concern that was evident in, for example, *Amorosa
Visione*, XIV and *Decameron*, I, vi and urges once again the need for
the clergy as a whole to 'follow Christ's footsteps in poverty' (VII, 70;
p. 425).

Whether and to what extent Chaucer evinces a corresponding
complexity of attitude is a question that will be returned to once we
have considered more fully the factors that might have influenced the

form of his antifraternalism. But we should first attempt to determine what major sources and traditions could have affected both these authors' representation of the friars.

Amongst the writers I have so far mentioned in connection with Boccaccio, the one most indisputably familiar to Chaucer is, of course, the 'grete poete of Ytaille / That highte Dant'. Chaucer's Friar Hubert himself acknowledges the pre-eminence of the poet of *Inferno* when the devil in the *Friar's Tale* prophesies that the summoner will be able to teach about Hell from his own experience

> 'Bet than Virgile, while he was on lyve
> Or Dant also...'
>
> (III, 1519–20)

– and the devil's assurance here, together with his promise to 'holde compaignye' with his 'brother deere' (1521) suggests that the relationship could indeed be seen as a grotesque parody of that between Dante the pilgrim and his 'dolcissimo padre', Virgil. The Summoner may be making a somewhat similar kind of allusion when he, in turn, shows a friar making a visionary pilgrimage through hell (Prologue to the *Summoner's Tale*, III, 1675f), in which he inquires about and encounters familiar figures, and witnesses – as they swarm out of their nest in 'the develes ers' – a peculiarly bizarre form of the *contrapasso* (1692–1706). But although they may thus at moments be viewed within a broadly Dantean perspective, Chaucer's friars do not appear to be portrayed in terms that are specifically indebted to anticlerical utterances in the *Comedy*.

Both Chaucer and Boccaccio, however, were in their different ways influenced by the French antifraternal tradition deriving largely from the *evènements* at the University of Paris in the mid thirteenth century. They would both have known about Guillaume de Saint-Amour's work, at least through such vernacular channels as the polemical poems of Rutebeuf and (especially) the portrait of Faus Semblanz in Jean de Meun's *Roman de la Rose*.[16] Rutebeuf's satire appears not to have had a direct effect upon either the *Decameron* or the *Canterbury Tales*.[17] The influence of the *Roman*, however, is already apparent in the romances Boccaccio wrote during his years in Naples and its major allegorical figures, including Faus Semblanz, had long been known to Italian readers through the 232 sonnets of *Il Fiore* (a redaction attributed to Dante).[18] Some of Faus Semblanz' more aggressive tactics as an extortioner (*Roman*, 11,693–756 in F. Lecoy's edition (Paris, 1970); cp. *Fiore*, CXXIV–CXXVI) could even have provided a model for some features of the ferociously venal Franciscan inquisitor in *Decameron*, I, vi, and for the threats he employs against the 'good man who had much more wealth than sense' (5, 8).[19]

The presence of Faus Semblanz is of course much more pervasive in Chaucer's work. Friar Hubert shows distinct affinities with him, both in abandoning the *poraille* in favour of the 'riche and selleres of vitaille' (General Prologue, I, 243–8 – cp. *Roman*, 11,208–38) and in busying himself with marriages and legal affairs (General Prologue, I, 258; cp. *Roman*, 11,649–62). And such indeed appears to have been the hold that the *Roman's* antifraternalism exercised over Chaucer's imagination that his most sophisticated hypocrite, the Pardoner – although not himself a friar – speaks of his solidarity with his 'brethren' (Prologue to the *Pardoner's Tale*, VI, 415–16), the purpose of his preaching (403, 423f) and his resolute avoidance of manual labour and apostolic example (444f) in terms that bear a marked resemblance to some of the assertions of Jean de Meun's friar (*Roman*, 11,607f, 11,535, 11,490f and 11,351–8).

Yet, despite this fascination with Faus Semblanz, Chaucer's actual acquaintance with actual friars and Orders is far less well-attested than is the case with Boccaccio. Thomas Speght's account of how, according to the records of the Inner Temple, the poet was once 'fined two shillings for beating a Franciscane fryer in Fleetstreete' has a certain proleptic appropriateness perhaps (in view of the location), but nothing more is known about either the cause of the assault or the identity of the victim.[20] In the absence, then, of either named opponents (like Langland's William Jordan) or known mentors (like Boccaccio's Dionigi da Borgo San Sepolcro) what factors in Chaucer's milieu could have influenced his attitude towards the mendicant orders?

As a poet connected with the Court Chaucer could hardly have failed to be aware of the privileged position held by certain mendicant groups within the royal households. The Dominicans enjoyed an especially high degree of patronage from this source, and indeed monopolized the post of confessor to the king from Henry III's time to that of Richard II.[21] And if we bear in mind, for instance, that at Christmas 1395 Richard II paid 40s. for a sermon preached by a Dominican friar of King's Langley and at the feast of the Epiphany offered the convent a noble of gold with frankincense and myrrh[22] – then the poet's account of his own poverty in the final stanza of the *Complaint to his Purse* may perhaps gain further ironic poignancy, especially when he ruefully explains that: 'I am shave as nye as any frere' (19).

The Carmelites were also conspicuous recipients of royal favour in

Chaucer's time. The poet's patron, John of Gaunt, was also a patron of this Order, and both he and the first two kings of the House of Lancaster employed them as confessors.[23] The Carmelites were active exponents of the popular sermon in the later fourteenth century and some of them were highly successful preachers at Court. Some, indeed, gained bishoprics as a direct result of their prowess in this field,[24] and it is perhaps not without relevance in such a context that Friar John, whose sermons in the *Summoner's Tale* seek more obviously material rewards, should associate himself at one point with the Carmelite Order (*Summoner's Tale*, III, 2115–17).

Several of the Austin friars also gained royal recognition during Chaucer's time;[25] and, whilst the mendicants in general were no longer so prominent in English learning as they had been before Ockham's departure from the country in 1324, some fresh intellectual impetus was however apparent among the Austins during the second half of the century (Knowles, *Religious Orders*, vol. I, p. 242 and vol. II, p. 150). This Order also appears to have provided one of the links between England and Italy at the time. Italian friars came to study at Oxford and Cambridge, where the Austins had two of their *studia generalia* (the only two from 1355 to 1365),[26] and the Order's traditional association with Italy led several of its prominent members to travel and even to settle there.[27]

There is at present no hard evidence that Chaucer was acquainted with any individual Austins – itinerant or otherwise – or indeed that he had particular contacts with friars of other Orders – except, perhaps, for that Franciscan in Fleet Street. He would, on the other hand, have been well aware of the controversies concerning the mendicants that recurred at intervals throughout the century. For example, the 'demarcation disputes' between the friars and the parish clergy had in principle been resolved by the papal bull *Super cathedram* (issued in 1300 and again in 1311). But an attempt to revive the controversy and sway the balance in favour of the parish priests had been launched by Richard FitzRalph, Archbishop of Armagh, first at Avignon (from 1350 onwards), and later, during 1356, through a series of popular sermons in London that might even, as Gwynn suggests, have been attended by the adolescent Chaucer (*English Austin Friars*, p. 87). Fitzralph's polemic, like that of Guillaume de Saint-Amour, also provided material for later antifraternal critics – such as Wyclif and his followers – who were ascertainably closer to the poet's main social and intellectual milieu. Wyclif's views about ecclesiastical wealth had earned favour and protection from Chaucer's early patron, John of Gaunt, during the 1370s. His vituperative assaults upon the four 'Orders of Caim' date from his later years of extreme anticlericalism and were subsequently echoed by the Lollards and some (presumably) of their sympathizers. The precise nature of Chaucer's attitude towards Wyclif and of his acquaintance with 'Lollard Knights' at Court (such as Clanvow, Clifford, Nevill and Sturry) is difficult to assess,[28] but he can hardly have failed to notice the intensification of antifraternal criticism from such quarters during the 1380s.

Despite hostility of this kind the mendicants – as the evidence of gifts and bequests makes clear – continued to command support not only at Court but in the country at large. This material prosperity can, in the Franciscan Order at least, be associated with a growing tendency 'towards a withdrawal from the world into the cloister, where the friar lived more and more the traditional monastic life'.[29] This tendency was predictably greeted with an increasing recurrence of one of the most vivid traditional charges against the friars. Already in the mid thirteenth century Matthew Paris had deplored the ostentatiousness of both Franciscan and Dominican convent buildings (*Chronica Majora*, IV, 279f and V, 194–5), and a little later Guillaume de Saint-Amour had, as J. V. Fleming points out, made this the subject of one of his 'few examples of wit'.[30] In Chaucer's own time the growth of these so-called 'Caim's castles' was of course exploited by Lollard propagandists, and a striking vernacular depiction is to be found in *Peres the Ploughman's Crede* (155–218).[31] But concern with such building programmes is also frequently evinced by less obviously partisan poets of the later fourteenth century. The poet of *Wynnere and Wastoure* portrayed the friars not only as allies of the mercantile classes (156–92) but also, later on, as their legatees, making use of bequests from such sources 'to paint their pillars and plaster their walls' (301). Langland shows a friar offering to immortalize Lady Meed's name in glass (*Piers Plowman*, B, III, 48–50) and Gower in the *Mirour de l'Omme* makes a similar satirical point when he describes the friars' convents as being raised upon the sins of those who have confessed to them (21,397–405). Chaucer's portrayal of Friar Hubert as both a 'noble post' of his order and a pedlar, and his account of how Friar John goes about 'oure cloystre for to reyse' (*Summoner's Tale*, III, 1718, 1977, 2102), thus reflects a preoccupation of antifraternal criticism that held a particular fascination for imaginative writers at this time. Like Langland, however, he does not present the prosperity of the established mendicants as a merely static condition – but through the restless activity of his friars he conveys a lively sense of the interdependence of the hive and the swarm.

Chaucer's portrayal of the friars therefore appears to be in part a response to social and intellectual conditions in which the mendicant Orders, though diminished in vigour and even in numbers,[32] still wielded considerable influence. Unlike Boccaccio he does not on present evidence appear to have been associated with or indebted to any particular Orders or friars – yet like Boccaccio's his characterization of the movement stems from a branch of anticlericalism that had continued to put forth new shoots throughout the fourteenth century. As well as being discernibly influenced by the antifraternalism of the *Roman de la Rose* (and hence aware of the importance of Guillaume de Saint-Amour), Chaucer would certainly have known about the polemical work of FitzRalph, Wyclif and the Lollards (as did a variety of lesser vernacular poets) – whilst he was also probably conscious of the strong antifraternal vein in the satires of his friend Gower (the *Mirour de l'Omme* and the *Vox Clamantis*) and in the apocalyptic vision of his contemporary Langland.

It is also of course possible that Chaucer may have been directly acquainted with Boccaccio's own portrayal of friars in the *Decameron*. The general view of the subject adopted, for example, by Farnham in 1924 was based largely upon lack of evidence concerning the wider availability of *Decameron* manuscripts in Chaucer's time, and its caution now appears somewhat exaggerated.[33] More recently some scholars have inclined to the opinion that the English poet's well-attested contacts with Italian merchants would have made it quite possible for him to have known about and even obtained a copy of Boccaccio's tales, since it was among this class that the earlier manuscripts of the work chiefly circulated.[34] Furthermore – with regard to the anticlericalism of the two authors – some comparative criticism of the *Shipman's Tale* has credited Chaucer with knowledge of the *Decameron*;[35] whilst Frate Cipolla's methods of exploiting the superstitions of countryfolk (*Decameron*, VI, x) could in some ways be seen as analogous to the procedures of Chaucer's Pardoner.

But apart, perhaps, from the case of the *Shipman's Tale* instances of direct or specific indebtedness to the *Decameron* on the English poet's part have not yet been securely established. And, whilst it remains likely that Boccaccio's antifraternalism would have been an added incentive for Chaucer to acquire a copy of the work once he had heard of it, the diligent seeker after positive evidence of 'influence' – especially in a region of satire so densely populated with traditional stereotypes, allusions and accusations – still risks turning into the kind of source-hunter who has been described as 'the indefatigable in pursuit of the untenable'.[36] Thus, since most of the attention so far in this discussion has been given to the various traditions and circumstances that could have contributed towards the two writers' anti-fraternalism, it may be more appropriate and productive to conclude with some specific suggestions about the ways in which their representation of friars could be compared.

Of the seven deadly sins, lechery, gluttony, avarice and pride are those most amply illustrated in both Boccaccio's and Chaucer's mendicants. Wrath and envy were often attributed to the friars,[37] and it is characteristic that Chaucer's Friar John should both preach against and practise the former whilst displaying the latter through his comments on monks and parish priests. Boccaccio's mendicants are, by comparison, a somewhat less violent and vindictive fraternity – with the exception, that is, of the choleric Franciscan Inquisitor (*Decameron*, I, vi).

On the other hand, several of the friars in the *Decameron* are more obviously and committedly lecherous than those in the *Canterbury Tales*. Of these Frate Rinaldo (VII, iii) perhaps shows most affinities with the stereotyped clerical seducer; yet even in this case his initial portrayal as 'a most elegant young man' (4) who dons the habit for the sake of more extensive *pastura* (7) reflects ironically – as does the 'conversion' of Frate Alberto – upon the decadence of the Orders. And Frate Alberto's own role as seducer – like the lecherous designs attributed to Friar Hubert and Friar John – needs to be seen in relation to his performing skills in general and to the broader implications of his dealings with the laity.

The traditional accusation of gluttony not unexpectedly recurs during both the antifraternal tirades in the *Decameron* (III, iii, 36 and 52 and VII, iii, 10–11), is hinted at in Friar Hubert's portrait (General Prologue, I, 241 and 248) and is of course a dominant feature in the characterization of Friar John. But the vice begins to take on richer connotations in the *Summoner's Tale*, when feeding and feasting come to be associated both literally with the friar's material motives and symbolically with his role as a 'glutton of words'.

Avarice and pride are likewise manifested by such friars in both straightforward and complex ways. The former provides an obvious motive for the activities of Boccaccio's Franciscan Inquisitor, as it does for the hawking of absolution, 'trentals' and other fraternal facilities on the part of Friar Hubert and Friar John; but like the friars' lechery it also reflects, as we shall see, upon an aspect of their relationship with the mercantile laity. Similarly, manifest pride is attributed to the mendicants in the *Decameron* (e.g. III, vii, 34 and VII, iii, 9) and is demonstrated also by Friar Hubert's appearance (General Prologue, I, 259–63) and by Friar John's assertions about 'charitable and chaste bisy freres'. But, as a more implicit vice, the sin of Lucifer seems to precede both Frate Alberto's literal fall (as a wingless angel) and the humiliation of Chaucer's two pretentiously 'curteis' friars.

The variety of forms in which such vices are embodied reinforces the impression that for these two authors antifraternal satire was one of the most fruitful branches of fourteenth-century anticlericalism – an impression that can be further substantiated by comparing their satirical treatment of the friars with their characterization of other clerics.[38] Boccaccio's friars, as practitioners of fraud and hypocrisy, mostly inhabit the *malebolge* of his comedy's underworld, whilst monks, nuns and hermits, on the other hand, seem to be consigned only to its outer circles.[39] Indeed the story of the monk, the abbot and the country girl could be construed not so much as an exemplification of *senno* (cunning), but rather as the triumph of appetite and vigour over the constraints of abstinence, and it thus strikes the keynote for much of the *Decameron*'s treatment of the cloistered or eremitical life. Chaucer infuses a similar kind of irony into the General Prologue portrait of the Monk as well as the Host's less subtle innuendoes in the Prologue to the *Monk's Tale* (VII, 1928–64). Monks in both the *Canterbury Tales* and the *Decameron* (notably III, viii) also engage in deception of the laity, but Chaucer's astute, commercially-minded Daun John in the *Shipman's Tale* is by far the most friar-like of them.

Certain priests in the *Decameron* also show some affinity with the friars – for example the priest of Varlungo (VIII, ii), whose dealings closely parallel those of Daun John in the *Shipman's Tale*, and Donno Gianni, whose living is mainly gained through 'buying and selling' (IX, x, 6). These small-scale operators are reasonably successful on their own (mostly rural) patches, but none of them is so spectacularly fraudulent as, say, Frate Alberto. Chaucer's friars on the other hand are equalled or excelled in stature and ambition by certain of the satanic majesties among his clerics. The Summoner, for instance, is capable of meeting and, arguably, beating the Friar on his own ground. The alchemist Canon, although he claims to share his secrets with a friar (*Canon's Yeoman's Tale*, VIII, 1355), is ultimately a more elusive and successful 'praktisour'. And the Pardoner is Chaucer's true false Apostle for whom even Friar John appears a kind of harbinger.

Some comparable features are also apparent in the two writers' representation of relationships between the mendicants and the merchant class. 'Without the towns', as R. W. Southern says, 'the friars would never have come into existence'; and their significance from this point of view is evident both from the urban settings in which Boccaccio usually shows them operating[40] and from his explicit references to their role as confidants of the bourgeoisie. Thus Frate Alberto on arrival in Venice quickly establishes himself as confessor, adviser and banker even in this capital of commerce (IV, ii, 11) – and both he and Frate Rinaldo (VII, iii, 4) make the wives of wealthy men the particular objects of their attention. The traditional accusation that friars as confessors colluded with merchants (and usurers especially) with a view to making a profit from the proceeds of restitution is explicitly lodged in Tedaldo's antifraternal sermon (III, vii, 38),[41] but it is earlier implied in the first story of the *Decameron*, where several of Ser Ciappelletto's exchanges with the friar, even at the brink of the grave, have the look of well-worn formulae current between the busy merchant and his accommodating confessor (44–6 and 54–5). A similarly ironic effect is achieved in Chaucer's account of how Friar Hubert's arguments almost alchemically transmute the tears that the insincere penitent cannot shed into silver for 'the povre freres' (General Prologue, I, 225–32).

I have shown elsewhere how Friar Hubert is portrayed as the first and one of the most active of Chaucer's mercantile pilgrims,[42] and both authors associate friars with merchants early on in their collections of tales. But whilst Boccaccio focuses primarily upon the symbiotic relationship between mendicants and town-dwellers, Chaucer on the other hand shows his friars ranging more widely through the land (even to the remote marshlands of Holderness) and operating more independently as traders. Of Boccaccio's more numerous mendicants only that hybrid monk-cum-friar, Frate Cipolla, expands the scope of his dealings to a similar degree.

As Chaucer's friars amply illustrate, however, the mendicant's main stock in trade was not knives, pins and parrots' feathers but words.[43] This aspect of their relationship to the laity seems above all to have concerned both authors. In the *Decameron* the mendicants' educative role is parodied for example through the account of how Frate Rinaldo's colleague teaches Madonna Agnesa's maid her paternoster (VII, iii, 23 and 39); but the credulity of the friars' lay associates is also ironically exposed in two earlier tales. Both Fra Puccio the Franciscan tertiary (III, iv) and Gianni Lotteringhi the leader of the Dominican *laudesi* (VII, i) exemplify certain features of bourgeois piety.[44] Gianni is not only deceived by his wife and her lover but is also exploited by the Dominican friars, who keep him well-nourished with works of vernacular piety in return for generous donations of food and clothing (VII, i, 5).

Both of these figures, caricatured as they are, represent a genuine appetite on the Italian laity's part which the friars' 'third orders', their popular preaching and their dissemination of devotional material were all designed to serve.[45] Tertiary orders as such were less common in England,[46] but the friars had helped to foster the growth of an educated laity (and a public for writers) in various ways, not least through their development of the art of preaching and the use of *exempla*. When Chaucer mocked this aspect of mendicant activity he was therefore, in B. Smalley's phrase, 'biting the hand that fed him'.[47] But he also seems to be demonstrating the very process by which educated laymen themselves might have come to do so, when, in the *Summoner's Tale*, he shows a friar who has vaunted his prowess as a teacher being progressively outwitted by the 'ymaginacioun' of a cunning churl, mildly teased by the learned language of a nobleman whose confessor he is, and utterly befooled by the applied 'ars-metryk' through which a sharp-witted squire solves the problem Thomas has posed.

The festive resolution of the *Summoner's Tale* invites us finally to compare the judgements upon friars as hidden or revealed persuaders in the *Canterbury Tales* and the *Decameron*. In the former the *Summoner's Tale*, as we have seen, not only holds Friar John up to scorn but also leaves the 'curteis' pilgrim-Friar humiliated by his churlish adversary and allowed no right of reply; and this perhaps, as E. T. Donaldson contends, 'is the harshest judgment visited by the author on any pilgrim except the Pardoner'. In the *Decameron* such judgements range from the savage, *Volpone*-like justice, Venetian-style, that is inflicted on Frate Alberto, to the ironic acquiescence implied by the convivial conclusion to the escapades of Frate Rinaldo, the final figure in Boccaccio's antifraternal gallery.

In general Boccaccio, unlike Chaucer, does not incorporate pretensions to learning into his satirical assessment of the mendicants, and perhaps his very respect for their scholarship prevented him from doing so. Indeed some of his friars are of distinctly limited intelligence. Boccaccio, does, however, manifest considerable interest in these characters as preachers, performers and story-tellers. Mendicants such as the Austin Simone Fidati, the Franciscan Filippo of Oltrarno and (especially) the Dominicans Remigio Girolami and Giordano da Rivalto had been the leading exponents of the popular sermon in Florence during the first half of the fourteenth century[48] – and this aspect of their reputation is reflected on a number of occasions in the *De-*

cameron. Even a relatively stupid friar like the credulous confessor of the Third Day can muster 'a variety of *exempla*' in order to encourage pious donations (III, iii, 33) – whilst star performers like Frate Alberto make story-telling a major element in their designs.

Chaucer also turns his friars into tale-tellers in the traditional mendicant mould. Friar Hubert's story of the devil and the summoner has obvious analogues in collections of material for preachers, and, as R. A. Pratt has shown, the poet appears to be nipping the mendicant hand yet more sharply when he equips the friar in the *Summoner's Tale* with a repertoire of classical *exempla* that he could have culled from a compendium put together by one of his own colleagues.[49] But whereas Boccaccio does little more than imply a certain degree of pride on the part of performers like Frate Alberto, the voices of Chaucer's friars loudly and clearly proclaim their confidence in their powers as preachers and glosers. Friar Hubert of course disclaims concern with 'scole-matere', 'auctoritees' and 'clergye' at the beginning of his Tale (III, 1271–7), but the devil who is, as it were, his instrument within it shows a distinctly academic turn of phrase and taste in humour (e.g. in 1480–1522), and the narrator's conclusion does indeed reveal that he has his 'auctoritees' ready up his sleeve (1645–9 and 1656–8). Friar John in the *Summoner's Tale* takes considerable pride in his alleged skills as teacher, preacher and scholar; indeed, as well as advertising that 'glosynge is a glorious thyng' (1793) and making certain that his own qualifications to do so are recognized (2186) – he also paints a near-apocalyptic picture of what the world would be like without the preaching that he and his colleagues provide (2109–14). Furthermore, the very form of the *Summoner's Tale* could be said to enact a judgement upon the kind of friar who tries to trade upon his skill with sermon *exempla*. The pilgrim-Friar has attempted to discredit the Summoner by means of a neatly devised 'game', which he retrospectively seeks to incorporate as an *exemplum* within a piously homiletic design. With typically violent contempt for such tactics, however, the Summoner in effect turns the Friar's whole procedure inside out and traps the mendicant sermon, *exempla* and all, within the framework of his (and Chaucer's) 'game'.

This evident fascination with the friar as word-spinner and tale-teller might imply that both writers regarded them as in some respects rivals for the ear of the educated laity; but there may be other reasons for it as well. Boccaccio already in the Introduction to the Fourth Day of the *Decameron* (par. 6) shows a wry awareness of how his own stories might be dismissed as 'trifles' or 'frivolities' (*ciance*). He also implies some analogy between the friars' dealings with their female devotees and the approach of the author to the ladies for whom he writes; and at the end of the *Conclusione dell' Autore* (22–3) he draws an explicit comparison between his own alleged *ciance* and those employed by the friars in their sermons. Of course neither of these passages is exactly solemn in tone, but the allusions in both to Dante's condemnation of false preachers (*Par.*, XXIX, 91–126) suggest that there is at least an undercurrent of concern.

Chaucer is characteristically more oblique in his approach to such analogies and comparisons; but, as we have seen, his work shows as much if not more engagement with the traits and tactics of mendicant rhetoric. Moreover, he introduces his Friar at the start of the Canterbury pilgrimage as a skilled entertainer who is accomplished in singing and harping as well as 'daliaunce and fair langage' (General Prologue, I, 253–7 and 266–8). And through the Parson's words at the end of the journey (Prologue to the *Parson's Tale*, X, 31–4) he also identifies purveyors of 'fables' with St Paul's false teachers (1 Tim. 1.3–7 and 2 Tim. IV. 3–4). All this suggests that, like Langland, he was well aware of the possible affinities between 'frere faytour' and other 'folk of that ordre' with a talent to amuse or beguile their listeners.

The 'meddling' of the friars with these two authors' minds thus appears to have been a far-reaching process. Chaucer and Boccaccio may well have approached the traditional figure of the 'bisy frere' as a comic stereotype, a social parasite, a false Apostle or a 'harlotry player'. But they also seem to have recognized in such a figure a possible, if distorted, image of the story-teller who, having set out to banish *malinconia* or provide 'merthe' and 'solas', could at some point along the way find himself criticized either for 'feeding upon wind' (*Decameron*, Introduction to Fourth Day, 7) or – like Friar John – for serving his hearers 'with nyfles and with fables'.

Notes

1 *Decameron*, I, i and vi; III, iii, iv and vii; IV, ii; VII, i and iii. Frate Cipolla in VI, x behaves very much as a mendicant, although his Order (founded 1095) was monastic.

2 R. Davidsohn, *Geschichte von Florenz*, vol. IV, 3 (Berlin, 1927), p. 84.

3 See, for example: Dante, *Inf.*, XIX; *Purg.*, XIX, 97f; *Par.*, XXI, 124f and XXVII, 19f; and Petrarch, *Canzoniere*, CXXXVI–VIII; *De Rebus Familiaribus*, VI, i, and the *Liber sine Nomine*, esp. letters 1, 5, 6, 8, 10 and 14–19.

4 Penn R. Szittya, '"Caimes Kynde": the Friars and the Exegetical Origins of Medieval Antifraternalism' (Ph.D. thesis, Cornell, 1971). See also his article on 'Antifraternal Exegesis and the *Summoner's Tale*', *Studies in Philology*, LXXI (1974), 19–46; and, for a general introduction, A. Williams, 'Chaucer and the Friars', *Speculum*, XXVIII (1953), 499–513.

5 F. R. H. Du Boulay, 'The Historical Chaucer', in *Geoffrey Chaucer*, Writers and Their Background, ed. D. S. Brewer (London, 1974), p. 44.

6 See for instance: Rutebeuf's *Frère Denise*, in *Oeuvres complètes de Rutebeuf*, ed. E. Faral and J. Bastin (Paris, 1959–60), vol. II, pp. 281–91 – translated in *Fabliaux*, ed. R. Hellman and R. O'Gorman (London, 1965), pp. 135–43; and Jacques de Baisieux's *Dis de le Vescie a Prestre*, in *Receuil général et complet de Fabliaux des xiiie et xive siècles*, ed. A. de Montaiglon and G. Raynaud, vol. III (Paris, 1878), pp. 106–17 – translated in *The Literary Context of Chaucer's Fabliaux*, ed. L. D. Benson and T. M. Andersson (Indianapolis–New York, 1971), pp. 344–59. Examples of short satirical poems featuring such stereotypes are nos. 65–8 in *Historical Poems of the 14th and 15th Centuries*, ed. R. H. Robbins (New York, 1959).

7 See A. E. Quaglio, 'Tra fonti e testo del Filocolo', *Giornale storico della letteratura italiana*, CXL (1963), 490–513. Boccaccio, however, spoke somewhat dismissively of Paolino later on, e.g. in *Genealogie*, XIV, 8.

8 See V. Branca, *Boccaccio: The Man and his Works* (New York, 1976), pp. 181–4; and U. Mariani, *Il Petrarca e gli Agostiniani* (Rome, 1946), esp. pp. 31–49 (on Dionigi) and 66–96 (on the Austins at Florence).

9 See Branca, *Boccaccio*, p. 184; Davidsohn, *Geschichte*, vol. IV, 3, pp. 28–9, 37–8 and 122–8; and C. T. Davis, 'Education in Dante's Florence', *Speculum*, XL (1965), esp. pp. 420–8.

10 Like King Robert (or his ghost-writer), Boccaccio's Fiammetta refers to Diogenes' rejection of wealth in *Filocolo*, IV, xxxiv, 13 (cp. Valerius Maximus, IV, iii, 4).

11 See H. Baron, 'Franciscan Poverty and Civic Wealth in Humanistic Thought', *Speculum*, XIII (1938), esp. pp. 15–17 and 21–2.

12 *Ibid.* pp. 15–16.

13. *Ibid.* pp. 4–5.

14 *Policraticus*, VII does not, of course, refer to friars, but as Branca shows (*Decameron*, p. 1212) the language of its invective appears to have influenced the generalizations about mendicant hypocrisy in *Decameron*, IV, ii, 5–6.

15 For examples of both Bonichi's and Pucci's antifraternal satire see G. Corsi (ed.), *Rimatori del '300* (Turin, 1969), pp. 670 and 815–17, and for further references V. Cian, *La Satira*, vol. I (Florence, 1923), pp. 240 and 247, as well as Corsi, p. 815n.

16 They may also have been interested in how some of the fourteenth-century French estates poems represent the mendicants; for examples see J. Mann, *Chaucer and Medieval Estates Satire* (Cambridge, 1973), pp. 305–9. They were also familiar with the French *fabliaux*, but apart from the examples cited above (n. 3) friars in general do not figure very frequently or interestingly in this genre. Some reasons for their absence are suggested by P. Nykrog in *Les Fabliaux* (Geneva, 1973), p. 134.

17 But for a possible parallel between Rutebeuf's *Frère Denise* and Chaucer's portrait of Friar Hubert see Roy J. Pearcy, 'The Marriage Costs of Chaucer's Friar', *Notes and Queries*, n.s. XVII (1970), 124–5.

18 On the influence of Guillaume de Lorris' part of the *Roman* upon Boccaccio's earlier works see L. F. Benedetto, *Il 'Roman de la Rose' e la letteratura italiana*, Beihefte zur Zeitschrift für Romanische Philologie, XXI (Halle, 1910), pp. 171–6. Benedetto also considers the broader affinities between Boccaccio and Jean de Meun (pp. 176–9) and the treatment of the *Roman* in *Il Fiore* (chapter 2).

19 As Branca suggests (*Decameron*, p. 1027), Boccaccio may also have had in mind a particular mendicant Inquisitor whose rapacity was a matter of recent memory in Florence.

20 On the authenticity of the reference to the Inner Temple records (now no longer extant) see R. A. Caldwell, 'Joseph Holand, Collector and Antiquary', *Modern Philology*, XL (1943), 295–301.

21 For an account of the English Dominicans' role as royal confessors and diplomats see W. A. Hinnebusch, *The Early English Friars Preachers* (Rome, 1951), chapters 22–3, and esp. pp. 460–3.

22 See B. Jarrett, *The English Dominicans* (London, 1937), p. 9. Richard also said divine office daily according to the Dominican rite (*ibid.* p. 15).

23 See D. Knowles, *The Religious Orders in England*, vol. II (Cambridge, 1955), p. 145. Prominent among Gaunt's Carmelite protégés were William Badby and Richard Maidstone. Badby's preaching is described as being so popular that people flocked to hear him 'as to a show' (G. R. Owst, *Preaching in Medieval England* (Cambridge, 1926), p. 221 and n. 2).

24 Knowles, *Religious Orders*, vol. II, pp. 152–3.

25 Notably Robert Waldeby, Archbishop of York from 1397 to 1398. On his earlier association with the royal family see F. Roth, *The English Austin Friars, 1249–1538* (New York, 1966), p. 87.

26 See A. Gwynn, *The English Austin Friars in the Time of Wyclif* (Oxford, 1940), pp. 96–105, and Roth, *Austin Friars*, pp. 68–9.

27 Knowles, *Religious Orders*, vol. II, pp. 118–20 and 150; Gwynn, *English Austin Friars*, Part IV; and Roth, *Austin Friars*, pp. 40, 69–72, 83 and 156. On clerical travellers to Italy in general see Wendy Childs' essay in this volume and G. B. Parks, *The English Traveller to Italy*, vol. I (Rome, 1954), pp. 348–51.

28 See K. B. McFarlane, *Lancastrian Kings and Lollard Knights* (Oxford, 1972), pp. 180 and 182–4.

29 J. R. H. Moorman, *A History of the Franciscan Order* (Oxford, 1968), p. 365.

30 *Opera Omnia* (Constance, 1632), p. 462, cited by Fleming in *Journal of English and Germanic Philology*, LXV (1966), 696–7. At about the same time the Franciscan Bonaventura was acknowledging the culpability of those 'qui superflua in aedificiis et aliis...procurant et acquirunt' or engage in 'aedificiorum constructio sumtuosa et curiosa' (*Opera*, vol. VIII (Quaracchi, 1898), pp. 341–2 and 469). Also during the later thirteenth century comments on the scale of mendicant buildings appear in Rutebeuf's *Des Jacobins* (27–8) and the *Roman de la Rose*, 11,285–6, 11,523–31 and 11,671–82.

31 The mendicants' churches and convents had contributed striking new features to the urban scene in England (especially London) during the late thirteenth and early fourteenth centuries. For descriptions see: G. Webb, *Architecture in Britain: the Middle Ages* (Harmondsworth, 1965), pp. 171–2; A. W. Clapham and W. H. Godfrey, *Some Famous Buildings and their Story* (Westminster, 1913), chapter 15; E. Hutton, *The Franciscans in England* (London, 1926), chapter 12; Hinnebusch, *Early English Friars*, chapters 8–9 and Gwynn, *English Austin Friars*, pp. 78–9.

32 See D. Knowles and R. N. Hadcock, *Medieval Religious Houses: England and Wales* (London, 1953), Appendix, p. 363.

33 W. E. Farnham, 'England's Discovery of the Decameron', *Publications of the Modern Language Association of America*, XXXIX (1924), 123–39. For an opposing view see T. H. McNeal, 'Chaucer and the Decameron', *Modern Language Notes*, LIII (1938), 257–8.

34 See M. F. Bovill, 'The "Decameron" and the "Canterbury Tales"' (B.Litt. thesis, Oxford, 1966), chapter 1, and more recently D. McGrady, 'Chaucer and the Decameron Reconsidered', *Chaucer Review*, XII (1977–8), 1–26. Both make use of Branca's work on the early dissemination of the *Decameron* manuscripts (*Studi di filologia italiana*, VIII (1950), 29–143).

35 See M. Copland, 'The Shipman's Tale: Chaucer and Boccaccio', *Medium Aevum*, XXXV (1966), 11–28, and R. Guerin, 'The "Shipman's Tale": The Italian Analogues', *English Studies*, LII (1971), 412–19.

36 H. Schless, 'Transformations: Chaucer's Use of Italian', in Brewer (ed.), *Geoffrey Chaucer*, p. 184.

37 E.g. in *Piers Plowman* (B-text), V, 136 and 143f, and XX, 271.

38 Neither author appears to be greatly concerned with the shortcomings of prelates, although Boccaccio approaches the subject in general terms in *Decameron*, I, ii and (less seriously) in VI, iii.

39 Indeed, the way the Abbot of Cluny overcomes his physical and moral ailments (*Decameron*, X, ii) puts him in a position somewhat akin to that of Dante's Pope Adrian V (*Purg.*, XIX, 97f). Frate Cipolla, however, remains a special case (see above, n. 1).

40 Florence in *Decameron*, I, vi; III, iii; III, vii and VII, i; Venice in IV, ii; and Siena in VII, iii. See R. W. Southern, *Western Society and the Church in the Middle Ages* (Harmondsworth, 1970), pp. 273–7, and, for a defence of the friars' attention to towns, Bonaventura's *Determinationes Questionum circa Regulam fratrum minorum*, I, v (Opera, vol. VIII, pp. 340–1).

41 See B. M. Nelson, 'Italian Businessmen and the Ecclesiastical Law of Restitution', *Journal of Economic History*, VII (suppl., 1947), 109. On the friars' alleged exploitation of sick and dying usurers see the *Roman de la Rose*, 11,225–30 (and *Fiore*, CVIII).

42 In 'Chaucer's Friar and Merchant', *Chaucer Review*, XIII (1979), 337–45.

43 See for example the sources cited and quoted by Mann in *Chaucer and Estates Satire*, pp. 37–9 and nn. 66–86. I am much indebted to Dr Mann for advice about this essay as a whole.

44 C. Delcorno, *Giordano da Pisa e l'antica predicazione volgare* (Florence, 1975), p. 67 and n. 90.

45 See J. Larner, *Culture and Society in Italy, 1290–1420* (London, 1971), pp. 39, 47 and 59–60; B. Pullan, *A History of Early Renaissance Italy* (London, 1973), pp. 72–6; and Davidsohn, *Geschichte*, vol. IV, 3, pp. 66–78 and 97–103. On the 'third orders' see also G. G. Coulton, *Five Centuries of Religion*, vol. II (Cambridge, 1927), chapter 10.

46 See Moorman, *A History of the Franciscan Order*, p. 418 and n. 1.

47 *The English Friars and Antiquity* (Oxford, 1960), p. 307. Accounts of the English mendicants as collectors of *exempla* can be found in Owst, *Preaching in England*, pp. 6of, 8of and 299–305; Hinnebusch, *Early English Friars*, pp. 300–6; and J. Coleman, *English Literature in History, 1350–1400: Medieval Readers and Writers* (London, 1981), pp. 174–84.

48 See Davidsohn, *Geschichte*, vol. IV, 3, pp. 66–76. For recent accounts of mendicant preaching in Italy see the contributions by C. Delcorno and L. Bataillon to 'Les ordres mendiants et la ville en Italie centrale' in *Mélanges de l'Ecole française de Rome*, LXXXIX (1977), 679–89 and 691–4; and for source-material on the subject see R. Rusconi, *Predicazione e vita religiosa nella società italiana* (Turin, 1981), esp. section III. A recent survey of Remigio's life and writings (with some attention to the forms and sources of his *exempla*) is by E. Panella in *Memorie domenicane*, vol. X (Pisa, 1979), esp. pp. 82f; and a collection of Giordano's *exempla* is provided in Delcorno, *Giordano da Pisa*, pp. 241–88.

49 R. A. Pratt, 'Chaucer and the Hand that fed him', *Speculum*, XLI (1966), esp. 619, 627 and 639.

Chaucer and Boccaccio's Latin Works

But God forbede but men shulde leve
Wel more thing then men han seen with ye!
Men shal not wenen every thing a lye
But yf himself yt seeth, or elles dooth;
For, Got woot, thing is never the lasse sooth,
Thogh every wight ne may it nat ysee.
(Chaucer, *Legend of Good Women*, Text F, Prologue, 10–15)

In two of his most allusive poems – the *Canterbury Tales* and the *Legend of Good Women* – Chaucer draws on Boccaccio's *De Casibus Virorum Illustrium, De Mulieribus Claris* and *De Genealogia Deorum*.[1] A simple catalogue of the points of verbal resemblance between these works can establish little about Chaucer's methods of borrowing and adaptation, because they are both more specific and less limited than has sometimes been assumed.

None of Chaucer's poems is solely dependent upon Boccaccio's Latin. Even those parts of the *Canterbury Tales* and the *Legend of Good Women* which owe a primary debt to Boccaccio are informed and enriched by a wide range of other sources, both classical and medieval. The problem of what Chaucer made of *De Casibus Virorum Illustrium, De Mulieribus Claris* and *De Genealogia Deorum* is thus linked to the larger question of how he refashioned his multiple inherited materials. My first task is to distinguish what Boccaccio's Latin prose offered to its earliest English adaptor.[2]

Extant in two redactions, the one (A) of 1355–60 and the other (B) of 1373–4,[3] Boccaccio's *De Casibus Virorum Illustrium* enjoyed a broad and swift diffusion in late medieval and early Renaissance Europe.[4] This moralistic and monotonous compilation of the biographies of men and women famed for their high good fortune and tragic adversity ranges from the age of Adam to the lifetimes of Boccaccio's contemporaries. It finds a natural complement in *De Mulieribus Claris* of 1361–75,[5] an anecdotal account of 104 celebrated women, from Eve to Boccaccio's own day. *De Genealogia Deorum*, Boccaccio's major work of erudition, occupied him from before 1350 until his death in 1375.[6] This immense mythological encyclopedia is best known for the defence of poetry contained in its fourteenth book and for Boccaccio's autobiographical apologia in Book XV.

These three Latin works share a number of common aims and methods. With repeated and often random illustration they interpret the mythical and historical past in a firmly moral light. Boccaccio's declaration at the beginning of Book I of *De Casibus Virorum Illustrium*:

When I was wondering what I might contribute from my laborious studies that might perhaps add something of value to the common good, many things – contrary to what I had believed – sprang to mind; but the obscene lusts, barbarious acts of violence, wasted hours of leisure, unsatisfied avarice, bloody feuds, sudden vendettas and many more wicked crimes of princes and leading men impinged with particular force on my consciousness. Since I saw these things flying about on all sides, aided and abetted by criminals, and the probity of the state thereby being defiled, the most holy laws of justice lying in ruins and all virtues being undermined and – this is quite unspeakable – the minds of the ignorant masses being incited to vice by loathsome examples, I thought that fortune had impelled me to do what I had been intending, and I swiftly took up my pen to write against such men. For what could be better than to employ all one's strength so that erring souls may be brought back to enjoy a better life, so that the sleep of death may be shaken from those who have fallen asleep in their idleness, so that vice may be repressed and virtue extolled?[7]

is matched by his letter to Andreola Acciaiuoli, Countess Altavilla, prefatory to *De Mulieribus Claris*:

I send to you and dedicate to your name what I have so far written about famous women; ... Nor, I think, will it be a waste of time, if you read through the work, and, forming an aversion to the crimes of women of the past, incite your excellent spirit to better things.[8]

So too in *De Genealogia Deorum*. The new Prometheus, as Boccaccio styles himself in Book I,[9] adopts from the outset a didactic and determined tone, and goes on, in Book XIV of *The Genealogy of the Gods*, to defend the suspect matter of imaginative verse, drawing on arguments that exegetes and theologians before him had used to explain and to justify Scripture.[10] Claiming poetry to be a kind of fiction that resembles the philosopher's truths and the facts of history,[11] Boccaccio attributes to it exemplary force and moral authority.

Similar attitudes are reflected in *De Casibus Virorum Illustrium* and *De Mulieribus Claris*. There illustrations from classical poetry, loosely systematized and expounded at length in *De Genealogia Deorum*, are placed side by side with *exempla* derived from the Bible, from ancient and medieval history and from contemporary events.[12] For Boccaccio, the immediate impulse to this genre was provided by the work of Petrarch, and in particular by Petrarch's *De Viris Illustribus*.[13] But Boccaccio goes beyond his acknowledged master's original design. He deals not only with the famous men and women of the past but also with the lives of his contemporaries,[14] and he treats his sources eclectically.

To both of these features of Boccaccio's writing Chaucer was alive. Boccaccio's eclectic use of his material is matched by Chaucer's eclectic use of Boccaccio's Latin works. A comparison of Boccaccio's treatment of his sources in his Latin biographies with Chaucer's treatment of him in the *Monk's Tale* and the *Legend of Good Women* will illustrate how these two individualists selected and combined disparate material into independent narratives that they made their own. Boccaccio and Chaucer, in this regard, are most readily comparable in their accounts of Cleopatra and Zenobia.

The names of Zenobia and Cleopatra are linked by ancient tradition. Ammianus Marcellinus (XXVIII, 4, 9) snidely cites them as respective heroines of the peoples of Egypt and Palmyra. The anonymous author of the *Historia Augusta* (XXIV, 30, 2)[15] records Zenobia's claim that she was descended from Cleopatra. Petrarch refers to these two famous women in an *exemplum* at *Trionfi*, 103–11. Boccaccio, drawing chiefly on the *Historia Augusta* for his account of Zenobia[16] and on a variety of sources for his portrait of Cleopatra,[17] is adapted in turn by Chaucer.

The influence of Boccaccio on the *Monk's Tale*, and the differences between *De Casibus Virorum Illustrium* and Chaucer's poem, have been ably discussed by Piero Boitani. Boitani, following and extending the study of R. K. Root,[18] points out that both works contain *exempla* of the 'falls' of men and women 'that stood in high degree'. *De Casibus Virorum Illustrium* is the subtitle given to the *Monk's Tale* in fifteen of the manuscripts that contain it. Divine providence, in Boccaccio, directs human affairs, and human downfall is sometimes caused by mortal vice. Fortune alone is dominant in Chaucer, and to that subject he directs the moralistic reflections of the Monk. Boccaccio's views on the importance of particular political ideas or of specific human failings in the assessment of adversity are eliminated in Chaucer's poem, as is the dream-setting of *De Casibus Virorum Illustrium*.[19] The *Monk's Tale* finds its idiosyncratic internal order through the development of the theme of fortune, without regard to chronology.[20] Boccaccio's stories, by contrast, are recounted chronologically. Where Chaucer's narrative is compressed and breathless, Boccaccio's is slow and calm.

Boitani lays stress on the similarities between the two works. Six of the seventeen stories in the *Monk's Tale* treat of characters prominent in *De Casibus Virorum Illustrium*; two present the tales of people mentioned several times by Boccaccio; four record figures who appear cursorily in the Latin. Only four of Chaucer's characters are not mentioned by Boccaccio. In the Zenobia episode, Boitani points out,[21] Chaucer contaminated a passage of *De Casibus Virorum Illustrium* with a chapter of *De Mulieribus Claris*. Boitani discusses the English poet's interest in this exotic subject, his preference for decorative detail, his distaste for historical fact, and his simplification of Boccaccio's dignified prose into an idiom comparable, in its epigraphical quality, to the language of *Troilus* and of the *Knight's Tale*.[22]

Boitani's brief pages on the Zenobia episode in the *Monk's Tale* represent incomparably the best study of the influence of Boccaccio's Latin works on Chaucer. They show us a Chaucer attentive to the distinctive qualities of his source, refashioning them into something new. And yet the example of Zenobia is, in one respect, as untypical as it is striking.

Only five other stories recounted in *De Casibus Virorum Illustrium* and *De Mulieribus Claris* occur as complete and distinct *exempla* in the *Monk's Tale*, and in none of these cases can Boccaccio be shown to be Chaucer's primary source. The tales of Adam, Samson and Antiochus in Chaucer's poem derive from the Bible. Croesus appears in Boethius and in the *Roman de la Rose*; Nero figures both in these works and in Suetonius.[23] The Zenobia episode is the only instance in the *Monk's Tale*, or in the *Canterbury Tales* as a whole, where Chaucer relies upon the Latin works of Boccaccio. Elsewhere his debts to *De Casibus Virorum Illustrium* and *De Mulieribus Claris* are highly eclectic and specific. How deep do they go? What did Chaucer find in Boccaccio's two accounts of Zenobia?

Boccaccio treats of Zenobia in chapter C of *De Mulieribus Claris* and at *De Casibus Virorum Illustrium*, VII, 6.[24] Before him lay the text of *Historia Augusta*, XXIV, 30.[25] This passage opens on a note of sharp disdain and unambiguous misogyny:

All shame had perished if things had come to such a pass in the weary state that, during Gallienus's vile reign, even women made excellent rulers, including a foreigner called Zenobia about whom many stories are current, who boasted that she descended from Cleopatra and the kin of the Ptolemies, and ruled as empress after her husband Odenatus.

A woman ruler, and a foreigner to boot 'de qua multa iam dicta sunt' – none of which, the tone implies, can be good.

A letter to the senate is quoted, defending the dubious taste of Aurelian's triumph over Zenobia on the grounds of her manifold achievements and erstwhile influence. Our author is somewhat mollified. He recounts her continence with evident interest and in physiological detail:

Such (they say) was her chastity, that, in bed, she would have nothing to do with her husband except for purposes of procreation. For once they had slept together she waited chastely for her period to discover whether she was pregnant; and, if not, she would again attempt to have children.

He describes Zenobia's regal pomp, her appearance and her justice. He begins to warm to his task, for her qualities were so imposing as to be almost masculine:

Her voice was clear and manly. When necessity required it, she could summon up the harshness of a tyrant; or, when dutiful kindness demanded, she had the clemency of good princes. She combined liberality with prudence, and kept a tighter hold on her treasures than women normally do . . .

The jewels Zenobia was forced to wear as a captive in Aurelian's triumph were too much for even her to bear: the rigour and toughness reflected in her protest against their weight recall the upright austerity of Roman matrons of the past, like one of whom she ended her days on an estate near Hadrian's palace. The oriental adversary of the Roman Empire, as Zenobia appears at the beginning of *Historia Augusta*, XXIV, 30, has become a dignified reminder of those manly virtues found wanting in Roman emperors. Rome's enemies, by an elegant implication, possessed qualities that her rulers lacked.

Boccaccio's account of Zenobia at *De Mulieribus Claris*, C, derived chiefly from this passage of the *Historia Augusta* with minor supplements from Jerome's translation of Eusebius' *Chronicle*, is twice the length of its principal source. It begins on that note of approval with which the anonymous author of the *Historia Augusta* had ended. Zenobia's descent is recorded in admiring terms; and Boccaccio notes cautiously that the identity of her parents is unknown. The manly exploits of Zenobia arouse his interest. With a wealth of incidental detail he describes her hunting and her campaigns: names, places and features of military engagements are added to the more summary account of the *Historia Augusta*.

But what truly arrests the attention of Boccaccio is Zenobia's continence. After describing her restraint within marriage he exclaims:

O what admirable judgement that woman had! It is very clear that she thought sexual passion was sent to mortal men by nature for the sole purpose of providing for future generations with new supplies of children and that all else was sinful, if not superfluous.

And he goes on, a little pompously, to reflect:

You will find very few women of her mettle!

Boccaccio's account of Zenobia, and of other famous women,[26] bears the stamp of misogyny.

The differences between this chapter of *De Mulieribus Claris* and Boccaccio's treatment of Zenobia at *De Casibus Virorum Illustrium*, VIII, 6 are pronounced. The interest in qualities of Zenobia's character or in details of her career found in *De Mulieribus Claris* is largely absent from *De Casibus Virorum Illustrium*. There Boccaccio's account is simpler, more starkly factual and yet richer in pathos. Zenobia's humiliation in the triumph of Aurelius, for example, is the subject of a series of rhetorical contrasts between her past glory and her sudden reversal:

Once admired by emperors, she is now pitied by commoners. She, once accustomed to wear a helmet and to make speeches to soldiers, is now forced to don a veil and listen to the prattle of trivial women. She who once, bearing a sceptre, ruled over the East, is now at Rome reduced to carrying a distaff and spinning like other women ... Go then, forgetting the human condition, and mount the heights only to tremble at every breeze Fortune blows your way or to fall asleep and fall to certain death in a headlong rush!

In *De Casibus Virorum Illustrium* all is subordinated to the central fact of Zenobia's final defeat, itself the subject of a sententious admonition on the folly of ambition and the deceptiveness of Fortune – the central theme of Boccaccio's dedicatory letter to Mainardo Cavalcanti.[27] Zenobia, pattern of manly prowess and virtuous restraint in *De Mulieribus Claris*, appears in *De Casibus Virorum Illustrium* as the noble victim of Fortune.

In the *Historia Augusta*, with its engaging mixture of malice and grudging admiration for Zenobia, Boccaccio distinguished two features of that queen which he developed in separate ways in his own Latin biographies. For the Roman writer Zenobia mattered primarily as a political figure. Boccaccio, in *De Mulieribus Claris*, is concerned less with politics than with morality. For him the chief example set by Zenobia's career – her continence – made her an exception to the general run of women. Boccaccio lays stress on the importance of procreation and condemns sex to any other purpose as vicious lust. The author of the *Decameron* and biographer of noble women speaks in the austere tones of a puritanical antifeminist. *De Casibus Virorum*

Illustrium is hardly less impassioned, and treats Zenobia's achievements and misfortunes as evidence for its theses on mutability and reversal. Perceived by a partisan witness in the *Historia Augusta*, recreated and expanded to suit moralistic and misogynistic biography in *De Mulieribus Claris* and summarized with almost homiletic style in *De Casibus Virorum Illustrium*, the career of Zenobia is transformed by Boccaccio from an event in political history to a vehicle for two distinct types of polemical generalization. Both have some foundation in his source, but both go far beyond it.

Chaucer's *Monk's Tale* opens with a statement of the central theme of *De Casibus Virorum Illustrium*:

> I wol biwaille in manere of tragedie,
> The harm of hem that stoode in heigh degree,
> And fillen so that ther nas no remedie
> To brynge hem out of hir adversitee.
> For certein, whan that Fortune list to flee,
> Ther may no man the cours of hire withholde.
> Lat no man truste on blynd prosperitee;
> Be war by thise ensamples trewe and olde.
> (1991–8)

Chaucer proceeds through a number of Biblical and mythological examples of famous victims of Fortune to his account of Zenobia. In outline he sticks close to his sources – *De Mulieribus Claris* at the beginning of the Zenobia episode and at its end *De Casibus Virorum Illustrium*. But in detail and in emphasis there are marked and subtle differences.

Chaucer describes Zenobia's breeding and martial prowess. He claims (2252) that she was descended from the kings of Persia, for which there is no evidence in Boccaccio's account. Chaucer's qualified praise of Zenobia's looks gives one pause:

> I seye nat that she hadde moost fairness,
> But of his shap she myghte nat been amended.
> (2253–4)

Robinson (p. 745 *ad loc.*) comments on these lines: 'Fairness, beauty in general, seems to be contrasted with *shap*, beauty of figure.' This is not quite the point. Chaucer is not denying that Zenobia was the prettiest of women. He is conceding that although her complexion was not bright, her figure was faultless. This is made plain by Chaucer's source for lines 2253–4, *De Mulieribus Claris*, c, 5: 'Erat hec speciosa corpore, *esto paululum fusca colore*; sic enim urente sole, regionis illius omnes sunt incole ...'[28] 'Fairness', referring specifically to complexion and not generally to beauty, here figures among the

earliest uses of the word in this sense in Middle English.[29] It adds a
degree of mock delicacy to Boccaccio's tactful observation. Boccaccio
tells us that Zenobia was slightly swarthy. Chaucer, describing
Zenobia's charms, hints at their imperfection, wryly twisting the
concessive tone of his source.

   The account of Zenobia's exploits and chastity in youth closely
follows *De Mulieribus Claris*, c, 2–4:

From hire childhede I fynde that she fledde	Dicunt autem hanc a pueritia sua, spretis omnino muliebribus offitiis,
Office of wommen, and to wode she wente,	cum iam corpusculum eduxisset in robur, silvas et nemora coluisse
And many a wilde hertes blood she shedde	plurimum et accinctam pharetra, cervis capriisque cursu atque sagittis
With arwes brode that she to hem sente.	fuisse infestam. Inde cum in acriores devenisset vires, ursos amplecti
She was so swift that she anon hem hente;	ausam, pardos leonesque insequi, obvios expectare, capere et occidere
And whan that she was elder, she wolde kille	ac in predam trahere, et impavidam, nunc hos nunc illos saltus et
Leouns, leopardes, and beres al torente,	prerupta montium discurrere, lustra perscrutari ferarum et sub divo
And in hir armes weelde hem at hir wille.	somnos etiam per noctem capere, imbres, estus et frigora mira tolerantia
She dorste wilde beestes dennes seke,	superare, amores hominum et contubernia spernere assuetam et virgin-
And rennen in the montaignes al the nyght,	itatem summopere colere. Quibus fugata muliebri mollicie adeo eam
And slepen under a bussh, and she koude eke	in virile robur duratam aiunt, ut coetaneos iuvenes luctis palestricis-
Wrastlen, by verray force and verray myght,	que ludis omnibus viribus superaret.
With any yong man, were he never so wight.	
Ther myghte no thyng in hir armes stonde.	
She kepte hir maydenhod from every wight;	
To no man deigned hire for to be bonde.	

(2255–70)

The additions and subtractions Chaucer makes to Boccaccio's account
are, with one exception, slight. Boccaccio's 'cursu' barely hints at
'She was so swift...' (2259), 'sub divo somnos etiam per noctem
capere' is not exactly 'slepen under a bussh' (2265), nor does 'imbres,
estus et frigora mira tolerantia superare' figure in Chaucer's English.
Boccaccio's pleonastic but poetical 'amores hominum et contubernia

spernere assuetam et virginitatem summopere colere' is reduced at line 2269 to its bare essentials. What Chaucer adds to Boccaccio's account is Zenobia's wish for independence (2270). She is not just a virgin who excels at manly pursuits: she has a mind of her own. The tone of this line, as later verses make explicit, is not wholly respectful.

Chaucer describes Zenobia's marriage to Odenake (Odenatus, prince of Palmyra). He was a fitting match for her in more senses than one. Nonetheless – the qualification is deliberate – their marriage was a success:

> And ye shul understonde how that he
> Hadde swiche fantasies as hadde she.
> But natheless, whan they were knyt in-feere,
> They lyved in joye and in felicitee;
> For ech of hem hadde oother lief and deere.
>
> (2274–8)

Neither Zenobia nor Odenake, who shared her views, is treated here with total seriousness. Given to extremes, they were a well-suited couple – and nonetheless got on. For 'swiche fantasies' at line 2275, reinforced by 'natheless' at line 2276, there is no foundation in Boccaccio. The brisk note of homely amusement is Chaucer's own.

Chaucer dwells, as does Boccaccio, upon Zenobia's continence (2279–94). He discusses her refusal to allow Odenake to make love to her until she had ascertained that she was not pregnant from the last occasion:

> And also soone as that she myghte espye
> That she was nat with childe with that dede,
> Thanne wolde she suffre hym doon his fantasye
> Eft-soone, and nat but oones, out of drede.
>
> (2283–6)

The terms are those of *De Mulieribus Claris*,[30] save at line 2285, where 'fantasye' impishly echoes the same word at line 2275. Its earlier connotations were ones of extreme austerity; at line 2285 they are made unabashedly sexual.

Boccaccio's views on continence and procreation[31] are incorporated into Chaucer's narrative of Zenobia's behaviour in marriage. For Boccaccio's high-sounding generalizations Chaucer substitutes a series of earthy asides in the style of the Prologue to the *Wife of Bath's Tale*:

> Al were this Odenake wilde or tame,
> He gat namoore of hire, for thus she seyde,
> It was to wyves lecherie and shame,
> In oother caas, if that men with hem pleyde.
>
> (2291–4)

In Boccaccio these last two lines form an authorial expostulation. Chaucer attributes them instead to Zenobia. And Zenobia was, he implied earlier, a bit of a crank. Chaucer gently undermines the admonitory sternness of his source.

The end of the Zenobia episode in the *Monk's Tale* owes most to *De Casibus Virorum Illustrium*. Chaucer eliminates the pathetic details of *De Mulieribus Claris*: Boccaccio's account of her weary pause in Aurelian's triumph, weighed down by a heavy mass of jewels,[32] is reduced to the merely matter-of-fact:

> Biforen his triumphe walketh shee,
> With gilte cheynes on hire nekke hangynge.
> Coroned was she, as after hir degree,
> And ful of perree charged hire clothynge.
>
> (2363–6)

Nothing is said of her honourable end in the manner of a Roman matron.[33] Instead Chaucer borrows from *De Casibus Virorum Illustrium* Boccaccio's stress on the fickleness of Fortune. But where Boccaccio's account moves from a contrast between what Zenobia had been and what she had become to admonish the reader on the uncertainty of the human condition, Chaucer's closes with a simple and poignant detail:

> And she that helmed was in starke stoures,
> And wan by force townes stronge and toures,
> Shal on hir heed now were a vitremyte;
> And she that bar the ceptre ful of floures
> Shal bere a distaf, hire cost for to quyte.
>
> (2370–4)

Zenobia, the warrior-queen, paragon of chastity and victim of Fortune, ends as an impoverished woman.

The *Monk's Tale* has received a bad press. R. K. Root, for example, regarded the work as so boring that he could not believe that Chaucer had intended it seriously.[34] Root postulated another book of one hundred tragedies of which Chaucer had completed only 'some dozen or thirteen' when he chose to abandon them on account of their 'literary badness', later deciding to foist 'these discarded fragments ... upon the substantial shoulders of the defenceless Monk' and indicating his awareness of their inferiority by the critical judgements of the Knight and the Host. 'Here is a thrifty way of disposing of one's literary bastards!' exclaims Root.

One of Root's claims has withstood the test of time. 'A discussion of the literary merit of these "tragedies"', he claims, 'must resemble the famous chapter on the snakes of Ireland.' In many cases it does.[35] The most that appears to be said in favour of Chaucer's *Monk's Tale* is that its solemn pomposity is well suited to its narrator (a would-be nobleman, as some would have it,[36] whose obsession with power and dignity is betrayed by his stories), who is pilloried by the Host, justly censured by the Knight and implicitly satirized in the *Nun's Priest's Tale*.

None of this does justice to Chaucer's work. The Zenobia episode examined in this chapter provides grounds for a more sympathetic appraisal.[37]

In the Prologue to the *Monk's Tale* the Host sets out to provoke the Monk:

> 'My lord, the Monk', quod he, 'be myrie of cheere,
> For ye shul telle a tale trewely . . .
> I vowe to God, thou hast a ful fair skyn;
> It is a gentil pasture ther thow goost.
> Thou art nat lyk a penant or a goost:
> Upon my feith, thou art som officer,
> Som worthy sexteyn, or some celerer,
> For by my fader soule, as to my doom,
> Thou art a maister whan thou art at hoom;
> No povre cloysterer, ne no novys,
> But a governour, wily and wys,
> And therwithal of brawnes and of bones,
> A wel farynge persone for the nones.
> I pray to God, yeve hym confusioun
> That first thee broghte unto religioun!
> Thou woldest han been a tredefowel aright.
> Haddestow as greet a leeve, as thou hast myght,
> To parfourne al thy lust in engendrure,
> Thou haddest bigeten ful many a creature . . .'
>
> (1924–5, 1932–48)

The Host's praise of the Monk's appearance is as tactless as it is jolly. It makes bawdily obvious what is ambiguous and double-edged in the description of the Monk in the General Prologue (165–207).[38] A layman's parodic view of clerical self-indulgence, it states simply the links of anticlericalism with sexuality:

> 'Religioun hath take up al the corn
> Of tredyng, and we borel men been shrympes.
> Of fieble trees ther comen wrecched ympes.
> This maketh that oure heires been so sklendre
> And feble that they may nat wel engendre.'

The Monk replies with quiet dignity, but the subject that he proposes contains an implied threat to that brimming self-confidence so obtusely displayed by the Host:

> This worthy Monk took al in pacience,
> And seyde, 'I wol doon al my diligence,
> As fer as sowneth into honestee,
> To telle yow a tale, or two, or three.
> And if yow list to herkne hyderward,
> I wol yow seyn the lyf of Seint Edward;
> Or ellis, first, tragedies wol I telle,
> Of whiche I have an hundred in my celle.
> Tragedie is to seyn a certeyn storie,
> As olde bookes maken us memorie,
> Of hym that stood in greet prosperitee,
> And is yfallen out of heigh degree
> Into myserie, and endeth wrecchedly.'
>   (1965–77)

After a warning that he will tell his stories unsystematically and an apology for his ignorance, which is more than usually ironical in the light of the learned narrative that is to follow (1983–90), the Monk begins his pointed Tale.

The Zenobia episode takes its place in a series of splendidly barbed retorts to the Host. The Host asks for a tale of lustiness, and receives a story of chasteness. He alludes salaciously to sex and procreation, and hears in return a delicate account of continence and marital restraint. He is presented with an admonitory tale in which the austere extremes of the leading characters are treated with a gentle wryness and a homely good sense that are poles apart from his own dim heartiness. And when the Host responds to the Monk's work as a whole, he has plainly missed its point:

> 'Ye', quod oure Hooste, 'by seint Poules belle!
> Ye seye right sooth; this Monk he clappeth lowde.
> He spak how Fortune covered with a clowde
> I noot nevere what; and als of a tragedie
> Right now ye herde, and, pardee, no remedie
> It is for to biwaille ne compleyne
> That that is doon, and als it is a peyne,
> As ye han seyd, to heere of hevynesse . . .'
>   (2780–7)

The Host, like the critics,[39] interprets the Monk's Tale as a depressing disquisition on Fortune. But this is to read Boccaccio's Latin works, not the poetry of Chaucer. The Monk's tales are not simply directed to the general questions of Fortune and mutability. The Monk's tales are aimed, specifically, at the Host. They offer him the very opposite of what he wished to hear, in a manner calculated to deflate him, if only he could grasp their sense. That object is partly achieved. The Host is muted, if not quite silenced. Having missed the point, he blunders on to another. That is why final victory does not lie, as the critics tell us, with the Knight or the Host. It lies with the Monk, and makes of the despised *Monk's Tale* a modest *tour de force*.

In the framework provided by *De Mulieribus Claris* and *De Casibus Virorum Illustrium* Boccaccio's sententious polemic is employed by Chaucer's Monk to an ironical end. A comparable pattern of selection and change can be traced in the *Legend of Good Women*.

The many debts of this work to different literary genres have obscured its true character. 'The *Legend*' writes Robinson,[40] 'falls at once into the ancient category of palinodes, known in literary history from the time of Stesichorus, who first wrote an ode against Helen of Troy and then composed his Palinodia in her praise.' Robinson cites the analogues of Horace and Ovid, Machaut and Hoccleve, and he goes on to add:

The form of the work imposed upon Chaucer as a penance is that of a legendary, or collection of lives of saints. The good women whose tragic stories he relates are heroines of classical antiquity who suffered or died out of devotion to their lovers. They are represented as saints or martyrs on Cupid's calendar. So the *Legend* may be regarded, in the words of a recent critic, as 'a cross between the Heroides of Ovid and the Legenda Aurea'.

A palinode and a legendary, in the tradition of Stesichorus, Ovid, Machaut and the *Golden Legend*: if this is what the *Legend of Good Women* is, what it is not seems very unclear.

Chaucer's apparent hybrid can be regarded more simply as one of the earliest instances in Middle English of a class of exemplary literature that had gained currency with Boccaccio's Latin works, from which it takes its inspiration and some of its details. As in the *Monk's Tale*, so in the *Legend of Good Women*, Boccaccio is Chaucer's primary source for only one story – that of Cleopatra – although he draws on *De Genealogia Deorum*[41] and *De Mulieribus Claris* for much supplementary information. These specific debts to Boccaccio are reinforced by a number of points of general resemblance between the *Legend of Good Women* and *De Mulieribus Claris*.

From Boccaccio Chaucer took the model for a series of feminine portraits, confining himself to virtuous women of classical antiquity, where Boccaccio had included examples from the present.[42] In both the *Legend of Good Women* and *De Mulieribus Claris* these stories follow one another without intervening passages of authorial comment. The structure of both works is outlined in their Prologues, which are informed by similar purposes of commendation. Chaucer's incomplete final legend would have referred to Alcestis – Queen Anne herself – just as Boccaccio's last chapter is about Queen Joanna.[43] All of Chaucer's finished tales, except those of Ariadne, Philomena and Phyllis, occur in *De Mulieribus Claris*, and in at least two of these exceptions Chaucer drew on Boccaccio's *De Genealogia Deorum* as well as Ovid.[44] The allegations that *De Mulieribus Claris* stands in the same relation to the *Decameron* as the *Legend of Good Women* does to *The Canterbury Tales*[45] and that the Latin titles of individual legends in Chaucer may have been developed from Boccaccio's chapter headings[46] need not be pressed to make the point that Chaucer wrote with Boccaccio in mind.

De Casibus Virorum Illustrium, VI, 15 and *De Mulieribus Claris*, LXXXVIII, have been advanced as Chaucer's sources for his own legend of Cleopatra.[47] These two accounts may be distinguished from one another. Only the chapter in *De Mulieribus Claris* is primarily concerned with Cleopatra. *De Casibus Virorum Illustrium* deals chiefly with Antony. In both Boccaccio employed a number of ancient writers, the three most important of whom were Suetonius, Florus and 'Hegesippus'.[48]

Florus (*Epitomae*, II) and Suetonius (II, 17) provided Boccaccio with a skeleton of Cleopatra's career, which he fleshed out from other authors. Chief among these was the first book of the translation and adaptation of Josephus attributed to Hegesippus.[49] One of the points at which Hegesippus offered Boccaccio information unavailable to him from elsewhere is his account of Cleopatra's ambitions in Arabia and of her dealings with Herod, King of Judaea, at *Historiae*, I, xxxii, 1–2.

The picture of Antony and Cleopatra presented by Hegesippus contains much that Boccaccio was to adopt. Antony, enslaved by his lust for Cleopatra, is depicted with cordial distaste. But the full force of Hegesippus' animus is directed at Cleopatra, who united avarice with ambition and corruption with cruelty in her plans to annex Judaea and Arabia and to murder their kings. Worse still, all of this was the plot of a mere pushy woman to whom Antony, for once, had the sense to say no:

Antony became a mere bondsman to his love for Cleopatra and slavishly ministered to her lusts, but he was incapable of overcoming her feminine greed and especially the zest of that woman for slaughtering her kinsmen ... She greedily thought that the kingdoms of Judaea and Arabia should be joined to her realms, after their rulers had been killed. But, at least in this respect, Antony came to his senses, although drunk with lust and heavy with sleep, and refused to slaughter men of such quality and powerful kings to enlarge the empire of a headstrong woman.[50]

Hegesippus describes Antony's gift of other territories to Cleopatra, her journey to the Euphrates accompanying him on his Parthian expedition, and her return through Judaea, where she was loaded with gifts by a Herod anxious to curry favour. Success increased her arrogance. Antony made her a present of the Parthian king, who had been captured in battle and was to be her lowly slave. The splendour of the victory was marred by the baseness of this gift:

Holding the monarch captive, with all the plunder and spoils from the Persian campaign, Antony led him a lowly slave in triumph to that woman, his illustrious victory matched by his abject gift which disgraced kings in such an ignominious manner.[51]

None of the Latin accounts of Cleopatra available to Boccaccio equals this in vehemence. Throughout Hegesippus' work a specific hostility to Cleopatra is linked to a deeper indignation at her presumptuousness in trespassing beyond what was expected of her as a woman. The highly-charged diction of Book I of Hegesippus' *Histories* contains few terms more censorious than 'mulier' and its cognates.

Boccaccio opens *De Mulieribus Claris*, LXXXVIII in a spirit of equal hostility:

Cleopatra, an Egyptian woman, was the talk of all the world ... for she came to rule over that kingdom by her wicked crimes and had no mark of true distinction except the beauty of her face, since she was instead everywhere renowned for avarice, cruelty and luxury.

It does not take him long to surpass Hegesippus in venom and bile. After poisoning her young brother, seducing Caesar and securing the Egyptian throne, Cleopatra set about winning Antony's favour when her previous protector had been murdered. Boccaccio revels in imagining her as a whore. The mild picture of feminine seductiveness at LXXXVIII, 7:

She seduced the ruler of the world, since she was very beautiful and, by her artful, sparkling eyes and the eloquence of her words, could win over whoever she wanted.

soon gives way to the biting contempt of LXXXVIII, 9:

So Cleopatra gained her kingdom by a two-fold crime and gave free rein to her lust for pleasure, becoming a kind of whore to the kings of the East, greedy for gold and for enjoyment ...

This carries through to the paragraphs that owe most to Hegesippus: *De Mulieribus Claris*, LXXXVIII, 10–16. Boccaccio recounts what he found in his source: Cleopatra's demands and her lover's refusal, Antony's gifts of cities and his expedition against the Parthians (or Armenians – Boccaccio is unsure). But when he describes Cleopatra's return journey to Egypt and her encounter with Herod, Boccaccio departs significantly from Hegesippus:

> As she was returning to Egypt through Syria she was magnificently received by Herod . . . then king of Judaea, and felt no shame at urging him, through intermediaries, to sleep with her, intending, if he agreed, to steal from him the kingdom of Judaea which he had acquired not long ago from Antony. Herod resisted the temptation not only out of respect for Antony, and would have freed him from this tainted and evil woman by arranging to have her put to death by the sword, had not his friends dissuaded him.

None of this is to be found in Boccaccio's sources, or in any other extant author. It is an invented detail, in perfect keeping with Boccaccio's hostile view of Cleopatra as an unscrupulous whore.[52]

Boccaccio goes on to describe the scenes of senseless prodigality and lust for power that precipitated Antony's downfall and Cleopatra's ruin. He recounts the variant versions of her death, each of them more degrading than the next, and concludes with the detail taken from Suetonius that Antony and she were buried in the same mausoleum. In his letter to Andreola Acciaiuoli, prefatory to *De Mulieribus Claris*,[53] Boccaccio warned that he would deal with 'crimes of women of the past'. His account of Cleopatra amply fulfils this description. Rarely does Boccaccio present a darker picture of female turpitude, blackening the already sombre tones of his source.

In *De Casibus Virorum Illustrium*, VI, 15, Boccaccio is less concerned with the wickedness of an evil woman than with the career of a vicious man. Antony is at first described in a style hardly more measured than that employed in *De Mulieribus Claris* to censure Cleopatra:

> Mark Antony, the nephew of Julius Caesar by his sister, came to the greatest, most splendid and highest power by savagery, rampant cruelty and debauchery.

Boccaccio narrates the couple's various excesses, errors and crimes. Antony finally emerges less as a monster of depravity than as a victim of his lover's ambition, of his own misplaced self-assurance and of Fortune. On Antony's suicide he comments:

> And so that unbalanced man, a prey to overweening ambition, despaired

about the high good fortune which he had ill-deserved and fell into the unhappy state which his shamelessness had earned him.

Unsavoury, flawed and over-ambitious Antony was, but his limitations prevented him from being an incarnation of evil. That title in *De Casibus Virorum Illustrium*, as in *De Mulieribus Claris*, is reserved for Cleopatra. Boccaccio relishes his subject. He dwells on the bite of the serpents' fangs into her limbs, accustomed only to luxury and lust; the suicide of Cleopatra draws from his otherwise ponderous prose an almost epigrammatic quality:

And so her blood was sucked by those creatures – she who had supped off draughts from melted pearls – and her beauty, which she had displayed with feminine fecklessness, deceived her when her fortunes changed so bitterly and grew foul while she was still alive to witness it and the empire which her measureless ambition had craved came to its end in the narrow confines of a mausoleum.

'Age cannot wither her, nor custom stale her infinite variety' for Boccaccio, too. The iniquity of Cleopatra is, in his eyes, an inexhaustible subject.

Cleopatra does not appear in Middle English literature before Chaucer's *Legend of Good Women*.[54] There his first story is devoted to her life and loves, and Boccaccio served as its principal source. The choice of Cleopatra was a surprising one, and surprising explanations have been devised to account for it. What really interested Chaucer about her career and that of her lover, argues W. H. Schofield,[55] was the battle of Actium. Threat of French invasion in 1386 and English victory at sea in 1387 had stimulated a lively interest in naval affairs. That is why Chaucer made Cleopatra appear in the *Legend of Good Women*. She 'gave him an opportunity to describe one of the decisive sea-battles of the world'.[56] The woman whose face did not launch a thousand ships provided the motive for a story not primarily concerned with a naval engagement in which she did not directly participate. This arresting hypothesis is perhaps a little oblique.

Chaucer's interest in Cleopatra remains a puzzle. The monster of *De Mulieribus Claris*, LXXXVIII and of *De Casibus Virorum Illustrium*, VI, 15 was not an obvious candidate with whom to begin a work intended to celebrate feminine virtue. Much attention has been paid to Chaucer's claim, in the Prologue, that the *Legend* was written to vindicate himself from the charges of having committed heresy against Love and of having maligned women in his earlier works. Equally important for assessing why he began the *Legend of Good Women*

with the story of Cleopatra is the attitude to written authority that
Chaucer displays in his Prologue.

Texts F and G of the Prologue to the *Legend of Good Women* both
stress that there are truths that cannot be proved by personal
experience:

> For, God wot, thing is never the lasse sooth,
> Thogh every wight ne may it not yse.
>
> (F, 14–15)

We also depend on books:

> Than mote we to bokes that we fynde,
> Thurgh whiche that olde thinges ben in mynde,
> And to the doctrine of these olde wyse,
> Yeve credence, in every skylful wise,
> That tellen of these olde appreved stories
> Of holynesse, of regnes, of victories,
> Of love, of hate, of other sondry thynges,
> Of which I may not maken rehersynges.
> And yf that olde bokes were aweye,
> Yloren were of remembraunce the keye.
> Wel ought us thanne honouren and beleve
> These bokes, there we han noon other preve.
>
> (F, 17–28)

In writing the *Legend* Chaucer claims to be doing no more than declaring a respectful belief in the authority of his written sources.
Here Text G contains a significant addition to the same declaration
in Text F. The common features of the two versions, together with
the supplement in G, are printed below:

> But wherfore that I spak, to yive credence
> To olde stories and doon hem reverence,
> And that men mosten more thyng beleve
> Then men may seen at eye, or elles preve, –
>
> (F, 97–100)

> But wherfore that I spak, to yeve credence
> To bokes olde and don hem reverence,
> Is for men shulde autoritees beleve,
> There as there lyth non other assay by preve.
> For myn entent is, or I fro yow fare,
> The naked text in English to declare
> Of many a story, or elles of many a geste,
> As autours seyn; leveth hem if yow leste.
>
> (G, 81–8)

G asserts the force of 'autoritees' when empirical proof is lacking, and
insists on the literal character of the narrative that is to follow. It is

worth recalling that these claims are advanced by the Prologue to the
Wife of Bath's Tale:

> Experience, though noon auctoritee
> Were in this world, is right ynough for me
> To speke of wo that is in marriage . . .
>
> Men may devyne and glosen, up and doun,
> But wel I woot, expres, withoute lye,
> God bad us for to wexe and multiplye;
> That gentil text kan I wel understande.
>> (Prologue, 1–3, 26–9)[57]

When Chaucer claims to be literal, we will do well to be on our guard.
The God of Love, in the G version of the Prologue, goes on to ask:

> Why noldest thow as wel han seyd goodnesse
> Of wemen, as thow hast seyd wikednesse?
> Was there no good matere in thy mynde,
> Ne in alle thy bokes me coudest thow nat fynde
> Som story of wemen that were goode and trewe?
>> (268–72)

His words are echoed in Alceste's command (F and G, 471–9), and
Chaucer responds with the legend of Cleopatra.[58]

Chaucer begins with Cleopatra's rule in Egypt as described in *De
Mulieribus Claris*. Like Boccaccio, he portrays Antony as Fortune's
favourite and, finally, as her victim:

> And soth to seyne, Antonius was his name.
> So fil it, as Fortune hym oughte a shame,
> Whan he was fallen in prosperite,
> Rebel unto the toun of Rome is he.
>> (588–91)

Chaucer acknowledges that Antony's passion for Cleopatra brought
about his downfall:

> But love hadde brought this man in swich a rage
> And hym so narwe bounden in his las,
> Al for the love of Cleopataras,
> That al the world he sette at no value.
> Hym thoughte there nas nothyng to hym so due
> As Cleopatras for to love and serve,
> Hym roughte nat in armes for to sterve
> In the defence of hyre and of hire ryght.
>> (599–606)

However, a tone of sympathetic extenuation runs through his account
and distinguishes it from Boccaccio's. Cleopatra's ambition and

whorishness, so prominent in *De Mulieribus Claris*, are eliminated;
her beauty is represented not as an unscrupulous snare but as an
innocent charm. And Antony's passion for her is merely an understandable mark of knightly *démesure*:

> This noble queene ek lovede so this knyght,
> Thourgh his desert, and for his chyvalrye,
> As certeynly, but if that bokes lye,
> He was of persone and of gentillesse,
> And of discrecioun and hardynesse,
> Worthi to any wyght that liven may,
> And she was fayr as is the rose in May.
>
> (607–13)

Where Boccaccio describes Cleopatra as 'Antonii primo pellex, deinde
coniunx', Chaucer discreetly comments:

> And, for to make shortly is the beste,
> She wax his wif, and hadde hym as hire leste.
>
> (614–15)

He does not falsify his source. Cleopatra *was* Antony's wife. Chaucer
merely omits to say that she had been Antony's mistress.

Boccaccio's account of the luxury and debauch of Antony and
Cleopatra is treated in a similar manner by Chaucer who passes it by,
refusing, in an ingenious *topos* of brevity (581–9), to burden his
narrative with the story of their wedding-feast. Again, the omission
is deliberate, for what he found in Boccaccio cast no credit on his hero
or heroine.

Chaucer passes to the war between Antony and Octavian. He inserts
into his tale a description of the battle of Actium, on the length and
nautical interest of which Schofield has so graphically written.[59] It is
possible that Chaucer wished to describe 'methods of naval warfare . . .
used by mariners of his own land',[60] although sixteen lines (638–53)
of the *Legend of Good Women* hardly seem the ideal context in
which to achieve this purpose. Chaucer wrote about Actium because
the subject was a safe one. Far from disgracing Antony, it heightened
the pathos of his defeat and death.

Chaucer has Antony commit suicide in the rout of Actium. Cleopatra's attempt to seduce the victor, to which much attention is paid
both by *De Mulieribus Claris* and by *De Casibus Virorum Illustrium*,
is veiled in tactful euphemism:

> His wif, *that coude of Cesar have no grace*
> To Egipt is fled for drede and for destresse.
>
> (663–4)

Her grief and her suicide after Antony's death become the subjects
of an expostulation on women's loyalty:

> But herkeneth, ye that speken of kyndnesse.
> Ye men that falsly sweren many on oth
> That ye wol deye, if that youre love be wroth.
> Here may ye sen of wemen which a trouthe!
>
> (665–8)

The remaining details that Chaucer borrows from Boccaccio, such as
the splendour of the mausoleum that Cleopatra shared with Antony,
are incidental to her final speech. Cleopatra addresses her dead lover,
laying claim to loyalty, constancy and 'wyfhood' (681–95). She kills
herself not by applying serpents to her veins, as in Boccaccio's version,
but by walking, naked and willing, into a pit of adders (696–700).[61]
Where Boccaccio ends both his Latin accounts of Cleopatra with a
bitterly hostile judgement on her misdeeds, Chaucer concludes:

> And this is storyal soth, it is no fable,
> Now, or I fynde a man thus trewe and stable,
> And wol for love his deth so frely take,
> I preye God let oure hedes nevere ake.
>   Amen.
>
> (702–5)

The last lines of the legend of Cleopatra recall the language of the
Prologue, and we are now in a position to assess their implications.

In his legend of Cleopatra Chaucer transforms the envenomed
narratives of Boccaccio, abbreviating and expanding them to present
the queen in a favourable light. In outline and at a number of specific
points Chaucer follows what he found in *De Mulieribus Claris* and *De
Casibus Virorum Illustrium*, but 'storyal soth' his legend most
certainly is not. It stands the transmitted image of Cleopatra on its
head, making an archetype of women's iniquity into a paragon of
feminine fidelity.

The daring of Chaucer's work has been little appreciated. One of
the most recent critics of the *Legend of Good Women* takes pains to
enumerate the reasons why Chaucer's story of Cleopatra is a failure:
'The poem ... lacks imaginative unity ... lacks an ethic to bind it
together ... lacks a strong central emotion to make it coalesce. It
remains a heap of fragments ... it fails also in some part because of
its brevity ...'[62] But there is more than this in the legend of Cleopatra.
Considered in relation to Boccaccio's Latin works and to Chaucer's own
Prologue, the tale is less dull than some would have us believe.

To illustrate his allegiance to the causes of Love and of ladies,
Chaucer attempts a radical revaluation of the worst of women. The

violent misogyny of Boccaccio's account is transformed into a lesson of female superiority over men. And in fulfilling one of the objects defined in his Prologue, Chaucer consciously undercuts the other.

To vindicate feminine virtue by the example of Cleopatra Chaucer undercuts, in the very first of his stories, the authority of the sources that his Prologue asserts. The legend of Cleopatra may be 'som story of women that were goode and trewe' (G, 272) but it does not set out to 'yeve credence / To bokes olde and don hem reverence' (G, 81–2). When Chaucer proclaims 'as certeynly, *but if that bokes lye*' (609) the high qualities of an Antony unfavourably presented by Boccaccio, the claim is tongue-in-cheek. After inviting us to rely on written authority, Chaucer goes on to show, by his own example, how un-reliable it can be. His assurance that 'this is storyal soth' is deliberately unreassuring. Mimicking the ostensibly cautious style and concern with accuracy of Boccaccio's Latin biographies, Chaucer adapts one of the chief contentions of Boccaccio's *De Genealogia Deorum*: the truth of poetry.

Boccaccio first asserts the truths that poetry can offer under the guise of fable at *De Genealogia Deorum*, I, 3 and then, more ex-tensively, at Book XIV, 9, 10, 13 and 18. There he launches into a spirited defence of poets against the charge of mendacity. Boccaccio is particularly anxious to vindicate fiction from the criticisms of its detractors. A discussion of the term 'fable' (*fabula*) stands at the centre of his argument. Boccaccio denies that its long-standing, pejora-tive, overtones are warranted: 'poets, like historians, philosophers and theologians, express moral truths under the guise of fable. Remove its external trappings, and the significance of the poet's fable becomes clear'.

An echo of this argument is heard in Chaucer's claim that his legend of Cleopatra: '. . . is storyal soth, it is no fable' (702). Through-out the *Legend of Good Women* Chaucer uses Boccaccio's *De Genealo-gia Deorum* to supplement the accounts of ancient heroines that he found in other works:[63] here he claims for his own poem the veracity that Boccaccio had attributed to poetry in general.

In Boccaccio's Latin biographies the classical poets are employed as historical sources,[64] and the myths related there are invested with moral and pedagogical meaning. But, as the accounts of Cleopatra and Zenobia in *De Mulieribus Claris* and *De Casibus Virorum Illustrium* show, Boccaccio follows his sources when it suits him. When it does not, he alters them to his own ends. Where they lack a graphic fact, he is not above inventing it. The truths of Boccaccio's Latin biographies are the partial truths of polemic.

Chaucer shares Boccaccio's concern with the appearance of accuracy, and he attributes to his own narrative each of the properties Boccaccio discusses in his Latin works: exemplary force, moral authority and historical veracity. But Chaucer makes these claims with a wryer, less ingenuous purpose than Boccaccio's.

Chaucer takes Boccaccio's exemplary account of Zenobia and uses it, in the *Monk's Tale*, to thwart and pillory the Host. In the *Legend of Good Women* he asserts the authority of the texts upon which he draws, yet employs Boccaccio's account of Cleopatra to reverse Boccaccio's interpretation of her. Chaucer understood all too well the example of *De Mulieribus Claris*, *De Casibus Virorum Illustrium* and *De Genealogia Deorum*. Affirming the literal truth of his poetry and its fidelity to his sources, he makes what he had inherited wholly his own. An appearance of deference to written authority is maintained, but in the absence of empirical proof, that authority is shown to be only as good as the use to which it is put. Record and report, as the *House of Fame* had showed, might misrepresent reality. What mattered was the moral that the histories of Zenobia and Cleopatra could be made to illustrate. The 'storyal soth' of Chaucer's treatment of Boccaccio's Latin works derives from independent adaptation.

Notes

1 Cf. J. A. W. Bennett, p. 101. Valuable studies of this question by P. Boitani, 'The *Monk's Tale*: Dante and Boccaccio', *Medium Aevum*, XLV (1976), 50–69; R. K. Root in W. F. Bryan and G. Dempster (eds.), *Sources and Analogues of Chaucer's 'Canterbury Tales'* (Chicago, 1941), pp. 615ff; E. F. Shannon, *Chaucer and the Roman Poets* (repr. New York, 1964), especially pp. 182ff; and M. Bech, 'Quellen und Plan der "Legende of Goode Women" und ihr Verhaeltniss zur "Confessio Amantis"', *Anglia*, V (1881), 314ff (summarized, with brief supplements, in W. W. Skeat, *The Complete Works of Geoffrey Chaucer*, vol. III (Oxford, 1894), pp. xxvii–xxix). Recent accounts of research in T. Pisanti, 'Boccaccio in Inghilterra tra Medioevo e Rinascimento' in *Boccaccio in Europe: Proceedings of the Boccaccio Conference, Louvain, December 1975*, ed. G. Tournoy (Leuven, 1977), pp. 199–200; and E. Reiss, 'Boccaccio in English Culture of the Fourteenth and Fifteenth Centuries' in *Il Boccaccio nella cultura inglese e anglo-americana*, ed. G. Galigani (Florence, 1974), pp. 19–20. The survey of H. G. Wright, *Boccaccio in England from Chaucer to Tennyson* (London, 1957), is still useful. I have learnt nothing from J. Raith, *Boccaccio in der englischen Literatur von Chaucer bis Painters Palace of Pleasure. Ein Beitrag zur Geschichte der italienische Novelle in England* (Leipzig, 1936) or F. P. Trigona, *Chaucer, Imitatore del Boccaccio* (Catania, 1923).

2 Pending V. Zaccaria's edition of *De Casibus Virorum Illustrium* (announced by A. Carraro, *Studi sul Boccaccio*, XII (1980), 198, n. 2) I have used the extracts published by P. G. Ricci in his *Giovanni Boccaccio. Opere in Versi. Corbaccio. Trattatello in Laude di Dante. Prose Latine. Epistole. La Letteratura Italiana. Storia e Testi*, V (Milan–Naples, 1965), pp. 786–893 and the facsimile reproduc-

tion of the Paris edition of 1520, ed. L. B. Hall (Gainesville, Florida, 1962). For the A Text I have consulted London, British Library MS Harley 3565 (saec. xiv) and for the B Text Oxford, Bodley MS Laud. Misc. 721 (saec. xv). Quotations from *De Mulieribus Claris* follow the edition of V. Zaccaria in *Tutte le Opere di Giovanni Boccaccio*, ed. V. Branca, vol. x (Milan, 1970). Quotations from *De Genealogia Deorum*, XIV follow Ricci, pp. 894–1063. For other books I cite the edition of V. Romano, *Giovanni Boccaccio. Genealogie Deorum Gentilium Libri*, Scrittori d'Italia, CC, CCI (2 vols., Bari, 1951). J. J. Reedy, *Boccaccio in Defense of Poetry. Genealogiae Deorum Gentilium Liber XIV*, Toronto Medieval Latin Texts, VIII (Toronto, 1978), and C. G. Osgood, *Boccaccio on Poetry, Being the Preface and the fourteenth and fifteenth Books of Boccaccio's 'Genealogia deorum gentilium...'* (Princeton, 1930) may be consulted with profit. A. Hortis' *Studj sulle opere latine del Boccaccio* (Trieste, 1879) remains indispensable.

3 See P. G. Ricci, 'Studi sulle opere latine e volgari del Boccaccio', *Rinascimento*, XIII (1962), 11–20.

4 For the manuscript tradition see V. Branca, *Tradizione delle opere di Giovanni Boccaccio* (Rome, 1958), pp. 84–9. For translations of *De Casibus* see Hortis, *Studj*, pp. 821–47.

5 See V. Zaccaria, 'Le fasi redazionali del *De Mulieribus Claris*', *Studi sul Boccaccio*, I (1963), 253–332.

6 See G. Martellotti, *Le due redazioni delle Genealogie del Boccaccio* (Rome, 1951).

7 Ed. Ricci, p. 794.

8 Ed. Zaccaria, p. 20.

9 Ed. Romano, p. 3 and see L. Marino, 'Prometheus, or the Mythographer's Self-Image in Boccaccio's *Genealogie*', *Studi sul Boccaccio*, XII (1980), 263–73.

10 See E. Gilson, 'Poésie et Vérité dans la *Genealogia* de Boccacce', *Studi sul Boccaccio*, II (1964), 253–82, especially pp. 278ff; and A. Buck, 'Boccaccios Verteidigung der Dichtung in den *Genealogiae deorum*', in Tournoy (ed.), *Boccaccio in Europe*, pp. 53–66.

11 Especially *De Genealogia Deorum*, XIV, ix, 13. (The argument is borrowed and ancient. Cf. Seneca, *Epistolae*, LXXXVIII and John of Salisbury, *Metalogicon*, I, 22.) See further below, pp. 290–1.

12 See the excellent study of A. Carraro, 'Tradizioni culturali e storiche nel *De Casibus*', *Studi sul Boccaccio*, XII (1980), 197–262, and Zaccaria (ed.), *De Mulieribus*, pp. 8–9.

13 See Boccaccio's reference to Petrarch at, e.g., *De Mulieribus Claris*, Prologue (ed. Zaccaria, p. 22) and at *De Casibus Virorum Illustrium*, IX (ed. Ricci, p. 798). Cf. the preface to Petrarch's *De viris illustribus*:
'Illustres itaque viros, quos excellenti quadam gloria floruisse doctissimorum hominum ingenia memorie tradiderunt, eorumque laudes, quas in diversis libris tamquam sparsas ac disseminatas inveni, colligere locum in unum et quasi quodammodo constipare arbitratus sum... Hic enim, nisi fallor, fructuosus historici finis est, illa prosequi vel sectanda legentibus vel fugienda sunt, ut in utranque partem copia suppetat illustrium exemplorum...' (Francesco Petrarca, *Prose*, ed. G. Martellotti, La Letteratura Italiana (Milan–Naples, 1955), pp. 218, 224.)
There is a useful discussion of this subject in E. Kessler, 'Geschichtsdenken und Geschichtsschreibung bei Francesco Petrarca', *Archiv für Kulturgeschichte*, LI (1959), 109–36.

14 To the article cited at n. 12 add M. Miglio, 'Boccaccio biografo' in Tournoy (ed.), *Boccaccio in Europe*, pp. 149–63; and Miglio, 'Biografia e raccolte biografiche nel Quattrocento italiano', *Atti dell' Accademia delle Scienze dell' Istituto di Bologna, Classe di Scienze Morali*, LXIII (1974–5), 166–99.

15 See pp. 272ff. Following Sir Ronald Syme (*Ammianus Marcellinus and the Historia Augusta* (Oxford, 1968) and *Emperors and Biography. Studies in the Historia*

Augusta (Oxford, 1971)) I do not refer to Trebellius as the author of this part of the work.

16 For the sources of Zenobia at *De Mulieribus Claris*, see Zaccaria, pp. 549–50.

17 *Ibid.* pp. 538–40. On Boccaccio's use of historical source see further J. Schuck, 'Boccaccios lateinische Schriften historischen Stoffes besonders in Bezug auf die alte Geschichte', *Neue Jahrbucher für Philologie* (1874), 497ff; Hortis, *Studj*, pp. 68ff, and V. Zaccaria, 'Boccaccio e Tacito', in Tournoy (ed.), *Boccaccio in Europe*, pp. 221–38.

18 See n. 1.

19 Boitani, 'The *Monk's Tale*', pp. 50–2. These last two points summarize A. W. Babcock, 'The Mediaeval setting of Chaucer's *Monk's Tale*', PMLA, XLVI (1931), 205–13.

20 See lines 1984–9 and E. M. Socola, 'Chaucer's Development of Fortune in the *Monk's Tale*', *Journal of English and Germanic Philology*, XLIX (1950), 150–71.

21 'The *Monk's Tale*', pp. 52–4.

22 *Ibid.* pp. 64–8.

23 Cf. Root, in Brian and Dempster (eds.), *Sources and Analogues*, pp. 625–44; A. Minnis, 'Aspects of the Medieval French and English Traditions of the *De Consolatione Philosophiae*', in *Boethius, His Life, Thought and Influence*, ed. M. Gibson (Oxford, 1981), pp. 334ff.

24 For a brief survey of the literature on Zenobia see R. Asmus, 'Zenobia von Palmira in Tradition und Dichtung', *Euphorion*, XVIII (1911), 1–14. Asmus discusses Boccaccio and Chaucer at pp. 10–11.

25 References are to the edition of E. Hohl, *Scriptores Historiae Augustae*, vol. II (Leipzig, 1927), pp. 127–30.

26 Cf. L. Torretta, 'Il *liber de claris mulieribus* di Giovanni Boccaccio', *Giornale storico della Letteratura Italiana*, XXXIX (1902), 264ff.

27 Ed. Ricci, p. 794.

28 Ed. Zaccaria, p. 408. 'She had a beautiful figure, although her complexion was a trifle swarthy; that is what all the inhabitants of that region are like from the blazing sun.'

29 For other contexts see *The Middle English Dictionary*, ed. H. Kurath and S. M. Kuhn, vol. III, p. 372 s.v. *fair 2a*.

30 Ed. Zaccaria, p. 410:

> 'Fuit tamen adeo pudicitie severa servatrix, ut nedum ab aliis abstineret omnino, sed etiam Odenato viro suo, dum viveret, se nunquam exhibere, preter ad filios procreandos, voluisse legimus; hac in hoc semper habita diligentia, ut post concubitum unum, tam diu abstineret ab altero, donec adverteret utrum concepisset ex illo; quod si contigerat, nunquam preter post partus purgationes a viro tangi patiebatur ulterius; si autem non concepisse perceperat, se ultro poscenti viro consentiebat.'

31 See p. 274 above.

32 Ed. Zaccaria, p. 414: 'Verum ipsa catenis aureis collo manibus pedibusque iniectis corona et vestimentis regiis ac margaritis et lapidibus pretiosis honusta, adeo ut, cum roboris inexhausti esset, pondere fessa persepe subsisteret.'

33 See p. 273 above.

34 *The Poetry of Chaucer* (Boston, 1906), pp. 206–7.

35 E.g. T. Whittock, *A Reading of the Canterbury Tales* (Cambridge, 1970), pp. 218ff; J. O. Brown, 'Chaucer's Daun Piers: One Monk or Two?', *Criticism*, VI (1964), 49ff; D. R. Howard, *The Idea of the Canterbury Tales* (Berkeley–Los Angeles–London, 1976), pp. 273ff. For an attempt to interpret this Tale in a light more sympathetic to Chaucer see W. C. Strange, 'The *Monk's Tale*: A Generous View', *Chaucer Review*, I (1967), 167–80.

36 Howard, The Idea, pp. 280–1.

37 For another see Boitani's discussion of Chaucer's Hugelyn and Dante's Ugolino, 'The Monk's Tale', pp. 54ff; and cf. M. Praz, 'Chaucer e i grandi trecentisti italiani', Macchiavelli in Inghilterra ed altri saggi (Rome, 1942), pp. 13–85.

38 See J. Mann, Chaucer and Medieval Estates Satire (Cambridge, 1973), pp. 17–37.

39 See n. 35 above.

40 p. 481.

41 To the bibliography cited at n. 1 add C. G. Child, 'Chaucer's Legend of Good Women and Boccaccio's De Genealogia Deorum', Modern Language Notes, XI, 8 (1896), cols. 476–90.

42 For the arguments cited in this paragraph see Bech, 'Quellen und Plan'; and Skeat, pp. xxiii–xxix.

43 Boccaccio speaks of dedicating De Mulieribus Claris to Joanna, Queen of Jerusalem and Sicily; Chaucer addresses Queen Anne.

44 See Child, 'Legend of Good Women and De Genealogia'.

45 Skeat, p. xxviii.

46 A. Brusendorff, The Chaucer Tradition, 2nd edn. (Oxford, 1967), pp. 144–5.

47 Cf. Shannon, Chaucer and the Roman Poets, pp. 182ff and n. 58 below.

48 Zaccaria (ed.), De Mulieribus, pp. 535–40.

49 References are to the edition of V. Ussani, Hegesippi qui dicitur Historiae Libri V, Corpus Scriptorum Ecclesiasticorum Latinorum (Vienna–Leipzig, 1932). On Boccaccio's use of Hegesippus see D. di Benedetto, 'Considerazioni sullo Zibaldone Laurenziano e restauro testuale della prima redazione del Faunus', Italia Mediœvale e Umanistica, XIV (1971), 107ff; and G. Padoan, Il Boccaccio, Le Muse, il Parnasso e l'Arno (Florence, 1978), pp. 123–50.

50 Ed. Ussani, p. 59.

51 Ibid. p. 60.

52 Cf. Carraro, 'Tradizioni Culturali', p. 236.

53 See p. 270 above.

54 J. L. Lowes, 'Chaucer's Legend of Good Women a Travesty?', Journal of English and Germanic Philology, VIII (:909), 513–69, discusses the treatment of Cleopatra in authors influenced by Chaucer, including Gower and Lydgate.

55 'The Sea-Battle in Chaucer's Legend of Cleopatra', Anniversary Papers by Colleagues and Pupils of George Lyman Kittredge (Boston, 1913), pp. 139–52.

56 Ibid. p. 152.

57 See discussion by J. Mann, 'Chaucer and the Medieval Latin Poets', Geoffrey Chaucer, Writers and their Background, ed. D. Brewer (London, 1974), pp. 176–9, 182–3.

58 The best account of this legend remains that of Shannon, Chaucer and the Roman Poets, pp. 179–90. See, recently, R. W. Frank, Jr, Chaucer and the 'Legend of Good Women' (Cambridge, Mass. 1972), pp. 37–46 and, in general, his 'The Legend of the Legend of Good Women', Chaucer Review, I (1967), 110–33. Other sources are discussed by B. Taylor, 'The Medieval Cleopatra: the Classical and Medieval Tradition of Chaucer's Legend of Good Women', Journal of Medieval and Renaissance Studies, VII (1977), 249–69; W. K. Wimsatt, Jr, 'Vincent of Beauvais and Chaucer's Cleopatra and Crœsus', Speculum, XII (1937), 375–81; and P. Aiken, 'Chaucer's Legend of Cleopatra and the Speculum Historiale', Speculum, XIII (1938), 232–6.

59 See n. 55.

60 Schofield, 'Sea-Battle', p. 151.

61 The iconography of this scene is discussed in V. A. Kolve, 'From Cleopatra to Alceste: An Iconographic Study of The Legend of Good Women' in Signs and

Symbols in Chaucer's Poetry, ed. J. P. Hermann and J. J. Burke, Jr (Alabama, 1981), pp. 130–78, especially figs. 1–11.

62 Frank, Chaucer and the 'Legend of Good Women', pp. 44–5.

63 Cf. n. 41, Shannon, Chaucer and the Roman Poets, pp. 228ff.

64 See Carraro, 'Tradizioni Culturali', especially pp. 202, 208–9.

Chaucer and the Italian Trecento: a Bibliography

Although the aim of this bibliography – which concentrates on the purely literary aspects of the relationship between Chaucer and the Italian Trecento – is *not* to provide a thoroughly exhaustive list of all the existing critical material on the subject, ample efforts have been made not to leave out any item that might be of some significance. I have therefore taken care also to include those studies which, for various reasons, may not be immediately available to the general reader – as, for instance, the results of research carried out by Italian scholars and critics in the first decades of the century, prior to Mario Praz' milestone essay of 1927. Some of these 'pioneer' works may now appear to be of no great consequence, but it should not be forgotten that Chaucerian studies in Italy are of relatively recent development, and still not so widespread as one could wish.

In this perspective, a certain selection had to be made, and this particularly shows in the decision to omit all unpublished material; one exception, however, was felt to be unavoidable – H. Schless' fundamental 1956 dissertation on Chaucer and Dante.

Section I, far from pretending to be a complete, or even a selective, bibliography of all the most important general works on Chaucer, aims only at presenting the non-specialist reader with a short list of 'indispensable' book-length studies in which the relationship between Chaucer and the Italian Trecento has been investigated with special care and success.

I General Studies

Bennett, H. S. *Chaucer and the Fifteenth Century* (Oxford, 1947).
Bennett, J. A. W. *The Parlement of Foules. An Interpretation* (Oxford, 1957).
Chaucer's Book of Fame (Oxford, 1968).
Bryan, W. F., and Dempster, G. (eds.) *Sources and Analogues of Chaucer's 'Canterbury Tales'* (Chicago, 1941).
Clemen, Wolfgang H., trans. C. A. M. Sym *Chaucer's Early Poetry* (London, 1963).

Everett, D.   *Essays on Middle English Literature*, ed. P. Kean (Oxford, 1955).

Howard, D. R.   *The Idea of the Canterbury Tales* (Berkeley, Los Angeles and London, 1976).

Hussey, S. S.   *Chaucer, An Introduction* (London, 1971).

Koonce, B. G.   *Chaucer and the Tradition of Fame* (Princeton, N.J., 1966).

Legouis, E.   *Geoffrey Chaucer* (Blond, 1910).

Lowes, J. L.   *Geoffrey Chaucer* (Boston, 1934).

Muscatine, Charles   *Chaucer and the French Tradition* (Berkeley and Los Angeles, 1957).

Payne, R. O.   *The Key of Remembrance: A Study of Chaucer's Poetics* (New Haven, 1963).

Preston, R.   *Chaucer* (London, 1952).

Robertson, D. W., Jr   *A Preface to Chaucer. Studies in Medieval Perspectives* (Princeton, N.J., 1962).

Root, R. K.   *The Poetry of Chaucer* (Boston, 1906).

Ruggiers, P.G.   *The Art of the Canterbury Tales* (Madison and Milwaukee, 1965).

Shelly, P. V. D.   *The Living Chaucer* (Philadelphia, 1940).

Speirs, J.   *Chaucer the Maker*, 2nd edn. (London, 1960).

Tatlock, J. S. P.   *The Mind and Art of Chaucer* (Syracuse, N.Y., 1950).

II Chaucer and Italy

Braddy, H.   'New Documentary Evidence Concerning Chaucer's Mission to Lombardy', *Modern Language Notes*, XLVIII (1933), 507–11.

Brown, E., Jr   'The Merchant's Tale: Why Was Januarie Born of Pavye?', *Neuphilologische Mitteilungen*, LXXI (1970), 654–8.

Cook, A. S.   'Chaucerian Papers', *Transactions of the Connecticut Academy of Arts and Sciences*, XXIII (1919), 39–44.

Crow, M. M., and Olson, C. C. (eds.)   *Chaucer Life-Records* (Oxford, 1966).

Dorris, G. E.   'The First Italian Criticism of Chaucer and Shakespeare', *Romance Notes*, VI (1964), 141–3.

Galway, M.   'Chaucer's Journeys in 1368', *The Times Literary Supplement*, 4 April 1958, p. 183.

Hutton, E.   'Chaucer and Italy', *Nineteenth Century*, CXXVIII (1940), 51–9.

Kuhl, E. P.   'Why Was Chaucer Sent to Milan in 1378?', *Modern Language Notes*, LXXII (1947), 42–4.

Manly, J. M.   *Some New Light on Chaucer* (New York, 1926).

'Chaucer's Mission to Lombardy', *Modern Language Notes*, XLIX (1934), 209–16.

Olson, P. A.   'The Merchant's Lombard Knight', *Texas Studies in Literature and Language*, III (1961), 259–63.

Parks, G. B.   'The Route of Chaucer's First Journey to Italy', *English Literary History*, XVI (1949), 174–87.

The English Traveler to Italy, vol. I: 'The Middle Ages (to 1525)' (Rome and Stanford, Cal., 1954).

Pearsall, R. B.   'Chaucer's Panik', Modern Language Notes, LXVII (1952), 529–31.

Pratt, R. A.   'Geoffrey Chaucer, Esq. and Sir John Hawkwood', English Literary History, XVI (1949), 188–93.

Rickert, E.   'Chaucer Abroad in 1368', Modern Philology, XXV (1928), 511–12.

Rokutanda, O.   'L'incontro del Chaucer e la letteratura italiana', Studi Italici (Kyoto), XVII (1969), 63–77.

Ruggiers, P. G.   'The Italian Influence on Chaucer', in B. Rowland (ed.), Companion to Chaucer Studies, rev. edn. (New York and Oxford, 1979), pp. 160–84.

Sells, A. L.   The Italian Influence in English Poetry from Chaucer to Southwell (Bloomington, Ind., 1955).

Spout, A.   'Chaucer's Lombardy Journey', The Athenaeum, 9 September 1893, p. 356.

Tatlock, J. S. P.   'The Duration of Chaucer's Visits to Italy', Journal of English and Germanic Philology, XII (1913), 118–21.

III Chaucer and Dante

Bennett, J. A. W.   'Chaucer, Dante and Boccaccio', Medium Aevum, XXII (1953), 114–15.

Boitani, P.   'The Monk's Tale: Dante and Boccaccio', Medium Aevum, XLV (1976), 50–69.

Chapman, C. O.   'Chaucer and Dante', The Times Literary Supplement, 29 August 1952, p. 565.

Chiarini, C.   Di un 'imitazione inglese della Divina Commedia: 'La Casa della Fama' di Chaucer (Bari, 1902).

Clark, J. W.   'Dante and the Epilogue of Troilus', Journal of English and Germanic Philology, L (1951), 1–10.

Cope, J. I.   'Chaucer, Venus and the Seventhe Sphere', Modern Language Notes, LXVII (1952), 245–6.

Dedeyan, C.   'Dante en Angleterre', Les Lettres Romanes, XII (1958), 367–88; XIII (1959), 45–68.

Dilts, D. A.   'Observations on Dante and The House of Fame', Modern Language Notes, LVII (1942), 26–8.

Dronke, P.   'The Conclusion of Troilus and Criseyde', Medium Aevum, XXXIII (1964), 47–52.

Foster, K.   'Italy and the English Poets: Chaucer, Dante and Boccaccio', The Tablet, CCVI (1955), 476–7.

Guerin, R.   'The Nun's Priest and Canto V of Inferno', English Studies, LIV (1972), 313–15.

Hammond, E. P.   'Chaucer and Dante and Their Scribes', Modern Language Notes, XXXI (1916), 121.

Kellett, E.   'Chaucer as a Critic of Dante', The London Mercury, IV (1921), 282–91.

Kellogg, A. L.   'Chaucer's Self-Portrait and Dante's', Medium Aevum, XXIX (1960), 119–20.

Koeppel, E. 'Chauceriana', *Anglia*, XIII (1891).

Lange, H. 'Der heliakische Aufgang der Fixsterne bei Dante und Chaucer', *Deutsches Dante-Jahrbuch*, XXI (1939), 19–41.

Levy, B. S. 'Chaucer's Wife of Bath, the Loathly Lady, and Dante's Siren', *Symposium*, XIX (1965), 359–73.

Looten, C. 'Chaucer et Dante', *Revue de Littérature Comparée*, V (1925), 545–71.

Lowes, J. L. 'Chaucer and Dante's Convivio', *Modern Philology*, XIII (1915–16), 19–33.

'Chaucer and Dante', *Modern Philology*, XIV (1917), 705–35.

McCallum, M. W. *Chaucer's Debt to Italy* (Sidney, 1931).

McCracken, H. N. 'Dant in English: A Solution', *The Nation*, LXXXIX (1909), 276–7.

Pisanti, T. 'Influssi danteschi nell'Europa del Trecento e del Quattrocento', *Critica Letteraria*, III (1975), 637–61.

Pratt, R. A. 'Chaucer and the Visconti Libraries', *English Literary History*, VI (1939) 188–99.

'Words into Images in Chaucer's *House of Fame*: A Third Suggestion', *Modern Language Notes*, LXIX (1954), 34–7.

Praz, M. 'Chaucer e i grandi trecentisti italiani', in *Machiavelli in Inghilterra ed altri saggi*, 2nd edn. (Florence, 1960), pp. 29–91; a shorter version first appeared in English, 'Chaucer and the Great Italian Writers of the Trecento', *The Monthly Criterion* (1927), 18–39, 131–57, 238–42; repr. in *The Flaming Heart* (New York, 1958).

Rambeau, A. 'Chaucers *House of Fame* in seinem Verhältnis zu Dantes *Divina Commedia*', *Englische Studien*, III (1870), 209–78.

Ruggiers, P. G. 'Tyrants of Lombardy in Dante and Chaucer', *Philological Quarterly*, XXIX (1950), 445–8.

Schless, H. 'Chaucer and Dante: A Revaluation', unpub. Pennsylvania diss., 1956.

'Chaucer and Dante', in D. Bethurum (ed.), *Critical Approaches to Medieval Literature: Papers from the English Institute, 1958–9* (New York and London, 1960), pp. 134–54.

'Transformations: Chaucer's Use of Italian', in D. S. Brewer (ed.), *Geoffrey Chaucer*, Writers and Their Background (London, 1974), pp. 184–223.

Chaucer and Dante (Norman, Oklahoma, 1984).

Shoaf, R. H. 'Dante's *Commedia* and Chaucer's Theory of Mediation: A Preliminary Sketch', in D. M. Rose (ed.), *New Perspectives in Chaucer Criticism* (Norman, Oklahoma, 1981), pp. 83–103.

Dante, Chaucer, and the Currency of The Word (Norman, Oklahoma, 1983).

Spencer, T. H. 'The Story of Ugolino in Dante and Chaucer', *Speculum*, IX (1934), 295–301.

Steadman, J. M. 'The Prioress's Tale and "Granella" of *Paradiso*', *Medieval Studies*, XXIV (1962), 388–91.

Tatlock, J. S. P. 'Chaucer and Dante', *Modern Language Notes*, XXX (1906), 367–72.

'Dante and Guinicelli in Chaucer's Troilus', *Modern Language Notes*, XXXV (1920), 443.

'The Epilog of Chaucer's Troilus', *Modern Philology*, XVIII (1920–1), 625–59.

Toynbee, P. *Dante in English Literature from Chaucer to Cary* (London, 1909).

IV Chaucer and Boccaccio

apRoberts, R. P. 'Love in the *Filostrato*', *Chaucer Review*, VII (1972), 1–26.

Bardelli, M. *Qualche Contributo agli Studi sulle Relazioni del Chaucer col Boccaccio* (Florence, 1911).

Beidler, P. 'Chaucer's *Merchant's Tale* and the *Decameron*', *Italica*, L (1973), 266–84.

Bloomfield, M. W. 'The Source of Boccaccio's *Filostrato* III, 74–79 and its Bearing on the MS Tradition of Lucretius, De Rerum Natura', *Classical Philology*, XLVII (1952), 162–5.

Boitani, P. *Chaucer and Boccaccio* (Oxford, 1977).

Brown, M. L. 'The *House of Fame* and the *Corbaccio*', *Modern Language Notes*, XXXII (1917), 411–15.

Capone, G. *La Novella del Cavaliere di Geoffrey Chaucer e la Teseida di Giovanni Boccaccio* (2 pts, Sassari, 1907–9).

Child, C. G. 'Chaucer's *House of Fame* and Boccaccio's *Amorosa Visione*', *Modern Language Notes*, X (1895), 379–84.

Coleman, W. E. 'Chaucer, the *Teseida*, and the Visconti Library at Pavia: a Hypothesis', *Medium Aevum*, LI (1982), 92–101.

Copland, M. 'The *Shipman's Tale*: Chaucer and Boccaccio', *Medium Aevum*, XXXV (1966), 11–28.

Cummings, H. M. *The Indebtedness of Chaucer's Works to the Italian Works of Boccaccio* (Cincinnati, 1916).

Farnham, W. E. 'Chaucer's *Clerk's Tale*', *Modern Language Notes*, XXXIII (1918), 193–203.

'England's Discovery of the *Decameron*', *Publications of the Modern Language Association of America*, XXXIX (1924), 123–39.

Forster, M. 'Boccaccios De Casibus Virorum Illustrium in englischer Bearbeitung', *Deutsche Literaturzeichtung*, XXVII (1924), 1943–6.

Giaccherini, E. 'The *Reeve's Tale* e *Decameron*, IX, 6', *Rivista di Letterature Moderne e Comparate*, XXIX (1976), 99–121.

Goffin, R. C. 'Quiting by Tidinges in the *House of Fame*', *Medium Aevum*, XII (1943), 40–4.

Kean, P. M. 'Chaucer's Dealings with a Stanza of Il *Filostrato* and the Epilogue of Troilus and Criseyde', *Medium Aevum*, XXXIII (1964), 36–46.

Knapp, P. A. 'Boccaccio and Chaucer on Cassandra', *Philological Quarterly*, LVI (1977), 413–17.

Koeppel, E. 'Chauceriana', *Anglia*, XIV (1891–2), 233–8, 245–7.

Korthen, H. *Chaucers literarische Beziehungen zu Boccaccio: Die künstlerische Konzeption der Canterbury Tales und das Lolliusproblem* (Rostock, 1920).

Lange, M. *Vom Fabliau zu Boccaccio und Chaucer. Ein Vergleich zweier Fabliaux mit Boccaccios Decamerone IX, 6 und mit Chaucers Reeve's Tale* (Friederichsen, 1934).

Lewis, C. S. 'What Chaucer really did to Il Filostrato', *Essays and Studies by Members of the English Association*, XVII (1932), 56–75.

Lowes, J. L. 'The Prologue to the Legend of Good Woman as Related to the French Marguerite Poems and to Il Filostrato', *Publications of the Modern Language Association*, XIX (1904), 593–683.

'The Franklyn's Tale, the Teseida and the Filocolo', *Modern Philology*, XV (1918), 689–728.

Lumiansky, R. M. 'Aspects of the Relationship of Boccaccio's Il Filostrato with Benoît's Roman de Troie and Chaucer's Wife of Bath's Tale', *Italica*, XXXI (1954), 1–7.

McGrady, D. 'Chaucer and the Decameron Reconsidered', *Chaucer Review*, XII (1977), 1–26.

McNeal, T. H. 'Chaucer and the Decameron', *Modern Language Notes*, LIII (1938), 257–8.

Mather, F. J. *The Prologue, the Knight's Tale and the Nun's Priest's Tale* (Houghton, 1908).

Morsback, L. 'Chaucers Plan der Canterbury Tales und Boccaccios Decamerone', *Englische Studien*, XLII (1910), 43–52.

Pisanti, T. 'Boccaccio in Inghilterra tra Medioevo e Rinascimento', in G. Tournoy (ed.), *Boccaccio in Europe: Proceedings of the Boccaccio Conference, Louvain, December 1975* (Leuven, 1977), pp. 197–208.

Pratt, R. A. 'Chaucer's Use of the Teseida', *Publications of the Modern Language Association*, LXII (1947), 598–621.

'Chaucer and Le Roman de Troyle et de Criseida', *Studies in Philology*, LIII (1956), 509–39.

Prestifilippo Trigona, F. *Chaucer Imitatore del Boccaccio* (Catania, 1923).

Raith, J. *Boccaccio in der englischen Literatur von Chaucer bis Painters Palace of Pleasure. Ein Beitrag zur Geschichte der italienische Novelle in England* (Leipzig, 1936).

Rajna, P. 'Le origini della novella narrata dal Frankeleyn nei Canterbury Tales del Chaucer', *Romania*, XXXII (1903), 204–67.

Reiss, E. 'Boccaccio in English Culture of the Fourteenth and Fifteenth Centuries', in G. Galigani (ed.), *Il Boccaccio nella cultura inglese e anglo-americana* (Florence, 1974), pp. 15–26.

Root, R. K. 'Chaucer and the Decameron', *Englische Studien*, XLIV (1911), 1–7.

Rossetti, W. M. *Chaucer's 'Troylus and Cryseide' compared with Boccaccio's 'Filostrato'* (London, 1873).

Schirmer, W. F. 'Boccaccios Werke als Quelle Geoffrey Chaucers', *Germanisch-Romanische Monatschriften*, XII (1924), 288–305.

Scott, P. S. 'The Seventh Sphere: A Note on *Troilus and Criseyde*', *Modern Language Review*, LI (1956), 2–5.

Sharrock, R. 'Second Thoughts: C. S. Lewis on Chaucer's *Troilus*', *Essays in Criticism*, VIII (1958), 123–37.

Tatlock, J. S.P. 'Boccaccio and the Plan of the Canterbury Tales', *Studia Romanica et Anglica Zagabriensia*, XXXIII–XXXVI (1972–3), 849–72.

Taylor, P. B. '*Peynted Confessiouns*: Boccaccio and Chaucer', *Comparative Literature*, XXXIV (1982), 116–29.

Torraca, F. 'Knightes Tale e la Teseida', *Società Reale di Napoli; Atti dell'Accademia di Archeologia, Lettere e Belle Arti*, X (1928), 199–217.

Utley, F. L. 'Boccaccio, Chaucer and the International Popular Tale', *Western Folklore*, XXXIII (1974), 181–201.

Velli, G. 'L'apoteosi di Arcita: ideologia e coscienza storica nel "Teseida"', *Studi e problemi di critica testuale*, V (1972), 33–66.

Walker, I. C. 'Chaucer and *Il Filostrato*', *English Studies*, XLIX (1967), 318–26.

Whitfield, J. H. 'Chaucer fra Dante e Boccaccio', in G. Galigani (ed.), *Il Boccaccio nella cultura inglese e anglo-americana* (see p. 302), pp. 137–53.

Wilkins, E. H. 'Criseida', *Modern Language Notes*, XXIV (1909), 65–7.

Wilson, H. S. 'The Knight's Tale and the Teseida Again', *University of Toronto Quarterly*, XVIII (1949), 131–46.

Wright, H. G. *Boccaccio in England from Chaucer to Tennyson* (London, 1957).

Young, Karl *The Origin and Development of the Story of Troilus and Criseyde* (London, 1908; repr. New York, 1968).

V Chaucer and Petrarch

Bellezza, P. *Irradiazioni e Reverberi dell'Anima Italiana. Saggi Culturali. Il Presunto Convegno del Chaucer col Petrarca* (Milan, 1926).

Capone, G. *Marginalia a la Novella del Cavaliere di Goffredo Chaucer: La Concezione de la Storia nel Petrarca e nel Chaucer* (Sassari, 1912).

Cate, W. A. 'The Problem of the Origin of the Griselda Story', *Studies in Philology*, XXIX (1932), 389–405.

Cook, A. S. 'The First Two Readers of Petrarch's Tale of Griselda', *Modern Philology*, XV (1918), 633–43.

Dempster, G. 'Chaucer's Manuscript of Petrarch's Version of the Griselda Story', *Modern Philology*, XLI (1943), 6–16.

Griffith, D. D. *The Origin of the Griselda Story* (Washington, 1931).

Hamilton, G. L. 'Chauceriana I: The Date of the Clerk's Tale and Chaucer's "Petrak"', *Modern Language Notes*, XXIII (1908), 169–72.

Hendrickson, G. L. 'Chaucer and Petrarch: Two Notes on the *Clerkes Tale*', *Modern Philology*, IV (1906–7), 179–92.

Hornstein, L. H. 'Petrarch's Laelius Chaucer's Lollius?', *Publications of the Modern Language Association*, LXIII (1948), 64–84.

Hutton, E. 'Did Chaucer meet Petrarch and Boccaccio?', *Anglo-Italian Review*, I (1918), 121–35.

Pratt, R. A. 'A Note on Chaucer's Lollius', *Modern Language Notes*, LXV (1950), 183–7.

Severs, J. B. *The Literary Relationships of Chaucer's Clerkes Tale*, Yale Studies in English, XCVI (New Haven, 1942).

Thomson, P. 'The *Canticus Troili*: Chaucer and Petrarch', *Comparative Literature*, XI (1959), 313–28.

Wilkins, E. H. 'Cantus Troili', *English Literary History*, XVI (1949), 167–73.

'Descriptions of Pagan Divinities from Petrarch to Chaucer', *Speculum*, XXXII (1957), 511–22.

VI Varia

Dempster, G. 'On the Source of the Deception Story in the Merchant's Tale', *Modern Philology*, XXXIV (1936), 133–54.

Guerin, R. 'The "Shipman's Tale": The Italian Analogues', *English Studies*, LII (1971), 412–19.

Looten, C. *Chaucer, ses Modèles, ses Sources, sa Religion* (Lille, 1931).

Meech, S. B. 'Chaucer and an Italian Translation of the Heroides', *Publications of the Modern Language Association*, XLV (1930), 110–28.

Nicholson, P. 'The Two Versions of Sercambi's "Novelle"', *Italica*, LIII (1976), 201–13.

Pace, G. B. 'Giraldi on Chaucer', *Chaucer Review*, VII (1973), 295–6.

Pratt, R. A. 'Giovanni Sercambi Speziale', *Italica*, XXV (1948), 12–14.

'Chaucer's Shipman's Tale and Sercambi', *Modern Language Notes*, LV (1940), 142–5.

The two volumes devoted by G. Billanovich to *La Tradizione del Testo di Livio e le Origini dell'Umanesimo* (Padua, 1981 and 1985) are absolutely indispensable for a reconstruction of Anglo-Italian contacts in the fourteenth century.

Index